**50** YEARS OF EXPONENT II

# YEARS OF EXPONENT II

Katie Ludlow Rich
Heather Sundahl

Afterword by
Laurel Thatcher Ulrich

SIGNATURE BOOKS | 2024 | SALT LAKE CITY

*Exponent II would not exist without its volunteers. It is to them that we dedicate this book, which documents fifty years of sharing stories in a spirit of trust and belonging.*

© 2024 Signature Books. All rights reserved. Signature Books is a registered trademark of Signature Books Publishing, LLC.
Printed in the USA using paper from sustainably harvested sources.

Join our mail list at www.signaturebooks.com for details on events and related titles we think you'll enjoy.

Design by Jason Francis

FIRST EDITION | 2024

LIBRARY OF CONGRESS CONTROL NUMBER: 2024942318

Paperback ISBN: 978-1-56085-477-7
Ebook ISBN: 978-1-56085-496-8

# CONTENTS

List of Selections . . . . . . . . . . . . . . . vii

Key Events in Exponent II History . . . . . . . . . . . xi

Introduction . . . . . . . . . . . . . . . . . xvii

1: *A Beginner's Boston* and Beyond . . . . . . . . . . 1

2: "Wonderful Darling Upstarts" . . . . . . . . . . . 9

3: Editing out the Anger . . . . . . . . . . . . . 21

4: Pilgrimage, Reunion, Retreat . . . . . . . . . . . 33

5: Turning Expectations into Intentions . . . . . . . . 41

6: "Dangerous History" . . . . . . . . . . . . . 51

7: "Mormonism's Stealth Alternative" . . . . . . . . . 61

8: *Exponent II* Goes Digital . . . . . . . . . . . . 69

9: Expanding Geographically and Thematically . . . . . . 79

10: Implementing Sustainable Processes and Financial Safeguards . . 91

11: Looking to the Future . . . . . . . . . . . . 103

Epilogue: *Exponent II*'s Legacy . . . . . . . . . . 109

Unit 1: 1974–1984 . . . . . . . . . . . . . . . 111
*Introduction by Heather Sundahl*

Unit 2: 1984–1997 . . . . . . . . . . . . . . . 157
*Introduction by Katie Ludlow Rich*

Unit 3: 1997–2009 . . . . . . . . . . . . . . . . . 201
*Introduction by Heather Sundahl*

Unit 4: 2010–2015 . . . . . . . . . . . . . . . . . 245
*Introduction by Aimee Evans Hickman*

Unit 5: 2015–2024 . . . . . . . . . . . . . . . . . 285
*Introduction by Pandora Brewer*

Unit 6: Reflections on Nearly Two Decades of the Exponent II Blog . 335
*Introduction by Caroline Kline*

An Afterword in the Form of a Personal Essay . . . . . . . . . 379
*Laurel Thatcher Ulrich*

Acknowledgments . . . . . . . . . . . . . . . . . 383

Cover Artist Acknowledgments . . . . . . . . . . . . 385

Index . . . . . . . . . . . . . . . . . . . . . . 389

About the Authors . . . . . . . . . . . . . . . . . 405

## List of Selections

116 Exponent II: Why?
**Claudia L. Bushman**

117 In the Mission but Not of the Mission (excerpts)
**Kathleen Flake**

119 "Line Upon Line" (excerpts)
**Susan Arrington Hill**

122 Mormon Denial (excerpts)
**Rebecca Cornwall**

123 From Vanguard to Rearguard (excerpts)
**M. and W. Woodworth**

125 Mother's Day
**Margaret Munk**

127 Blacks, Priesthood and Sisterhood
**Chris Rigby Arrington**

129 Patti Perfect
**Margaret B. Black and Midge W. Nielsen**

131 To Mother
**Kristine Barrett**

133 One Woman's Perspective: Eliza R. Snow
**Jill Mulvay Derr**

137 Wind
**Susan Howe**

138 Heritage
**Vernice Wineera Pere**

139 On Being Happy: An Exercise in Spiritual Autobiography (excerpts)
**Lavina Fielding Anderson**

141 Coming Apart Together
**Mary L. Bradford**

141 Scouting
**RevaBeth L. Russell**

142 Ode to Autumn
**Laurel Thatcher Ulrich**

143 Milk and Honey Motherhood
**Emma Lou Thayne**

145 The Good Woman Syndrome: Or, When is Enough, Enough?
**Helen Candland Stark**

148 Community Involvement (excerpts)
**Lorie Winder**

149 Depression (excerpts)
**Heather Cannon**

150 Some Positive Repercussions
**Cindy L. Barlow**

151 The Founding Foremothers

162 Substance of Things Unseen
**Helen Mar Cook**

163 Wife #3
**Violet Tew Kimball**

164 Birth Control: My Choice, Your Choice (excerpts)
**Diane McKinney Kellogg**

166 Cheese and Crackers (excerpts)
**Cheryl Davis Howard DiVito**

168 Creativity: A Constant Renewal
**Susan Howe**

172 The Abuse of Women: An Interview with "Jane" (excerpts)

174 Don't Look to Me for Direction (excerpts)
**Claudia W. Harris**

177 Looking Back: Reflections on President Benson's Talk (excerpts)
**Margaret Blair Young**

179 Unheard
**Carrel Sheldon**

180 The Adoptive Mother (excerpts)
**Robin Zenger Baker**

183 The Light's Still On—Spring 1991
**Claudia Knight-Zimmer**

186 Editorial: Annus Horribilis
**Sue Paxman and Jenny Atkinson**

189 Women's War
**Shari Siebers Crall**

191 Editorial: First Hands and Backs, Now Feet and Voices
**Sue Paxman**

194 Editorial: Embracing All of Our Sisters and Brothers
**Judy Dushku**

197 Affirmation and Supporting Mormon Lesbians
**Ina Mae Murri**

198 Living With Disabilities (excerpts)
**Joan D. Groesbeck**

199 On Learning to Recognize Spousal Abuse (excerpts)
**Dennis Lythgoe**

207 Known to Your Bones: Living in the Company of Women
**Pandora Brewer**

212 Minus Motherhood
**Karen Rosenbaum**

216 From Victoria's Secret to Beehive Clothing
**Sylvia Cabus**

218 Love Making
**Ann Gardner Stone**

218 Period
**Ann Gardner Stone**

219 Personal Revelation in an Authoritarian Church—Balance of Power or Detente?
**E. Victoria Grover**

222 Editorial: Something Old, Something New
**Nancy T. Dredge**

223 Christmas in a Changed World
**Linda Hoffman Kimball**

226 As Regards Touching
**Kate Holbrook**

229 Encircling
**Kylie Nielson Turley**

230 The Stump's Last Stand
**Julie Paige Hemming Savage**

232 Holding My Grandchild, Come to Land this Morning
**Judith Curtis**

233 Life is Good: An Interview with Cathy Stokes (excerpts)
**Linda Hoffman Kimball**

238 Cap of Many Colors
**Heather Sundahl**

240 In the Shadow of His Wings
**Deborah Farmer Kris (as "Deborah")**

241 Dress
**Brooke Jones (as "Brooke")**

242 Staking My Claim, Claiming My Stake: Mid-Singles
**Sandra Lee (as "Dora")**

250 Waiting
**Lisa Van Orman Hadley**

252 Letter from the Guest Editor
**Lisa Butterworth**

253 Mourn with those that Mourn: Being a Hospital Chaplain
**Emily Clyde Curtis**

256 A Letter to the Brethren
**Amy McPhie Allebest**

## LIST OF SELECTIONS

261 Reinventing Emma Smith
**Jana Riess with Linda King Newell**

263 Artist Spotlight: The Sacred
History of Remnants
**Page Turner**

266 So Many Words
**Diane Pritchett**

270 Deployed Without the Priesthood
**Abby Maxwell Hansen**

272 Remembering *Exponent II*:
A Beacon in the East
**Maxine Hanks**

275 The Radical Mission of Exponent II
**Aimee Evans Hickman**

279 As I Am
**Averyl Dietering**

282 The Color-Blind Conundrum
**Kalani Tonga**

291 Unfinished Business
**Melody Newey**

292 Arithmetic Rhetoric
**Emily Parker Updegraff**

295 Claiming Space:
A Spiritual Autobiography
**Margaret Olsen Hemming**

299 Jael
**Ellen McCammon**

306 Wendell
**Susan Christiansen**

308 Persisters in Zion/Daughters of
Exponent: a Medley
**Heather Sundahl**

309 Wonder Women
**Rachel Rueckert**

312 Letter from the Editor:
Exponent Wrapped
**Rosie Gochnour Serago**

314 The Folly of Hedges
**Tracy McKay Lamb**

318 Gingerbread Girl
**Falencia Jean-Francois**

319 Family History: Made for You
But Not For Me
**Ramona Morris**

321 On Saying Yes to Boys
**Hannah MacDonald (pseudonym)**

323 During the Sacrament
**Carol Lynn Pearson**

324 Letter from the Editor:
Holy in All its Forms
**Carol Ann Litster Young**

326 Shifting Sands
**Andee Bowden**

328 The Place that Doesn't Exist
**Allison Pingree**

329 After Dobbs
**Alixa Brobbey**

330 The Trench Coat of Multiple Colors
**Allison Hong Merrill**

341 Radical Mormon Feminist Manifesto
**Jana Remy (as "Jana")**

342 Baby Killer
**Heather Sundahl (as "Heather")**

345 The Modesty Myth: Why Covering
Up Just Won't Do (excerpts)
**Amelia Parkin (as "Amelia")**

347 Now I Have the Power
**Meghan Raynes (as "MRaynes")**

349 What I First Learned About
Heavenly Mother (excerpts)
**Rachel Hunt Steenblik (as "Rachel")**

352 After
**Sherrie Gavin (as "Spunky")**

354 Rejected Offerings
**April Young-Bennett**

356 Neckties: Priesthood Attire or
Lucifer's Lust Pointer? (excerpts)
**April Carlson (as "Cruelest Month")**

359  Poems of Exclusion
    **Nancy Ross and Emily Holsinger Butler (as "EmilyHB")**

360  The Harms of Projecting the Mormon Male Gaze Onto Young Women (excerpts)
    **Caroline Salisbury (as "Violadiva")**

362  Come Come Ye Queer Saints: Pride, Prejudice, Persecution
    **Melissa-Malcolm King**

364  Freedom of Religion Under Attack Again
    **Emily Gilkey Palmer (as "Em")**

367  Acknowledging Institutional Mistakes is a Strength Not a Weakness: Wisdom from Oral Histories with Mormon Women of Color
    **Caroline Kline (as "Caroline")**

370  The Unconditional Act of Hugging (excerpts)
    **Jody England Hansen**

373  Gender Affirming Care: Simple Words, Complex Emotions (excerpts)
    **Valerie Nicole Green**

375  #hearLDSwomen series
    **edited by Lindsay Denton**

# Key Events in Exponent II History

1966     *A Beginner's Boston,* edited by Laurel Thatcher Ulrich and illustrated by Carolyn Peters (Person), is published as a fundraiser for the Cambridge Ward Relief Society; *Dialogue: A Journal of Mormon Thought* founded

1970     First consciousness-raising meeting of Boston-area Mormon women at the home of Laurel Thatcher Ulrich in Newton, Massachusetts (June); *Relief Society Magazine* discontinued

1971     Women's "Pink Issue" of *Dialogue: A Journal of Mormon Thought,* edited by Claudia Bushman and Laurel Thatcher Ulrich

1972     Equal Rights Amendment (ERA) passes both houses of Congress and goes to the states for ratification

1972–73 Boston women prepare and then deliver a spring 1973 course on Mormon women's history for the LDS Cambridge Institute of Religion; Susan Kohler uncovers copies of the (surprisingly suffragist!) Utah-based periodical the *Woman's Exponent* (1872–1914) at Harvard's Widener Library

1973     First Boston-area Mormon women's retreat at Camp Windigo in western Massachusetts (attended by eleven women and three nursing babies)—they discuss publishing a Mormon women's newspaper; First Exponent Day Dinner—an event meant to celebrate the *Woman's Exponent*—with Maureen Ursenbach as guest speaker; Subsequent Exponent Day speakers include Juanita Brooks ('74), Emma Lou Thayne ('75), Lela B. Coons ('76), Claudia Bushman ('77), Jill Mulvay Derr ('78), Mary Bradford ('79), Christine Durham ('80), Linda King Newell ('81), Lavina Fielding Anderson ('82)

1974     *Exponent II* begins publication (July), with Claudia Bushman as editor; Retreat with thirty women at Laurel Thatcher Ulrich's home in Durham, New Hampshire; Sunstone Education Foundation founded

1975     *Exponent II* celebrates its first birthday with about 2,000 subscribers; Claudia Bushman cautioned about being editor of *Exponent II* by two general authorities (Hales and Perry), who suggest that *Exponent II* close operations; Nancy Dredge becomes second editor of *Exponent II* (December); *Sunstone* magazine begins publication

1976     First BYU Women's Conference; Elouise Bell guest edits the Provo issue (vol. 3, no. 1); *Mormon Sisters: Women in Early Utah,* edited by Claudia L. Bushman, is published by Emmeline Press, a publishing company formed by the Boston women; LDS Church First Presidency takes official stand against the ERA

1977     Feminists in Virginia (Maida Rust Withers, Teddie Wood, Hazel Rigby, and Sonia Johnson) organize Mormons for ERA; *Exponent II* publishes reactions to the disruptions to the Utah International Women's Year conference and the LDS Church's increasing anti-ERA activity (vol. 4, no. 1; vol. 4, no. 2); Exponent II begins sending documents, correspondence, etc., to the university archives at BYU (now called the L. Tom Perry Special Collections)

1978     Official Declaration 2 removes the LDS Church's racial restrictions on priesthood and temple participation for Black church members; Mary Bradford becomes the first woman editor of *Dialogue*; Chris Rigby Arrington guest edits the New York issue (vol. 4, no. 3)

1979     *Exponent II* publishes issue on Mormon women and depression (vol. 5, no. 3) following Louise Degn's documentary, *Depression and Mormon Women*, which airs on KSL TV in Salt Lake City; Lael J. Littke guest edits the Pasadena issue (vol. 5, no. 4); Sonia Johnson is excommunicated for her public, provocative criticism of the LDS Church's covert anti-ERA activity

1980     Connie D. Cannon guest edits the Denver issue (vol. 6, no. 3); Susan Sessions Rugh guest edits the Chicago issue (vol. 7, no. 1); Peggy Fletcher Stack becomes the first woman editor of *Sunstone*

1981     Susan Elizabeth Howe becomes the third editor of *Exponent II*; Rebecca Chandler guest edits the Ohio issue (vol. 7, no. 4)

1982     First "Pilgrims" retreat held in Nauvoo, Illinois (May 15–17), organized by Lavina Fielding Anderson, Maureen Ursenbach Beecher, Jill Mulvay Derr, Carol Cornwall Madsen, and Linda King Newell

KEY EVENTS IN EXPONENT II HISTORY

| | |
|---|---|
| 1983 | Chicago Hyde Park-area Mormon feminists organize first Midwest Pilgrims retreat (June); First national Exponent II retreat (called a "reunion") held in Hillsboro, New Hampshire, celebrating the paper's tenth anniversary (October); C. Brooklyn Derr guest edits the Mormon Male issue (vol. 9, no. 3) |
| 1984 | Susan Larsen Paxman (Booth-Forbes) becomes the fourth editor of *Exponent II* |
| 1987 | Ezra Taft Benson's high-profile address "To the Mothers in Zion" presents stay-at-home motherhood as a religious obligation for Mormon women; *Exponent II* publishes an issue on the abuse of women (vol. 13, no. 3) |
| 1990 | *Exponent II* publishes issues on the topics of abortion (vol. 15, no. 4) and adoption (vol. 16, no. 2) |
| 1993 | Boyd K. Packer declares feminists, intellectuals, and homosexuals as enemies of the church and coordinates with local leaders the discipline of the September Six, including the excommunications of Lavina Fielding Anderson, Maxine Hanks, Paul Toscano, D. Michael Quinn, Avraham Gileadi, and the disfellowshipment of Lynne Kanavel Whitesides |
| 1995 | *All God's Critters Got a Place in the Choir,* a collection of essays mainly from the East/West column of *Exponent II* by Laurel Thatcher Ulrich and Emma Lou Thayne, is published by Aspen Books; Gordon B. Hinckley presents "The Family: A Proclamation to the World" at the September women's meeting of general conference |
| 1996 | *Exponent II* publishes an issue on the experience of LGBQ Mormons (vol. 20, no. 1) |
| 1997 | Jenny Atkinson becomes the fifth editor of *Exponent II* |
| 2000 | Nancy Dredge becomes sixth editor of *Exponent II;* Hillsboro Camp closes |
| 2005 | Caroline Kline and Jana Remy guest edit the Southern California issue (vol. 27, no. 3) |
| 2006 | Exponent II blog (long called *The Exponent*) co-founded by Caroline Kline, Jana Remy, Deborah Farmer Kris, Emily Clyde Curtis, Sandra Lee, Brooke Jones, and Amelia Parkin |

| | |
|---|---|
| 2007 | *Exponent II* moves to an annual, online-only publication for three years |
| 2009 | Aimee Evans Hickman and Emily Clyde Curtis become the seventh editors of *Exponent II* |
| 2010 | *Exponent II* comes back in print as a full-color quarterly magazine |
| 2011 | Lisa Butterworth guests edits the *Feminist Mormon Housewives* issue (vol. 31, no. 2) |
| 2012 | *Exponent II* publishes an issue on Mormons and politics (vol. 32, no. 3); Exponent II publishes the book *Habits of Being: Mormon Women's Material Culture,* edited by Elizabeth Pinborough, a collection of essays and poetry about objects Mormon women inherited from their ancestresses; Neylan McBaine guest edits the Mormon Women Project issue (vol. 32, no. 3) |
| 2013 | Linda Hoffman Kimball and Nancy Harward guest edit the Midwest Pilgrims issue (vol. 33, no. 2); Kate Kelly, Lorie Winder Stromberg, and others organize Ordain Women to advocate for Mormon women's priesthood ordination |
| 2014 | Kate Kelly's bishop excommunicates her for "openly, repeatedly and deliberately acting in public opposition to the church and its leaders"; *Exponent II* celebrates forty years of publishing and holds a gala in Cambridge, Massachusetts, the night before the retreat |
| 2015 | Margaret Olsen Hemming becomes eighth editor of *Exponent II*; LDS Church's "Policy of Exclusion" leaked online, revealing the church will deny ordinances to the children of homosexual couples and deem homosexual cohabitation as apostasy—bloggers quickly respond |
| 2016 | *Exponent II* publishes a contest issue on Feminist Midrash (vol. 35, no. 3); *Exponent II* responds to "Policy of Exclusion" (vol. 35, no. 4) |
| 2017 | Exponent II publishes *Illuminating Ladies: A Coloring Book of Mormon Women,* illustrated by Molly Cannon Hadfield (with a second edition in 2020); Exponent II discovers its treasurer had embezzled large sums over several years |
| 2019 | Exponent II announces the "LDS Women of Color Art Scholarship"—first recipients include Kwani Povi Winder, Gifty Annan-Mensah, DeTiare Leifi, Karyn Dudley, Hanna Choi, Marlena Wilding, and |

KEY EVENTS IN EXPONENT II HISTORY

Esther Hiʻilani Candari; *Exponent II* publishes an issue on Mormon women and poverty (vol. 39, no. 1)

2020 Margaret Olsen Hemming guest edits the Spring 2020 issue of *Dialogue*; *Exponent II* publishes an issue on Mormon women's activism (vol. 40, no. 1); Annual retreat canceled due to COVID-19 pandemic

2021 Rachel Rueckert becomes ninth editor of *Exponent II* magazine; bimonthly writing workshop series begins; Exponent II expands art scholarship to become the "BIPOC Writer and Artist Scholarship" and begins offering modest honorariums to magazine contributors; Annual retreat canceled due to COVID-19 pandemic

2023 Exponent II launches upgraded website with the organization (magazine, blog, retreat registration) under one digital roof

2024 Exponent II celebrates its fiftieth anniversary and publishes a special double issue for the anniversary (vol. 43, no. 4)

**Exponent II Annual Retreat Keynote Speakers:**

1983 Virginia Sorenson and Esther Peterson[1]
1986 Susan Howe
1987 Mary Beth Raynes
1989 Susan Howe
1990 Claudia Bushman
1991 Linda Sillitoe
1992 Camille DeLong
1993 Emma Lou Thayne
1994 Anna-Kaarina Roto
1995 Peggy Fletcher Stack
1996 Louise Plummer
1997 Elouise Bell
1998 Wendy Ulrich
1999 Grethe Peterson
2000 Aileen Clyde
2001 Laurel Madsen
2002 Ann Gardner Stone
2003 Kathleen Flake

---

1. The retreat's format took shape over time, and the term "keynote" was not used until 1986. In 1983, Virginia Sorensen and Esther Peterson were welcomed as "special guests."

2004  Linda Hoffman Kimball
2005  Pandora Brewer
2006  Sharon Swenson
2007  Sue Booth-Forbes
2008  Kate Holbrook
2009  Marion Bishop
2010  Margaret Blair Young
2011  Jana Riess
2012  Claudia Bushman
2013  Emma Lou Thayne, in absentia
2014  Joanna Brooks
2015  Fiona Givens
2016  Carol Lynn Pearson
2017  Fatimah Salleh
2018  Andrea Radke Moss
2019  Rebecca van Uitert
2020  Canceled due to the COVID-19 pandemic
2021  Canceled due to the COVID-19 pandemic. Laurel Thatcher Ulrich writes essay "Retreating" in lieu of her keynote, vol. 40, no. 2
2022  Allison Hong Merrill
2023  Lacey Bagley
2024  Heather Sundahl

For a broader timeline of key events in Mormon feminist history, see Joanna Brooks, Rachel Hunt Steenblik, and Hannah Wheelwright, eds. *Mormon Feminism: Essential Writings* (New York: Oxford University Press, 2016), 24–32; see also Laurel Thatcher Ulrich, "Mormon Women in the History of Second Wave Feminism," *Dialogue: A Journal of Mormon Thought* 43, no. 2 (Summer 2010): 45–63. Special thanks to Nancy Dredge for assembling a timeline for Exponent II's fortieth anniversary that became the basis for these events and list of keynote speakers.

# Introduction

On a sweltering day in June 1974, women of the newly incorporated Mormon Sisters, Inc., gathered in the Boston suburbs. The occasion was the first paste-up party for a "modest but sincere" newspaper, *Exponent II*.[1] After months of effort, the content was ready for the eight-page inaugural issue. The women had their work cut out for them, as the copy was literally in pieces—a paragraph here, a single retyped line there. It all had to be meticulously assembled and proofread before being sent for printing. The Mormon women—a mix of housewives, graduate students, and young professionals—knew they could not wait for conditions to be perfect. With babies and toddlers underfoot, they began.

Editor Claudia Bushman, a mother of six and a doctoral student at Boston University, set forth the purpose and hope of the paper in its first two issues. "*Exponent II*, poised on the dual platforms of Mormonism and Feminism, has two aims: to strengthen The Church of Jesus Christ of Latter-day Saints and to encourage and develop the talents of Mormon women. That these aims are consistent we intend to show by our pages and our lives."[2] The women considered themselves faithful members of the church and saw no conflict in writing about their interests and connecting with other Mormon women. The quarterly would arrive in mailboxes "like a long letter from a dear friend."[3] The paper's founders were proud of their work and naïve about the cold reception they would soon receive from top church leaders.

The greater Boston area, a hub of the Mormon diaspora, served as fertile ground for such a project and nurtured the talent and intellect of transplants from the Intermountain West. It was also a hub of second-wave feminism, home to organizations such as the Cambridge Women's Center, founded in 1971 after a group of feminists staged a ten-day occupation of a Harvard-owned building, demanding affordable housing, childcare, and education.[4] Few of the Boston-area Mormon feminists, or "Boston group," were

---

1. Claudia Bushman, "*Exponent II* is Born," *Exponent II* 1, no. 1 (July 1974): 2.
2. Bushman.
3. Bushman, "*Exponent II*: Why?" *Exponent II* 1, no. 2 (October 1974): 2.
4. "History," Cambridge Women's Center, cambridgewomenscenter.org.

inclined to participate in political demonstrations. However, they engaged in the consciousness-raising era by meeting in living rooms with fellow Relief Society sisters to discuss the women's movement. In *Exponent II*, they created a national platform that cultivated connections among Mormon feminists across the United States and beyond through individual contributions and regional guest-edited issues. But for participants of a conservative, patriarchal religious tradition, might engaging in even mild feminist activism pose a risk to one's church standing? This was never more threatening than in the early nineties during an era of LDS Church retrenchment against intellectualism, feminism, and homosexuality, wherein the church excommunicated several writers and scholars.

As the era of retrenchment cooled, Jan Shipps, the acclaimed non-LDS scholar of Mormon history, visited Boston. She spoke at an Exponent II event in October 1997 and shared her perspective on the paper's unique position among the "unsponsored sector" of Mormon publications. *Exponent II* was founded in an era of intellectual excitement in the burgeoning field of Mormon studies in which several organizations and publications emerged: the Mormon History Association (1965)[5] and its publication, the *Journal of Mormon History* (1974); *Dialogue: A Journal of Mormon Thought* (1966); and the Sunstone Education Foundation (1974) and its magazine, *Sunstone* (1975). Shipps dubbed *Exponent II* as "Mormonism's Stealth Alternative."[6] Like a military plane that flies without radar detection, the paper had managed to publish for decades without its staff members facing the church discipline that some writers of *Sunstone* and *Dialogue* had recently experienced. Shipps argued that while *Exponent II* was interested in the past, it did not set out to reconstruct or get at the truth of the past. *Exponent II* did history through "consistently adding to the body of evidence of what it is like to be a Mormon woman." Geography facilitated their stealthiness—they carried out their work away from the shadow of LDS Church headquarters in Utah. Additionally, the staff focused on sharing individual perspectives and only occasionally engaged in direct advocacy. Because they recognized the span of political and religious beliefs among Mormon feminists, they chose connection and community over ideological purity. In this way, *Exponent II* also functioned as *feminism's* stealth alternative, holding space for Mormon feminists to wrestle with issues of equality despite their religious affiliation.

"Stealthy," however, does not mean inconsequential. How has *Exponent II* transformed the lives of its participants? For many, it helped them

---

5. The Mormon History Association was initially founded under the umbrella of the American History Association in 1965 and became an independent organization in 1972.

6. Jan Shipps, "*Exponent II*: Mormonism's Stealth Alternative," *Exponent II* 22, no. 4 (Summer 1999): 28–33.

launch careers, pursue graduate school, impact their communities, or make it through years at home as a caregiver with a greater sense of camaraderie. While some discover the organization in a time of transition and leave empowered for their next stage, others engage in the reciprocal community throughout their lives. Participants have embraced their Mormonism and feminism, at times viewing them as complementary dual identities but just as often wrestling with them as dueling identities. *Exponent II* has partly navigated this tension by resisting static definitions of Mormonism, feminism, and even womanhood, eventually embracing the expansiveness of gender and sexuality in a gendered space. The organization has stretched and morphed those labels to make room for individuals to show up with their full identities and witness one another. With a run of fifty years, *Exponent II* has become the longest-standing independent publication by and for Mormon women and gender minorities. The organization has grown from a quarterly newspaper to a quarterly print magazine, a blog with multiple weekly posts, and an annual retreat in New England.

This book includes the first-ever comprehensive history of this organization and an anthology of selected works from the quarterly publication and blog. The authors conducted over three dozen oral history interviews, reviewed every issue and thousands of blog posts, consulted secondary histories, and performed archival research. Exponent II began sending material to the Brigham Young University (BYU) archives in Provo, Utah, now called the L. Tom Perry Special Collections, in 1977.[7] The authors accessed decades of meeting minutes, financial and organizational records, correspondence, content drafts, scrapbooks, and miscellaneous materials through that archive. For recent content, the authors collected documents from the organization's board members and volunteers. The anthology of selected works includes a sampling of *Exponent II*'s best writing, dominant themes, and most memorable and historically significant pieces. The selections span a range of topics, including sexism, motherhood, abortion, adoption, infertility, domestic and ecclesiastical abuse, war, mental health, marriage, singlehood, queer identity, racial identity, the divine feminine, and more.

It is challenging to write the perilously recent past for an ongoing organization whose participants are mostly still living and deserving of dignity and appropriate privacy.[8] As authors, we opted to write a chronological history following the paper's editor eras, tracing the organization's transitions, successes, and most significant challenges. We hope that scholars and the

---

7. "Exponent II Papers to BYU," *Exponent II* 3, no. 4 (June 1977): 3.
8. Heather Ann Thompson, "Writing the Perilously Recent Past: The Historian's Dilemma," American Historical Association, October 1, 2013, historians.org.

Exponent II community alike will view gaps in this history as opportunities for further research and writing. There is much to explore from *Exponent II*, and its writing and art are more accessible now than ever before. BYU library's staff has scanned and uploaded to Internet Archive (archive.org) the entire backlog of *Exponent II*'s quarterly publication; only the most recent years are behind a paywall on exponentii.org, where the blog is accessible for free, and readers can purchase a print or online-only annual subscription.

In these pages, readers will find the founders' excitement of discovering and leaning into their Mormon history to create a platform to connect the blossoming network of Mormon feminists and their agentive decision to persist when male church leaders encouraged them to shut down. They will see the *Exponent II* staff learn hard lessons on how friendship and trust are not enough to run a nonprofit organization and watch them navigate volunteer burnout, disagreements, and betrayal. Readers will follow the paper to the brink of closing before successfully bridging the gap of the digital revolution. They will witness the struggle of foundational leaders handing off the organization to a new, geographically dispersed generation eager to engage in the resurgence of the women's movement. They will see the volunteers' grit, determination, and tenacity. Technology has evolved, and its community has expanded, but the can-do impulses that led the founders to plant the seeds of *Exponent II* are the same impulses that allow the community to grow and flourish today.

The organization emerged from a group of project-oriented women who learned they "could use small bits of time to accomplish something useful."[9] They started by creating a guidebook to navigating their city: *A Beginner's Boston*.

---

9. Laurel Thatcher Ulrich, "Mormon Women in the History of Second-Wave Feminism," *Dialogue: A Journal of Mormon Thought* 43, no. 2 (Fall 2010): 49.

# 1  *A Beginner's Boston* and Beyond

Bishop van Uitert had had enough. Nearly a decade before the first issue of *Exponent II*, Laurel Thatcher Ulrich, Bonnie Horne, and their husbands met for dinner at the home of LuAnne and Bert van Uitert, then bishop of the Cambridge Ward. In the latter half of the twentieth century, the Boston area, rife with institutions of higher education, became one of several diasporic sites that Latter-day Saints migrated to from the Intermountain West for school or work. Ulrich recalls Bishop van Uitert saying he was tired of church members moving out to Boston and complaining for the first two years before they adjusted to living in a new place. He suggested the ward produce a practical guidebook for living in Boston to help with the problem, one that could be sold and double as a ward fundraiser.[1] Ulrich, then a stay-at-home mother of four children, had published some pieces in the *Relief Society Magazine*, a periodical sponsored by the church for the women's organization. She was interested in the task. When the bishop introduced the idea to the ward council, the elder's quorum leaders rejected it, certain the book wouldn't make money. Horne, as ward Relief Society president, said the women would do it.[2]

With Ulrich at the helm, the 1966 publication of *A Beginner's Boston* became a collective fundraiser for the Cambridge Ward Relief Society. Ulrich brought on Carolyn Peters (now Person), a woman she visit taught, to do the artwork.[3] LuAnne van Uitert did the typing. Dozens of ward members made recommendations, wrote small sections, and assisted in the book's production and distribution. The women scraped together enough money to print 1,000 copies and sent an advanced copy to the *Boston Globe*. Citing the effort of "several young housewives," the reviewer praised the book as "a thorough, wonderfully readable, imaginative and practical guide to just about

---

1. Laurel Thatcher Ulrich, interview with the authors, June 21, 2022.
2. Ulrich interview.
3. In LDS wards, each woman is assigned two "visiting teachers" whose job it is to visit monthly and offer support and friendship; in 2018 the program became known as "ministering."

The cover of *A Beginner's Boston* by Laurel Thatcher Ulrich and others, illustrated by Carolyn Peters (Person). First published in 1966, this guidebook was sold as a fundraiser for the Cambridge Ward Relief Society. *Courtesy, L. Tom Perry Special Collections, BYU Library, Brigham Young University*

everything in and around Boston."[4] With this glowing review, the women sold out the entire first run before the books arrived. They ordered another 5,000 copies and sold those too. Eventually, with a second edition that Ulrich took a year off from her graduate studies to complete and a third edition under the direction of Claudia Bushman, they sold nearly 23,000 copies.

The guidebook's smashing success raised money and gave the women confidence. At the time, ward Relief Society chapters were responsible for self-funding their activities and contributing to the ward's welfare fund and other needs.[5] The Cambridge Ward Relief Society had previously raised money by hosting bazaars and selling cookbooks but could now fund much of the ward's financial needs for years. They used the money to do things like replace the refrigerator in the Longfellow Park LDS chapel where they met, buy new drapes for the Relief Society room, and pay babysitters during weekday Relief Society meetings.[6] The Relief Society played a crucial part in

---

4. Diane White, "Splendid Way to Learn About Boston," *Boston Globe*, September 13, 1966.
5. Colleen McDannell, *Sister Saints: Mormon Women Since the End of Polygamy* (New York: Oxford University Press, 2019), 93–94.
6. Ulrich interview.

the social lives of these women. There, they built the relationships necessary to collaborate on group projects.

### Consciousness Raising among Boston Mormon Women

With the emerging women's movement raising questions about gender roles and equal rights, Ulrich invited a group of female friends from her ward to her home in June 1970 to discuss the issues. Their conversation included many of the same topics as other consciousness-raising groups around the country—birth control, family size, women in the workplace—but also issues unique to their lives as Latter-day Saints. For instance, were they obligated to accept any church job requested of them?[7] Ulrich reflected a decade later:

> I remember Claudia Bushman sitting on a straight oak chair near my fireplace telling us about women's lives in the nineteenth century. Since she had just begun a doctoral program in history, she was our resident scholar. If we had a resident feminist, it was Judy Dushku, who came to that first meeting with a rhymed manifesto she had picked up at the university where she taught. We laughed at the poem's pungent satire, then pondered its attack on 'living for others.' 'Isn't that what we are supposed to do?' someone said. Our potential for disagreement was obvious, yet on that bright morning we were too absorbed in the unfamiliar openness to care. The talk streamed through the room like sunshine.[8]

Their shared faith united the women, but they came to feminism from different entry points and perspectives. Ulrich had been introduced to Betty Friedan's groundbreaking 1963 book *The Feminine Mystique* by her ward organist.[9] Judy Rasmussen (later Dushku) was a new professor of government and comparative politics at Suffolk University on Beacon Hill; she came to feminism by way of the civil rights and anti-war movements of the 1960s. She often took her students to observe the protests and demonstrations held at the nearby Boston Commons.[10] The women had frequent, intense disagreements, usually rooted in differences in their life stages and experiences. Dushku was single when they began meeting. She later married a man who was not a church member, granting her greater space away from the church's expectations that women stay home with their children. Other women in the group already had several children and husbands who were bishops or serving in other time-intensive church callings. How did the feminist movement

---

7. Bushman, "My Short Happy Life with Exponent II," *Dialogue: A Journal of Mormon Thought* 36, no. 3 (Fall 2003): 183.

8. Ulrich, "The Pink Dialogue and Beyond," *Dialogue: A Journal of Mormon Thought* 14, no. 4 (Winter 1981): 28.

9. Ulrich, "Mormon Women in the History of Second-Wave Feminism," *Dialogue: A Journal of Mormon Thought* 43, no. 2 (Summer 2010): 49.

10. Judy Dushku, interview with the authors, January 30, 2022.

apply to these women when some critical life choices were behind them? The freedom to discuss these important issues in the context of their lives as Mormon women was deeply meaningful, no matter their differing circumstances.

While the Boston group pondered ways to expand women's choices, church leaders in Salt Lake City were streamlining the rapidly globalizing church in ways that ultimately eroded the autonomy of the Relief Society at both the general and local levels via the priesthood correlation movement. Significantly, in July 1970, the church's First Presidency sent two letters that ended the financial independence of the women's organization: Relief Society fund-raisers and dues were to stop, all assets were to be handed over to priesthood officers, and the society would thereafter be financed out of budgets under priesthood control.[11] Initially, many women felt relieved to no longer spend their limited time fundraising. It later became evident that LDS women had lost financial control of their organization and its accompanying decision-making power. Male leaders did not add women to the general financial committee and did not permit women to serve in bishoprics or as financial clerks on a local level.

Additionally, the correlation committee ended the *Relief Society Magazine* after a fifty-six-year run as part of an effort to economize and consolidate church-sponsored publications. The First Presidency and the Quorum of the Twelve would oversee a new trio of magazines—the *Ensign* for adults, the *New Era* for teens, and the *Friend* for children—to represent the entire church, not any particular auxiliary.[12] Mormon women received the implicit message to step back and let men make the decisions in finances and communication unless asked to contribute. However, it was not in the Boston group's nature to wait for calls that would never come.

### Editing the "Pink Issue" of *Dialogue*

Bushman wanted to channel her friends' energy into something productive. Always a project-oriented person, Bushman saw her friends' challenges and frustrations, as well as their talents and proven success in working together on *A Beginner's Boston*. When Eugene England, an editor of the newly-established independent publication *Dialogue: A Journal of Mormon Thought*, visited Boston, Bushman and Ulrich strolled with him through Harvard's red-brick campus. Bushman suggested that the women guest edit an issue of *Dialogue*. She recalled, "I expected more of a hard sell, but he just immediately agreed and said to go ahead with it."[13] Thus began the second significant publishing

---

11. Jill Mulvay Derr, Janath Russell Cannon, and Maureen Ursenbach Beecher, *Women of Covenant: The Story of Relief Society* (Salt Lake City: Deseret Book, 1992), 340–41.

12. Derr et al., 343.

13. Devery S. Anderson, "A History of *Dialogue*, Part Two: Struggle toward Maturity, 1971–1982," *Dialogue: A Journal of Mormon Thought* 33, no. 2 (Summer 2000): 14.

venture of the Boston group. Shortly thereafter, in fall 1970, the Ulrichs moved more than an hour away to Durham, New Hampshire, where Ulrich's husband, Gael, joined the University of New Hampshire's faculty. Ulrich continued to participate in writing and editing from afar as she began her part-time doctoral program in history. Bushman directed efforts locally.

Editing the women's issue of *Dialogue*, later called the "Pink Issue" for its bright magenta cover, proved to be a challenge both interpersonally and creatively. *Dialogue* was not a church-sanctioned publication. Ulrich recalled, "Some women didn't want to be associated with something that might seem critical of the church. Others thought we were not being bold enough"[14]—similar to criticisms that *Exponent II* encounters to this day. The Pink Issue was the first project of its kind for the women and involved a steep learning curve. Bushman solicited contributions from writers and scholars around the country, including Juanita Brooks in Utah, Charlotte Cannon Johnston in Chicago, and Mary Bradford in Washington, D.C. They printed poems by Blanche Berry, a recently deceased Black church member.[15] Church historian Leonard Arrington contributed an essay and continued to support and encourage the Boston group for years to come. Carolyn Peters again supplied artwork, including a woodcut image that the women later adopted as *Exponent II*'s first logo on the paper's masthead. The "Tree of Knowledge" holds a single apple, unbitten—Eve's choice to partake of the fruit and leave the garden was yet to be made.

As the Boston group worked on their issue, Eugene England stepped down as editor of *Dialogue*, and Robert Rees, an English professor at UCLA, took his place. While Rees honored the guest-editing arrangement, the women felt surprised by his criticisms of their work. Ulrich recalled, "He wanted us to tackle tough issues, like polygamy and the priesthood and was puzzled by our fascination with Juanita Brooks' nursing baby and her curdled tomato soup.... In our situation, Juanita Brooks' self-revelations were of immense value. To us it really mattered that the foremost female scholar in Mormondom once hid her typewriting under the ironing."[16] Here, the women brushed against how other people defined feminism. They were carving out a Mormon feminism that allowed them to embrace home and family while also gently pushing against proscriptive models that suggested their efforts should end at motherhood and church service. Locally, groups

---

14. Anderson, 15.

15. Blanche Berry was baptized into the LDS Church in 1963 and died in 1966 at the age of eighty. Before she passed, she gave a number of her poems to her home teacher, Tom Rogers, who submitted them to *Dialogue*. Through Mary Bradford, Berry's poems made their way to Bushman and Ulrich and were published in the *Dialogue* 1971 women's issue and *Exponent II* 1, no. 4.

16. Ulrich, "Pink Dialogue," 31–32.

"Tree of Knowledge" woodcut image by Carolyn Peters (Person). Created for the 1971 women's issue (the "Pink Issue") of *Dialogue: A Journal of Mormon Thought*, the image was adopted as *Exponent II*'s first logo in 1974.

such as Boston Female Liberation (also known as "Cell 16" because of their headquarters at 16 Lexington Avenue) and the Boston Women's Health Book Collective founded feminist publications, hosted seminars, and participated in demonstrations.[17] Bushman wrote in the Pink Issue's introduction, "Although we sometimes refer to ourselves as the L.D.S. cell of Women's Lib, we claim no affiliation with any of those militant bodies and some of us are so [strait-laced] as to be shocked by their antics. We do read their literature with interest."[18] The Boston group weaved through the tension of external criticism and internal disagreements to publish in summer 1971. Though ultimately a respected issue and what historian Benjamin E. Park terms as "arguably the first explicitly feminist publication in modern Mormonism,"[19] Bushman credits Rees' criticisms as a spur that led the Boston group to study the Mormon women of the past more deeply.

## Unearthing the *Woman's Exponent*

In fall 1972, the Cambridge LDS Institute of Religion director, Steve Gilliland, invited the Boston group to teach a spring 1973 lecture series on Mormon

---

17. Boston Female Liberation/Cell 16 published *No More Fun and Games* beginning in 1968 and launched a magazine called *Second Wave* in 1971. The Boston Women's Health Book Collective published the booklet "Women and their Bodies" in 1970 and the first edition of the book *Our Bodies, Ourselves* in 1973.

18. Bushman, "Women in *Dialogue*: An Introduction," *Dialogue: A Journal of Mormon Thought* 6, no. 2 (Summer 1971): 5.

19. Benjamin E. Park, *American Zion: A New History of Mormonism* (New York: Liveright Publishing, 2024), 299.

Guest speaker Maureen Ursenbach (Beecher) and Susan Kohler at the first Exponent Day Dinner in 1973, held in Cambridge, Massachusetts, as a celebration of the one-hundredth anniversary of the *Woman's Exponent* (1872–1914). Kohler found bound copies of the Utah periodical in Harvard's Widener library and shared her discovery with her Boston-area Mormon feminist friends. *Courtesy, L. Tom Perry Special Collections, BYU Library, Brigham Young University*

women's history.[20] Since the 1960s, American historians had been adopting new social history techniques that more closely examined the lives of "common people" with a new emphasis on women, children, families, class, and race. In line with this movement, the "New Mormon History" was garnering steam, though specialized Mormon women's history was in its infancy.[21] The Boston women divided topics and began research, but one discovery became a goldmine of inspiration. Susan Kohler used her access to Harvard's Widener Library as a faculty spouse to dig through its Mormon collection. There she found large, bound volumes of the all-but-forgotten *Woman's Exponent*, a bi-monthly, Utah-based newspaper that ran from 1872–1914. Kohler recounted, "Dragging a large volume into an unused carrel at the end of the corridor, I began by looking for family names. Every article I read was fascinating.... These women were feminists! They seemed so forthright, so sure

---

20. Bushman, "Women in *Dialogue*: A Retrospective," *Dialogue: A Journal of Mormon Thought* 53, no. 1 (Spring 2020): 125. LDS Institutes of Religion are local organizations connected to the Church Educational System that function outside of the ward structure and provide various religious courses, most often intended for university students and single adults under age thirty.

21. D. Michael Quinn, *The New Mormon History* (Salt Lake City: Signature Books, 1992), vii–x.

of themselves, so liberated!"[22] Thrilled by her discovery, she checked out the volumes and brought them to her friends. They shared her excitement about these Mormon suffragists and activists. The *Woman's Exponent* was not just a window to the past but a mirror. It reflected individuals who grappled with women's rights and worked to actualize their potential while navigating duty to home and church.

Kohler's unearthing of the *Woman's Exponent* intersected with and galvanized several concurrent projects. The Boston women taught their institute classes and then worked to turn their lectures into essays for a book. This became *Mormon Sisters: Women in Early Utah,* edited by Claudia Bushman and initially self-published in 1976 by Emmeline Press, a publishing company created by the women for this book. The women organized the first Exponent Day Dinner in 1973 to celebrate the one-hundredth anniversary of the *Woman's Exponent*'s founding. Judy Dushku invited historian Maureen Ursenbach (Beecher) from the Church History Department in Salt Lake City to present the keynote speech on Eliza R. Snow, a nineteenth-century poet and Relief Society leader.[23] The Exponent Day Dinner became an annual event for the next decade, including speakers such as Judge Christine Durham and historians Juanita Brooks and Jill Mulvay Derr. The dinners allowed the talents of non-literary women in the group to shine, such as Bonnie Horne and Finnish immigrant Mimmu Hartiala-Sloan, with the skills they had honed in Relief Society for organizing and managing large events.

They also started a newspaper.

---

22. Susan Whitaker Kohler, "Discovering the Woman's Exponent," *Dialogue: A Journal of Mormon Thought* 49, no. 2 (Summer 2016): 154.

23. Diary entry for April 24, 1973 in Gary James Bergera, ed. *Confessions of a Mormon Historian: The Diaries of Leonard J. Arrington, 1971–1977*, 3 vols. (Salt Lake City: Signature Book, 2018): 1:482.

# 2 "Wonderful Darling Upstarts"

The Boston Mormon feminists, delighted at discovering their pioneer foremothers' paper and knowledgeable of other local feminist groups producing kitchen-table-style publications, decided to start their own newspaper. Avoiding the more direct advocacy style of other feminist groups, they hoped to give Mormon women greater status, share news and life views, and foster friendships.[1] In short, they gave Mormon women a place to find themselves in feminism. They named their newspaper *Exponent II,* claiming its heritage as a spiritual descendent of the *Woman's Exponent* (1872–1914).[2] To the founders' surprise, church leaders repeatedly challenged the paper in its first year and a half. The staff had to measure their resolve to publish on the dual platforms of Mormonism and feminism.

## From Idea to Newspaper

Like most origin stories, perspectives differ on how the paper came into being. Some of the founders, including Heather Cannon, place the origin in fall 1973 when the women gathered for a retreat at Camp Windigo in western Massachusetts. They talked about the shape of their lives, their goals, and the need for a contemporary newspaper for Mormon women to write about important topics.[3] Alternatively, Claudia Bushman attributes the idea of the paper to a conversation with her husband, Richard, after she came home from a successful meeting with her friends. Claudia told him, "Everything we do turns to gold; what should we do next?" He encouraged her to start a newspaper.[4] Carrel Sheldon recalls that the women first looked to Stephanie Goodson to be the editor.

---

1. Claudia Bushman, "*Exponent II* is Born," *Exponent II* 1, no. 1 (July 1974): 2, and "*Exponent II*: Why?," *Exponent II* 1, no. 2 (October 1974).
2. In this volume, the *Woman's Exponent* will always be referred to by its full name. "*Exponent II*" will be used to refer to the quarterly print publication, "Exponent II" or "Exponent" without italics for the organization or its community, and "*The Exponent*" or "the Exponent II blog" for the blog.
3. Heather S. Cannon, "Fall Retreat," *Exponent II* 1, no. 1 (July 1974): 1.
4. Claudia Bushman, interview with the authors, June 27, 2022.

[Stephanie] had a degree in journalism, and she had worked many years on newspapers. She wanted to be the editor. She was Relief Society president at the time, and she felt that she had to be released. She couldn't do both. She went to her bishop and literally begged him to release her. She felt that she had been called to do this other work, to be editor of *Exponent II*. He refused to release her ... so she had to decline the editorship. Claudia very ably became our first editor.[5]

Like Goodson, Bushman could offer reasons why this wasn't the right time for her—she had six children ranging from ages three to eighteen, was a doctoral student, and was editing the book *Mormon Sisters*. But she accepted the role in line with her personal life philosophy, "You always have room for another big job, and you should always just say yes, no matter what."[6] The women did not envision their feminist paper as displacing church or home responsibilities but as a thoughtful addition to those roles.

Producing *Exponent II*'s inaugural issue called on the skills and labor of the entire staff—and some of their husbands. Bushman solicited content from friends around the country; Judy Dushku, Stephanie Goodson, Heather Cannon, Laurel Thatcher Ulrich, and others wrote articles. Connie Cannon's husband, Jim, prepared legal filings for the nonprofit. Carrel Sheldon opened the bank account and post office box. Carolyn Peters created witty and idiosyncratic drawings, and art director Joyce Campbell assisted in the paper's layout. Sheldon and Bonnie Horne managed production at the first paste-up party, held at Maryann MacMurray's home, which was in disarray as her family prepared to move. Horne set up lightboards of frosted glass with frames built by Sheldon's husband, Garret. Each frame rested on large wheat cans from the MacMurrays' year supply of food storage. The copy, which Susan Kohler typed and retyped on her husband's Selectric typewriter, was organized into columns on pages and then embellished with paste-on headlines, composed one character at a time.

Staff responsibilities took shape over the following months. Continuously inspired by their history, Kohler mined old issues of the *Woman's Exponent* for pertinent pieces to republish. From New Hampshire, Ulrich took on an advisory role, handled book reviews, and hosted some staff retreats. Heather Cannon edited the "Cottage Industry" column about women's home business ventures. Patricia Butler edited the "Frugal Housewife" column, which focused on Mormon women's domestic inclinations and featured subjects such as housework, canning, and food storage. Dushku edited the long-running

---

5. "The Founding Foremothers," *Exponent II* 10, no. 1 (Fall 1983): 8–9. This article, included on pages 151–56, includes additional perspectives on the paper's founding.

6. Busman interview.

Exponent II staff retreat at Grethe Peterson's farmhouse in Winchendon, Massachusetts, September 1975. Back row: Grethe Peterson, Claudia Bushman, Mimmu Haritala-Sloan, Laurel Thatcher Ulrich, Bonnie Horne, Kaye Clay, Vicki Clarke. Front row: Judy Dushku, Tricia Butler, Nancy Dredge, Connie Cannon. *Courtesy, L. Tom Perry Special Collections, BYU Library, Brigham Young University*

"Sisters Speak" column, where she posed a question in one issue and printed reader responses in the next. Poetry, short fiction, and reports of interesting events sat alongside profiles of prominent women.

Attracting subscribers and managing their nonprofit's finances became a new and persistent concern. The staff was all unpaid, but production was not free. The first issue tells readers, "We are currently operating out of our grocery budgets ... get in on the kitchen floor of this historic enterprise!"[7] The bulk of the funding for the first issue came from a $300 Church Historical Department grant that Leonard Arrington awarded the Boston group to turn their institute lectures into a book. Since they had only used part of the grant, they commandeered the remains for publishing and mailing costs.[8] To formulate a mailing list, staff collected addresses of family and friends who

---

7. *Exponent II* 1, no. 1 (July 1974): 8.
8. Claudia Bushman, "Looking Backwards," *Exponent II* 10, no. 1 (Fall 1983): 3, 9.

might each distribute a bundle of papers. The women asked if they could pass around copies in Relief Society and left stacks in the ladies' room at church.[9] Robert Rees shared *Dialogue's* mailing list.[10] By the end of the first year, the paper boasted over 2,000 subscribers from all fifty states as well as some foreign countries.[11]

From the outset, *Exponent II* refused to make Mormon women a monolith and sought balanced perspectives on divisive issues, such as mothers working outside the home. With increasingly widespread access to birth control, more college-educated women in the 1970s were delaying marriage and childrearing in favor of starting their careers. They were also more likely to continue working once they had children.[12] Some Mormon women feared that a feminist publication would seek to push women into the workforce and were wary of reading a paper they thought might contradict church leaders' teachings about women's roles.[13] *Exponent II*, however, desired to reflect the broader lived experience of Mormon women. On a single page, they might include one woman's argument for mothers of young children to stay at home alongside an article about a mother who was also a doctor and hired outside childcare.[14] They made these editorial decisions out of care for the women whose stories they shared and the range of opinions among their readers, not out of fear of church censure. Little did they know the fuss that was stirring at church headquarters.

## Conflicts with Salt Lake

Church leaders were unhappy with the emerging crop of unsanctioned Mormon publications. In early 1975, rumors of their displeasure reached Boston. Apostles Howard W. Hunter and Bruce R. McConkie had advised Leonard Arrington that the Church Historical Department was not to give the appearance of approving of *Dialogue*. They also told him that the brethren had "discussed Claudia Bushman's Women's Lib magazine, *Exponent II*," but did not elaborate on their opinion.[15] As a result, Arrington asked Maureen Ursenbach (Beecher) from his department to pull an article on Eliza R. Snow

---

9. Carrel Hilton Sheldon, "The Physical Process of Creation," *Dialogue: A Journal of Mormon Thought* 49, no. 2 (Summer 2016): 159.

10. Robert Rees to Claudia Bushman, August 1, 1974, Exponent II records, MSS 1527, L. Tom Perry Special Collections, Harold B. Lee Library, Brigham Young University, Provo, Utah. Hereafter Exponent II records.

11. Bushman, "Editorial: Exponent II is 1," *Exponent II* 1, no. 5 (June 1975): 2.

12. Claudia Goldin, *Career and Family: Women's Century-Long Journey toward Equity* (Princeton, NJ: Princeton University Press, 2021): 109–32.

13. Nancy Dredge, email to authors, December 13, 2023.

14. Kathryn Ann Anderson, "Truly Brave Women," and Judy Dushku, "A Working Mother," *Exponent II* 1, no. 3 (December 1974): 3.

15. November 17, 1974, entry in Bergera, ed. *Confessions of a Mormon Historian*, 1:753–54.

that she had recently submitted to *Dialogue*. Rees wrote to Bushman: "What do you think of that? I don't particularly like being blackballed, but Leonard Arrington thinks it is best not to make an issue of it at this time ... I certainly hope it is nothing more than that and that neither *Exponent II* nor *Dialogue* is the victim of an official censorship policy."[16] Bushman may have shared Rees's concerns, but she had not heard directly from Salt Lake.

The *Exponent II* staff gathered in June 1975 for a meeting at Vicky Boyack Clark's Belmont home, joined by atypical guests: the Cambridge Ward Bishop, John Romish, and Boston Stake President—Claudia's husband—Richard Bushman. Connie Cannon recorded detailed minutes of the meeting. Romish began hesitantly, not wanting "to upset the apple cart," but shared his concern that it needed to be clear that the paper was not "recognized by the church." He instructed the women not to use church buildings for Exponent activities or church bulletins for announcements. Further, "He questions why we make so much work for ourselves when the church keeps us so busy as it is."[17] Next, Richard Bushman relayed information from two phone calls he received from Elder L. Tom Perry, a new member of the Quorum of the Twelve. It had only been a few years since Perry had served as president of the Boston Stake, and his New England roots may have been why he was selected to speak for the Twelve.

Perry's phone calls identified what Claudia Bushman would later consider her two big mistakes that garnered the brethren's disapproval.[18] First, Perry called regarding a *Globe* article about the LDS Church in Boston; the article cited Claudia as saying that her husband "has tried without success to get [Black members] accepted as missionaries. There are many [white members] within the faith, she said, who wished the ban would be lifted."[19] At the time, the church's racial priesthood restrictions prevented Black male members from being ordained to the priesthood, as was typical for all non-Black male members beginning at age twelve; it also prevented male and female Black members from participating in most temple ordinances. Perry worried the comments indicated the Bushmans were being "restive." Perry's second call concerned the flood of *Exponent II*s that the women sent to the Church Office Building in Salt Lake City for general authorities to give to their wives. The women mistakenly assumed their paper would be pleasantly received. Perry feared the women were trying to "tweak their noses" at the brethren. To avoid any impression that the brethren approved of the

---

16. Robert A. Rees to Claudia Bushman, February 5, 1975, Exponent II records.
17. Exponent II Minutes, June 12, 1975, Exponent II records.
18. Bushman interview.
19. Kay Longcope, "The Mormon Experience," *Boston Globe*, April 13, 1975.

publication, he asked the women to cancel any subscriptions to general authorities, even gift subscriptions.[20]

Despite these rumblings, the *Exponent II* staff still felt confident that their brand of feminism was consistent with the church's aims. They determined to "1. Keep a low profile 2. Do visiting teaching faithfully 3. Make an all-out effort to befriend everyone at the ward 4. Accept and magnify all church callings." They decided to remove the phrase "Mormon Sisters, Inc." from the paper's cover in deference to the men offended by its suggestion of the paper's official status.[21] They hoped that, through their faithfulness to the church, leaders would take their efforts to share women's stories in a positive spirit. They had not yet realized what Mormon feminists repeatedly learn: deference to authority was the preferred evidence of faith. It was not the last they would hear from Salt Lake.

## Visit from Elder Hales

Something had been weighing on Claudia Bushman for weeks. In September 1975, managing editor Grethe Peterson hosted a retreat at her family's farm in Winchendon, Massachusetts. After dinner, Bushman opened the business meeting with unsettling news: Elder Robert D. Hales, a former counselor in the Boston stake presidency and newly called general authority, visited Boston for a stake conference and requested to meet with her. Hales told Bushman that "*Exponent II* should cease." He had submitted one issue of the paper to the Priesthood Correlation Committee, a group led by general authorities who oversaw all church materials, "and they had felt it was in no way objectionable except for the art. They felt that the art smacked of an underground newspaper.... But the actual content of the paper, while substandard in the way it was written, was given their approval." Regardless, Hales feared the paper might damage the reputations of those involved in the eyes of the church. Bushman interpreted the warning to mean that the paper might derail her husband's future callings. She worried that she had to resign, saying, "She is not repentant, but that she is obedient." The staff felt shocked by the news and at what they considered a double standard: Richard Bushman was on *Dialogue*'s board of editors even as he was stake president. To their knowledge, he was not pressured to resign like Claudia. "Is it a hang-up about women?" they wondered.[22]

---

20. Exponent II Minutes, June 12, 1975, Exponent II records. The women did indeed have to cancel some subscriptions to LDS general authorities, including to LeGrand Richards. He had written to accept a gift subscription, but later wrote to cancel as he had learned of the brethren's decision not to show support for *Exponent II*. LeGrand Richards letter to Claudia Bushman, June 17, 1975, Exponent II records.

21. Exponent II Minutes, June 12, 1975, Exponent II records.

22. Exponent II Minutes, September 12, 1975, Exponent II records.

The staff talked late into the night. They had not anticipated pushback from church leaders on a project they viewed as an act of devotion, not rebellion. Bushman felt that the church was wasting the women's talents. Joyce Campbell retorted that maybe they "could open a modeling agency" rather than a newspaper. When Connie Cannon suggested they examine their motives for the paper, Judy Dushku responded that she "feels lonely in the church and needs support" and "feels that the paper can reach a lot of people like herself." Heather Cannon concurred with the paper's ability to give a sense of belonging. After each woman had a chance to speak her mind, they decided to fast and pray about the issue—a common practice Mormons employed for spiritual clarity—and meet the following week.[23] After breaking their individual fasts, they gathered at Campbell's home in Belmont. Grethe Peterson opened the meeting with prayer, and the women discussed Hales' directives. Most felt that the Lord did not care one way or another if they continued with the project, suggesting it was their choice. Ultimately, the group decided to write letters to Hales to express what the paper meant to them.[24] They still hoped their faithfulness could resolve the brethren's concerns. The following month, they voted to change the name of their corporation from Mormon Sisters, Inc. to Exponent II, Inc. in hopes of avoiding further offense.[25] Then in November, the women got word that Elder Perry was flying to Boston and wanted to meet with them.

### LDS Apostle Meets with the *Exponent II* Staff

Perry's visit did not feel like a reunion among old friends, though many had known him for years from his time in stake leadership. The staff gathered at the Bushmans' home in Belmont on Sunday, November 23, 1975, eager to hear what the apostle had to say.[26] Hales had forwarded the women's letters to the Twelve, and Perry spoke on behalf of the brethren. He didn't deliver the death blow that some expected—he said he did not come to tell them to close, only to caution them. Except, that is, for Claudia Bushman: as the wife of the current stake president, he expected her to step down as editor to avoid the appearance that the publication was church-sanctioned.[27] The LDS

---

23. Minutes, September 12, 1975.
24. Minutes, September 12, 1975.
25. Exponent II Minutes, October 1975, Exponent II records.
26. Minutes from the meeting identify the following as present at the meeting: "Apostle L. Tom Perry, President Richard L. Bushman, Vicki Clarke, Judy Dushku, Carrel Sheldon, Joyce Campbell, Heather Cannon, Anzu Roto (visiting from Finland), Nancy Dredge, Susan Kohler, Grethe Peterson, Tricia Butler, Sandra Buys, Laurel Ulrich, Bonnie Horne, Claudia Bushman, Connie Cannon." Exponent II Minutes, November 23, 1975, Exponent II records.
27. Exponent II Minutes, November 23, 1975, Exponent II records, and Claudia Bushman, interview with Exponent II History Committee, June 27, 2022.

Several of *Exponent II*'s Founding Mothers posing at the John Harvard statue on Harvard University campus in 1974. Clockwise from top: Carrel Sheldon, Judy Dushku, Claudia Bushman, Carolyn Peters (Person), Bonnie Horne, Maryann MacMurray, Susan Kohler, Heather Cannon, Joyce Campbell, Stephanie Goodson. *Courtesy, L. Tom Perry Special Collections, BYU Library, Brigham Young University*

Church has a lay ministry with local leaders serving without formal training or pay; they work their regular jobs to support themselves and their families while in ecclesiastical office. There were no written rules about the appropriate activities for a stake president's wife, though it seems there were limits to her freedom. Unspoken rules and precarious power were not unusual for the wives of American Christian ministers in the 1970s who had no avenue for formal authority within their churches. It may have been women's restricted organizational roles, argues historian Kate Bowler, that drove so many of them into the marketplace of public speaking and publishing to begin with.[28]

Perry expressed concerns about unsanctioned publications that the brethren had deemed "disastrous." Perhaps recalling the *Globe* article quoting Bushman, he instructed the women to avoid situations "where the press could blow up our position and try to cause division within the ranks of the Church." Second, he urged them not to push for change in the church. Women should speak out and lead in their communities, but the prophet leads the church. Third, he told them to be careful "on what we say concerning the role of man and woman. It is different. Women must be in a position to touch the lives of small children in a way that only the mother can ... we must not tread on this doctrine." The staff—most of whom were wives and mothers and considered themselves moderate feminists—pushed back. For instance, Sheldon and Peterson raised how the church's view on gender was limiting and that both parents caring for children was a good thing. Perry, perhaps aware of the church's anti-Equal Rights Amendment (ERA) efforts that would soon launch, cautioned them not to "discuss volatile issues such as the ERA when they are at their peak" in order to stay within the bounds of the church. Sheldon wondered if their group was already "outside the bounds of the church" by existing. Perry suggested *that* would be up to the women.[29]

One of *Exponent II*'s explicit goals was to strengthen the church, but the brethren's position reflected a fundamental disagreement about what made the church strong. Bushman had written that Mormon women were trained to "limit their aspirations. Experienced teachers, speakers, and executives, our women could rise like cream in community organizations, yet they hide their talents under bushels."[30] The staff hoped to highlight women's triumphs and inspire more to benefit both the church and their communities. The brethren, in their efforts to streamline and grow the church, were leaning into a corporate model where strength came through consistent top-down messaging. In the decades to come, the brethren would repeatedly teach

---

28. Kate Bowler, *The Preacher's Wife: The Precarious Power of Evangelical Women Celebrities* (Princeton, NJ: Princeton University Press, 2019), 3.
29. Exponent II Minutes, November 23, 1975, Exponent II records.
30. Bushman, "*Exponent II*: Why?"

that a woman's focus should be on her home and children. They presented a singular model of righteous womanhood, with little consideration given to women who were single, childless, or who worked outside the home by necessity. Perry suggested that the women consider how their decision would impact their future callings. He shared that the general boards in Salt Lake (for the women's auxiliaries of Relief Society, Young Women's, and Primary) could no longer adequately represent the whole church. He said that the general boards would soon be dissolved in favor of regional boards and that the women's actions with *Exponent II* could brand them and deprive them of the opportunity to serve in these callings. Reflecting decades later, Laurel Thatcher Ulrich commented that these regional positions for women "never happened."[31] As the meeting concluded, Ulrich said, "Maybe Exponent isn't that important but the women of the Church are ... what if they need us?"[32] What Salt Lake saw as a threat, others saw as a lifeline.

On the one hand, the staff meaningfully considered Perry's cautions, but on the other hand, their post office box filled up with article submissions and letters from admirers. Susan J. Maas from Oregon wrote, "A newspaper for Mormon feminists? Far out! Maybe there is a place in the Church for women like me."[33] Jeffrey R. Holland, then Dean of Religious Instruction at BYU, received a subscription at his office and wrote to request one at home for his wife, Pat. He teased Bushman, "I have guilt-ridden visions of you running a hand-press from 7:00 a.m. to 8:00 p.m. You know—one of the Lowell girls"—referencing the Lowell, Massachusetts, factory workers Bushman was writing about in her dissertation.[34] After visiting the Exponent staff in Boston, poet Emma Lou Thayne wrote from Utah: "Dear Wonderful Darling Upstarts! ... If you ever have doubts about your right to exist, to promulgate the excitement of free expression, to examine and choose or not choose ideas and ways of doing, you must take heart that everywhere there are those of us who resonate to your kind of willingness to look and to be enriched for the looking."[35] Their project was larger than the staff in Boston—they had a growing national audience, and a significant portion of their submissions came from outside New England.

*Exponent II*'s staff did not make their decision about moving forward

---

31. Laurel Thatcher Ulrich, interview with the authors, June 21, 2022. In 2021, the First Presidency approved calling women as area organization advisers to work under male area authorities, but only outside of the United States and Canada. "Area organization advisers: Women leaders in international areas to provide instruction, mentoring," *Church News*, March 17, 2021, thechurchnews.com.

32. Minutes, November 23, 1975.

33. Susan J. Maas, "Letters to the Editor," *Exponent II* 1, no. 2 (October 1974): 10.

34. Jeffrey R. Holland to Claudia Bushman, December 23, 1974, Exponent II records.

35. Emma Lou Thayne letter to Exponent staff, June 14, 1975, Exponent II records.

lightly. Carrel Sheldon recalled, "We had long and anguished group discussions. Some thought we should quit. We began to plan the 'dead bird' issue, envisioning our last cover art as a crow on its back with its feet in the air, Xs for eyes. But some understood Elder Perry's words as giving us the OK to continue ... it was obvious that the general authorities didn't have confidence in us, but we had confidence in ourselves."[36] They weren't interested in staying inside proscriptive boxes of what it meant to be a Mormon or a feminist—they claimed both.

Bushman shared her official decision to follow the directives of the general authorities and step down as editor at their December 1975 meeting. She hoped that in doing so, "our record will be clear" in the eyes of the brethren. The women discussed their options for the next editor—should a committee of editors take Bushman's place? Could any of the women there take on the role? Bushman vouched for Nancy Dredge, who had helped her edit articles for *Mormon Sisters*.[37] Dredge had recently given birth to her third child and was concerned about taking on such a big responsibility, especially without Bushman's wide network of female friends. Nevertheless, she accepted the position, with Peterson and Ulrich serving in an advisory capacity for a couple of issues until Dredge transitioned to editor in chief. The paper would go on.

---

36. Sheldon, "The Physical Process of Creation," *Dialogue: A Journal of Mormon Thought* 49, no. 2 (Summer 2016): 161.

37. Exponent II Minutes, December 3, 1975, Exponent II records.

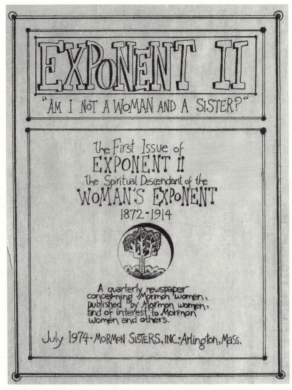

The cover of the first issue of *Exponent II*, published July 1974. Art by Carolyn Peters (Person).

Left: Nancy Dredge, second editor of *Exponent II*, types final edits at paste-up. 1978. Right: Katheleen Watt, art editor, adds detail to the paper. 1978.

# 3  Editing out the Anger

When general authorities insisted that *Exponent II*'s first editor resign due to her husband's role as stake president, they might have expected the paper to fold. Instead, the staff settled into new routines and sought opportunities to connect with Mormon feminists around the country and beyond. As tensions in the church rose over the debate surrounding the Equal Rights Amendment (ERA), *Exponent II* strove to be a place where women could discuss complex issues across the stark lines of identity politics—a place where Mormon feminists could reconcile their sometimes dueling identities.

## Producing the Paper

In retrospect, it seems remarkable that Nancy Dredge, someone so foundational to *Exponent II*, is not always named among its "Founding Mothers." The term gained popularity after the paper's tenth anniversary, and some considered only those named on the masthead of the first issue or in the first year to make the cut. Dredge had participated in the Boston group's Spring 1973 Cambridge Institute course, producing a lecture on the impact of federal anti-polygamy legislation on plural wives in late nineteenth-century Utah.[1] However, in March 1974, shortly after having her second baby, Dredge flew across the world with her children to join her husband, Paul, in a small South Korean village for his field research as part of a Fulbright scholarship.[2] While Dredge taught English classes and minded her children, her friends in Cambridge started the paper. Dredge's mother-in-law brought the second issue of *Exponent II* with her on a visit to South Korea. Dredge wrote to Claudia Bushman, "The 'little newsletter' you envisioned a year ago turned into quite a project! … I can hardly wait to get home and help you with it."[3]

---

1. Dredge, "Victims of Conflict," in *Mormon Sisters: Women in Early Utah*, ed. Claudia Bushman (Logan: Utah State University, 1997), 133–56.
2. Dredge, "A Day in a Korean Village," *Exponent II* 1, no. 5 (1975): 9.
3. Dredge to Claudia Bushman, November 8, 1974, Susan Paxman Collection of Exponent II records, MSS 6192, L. Tom Perry Special Collections, Harold B. Lee Library, Brigham Young University.

She returned to the United States in February 1975, a month before giving birth to her third baby. Back in Cambridge, Dredge held her newborn on her lap as she typed the copy—her first volunteer job for the paper. By the end of the year, she transitioned to editor.

*Exponent II* editors never again experienced such direct interference from LDS general authorities as Bushman did, though they occasionally heard from church leaders. In one instance, Elder Perry forwarded Richard Bushman a letter he had received from an anonymous woman, using Richard as an emissary to *Exponent II*. The woman wrote that she was new to Cambridge and felt both left out of the Cambridge sisterhood *and* afraid to be involved with the paper: "If one does not choose to affiliate with the Exponent women here one begins to feel the void of women friendships, any source of stimulation," though she also felt that joining the staff would require her to "compromise what I feel I should involve myself in."[4] No response was required, but the staff discussed the need to be "careful not to discuss Exponent business in front of those not involved" and to welcome all interested to join their efforts.[5] What the anonymous woman hoped to accomplish by writing Perry is uncertain.

Producing the paper required managing frequent turnover and shifting responsibilities. Dredge wrote, "*Exponent II*'s second year has been one of goodbyes, hellos, and changes. In a transient area like Boston, spring brings not only magnolias and flowering dogwood, but also the departure *en masse* of large numbers of the academic population."[6] Exponent bookkeeper Vicky Clarke left for Utah, art editor Joyce Campbell moved to Paris, and the availability of local staff undulated with the rise and fall of life and family demands. Moving forward demanded flexibility. Board meetings rotated homes, with the rare daytime meetings requiring "zooing it with children."[7] Many meetings took place in the evenings, at times going past midnight, though late nights did not mean an end to disruptions. At one meeting, "attention was then diverted to Muffin, Grethe's Golden Retriever, who just had six puppies and was being unruly. Muffin was disciplined and the meeting returned to order."[8]

The Petersons opened their residence to the paper's production. While Grethe Peterson's husband, Chase, worked in Harvard's administration, they lived in a large historic home at 95 Irving Street in Cambridge. The house provided space for discussion groups in the living room, board meetings in

---

4. Unsigned letter to Elder L. Tom Perry, January 30, 1976, Exponent II records.
5. Minutes, February 26, 1976, at Vicky Clarke's home, Exponent II records.
6. Dredge, "Transitions," *Exponent II* 2, no. 4 (June 1976): 2.
7. Minutes, February 26, 1976, at Vicky Clarke's home, Exponent II records.
8. Minutes, September 22, 1976, Exponent II records.

Exponent II staff photo from 1978 in Grethe Peterson's home library in Cambridge, Massachusetts. Back row: Linda Hoffman Kimball, Wendy Whitman, Sharon Miller, Janice McKinnon, Susan H. Porter, Grethe Peterson, Renee Tietjen, Diane McKinney, Helen Claire Sievers. Front row: Janna Haynie, Jeanne Decker, Robin Hammond, Saundra Buys, Carrel Sheldon, Bonnie Horne, Tricia Butler, Nancy Dredge, Judy Dushku, Kathleen Watt. *Image touchups by Abigail Coyle*

the library, and mailings of the paper prepared on the dining room table. They held quarterly paste-up meetings in the fourth-story, uninsulated attic space, utilizing a large ping-pong table as the central workstation. Peterson recalls, "We kept the lines straight with the help of graph paper taped to a light board ... so the blue lines wouldn't show up in the finished product but would help us line everything up. The ping pong table was soon littered with lamps, graph paper, scotch tape, scissors, and glue."[9] The staff tacked previous issues of the paper up on the walls as a visible template for design continuity. While Chase served in the bishopric of the student-attended Cambridge University Ward, Grethe found herself in a position to meet and invite younger women to join the staff, including Susan Howe, Renee Tietjen, Sharon Miller, and Diane McKinney (later Kellogg). As deadlines approached, Exponent women came and went freely, with Muffin taking on the role as eager receptionist.[10]

When the Petersons moved back to Utah in 1978, Grethe tapped McKinney to take over as the paper's managing editor. McKinney—an unmarried doctoral student studying organizational behavior at Harvard—had gotten to know Peterson through her calling as the Relief Society president in the

---

9. Grethe Peterson, *Growing Into Myself: A Memoir* (Salt Lake City, Utah, 2023), 87.
10. Peterson.

Cambridge University Ward. Despite their age gap, they became close friends and jogging partners. McKinney took advantage of the large kitchen in her second-story condo to host paste-up parties. She lived directly above Chris and Linda Hoffman Kimball, a back stairwell connecting their apartments. They arranged for McKinney to keep her door unlocked so that Kimball, then art editor, could come up anytime to work on the paper and add her custom hand-drawings.

The project nature of the paper brought together women who may not have otherwise socialized outside of church and allowed for ongoing conversations about significant issues. Much like the consciousness-raising meetings of prior years, they discussed sex, marriage, family planning, and national politics. The staff received letters from Mormon women across the country, giving them a deeper understanding of women's issues, including mental health challenges. Exponent women gathered to view the 1979 documentary *Mormon Women and Depression* reporter Louise Degn produced for Utah's KSL Channel 5 news. Dredge recalled how revolutionary it felt to openly discuss a taboo topic: "If you were a Mormon, you were supposed to be happy and not depressed because depression and happiness are opposite each other, right? No." They published an article on the documentary by Lavina Fielding (later Anderson) and personal responses in the Sisters Speak column. Exponent repeatedly found openings to bring shadow topics to light.

The paper connected dispersed pockets of Mormon feminists through regional guest-edited issues. When one of the paper's co-founders, Connie Cannon, moved to Colorado, she guest edited the Spring 1980 Denver issue. Most often, however, guest editors were subscribers or friends of staff who reached out with an offer to solicit content from their local network. Guest editing from Provo for the September 1976 issue, English professor Elouise Bell highlighted feminism at BYU and the lives of groundbreaking, now senior-aged Mormon women. From New York City, Chris Rigby Arrington focused on Mormon art and theater in the Spring 1978 issue. Lael J. Littke led the Summer 1979 Pasadena, California, issue, which centered on the lives of local, "everyday" women. Susan Sessions Rugh edited the Fall 1980 Chicago issue, exploring tension points of the feminist movement for Mormon women in decisions to work or stay home and the political causes they support. Rebecca Chandler's Summer 1981 Ohio issue sought to commemorate the LDS Church's sesquicentennial and argued that the "Kirtland era" is still underway.

Understanding each other's individual and regional contexts was important for Mormon feminists to forge relationships across differences, including race and politics. While *Exponent II* had published writing by Black women and other women of color beginning in its first year, its staff in Boston primarily consisted of white transplants from the western United States. The paper rarely discussed race explicitly; when it did, the writer was most often white. However, the 1970s was a significant decade for the LDS Church's reckoning with its treatment of Black members. In 1971, with approval from the First Presidency, three Black male converts in Salt Lake City—Ruffin Bridgeforth, Darius Gray, and Eugene Orr—founded the Genesis Group to support Black members of the church.[11] In June 1978, the First Presidency, led by Spencer W. Kimball, announced the Revelation on the Priesthood that reversed long-held discriminatory doctrines and extended LDS priesthood and temple ordinances to Black church members. Chris Rigby Arrington wrote about the 1978 Revelation for *Exponent II*, focusing on sisterhood and quoting Black Mormon women about what the change meant to them. Arrington wrote that of the church's 4.2 million members, estimates suggested that between 1,000–5,000 members were Black; she hoped that "as a renewed sisterhood grows up around these [B]lack women, it will help bind all Mormon sisters together."[12] A decade later, Scott Adams-Cooper, a rare male *Exponent II* staffer, spoke with participants of the Genesis Group and members of a local Boston branch in a Black community about the progress and ongoing prejudice that Black church members faced.[13] While *Exponent II* exulted in the 1978 Revelation after the fact, it did not advocate for change beforehand. The staff was perhaps cautious due to the censure that founding editor Claudia Bushman received from Elder Perry for speaking to the *Boston Globe* in 1975 about many white members' desires that the church lift the ban.[14]

The regional guest-edited issues of *Exponent II* found opportunities to discuss race in their local contexts after the 1978 revelation. In the Pasadena issue, Mary Ellen Romney MacArthur interviewed five white LDS teenagers about their experiences in the court-ordered desegregated Pasadena school district; they expressed that attending school with Black and other non-white students helped rid them of prejudice.[15] In the Chicago issue, Tom Rugh wrote about the church's new missionary efforts with the "predominantly Black population of Chicago's South Side"; he notes that efforts include both baptizing Black converts and intentionally exposing white church members

---

11. Benjamin E. Park, *American Zion: A New History of Mormonism* (New York: Liveright Publishing, 2024), 292–93.

12. Chris Rigby Arrington, "Blacks, Priesthood and Sisterhood," *Exponent II* 5, no. 1 (1978): 4. The full article is available in this volume on pages 127–29.

13. Scott Adams-Cooper, "All Worthy Male Members..." *Exponent II* 14, no. 2 (1988): 14–15.

14. See page 13.

15. Mary Ellen Romney MacArthur, "Mormons in an Integrated School System," *Exponent II* 5, no. 4 (Summer 1979): 6–7.

*Art editor sees to details.*

Art editor Sharon Miller checks column space during the paste-up of *Exponent II*, 1978.

to Black culture, music, and food.¹⁶ Also in that issue, Cathy Stokes, a recent Black convert in the Hyde Park Branch, writes that though she felt the Lord had led her to the LDS Church, she must confront the scarcity of what she terms "M.I.L.C.s (Mormons In Living Color)" in addition to the lack of members in nontraditional families and the young average age of her branch.¹⁷ Stokes was the first to publish in *Exponent II* about the challenge of being Black and Mormon.

### The ERA and International Women's Year

Could Mormons support the Equal Rights Amendment (ERA)? Early on, most did. But as national debates around the ERA became heated, Exponent staff confronted unsettling intersections of their dueling identities as feminists and Mormons. Though the ERA was first introduced half a century earlier, it gained new steam from the women's movement and passed both houses of Congress in 1972. The proposed constitutional amendment asserted that "equality of rights under the law shall not be denied or abridged by the United States or by any State on account of sex." Congress set an initial seven-year deadline for the requisite three-fourths of states (38) to ratify the amendment. By the end of 1972, twenty-two states had done so.

The amendment's passage slowed to a glacial pace as opposition led by Roman Catholic antifeminist Phillis Schlafly and her STOP ERA campaign

---

16. Tom Rugh, "The Field Is White," *Exponent II* 7, no. 1 (Fall 1980): 2.

17. Catherine M. Stokes, "A Black Woman's Perspective," *Exponent II* 7, no. 1 (Fall 1980): 14. An interview of Cathy Stokes by Linda Hoffman Kimball is included in this volume on pages 233–37.

*101, 102--Readers keep changing addresses!*

Circulation team member Susan H. Porter keypunches subscribers' mailing addresses to create shipping labels, 1978.

gained a broad conservative coalition and launched the country into identity politics over "family values" (STOP stood for Stop Taking Our Privileges). The growing "religious right" sought to reverse the gains of the civil, gay, and women's rights movements and fought a successful state-by-state campaign to kill the ERA.[18] Initially, LDS leaders did not comment on the amendment. The church entered the public debate after Schlafly visited the newly called General Relief Society president Barbara Smith. Schlafly persuaded Smith that the ERA was a moral issue of great concern to the family, and Smith took her concerns to LDS apostles.[19] With their support, Smith gave a speech on December 13, 1974, stating that "the Equal Rights Amendment is not the way."[20] In October 1976, the church released an official statement opposing the ERA and joined STOP ERA efforts by directing church members to engage in lobbying efforts in several battleground states.

The buzzing, high-nerve scene at the Utah International Women's Year (IWY) conference displayed perhaps the most dramatic demonstration of the church's anti-ERA efforts. Conference organizers, led by BYU professor

---

18. For a fuller history of the ERA fight, see Marjorie J. Spruill's book *Divided We Stand: The Battle Over Women's Rights and Family Values that Polarized American Politics* (New York: Bloomsbury, 2017) and for a detailed treatment on LDS involvement, see Martha Sonntag Bradley, *Pedestals & Podiums: Utah Women, Religious Authority, and Equal Rights* (Salt Lake City: Signature Books, 2005).

19. Colleen McDannell, *Sister Saints: Mormon Women Since the End of Polygamy* (New York: Oxford University Press, 2019), 102–3.

20. Lorie Winder, "LDS Positions on the ERA: An Historical View," *Exponent II* 6, no. 2 (Winter 1980), 6–7.

of education Jan Tyler, expected up to 2,000 participants. Each state was to hold a conference leading up to the National Women's Conference as part of Congress's effort to "assess the progress that has been made toward ensuring equality for all women [and] to set goals for the elimination of all barriers to the full and equal participation of women in all aspects of American life."[21] After LDS apostle Ezra Taft Benson sent a letter directing each Utah ward to select one woman as a spokeswoman and at least ten others to attend, the Salt Palace convention center was overwhelmed with nearly 14,000 women.[22] On the instruction of church leaders, many of the women participated in earlier meetings held by the Conservative Caucus wherein they were directed to vote "no" on all fourteen of the national commission's recommendations. These meetings and anti-ERA literature circulated in Relief Societies pit homemakers against feminists. While a portion of attendees supported the ERA or voted in favor of some of the measures, the Utah convention was overwhelmed by Mormon women who, believing they were voting to protect their families, rejected the resolutions ranging from equal pay to expansion of birth control access to more robust protections for victims of rape.[23]

Back in Massachusetts, which had ratified the ERA in 1972, Exponent staff heard about the events in Utah and other states. Peterson wrote that while summer was usually quieter, that was not the case in 1977: "We have heard from women all over the country. We have received letters, clippings, and more telephone calls from readers and friends, many of whom participated in their state meetings.... There seems to be little agreement as to what actually happened and why, and the implications of the conferences are still very much on the minds of the women."[24] The Fall 1977 and Winter 1978 issues responded to the IWY meetings and the church's apparent interference. Rebecca Cornwall wrote about her surprise at the intensity and hostility Mormon women expressed at the Utah convention. She wondered if it was an accumulation of festering feelings women felt unable to express at church or at home, including "the evolution of the Relief Society from a publicly significant force to a women's auxiliary," and whether this meeting channeled rage into denial.[25] M. and W. Woodworth wrote that Mormon women had moved from the "vanguard to the rearguard" of the women's movement. While women in early Utah worked with national suffragist leaders like Susan B. Anthony, the church was linking itself "with extremist fanatics such

---

21. PUBLIC LAW 94-167—DEC. 23, 1975.
22. Bradley, *Pedestals & Podiums*, 175–76.
23. Bradley, 185–86.
24. Peterson, "Summer of IWY," *Exponent II* 4, no. 1 (Fall 1977): 2.
25. Rebecca Cornwall, "Mormon Denial," *Exponent II* 4, no. 1 (Fall 1977): 5. Included on pages 122–23.

as the Eagle Forum, KKK, and so on" in its fight against the ERA.[26] As they had done in every issue, *Exponent II* reprinted selections from the *Woman's Exponent*. In Fall 1977, they published an 1876 quotation from editor Emmeline B. Wells: "Give (women) equality in all respects, and let each work with the same chance of success according to the labor performed, without the consideration of sex, and there would soon be a vast change which would be a material benefit to the existing state of society."[27] Could looking to their history help them move through the current tensions?

Desiring to remain balanced and uncritical of church leaders, the *Exponent II* staff found responding publicly to the church's STOP ERA efforts complicated. In-person conversations allowed for more openness, though not consensus. At a January 1978 meeting, Lorie Winder (later Stromberg), Susan Porter, Renee Tietjen, and Pam Bookstaber led a discussion on the IWY. Tietjen began the conversation with *Deseret News* articles on what happened in Utah. Winder shared the results of the Houston convention, including the "10,000 at a counter-rally led by Phyllis Schlafly, many from Utah."[28] Winder had been adamantly pro-ERA since a friend in the BYU dorms introduced her to the amendment; she had moved to Boston after graduating specifically to associate with other Mormon feminists and work on the paper.[29] Bookstaber, also a BYU graduate, joined the discussion from an anti-ERA perspective, and "freely admitted her bias" while offering arguments for and against the amendment. Helen Claire Sievers wrote in the meeting's minutes, "A certain tension was felt during the meeting, especially during Pam's discussion. Many left the meeting feeling quite uneasy about the night's discussion."[30] Holding disagreement while remaining in community with one another was both the challenge and the gift of this group. But tension among the staff grew as another Mormon feminist group from Virginia, Mormons for ERA, began making national headlines.

### The LDS Church Excommunicates Sonia Johnson

Sonia Johnson embraced the ERA upon reading it. A mother, wife, and lifelong church member who held a doctorate in education from Rutgers University, she felt shocked when she found herself in conflict with the church's position. Never before an activist, Johnson joined with her friends Hazel Davis Rigby, Maida Rust Withers, and Teddie Wood to found Mormons

---

26. M. and W. Woodworth, "From Vanguard to Rearguard," *Exponent II* 4, no. 2 (Winter 1978): 10. Included on pages 123–25.

27. Emmeline B. Wells, "Small Beginnings," *Woman's Exponent* (September 1, 1876), reprinted in *Exponent II* 4, no. 1 (Fall 1977): 18.

28. Exponent II Minutes, Discussion Group, January 12, 1978, Exponent II records.

29. Lorie Winder Stromberg, interview with the authors, May 17, 2023.

30. Minutes, January 12, 1978, Exponent II records.

for ERA.³¹ The group participated in a pro-ERA demonstration in Washington, D.C., in July 1978, and the following month, Johnson spoke before the Senate Constitutional Rights Subcommittee on behalf of her organization.³² Her speech, "The Church Was Once in the Forefront of the Women's Movement," met immediate opposition from fellow church member, Utah Senator Orrin Hatch; media coverage of their verbal sparring helped launch Johnson and Mormons for ERA into the national spotlight. Of particular concern to Johnson was how the church directed the activities of its members without registering as an anti-ERA lobbying group, thereby feigning that its members' actions in contacting legislatures or showing up at protests reflected organic grassroots activism by concerned citizens.³³ Mormons for ERA began highly publicized demonstrations, including chartering a plane to tow a banner reading "Mormons for ERA are everywhere!" over Temple Square in Salt Lake City during the April 1979 general conference.³⁴ Johnson's actions brought her into conflict with church authorities. After a series of fiery speeches that criticized the church as overly patriarchal, her local leaders initiated a church disciplinary council and excommunicated her in December 1979.³⁵

News of Johnson's excommunication sent shockwaves through the Mormon feminist community. Nancy Dredge and Diane McKinney upended their plans for the Winter 1980 issue. In a joint editorial, they wrote, "After much careful—and prayerful—thought, however, we decided to … carve out a role for the paper in dealing with two concerns: to provide some historical perspectives for those who have expressed confusion as to the facts involved in the Sonia Johnson case, and to allow our readers the chance to read the thoughts of individual committed Church members on various aspects of this event."³⁶ They hoped that by dealing with the divisive topic directly, they might strengthen the sisterhood of their readers. Lorie Winder wrote the historical view, tracking changes in the church's response to the ERA, ending with the church justifying direct intervention with the belief that "the ERA is a moral issue with many disturbing ramifications

---

31. Bradley, *Pedestals & Podiums*, 332.
32. Joanna Brooks, Rachel Hunt Steenblik, and Hannah Wheelwright, eds., *Mormon Feminism: Essential Writings* (New York: Oxford University Press, 2015), 68.
33. "The Issues in Review," *Exponent II* 6, no. 2 (Winter 1980): 9.
34. The LDS Church holds biannual general conferences where general authorities and auxiliary leaders speak to church members. The conferences are televised live (and now streamed) and written versions of the talks are printed in the *Ensign* magazine (and now online).
35. Brooks et al., *Mormon Feminism*, 71–73.
36. Dredge and Diane McKinney, "To Strengthen Sisterhood," *Exponent II* 6, no. 1 (Winter 1980): 7.

for women and for the family as individual members and as a whole."[37] The paper shared a range of responses from staff and readers, including those who were deeply troubled and those who were unsurprised by the results of Johnson's disciplinary council.

Johnson's excommunication pushed *Exponent II* to again wrestle with dueling aspects of feminism and faith. Excommunication is a spiritually violent act within LDS theology that cuts off an individual from covenants deemed necessary to be with their family in the eternities. With such huge ramifications, some found themselves considering both their views on the ERA and their relationship with the church. Judy Dushku wrote how the excommunication felt personal for many women. They wondered whether their questions or points of advocacy—such as protesting the lack of diaper changing tables in men's bathrooms in LDS chapels—put them at risk of church discipline.[38] Dushku's hyperbolic example highlights the uncertainty some feminists felt about where the church drew the line on activism. Was pushing for greater equity in the church acceptable as long as it didn't draw national media attention? When Dushku heard that Johnson would be coming to Boston for a radio interview, she offered to host Johnson in her home for a group discussion, though not as an Exponent event as she knew the board was divided. Dushku wanted Johnson to see that there were Mormon women who supported her, and she wanted her neighbors to see that she was unafraid of associating with Johnson.[39] Hearing Johnson's personal story proved softening for some women who had viewed her actions as too radical.[40]

Behind the scenes, deciding what and how much to say on the topic sparked intense debate and opened fissures among the staff. One challenge was deciding how to present the issues without inflaming tensions. "I was editing out the anger," reflected McKinney. "When Sonia was excommunicated, we were still trying to be the bridge between the church and women.... It was not a time when Exponent was welcomed in the church, and we were walking on eggshells. We were extremely careful with how we phrased things."[41] They wanted to give women a place to speak, but they also wanted women to be heard. The staff struggled with who made decisions about sensitive content: the editors alone, or the entire board? Years later, Dushku wrote about the board's agonizing, late-night discussions over this

---

37. Winder, "LDS Positions on the ERA: An Historical View," *Exponent II* 6, no. 1 (Winter 1980): 6–7.
38. Dushku, "Assessing the Situation," *Exponent II* 6, no. 1 (Winter 1980): 11.
39. Dushku, email to authors, May 31, 2023.
40. Cindy L. Barlow, "Some Positive Repercussions," *Exponent II* 6, no. 1 (Winter 1980): 10.
41. Diane McKinney Kellogg, interview with the authors, December 9, 2022.

issue and coming to vote on each article. Even after the careful decisions, two from the group asked for their names to be pulled from the masthead, and one person resigned from the board.[42]

Johnson's excommunication heightened the shadowy threat of church discipline. In Sasha Cluff's 1996 master's thesis comparing *Exponent II* to the evangelical feminist paper *Daughters of Sarah* founded in Chicago in 1974, she concluded that the strict hierarchical nature of the LDS Church and the threat of official recrimination constrained *Exponent II* from taking bolder social action. Though they emerged from a nearly identical social context, *Daughters of Sarah* had greater freedom to explore social change when no one authoritative body could cut them off from their broader tradition.[43] *Exponent II*'s founders emphasized social support and sisterhood out of care for their readers, not out of fear of church leaders' opinions. However, the looming threat of church discipline complicated their efforts to harmonize Mormonism and feminism. The phrase "the personal is political," popularized by Carol Hanisch's 1970 essay of the same name, was a rallying cry of second-wave feminism. Mormon women found that when religion became political, it also became personal.

---

42. Dushku, "Negotiating Controversy Over Forty Years," *Dialogue: A Journal of Mormon Thought* 49, no. 2 (Summer 2016): 143–52.

43. Sasha S. Cluff, "Christian Feminist Publications and Structures of Constraint: A Comparison of *Daughters of Sarah* and *Exponent II* within the Contexts of Neo-Evangelicalism and Mormonism" (master's thesis, Brigham Young University, 1996), 122–24.

# 4. Pilgrimage, Reunion, Retreat

In 1981, after six years as editor, Nancy Dredge passed the torch and stepped back into a supportive role with the paper. Her family demands were increasing as the oldest of her now five children entered their teen years. Having honed her skills, Dredge was also launching a career as a professional editor.[1] *Exponent II* found its next editor in chief in Susan Howe—a young writer and playwright. Howe moved to Cambridge on a whim after finishing her master's in creative writing at the University of Utah. Unmarried, she found her interest in living in Boston a compelling enough reason to move. Temp work led her to an editing job at Harvard's journal *Science, Technology and Human Values* and then to Houghton Mifflin.

Though Howe's day job was in professional editing, *Exponent II* did not have the budget or equipment of a major publishing house; its production methods continued much the same, even as it shifted locations. Roslyn (Roz) Udall took over the role of managing editor, hosting mailing parties in her unfinished basement in Belmont.[2] Paste-up, as well as many board meetings, moved to Carrel Sheldon's spacious Victorian home in Arlington. Nancy Dredge, Sue Paxman, and Linda Collins assisted as associate editors, divvying up responsibilities to share the workload. Renee Tietjen, a landscape architect student at Harvard, became art editor.

Embracing Exponent's progressive Mormon community, Howe picked up on threads the paper had touched on before and wove them into larger themes. Though tame compared to publications like Gloria Steinem's *Ms.* magazine, *Exponent II* broke new ground for LDS publications with their Fall 1982 issue, "Mormons and Sexuality." The cover was a black and white image of Nancy and Paul Dredge's hands just barely touching, an intentionally subtle suggestion of the issue's theme. Content included an interview with a marriage and family therapist, essays on the challenge of celibacy, passion within marriage, sexless marriage, sexual harassment, and poetry and fictional stories

---

1. Nancy Dredge, interview with the authors, August 17, 2022.
2. Roslyn Udall, interview with the authors, January 17, 2023.

exploring romance, fantasy, and mismatched sex drives.³ Having broached the topic, letters and related submissions flooded their mailbox, including a criticism from the group Affirmation/Gay & Lesbian Mormons that Exponent had missed the opportunity to discuss homosexuality.⁴ In Spring 1983, C. Brooklyn Derr, who had become friends with several Exponent women while attending Harvard, guest edited from Utah an issue on the "Mormon Male." Essays discussed the need to liberate men from traditional, stereotypical notions of masculinity, make greater room for men to experience the full range of human emotions, and shift the culture for men to partner in homemaking and parenting.⁵ These issues made room for readers to consider the topics of sexuality and gender in a more nuanced and expansive way.

Recognizing that the paper had a national reach to an audience of diverse perspectives, Howe launched the popular and long-running East/West column. For the East correspondent, she called upon the talents of *Exponent II* co-founder Laurel Thatcher Ulrich, then a doctoral student at the University of New Hampshire. For the West correspondent, she asked the Utah-based poet and novelist Emma Lou Thayne. Over the following decade, Ulrich and Thayne wrote about motherhood, faith, visiting teaching, feminism, and more. Their friendship was first sparked through reading each other's writing. Ulrich reviewed Thayne's novel *Never Past the Gate*.⁶ The following summer, Ulrich ran across Thayne in a bakery in Salt Lake City and immediately recognized her.⁷ When Thayne found herself in New Hampshire for a writing project, she called Ulrich to arrange a lunch.⁸ Their friendship blossomed through sharing the pages of their column and visiting together when possible. One such opportunity to connect was in Nauvoo.

## Pilgrimage

History called Mormon feminists on a pilgrimage. The landmark "Pilgrims" retreat took place in Nauvoo, Illinois, from May 15–17, 1982. Utah-based writers and historians Lavina Fielding Anderson, Maureen Ursenbach Beecher, Jill Mulvay Derr, Carol Cornwall Madsen, and Linda King Newell organized the gathering to celebrate the 140th anniversary of the Relief Society.⁹ With space limited to the number of bunk beds in the Nauvoo Mansion

---

3. *Exponent II* 9, no. 1 (Fall 1982). See cover of this issue on page 111.

4. Affirmation/Gay & Lesbian Mormons, Letter to the Editor, *Exponent II* 9, no. 2 (Winter 1983): 20.

5. *Exponent II* 9, no. 3 (Spring 1983).

6. Ulrich, "An Insider's Novel," *Exponent II* 2, no. 4 (June 1976): 14.

7. Laurel Thatcher Ulrich, interview with the authors, June 21, 2022.

8. Emma Lou Thayne, "On a Common Branch," in *All God's Critters Got a Place in the Choir* (Salt Lake City: Aspen Books, 1995), 1.

9. Hand Carré, "Women Retreat for Support, Strength," *Sunstone*, October 1989, 47.

House, the organizers invited a select group they knew to share their interests in feminism and Mormon women's history. But many invitees had a friend they thought must also be included, so the list of attendees grew from there.[10] Ultimately, the retreat consisted of about fifty-four women from around the country, including *Exponent II* staffers Nancy Dredge, Judy Dushku, Bonnie Horne, Diane McKinney Kellogg, Sue Paxman, Carrel Sheldon, and Laurel Thatcher Ulrich, along with many former staff and contributing writers.

The Pilgrimage intended to strengthen the women's connections to one another and to their past, but it required pushing through uneasiness to get to a place of trust.[11] On the first day, Nancy Richards Clarke led a tour of historic Nauvoo. In the evening, attendees gathered above Joseph Smith's red brick store where the Relief Society had been organized. Beecher directed a reader's theater based on the text of the original Nauvoo Relief Society minute book.[12] The women varied in their positionality to the church, and as discussions progressed, the event planners were startled by how much anger some of the women expressed about sexism in the church. Anderson reflected, "The Exponent women were among those most willing to bring up 'if we could change the Church, what would it look like?' proposals. The Salt Lake women, many of whom were employed by the Church or by Brigham Young University, were more hesitant since their jobs could have been affected."[13] There was a sense that it was risky to gather and speak openly about issues they may have with the church. With the anger aired and out of the way, the women went on to strengthen their friendships.[14] The following day, they had breakout sessions, singing led by Cathy Stokes, and late-night conversations. History was the driving force of the weekend, as these Mormon feminist pilgrims sought what so many women and scholars across the country were seeking—to "think back through their mothers" to discover a counter-heritage to the male-focused one that they had inherited.[15]

Many attendees found the pilgrimage deeply moving. The closing event consisted of a Quaker-style meeting. Melodie M. Charles wrote, "We gathered our chairs in a circle on the banks of the Mississippi on a morning newly brilliant after three days of rain near the place where Joseph and Emma had

---

10. Lavina Fielding Anderson, email to the authors, April 6, 2023.
11. Carré, "Women Retreat for Support."
12. Despite the efforts of some of the historians in attendance, the church did not make the minutes publicly available for a few more decades. The full text was published in *The First Fifty Years of Relief Society*, edited by Jill Mulvay Derr et al. (Salt Lake City: Church Historian's Press, 2016).
13. Anderson email.
14. Carré, "Women Retreat for Support."
15. Laurel Thatcher Ulrich, *Well-Behaved Women Seldom Make History* (New York: Vintage Books, 2008), xxxiv.

lived and Emma had died. Thoughts of our heritage made our hearts soar."[16] The women were used to LDS testimony meetings held monthly in sacrament and Relief Society meetings. This meeting, however, lacked hierarchy or priesthood oversight. All who felt moved to stand and speak could do so and share what was in their hearts. Over the following weeks, Ulrich spent time processing the experience in her diary: "Jill Derr said she hoped the conference would send women home *empowered*. It surely did.... What did happen at Nauvoo? A reunion, a retreat, a painful confrontation with my own need for validation, a tumbling down of revelations, personal & universal, a struggle, a giving in, a renewal."[17] When attendees suggested they gather again the following year, the event organizers recommended the women plan their own regional retreats. Seven attendees from the Chicago Hyde Park area organized the Midwest Pilgrims retreat for Spring 1983.[18] In the following years, a network of Mormon feminist "pilgrims" retreats launched around the country.

A few weeks after the Nauvoo pilgrimage, Exponent hosted Anderson as their speaker for the tenth—and final—Woman's Exponent Day Dinner. The dinners had been held annually since 1973 as a way to celebrate the founding of the *Woman's Exponent*. Anderson's speech was titled, "On Being Happy: An Exercise in Spiritual Autobiography." She introduced the genre of "spiritual autobiography" as one that had existed for centuries. She had become familiar with it in the Mormon tradition through reading hundreds of life stories and journals in the church archives. She continued with personal stories and lessons that had shaped her spiritual life.[19] The Nauvoo pilgrimage and Anderson's speech had an enduring impact. Exponent II adopted Quaker meetings and spiritual autobiographies as traditions into their own national retreats.

### "Reunion" in the New Hampshire Woods

Communities like to gather and celebrate. The *Exponent II* staff planned two projects to commemorate the paper's tenth anniversary. The first was a ten-year retrospective issue that contained the "best of" from previous issues.[20] The second project, chaired by Sue Paxman, was a "reunion"—a retreat in which both staff and readers from near and far would be invited to register and attend. Even before launching the paper, the Boston group held small retreats at each other's homes or vacation properties. This event, held from October 7–10, 1983, at Hillsboro Camp in New Hampshire, would be Exponent's first truly national retreat. Its format was inspired in part by

---

16. Melodie M. Charles, "The Pilgrimage," *Exponent II* 8, no. 4 (Summer 1982): 13.
17. Ulrich, diary entry, May 29, 1982, transcribed and shared with the authors.
18. Ann Stone, "Midwest Pilgrims," *Exponent II* 11, no. 2 (Winter 1985): 20.
19. Lavina Fielding Anderson, "On Being Happy: An Exercise in Spiritual Autobiography," *Exponent II* 8, no. 4 (Summer 1982): 1–4, 14. Excerpt on pages 139–40.
20. *Exponent II* 10, no. 4 (Summer 1984).

Jim Sloan talks with a group at Exponent II's first national retreat in 1983 in Hillsboro, New Hampshire. Special guests Virginia Sorensen and Esther Peterson sit back-to-back in the front right of the image.

the 1982 Nauvoo Pilgrimage. Significantly, unlike at previous retreats, the women would not need to plan or cook meals at Hillsboro. The retreat became a restorative place outside of both church structure and the typical concerns of their daily lives.

Months of planning culminated with Paxman, clipboard in hand, directing attendees aboard the bus at the Cambridge Ward chapel. Nearly 125 people, including five men, attended from around the country. Once at Hillsboro, they were assigned rudimentary cabins equipped with metal-frame bunk beds and screen-only windows and doors. Bathroom facilities consisted of wooden outhouses and cold-water sinks with a small outdoor shower house some distance away from the cabins. After settling in, campers made their way around the lake to the dining hall. Traveling from California, Lael Littke captured the camper's delight at the food: "Dinner was a surprise. We enjoyed a sturdy corn chowder and green salad, thinking that they were just right for our first night. *Then* the meal came ... we were in for a weekend of heaven because all the food was homemade. [Patricia] Puffy Nissen, who runs the camp with her sister Harriet, makes her own bread, ice cream, maple syrup, pickles, and so on."[21] Introductions and stories followed, going late into the night as temperatures dropped. Women ran to their bunks to grab sleeping bags to continue talking by the fire. The unheated cabins proved a challenge in the October chill; campers stuffed their sleeping bags into large

---

21. Lael J. Littke, "Our New Hampshire Weekend.... You Come, Too!" *Exponent II* 10, no. 1 (Fall 1983): 4–5.

Judy Dushku speaks at the 1983 retreat in Hillsboro, New Hampshire. Behind her, the camp slogan reads, "Here let the fire of ever-lasting friendship burn."

plastic trash bags to add insulation. The following year, Paxman moved the date up from October to July: "Never again would I sleep that cold."[22]

Saturday started off with aerobics led by Bonnie Wood and followed with breakout sessions and more incredible meals. Sessions mirrored the topics that *Exponent II* discussed in print: Ann Rhytting presented on "Mormons and Sexuality," Renee Tietjen discussed "Creative Crises," and Meg Wheatley spoke on "Mormonism and Feminism," among other options. Though the term "keynote" was not officially used for a few more years, a highlight was "An Evening with Virginia Sorensen and Esther Peterson," led by *Dialogue* editor and long-time *Exponent II* contributor, Mary Bradford. Peterson spoke from her experience as a consumer-rights and women's-rights advocate in Washington, D.C, and Sorensen of her career as novelist and writer. Sunday, the final day of camp, took on a more intentionally spiritual tone, starting with a sacrament meeting led by Dennis Lythgoe. Then five people—Marti Lythgoe, Mary Ellen MacArthur, Scott Cooper, Eunice Pace, and Judy Dushku—each shared their spiritual autobiographies.[23] They closed with a Quaker meeting. The retreat offered a place for attendees to harmonize their Mormonism and feminism.

Particularly for women who felt isolated or marginalized in their home wards, gathering with women who understood and accepted them was affirming and empowering. Eileen Lambert came on her own from Rhode Island, unsure of what to expect. She found the retreat deeply emotional and

---

22. Sue Booth-Forbes, interview with the authors, September 30, 2022.
23. Littke, "Our New Hampshire Weekend."

felt that, when she returned home, "something important inside of me had actually been *moved*—to a different place, a better space, larger than before and with more light. My prayers are better now. I am responding to other people, including myself, with more care, with less cynicism." Taking a moment to wander the woods alone, she surprised herself by climbing a tree, something she hadn't done since childhood.[24] The women paddled canoes, walked through fall leaves, talked, and sang hymns. "The singing," Anne Castleton Busath opined. "We sang hymns, we sang Utah suffrage anthems, and we listened to many folk songs from other cultures. Judy Dushku, chorister, many times led in tears to a group singing through tears."[25] Despite unbearably cold nights, the words written above the dining room fireplace served as the camp motto: "Here let the fires of everlasting friendship burn."

While smaller retreats for local staff continued at sporadic intervals, the success of the first year at Hillsboro established the annual retreat as a core part of the Exponent II organization. The paper had always solicited work from readers near and far, but the retreat provided a chance to gather in person and connect. Aware of the financial burden of such a weekend, they aimed to keep registration costs low and offered scholarships whenever funds allowed. With no sense of competition, *Exponent II* freely advertised other Mormon feminist retreats, and over time, participants might attend multiple iterations as cross-country moves or travel permitted. The retreat was not without some controversy, however. Shortly after the first retreat, Exponent staff heard complaints from local priesthood leaders and reports of bishops warning women to be careful of associating with the organization.[26] Caught in a double bind, Exponent was accused of creating cliques and not being welcoming enough while also having some male leaders work against them inviting others to join.

### Community off the Page

Though the paper acted as their ongoing group project, friendship and community made the volunteer labor doable. This included elaborate meals at events like the annual Finnish Christmas celebration at Mimmu Hartiala-Sloan's house and get-togethers for activities like swimming pool ballet.[27] They might host a baby shower one month and arrange a special fast for someone undergoing surgery the next. Carrel Sheldon could be strict with expectations at paste-up and board meetings but also liked to have fun. When Linda Collins (Othote) married a man who was an avid duck hunter, Sheldon arranged

---

24. Eileen Lambert, "Both Going and Coming Back," *Exponent II* 10, no. 1 (Fall 1983): 11.
25. Anne Castleton Busath, "The Only True Reunion," *Exponent II* 10, no. 1 (Fall 1983): 11.
26. Exponent II Minutes, February 9, 1984, and March 8, 1984, Exponent II records.
27. Susan Howe, interview with the authors, July 7, 2022.

a group gift of a Coleman canoe with a Mormon touch. Sheldon called the Coleman company to inquire how to refinish the exterior, and then had her husband take a blowtorch to the canoe's surface. She then invited the staff over to stencil quilt squares and paint the patchwork canoe. They loaded the canoe on a minivan and drove to the reception through a chorus of honks.[28]

New staff often joined due to social connections. Linda Andrews learned about the paper when her college roommate Mindy Ulrich, Laurel's daughter, brought her to a paste-up party. Andrews became a core volunteer after finding the organization to be a place where she felt truly accepted.[29] Cheryl Howard (later DiVito) had been friends with Susan Howe at BYU and reconnected when Howard moved to Boston. At a picnic, Howe pulled out a sheaf of papers to edit, and Howard asked about them. Knowing Howard's background in English, Howe invited her to assist. Among other responsibilities, Howard eventually became the organization's historian. She created scrapbooks of retreats and organized minutes and financial records into binders that made a significant contribution to the growing Exponent II archive at BYU Special Collections.

Few staff members had local extended family, so they learned to lean on each other. In 1981, Howe learned that her twenty-three-year-old sister Nancy, who had just given birth to her first child, was diagnosed with a terminal brain tumor. Howe shared the news at a board meeting.[30] She wrote, "Someone, as we were discussing what I planned to do, asked, 'Do you have the money to go home?' and I broke down and cried. Those dear sisters gave me, on the spot, the money for an airplane ticket to Utah, and then we all knelt together in prayer, asking a blessing on my sister."[31] She flew home to be with her sister and family in what would prove to be a year of loss.

Decades later, Howe reflected on what it meant to her to be in a community of women who supported one another, had fun together, and listened deeply to each other's honest experiences: "We had a group of women who enjoyed life.... I think that the closest you come to what's holy and to understanding people as the Savior does is when people are honest in sharing their lives and their hearts. And that really happened."[32] Feminism did not hinder the women's deeply Mormon spiritual practices. After three years as editor in chief, Howe accepted a position in a PhD program in Colorado. Having completed its first decade, the paper passed into Sue Paxman's capable hands.

---

28. Cheryl Howard DiVito, interview with the authors, September 21, 2022.
29. Linda Andrews, interview with the authors, February 10, 2023.
30. Exponent II Minutes, May 7, 1981, Exponent II records.
31. Howe, "To Promote Sisterhood," *Exponent II* 9, no. 2 (Winter 1983): 2.
32. Howe interview.

# 5  Turning Expectations into Intentions

Sue Paxman (later Booth-Forbes)[1] led *Exponent II* into its second decade and had the longest single run as editor in chief, serving from 1984 to 1997. Under her leadership, the paper favored themed issues over regional guest edits and tackled topics ranging from abortion to homosexuality to adolescent drug use. One subject—the abuse of women and children—became a rallying point where Exponent moved into direct advocacy. Paxman was not new to feminist advocacy. In 1971, while living in Charlottesville, Virginia, her career as an English teacher abruptly ended when she was denied a renewal of her contract due to her pregnancy with her first child. She became a named plaintiff in a legal action that made its way to federal court. While the case was ongoing, the Paxmans moved several times, including for their first stint in Boston where Sue volunteered on *Exponent II*'s staff in its inaugural two years. Finally, in 1980, the court declared the policies under which Paxman had lost her job to be unconstitutional and ordered her reinstatement, though without back pay.[2] While the 1980 judgment was essentially a symbolic victory—both federal law and Paxman's life had moved forward since the 1971 incident—it is one example of how feminism was more than just an intellectual exercise for her. It required both words and action.

## Advocating on Behalf of the Abused

The abuse of women and children became a central theme of Paxman's editorship. Exponent's focus on abuse aligned with national trends in which news media paid greater attention to home and workplace violence. Best-selling books such as Melonie Beattie's 1986 *Codependent No More* opened conversations about unhealthy relationships, Anita Hill's testimony against Clarence Thomas in his 1991 Supreme Court appointment hearings shined a spotlight on workplace sexual harassment, and a broad coalition of grassroots advocacy led to Congress passing the landmark 1994 Violence Against

---

1. Sue Paxman is at times identified in *Exponent II* as Susan L. Paxman and later, Sue Booth-Forbes.
2. Sue Booth-Forbes, interview with the authors, September 30, 2022.

*Exponent II*'s first four editors: Claudia Bushman, Nancy Dredge, Susan Howe, Sue Paxman (Booth-Forbes).

Women Act. In the mid-'80s, unsure of where else to turn, many Mormon women wrote to *Exponent II* about their personal experiences with abuse. The staff realized that even among Mormon families and wards, the problems were more pervasive than they had imagined.

Paxman and Judy Dushku wrote several editorials regarding domestic and ecclesiastical abuse and published essays and letters detailing women's experiences. The Spring 1987 issue focused on power imbalances within relationships. Dushku wrote, "The deadening effect that being controlled has on the coerced—both in body and in spirit—is the core of sin.... Inequity is dangerous because it allows for dominance and use of unrighteous force. It is the source of much of the 'ire' that must disappear before the lamb and the lion can lie down together in peace, harmony, mutual respect, and love."[3] The topic only took on greater urgency. Paxman editorialized in "We Can't Sit By" that she had become overwhelmed in reading the stories of domestic abuse that women sent to *Exponent II*. "My own righteous anger compels me to request further action. I am firmly convinced that until we eliminate all traces of our condoning violence toward women, it will continue to occur in our own culture." She called for church leaders to send a message that the

---

3. Dushku, "The Day of the Lambs and the Lions," *Exponent II* 13, no. 3 (1987): 2.

"abuse of women will not be tolerated" and to disfellowship or excommunicate priesthood-holding abusers.[4]

Frustrated at the inadequate resources for victims of domestic violence within the church, Exponent II began to gather and share its own resources. They reached out to BYU's Women's Research Institute for information and statistics about abuse throughout the church, which the department provided. They coordinated with local non-LDS groups that connected victims to resources and trained experts. At an Exponent-sponsored convocation at Brandeis University, several abuse victims spoke about their experiences and a therapist discussed what constitutes abuse and how to recognize it.[5] Their work opened the door for more conversations about abuse among church members in the Boston area. Paxman and Evelyn Harvill—an Exponent volunteer who had a history of severe childhood abuse—were invited with some frequency to speak with LDS groups.[6] Paxman eventually stopped accepting these local speaking requests because she was discouraged at how few resources she had to offer attendees, but she continued this work in the paper and with efforts such as leading a panel about abuse at the 1991 Washington D.C. Sunstone Symposium[7] and contributing a chapter to the 1993 book *Confronting Abuse: An LDS Perspective*, published by Deseret Book.[8]

Because local leaders were responsive to this advocacy on behalf of victims of abuse, Exponent saw some positive results from their efforts. Dennis Lythgoe, a friend of the paper and a local bishop, wrote about attending an Exponent event with guest speaker Sharon Fleishacher, who worked with abused women through the Women's Protective Services program in Framingham, Massachusetts. The meeting helped Lythgoe recognize the signs of abuse with people he counseled as bishop and opened his eyes to the need to do more. He invited Fleishacher to speak to bishops and Relief Society presidents in his stake.[9] In a move nearly unheard of in the LDS Church, Bishop Bob Chandler in the Arlington Ward called Mimmu Hartiala-Sloan as a counselor and liaison with women in the ward. Women could go directly to Hartiala-Sloan to discuss sensitive issues; she would direct them to professional or pastoral counseling as necessary and often attended meetings and

---

4. Sue Paxman, "We Can't Sit By," *Exponent II* 4, no. 1 (1987): 2.
5. Barbara Taylor, email to the authors, July 2, 2023.
6. Booth-Forbes interview.
7. Paxman, "Women as Victims—Women as Healers: The Presence of Violence in Our Society," 1991 Washington, DC, Sunstone Symposium.
8. Anne L. Horton, B. Kent Harrison, Barry L. Johnson, eds., *Confronting Abuse: An LDS Perspective on Understanding and Healing Emotional, Physical, Sexual, Psychological, and Spiritual Abuse* (Salt Lake City: Deseret Book, 1993).
9. Dennis Lythgoe, letter in "Sisters Help," *Exponent II* 14, no. 3 (1988): 14. Excerpt on pages 199–200.

therapy sessions with women who did not want to meet alone with men.[10] Managing editor Barbara Taylor served on a committee in the Boston Stake formed to provide feedback and suggestions on how the stake could better help victims of abuse; she recalls Stake President Mitt Romney reaching out to leaders in Salt Lake and receiving additional resources and training for local leaders.[11] However, local efforts yielded local results. Over the following decades, Mormons seeking structural changes at the general church level to protect abuse victims at times found their church membership at risk.

### "Learning to Speak from Experience"

It is not always easy to talk openly about abortion. Though *Exponent II* had long printed discussions about family planning and birth control, their first issue focused on abortion came in 1990. Unlike the Boston Women's Health Book Collective and their best-selling pamphlet-turned-book *Our Bodies, Ourselves*, which had spoken frankly about abortion rights for years, Exponent took a cautious approach. The LDS Church had more permissive policies than some conservative Christian traditions—allowing for abortion when pregnancy was the result of rape or incest, when the life or health of the mother was in jeopardy, or when the fetus had known terminal defects. However, in the 1980s, the Church's *General Handbook of Instruction* referred to abortion as "one of the most revolting and sinful practices of this day" and considered participating in elective abortion as a potential cause for excommunication.[12] Religious stigma and differing beliefs about abortion divided Mormon women on the topic. "At the Exponent reunion this summer, I asked people their feelings about abortion. No consensus emerged," Dushku wrote. "Then I asked women to tell their own stories about tough decisions to continue or terminate pregnancies. As they talked about their experiences and reflected on them and on what they had learned, a consensus began to surface.... These women felt like they had learned great and beautiful things about the process of making serious decisions with the companionship of the Lord."[13] *Exponent II* dedicated two issues for women, often unnamed, to share their experiences related to abortion and adoption.[14] The hope was that sharing and reading personal stories would give more room for a nuanced understanding beyond political divisions.

---

10. Mimmu Hartiala-Sloan, interview with the authors, January 21, 2024. She was later reclassified as an "advisor" when some leaders objected to her role as a bishopric "counselor" without holding priesthood office.

11. Barbara Taylor, interview with the authors, March 28, 2022.

12. "Abortion," *The General Handbook of Instruction No. 24* (Salt Lake City: The Church of Jesus Christ of Latter-day Saints, 1989), sections 10-4 and 11-4.

13. Dushku, "Abortion: Learning to Speak from Experience," *Exponent II* 15, no. 4 (1990): 2.

14. *Exponent II* 15, no. 4 and 16, no. 2.

Laura Fox and Eileen Lambert at a retreat in Hillsboro, New Hampshire.

Dushku's long-running columns Sisters Speak and Sisters Help exemplified *Exponent II*'s resistance to ideological purity and emphasis on allowing women to speak for themselves.[15] The columns were similar in topics, style, and format, with one main difference: in Sisters Speak, Dushku would pose a question, and in Sisters Help, she would share a letter from a reader asking the Exponent community for non-preachy, sympathetic advice. For both columns, she would publish reader responses to the question or letter in the following issue. This column style was not unique to *Exponent II,* but it allowed contributors to write without the restraints of a formal article or a litmus test of Mormon or feminist orthodoxy. This did not mean that the paper or the views it shared escaped criticism, but personal sharing was less threatening than overt agenda-setting or the appearance of leading a movement. This allowed Exponent to enter challenging conversations. When Carol Lynn Pearson's groundbreaking 1986 memoir *Goodbye, I Love You* about her mixed-sexual-orientation marriage and caring for her ex-husband as he died from AIDS became widely discussed in LDS circles, Dushku saw the opening to discuss homosexuality more directly and frankly.[16] Sisters Speak responses included women's experiences with their own sexuality, mixed-orientation marriages, or with gay family members.[17]

---

15. Dushku edited the Sisters Speak column from 1974 to 2004. She introduced Sisters Help in 1985 and it continued through the late '90s. At times the columns appeared as a combined Sisters Speak/Sisters Help.

16. Dushku, "Sisters Speak," *Exponent II* 13, no. 1 (Fall 1986): 18.

17. "Sisters Speak," *Exponent II* 13, no. 2 (Winter 1987): 16–19.

In one Sisters Help letter, a mother of six young children—whose family was struggling financially—wrote about the challenge of her husband's demanding calling: "My husband was called to be bishop less than a year ago, and I feel like I have been in hell ever since."[18] In the following issue, women who had been wives of bishops responded with empathy, offering recommendations on how to communicate honestly and practical tips for making it through.[19] Other Sisters Speak/Sisters Help columns discussed challenges such as excluding non-church members from temple weddings,[20] eating disorders,[21] and feeling unsafe at church.[22] These columns were a place for members of the Exponent community to speak to one another before email listservs and social media made connecting across distances more accessible. *Exponent II* expanded the limits of Mormon womanhood by facilitating honest personal sharing.

## Modernizing Production

Technology outpaced the paper's budget. Handwritten meeting notes from August 1983 lay the problem bare: "Rent typewriter—no money for word processor." Finding solutions demanded teamwork. By November 1983, a committee consisting of Roslyn (Roz) Udall, Garret Sheldon, and Barbara Taylor arranged to finance a computer that would be stored at Jan and Scott Adams-Cooper's house; the Adams-Coopers would need to explore renter's insurance to protect against loss or theft.[23] Updating production required investing in equipment and training for new skills. By the early '90s, through a combination of financing and thrifty purchases, Exponent II maintained a few computers and printers and requested that essay submissions include an IBM/WordPerfect compatible disk when possible.[24] From her home in Warwick, Rhode Island, Eileen Lambert took on the task of layout and graphic design after Exponent paid for her to take a PageMaker class.

Consequently, the paper's workflow dramatically changed. Paxman would lead the reader's committee for selecting articles, coordinate revisions with the authors, and deliver articles for typing by Ellen Patton or other volunteers. The articles would then be emailed to Lambert, who scanned the art and designed the layout. Former art editor Renee Tietjen had given Lambert a box of clipart books with Victorian-style drawings that Lambert relied on

---

18. *Exponent II* 13, no. 2 (Winter 1987).
19. Sisters Help, *Exponent II* 13, no. 3 (Spring 1987): 10–11.
20. "Sisters Speak," *Exponent II* 12, no. 3 (Winter 1986): 14–15.
21. "Sisters Speak," *Exponent II* 16, no. 2 (1991): 10–11 and *Exponent II* 17, no. 1 (1992): 16–17.
22. "Sisters Speak," *Exponent II* 17, no. 4 (1993): 16–17.
23. Exponent II Minutes, August 4, 1983, and November 3, 1983, Exponent II records.
24. "Call for Submissions," *Exponent II* 17, no. 1 (1992): 20.

for much of the paper's art in addition to original drawings by Linda Hoffman Kimball. Lambert's sister, April Perry, was a painter as well as the art editor of the church's *Ensign* magazine. Perry contributed bespoke paintings, designed a new logo for the paper, and encouraged her sister's efforts.[25] Unlike at the *Ensign*, which had very strict requirements for images, down to the length of Jesus' hair, Lambert had freedom to play and make mistakes.[26] When an issue was complete, Lambert would deliver the file on a disk to the Charles River printing company in Boston. Paxman would receive the "blue pages" to proofread, and after revisions, the issue would go to print. Managing the subscription database was still a demanding task, but Exponent began outsourcing the labor of adding mailing labels, postage, and sorting and bundling by zip code to a mailing service.

The move toward computer processing and design fundamentally shifted the paper's culture. Paste-up parties had allowed staff members to spend time in each other's homes, swapping stories and sharing food as they worked. But the process was labor-intensive and it became difficult to maintain a sufficiently large staff. Volunteer burnout was a perpetual problem. Still, the nostalgia had a strong pull. In August 1989, Carrel Sheldon wrote to the staff that while the "next issue of the paper is now with Eileen Lambert getting beautifully laid out," the following issue would be pasted-up "the old fashioned way with bodies working around lightboards."[27] However, layout was soon exclusively digital. Without the quarterly paste-up and mailing parties, the board entered a transition period.

Modernizing the paper's production required the board to reshape its function. Originally, the organization's work centered on the paper; board meetings were generally open to officers, staff, and friends. While Exponent II always technically maintained a corporate board with the required officers for a legally recognized nonprofit organization, the larger board's membership and function was fluid. Taking over as president from co-presidents Judy Dushku and Mimmu Hartiala-Sloan, Sheldon called a meeting in October 1989 to redefine the board in order to support the organization's current needs. The result was a more distinct separation of the "newspaper" and the "corporation." The newspaper included both the editorial department and the business department. The editorial department was made up by the editor in chief and the various assisting editors and subcommittees that worked together to produce the paper. The business department was responsible for

---

25. A painting by April Perry appeared in *Exponent II* 13, no. 2 (Winter 1987): 10. Perry also created a new logo depicting two female figures under a tree, first used in *Exponent II* 14, no. 4 (1989). See logo on page 387.
26. Eileen Lambert, interview with the authors, February 3, 2023.
27. Exponent II Minutes, August 23, 1989, Exponent II records.

Carrel Sheldon leads retreat goers through Friday night introductions.

managing subscriptions, hosting fundraisers, and creating financial reports. The corporation was responsible for annual events such as the fall open house, the staff Christmas party, and the retreat in New Hampshire. They would also host discussion meetings and oversee special projects.[28] While roles became more distinct on paper, a degree of fluidity still existed according to volunteer availability. This engendered conflict at times about who had final decision-making power. Formalizing roles was an ongoing struggle for years to come.[29]

## Retreat at Hillsboro Camp

The successful tenth-anniversary "reunion" at Hillsboro Camp in '83 initiated Exponent II's annual open-registration retreat. Retreat directors rotated, with Barbara Taylor, Jennifer Goodfellow, Nancy Dredge, Karen Haglund, and Lisa Tobler-Preece among its many organizers. Retreat directors coordinated thoughtful workshops, and the board voted on who to invite as the keynote speaker. They sometimes brought in well-known Mormon feminists but just as often drew on the wisdom of friends of the paper.[30] A core event

---

28. Carrel Sheldon letters to Exponent II staff, October 15 and October 21, 1989, Exponent II records.
29. Exponent II Minutes and Letters to Staff, September 13–November 22, 1991, Exponent II records.
30. A list of keynote speakers is included on pages xv–xvi.

was the Friday night ceremony led by Sheldon. After dinner, retreat attendees gathered around a fireplace for introductions. Each individual had the chance to share something "significant and real that happened to her in the last year" along with what it meant to her. With upward of seventy attendees, the introductions could last long into the night, especially before Linda Andrews took on the task of timing each speaker. Sheldon would ask the women about their expectations of the weekend—first, the unmet or unmeetable kind. "Once we bring these unmeetable expectations to awareness, we can let them go," she'd explain. Then she'd ask them to consider their intentions and what they want to be responsible for. "In choosing to be responsible for making something happen, they can transform those hopeful expectations into intentions." Finally, she would guide the women to offer trust as a gift. "In a setting like a retreat, trust isn't something each of us has a chance of earning. However, trust can be a gift we individually give to the group. We overcome our fears, concerns, excuses, and 'push through' to being willing to trust."[31] With their intentions set, the women could go throughout the weekend a bit more open and self-aware to help them connect with others.

For some women, the annual retreat was their only opportunity to escape household responsibilities and explore what it meant to be an individual. While the first retreat included a handful of male attendees, it was soon limited to only women, as some women found it easier to talk openly without men in the room. However, as only LDS priesthood holders were allowed to bless the sacrament, retreat organizers would invite one or two of the women's husbands to come on Sunday morning to facilitate a sacrament service before the Quaker meeting. It was sometimes challenging to find men available to make the drive. In a board meeting, Eileen Lambert quipped that perhaps the women could bring freeze-dried, pre-blessed sacrament bread.[32] A new tradition emerged with warmer July weather and exclusively women around: late-night skinny-dipping in the lake. They also added a talent variety show on Saturday nights. Evelyn Harvill, a frequent retreat attendee, struggled to be in large gatherings due to mental health challenges and often found she had to leave a room or remain on the edge; however, she gained legendary status for leading humorous musical numbers with a group she named the "Heavenly Bodies." Talent was optional, but feather boas were required.

During intimate and often secluded moments, the network of feminist retreats, including Exponent's, offered some women the opportunity to reclaim the beloved tradition of giving blessings by laying on hands for comfort or healing. LDS Church history is replete with narratives of women

---

31. Sheldon, Retreat Friday Nights, *Exponent II* 24, no. 1 (Fall 2000): 6.
32. Exponent II Minutes, October 2, 1994, Exponent II records.

bestowing blessings, notably in the diaries of prominent Mormon women such as Emmeline B. Wells.[33] Women generally invoked faith rather than priesthood as their source of authority. The practice waned in the first half of the twentieth century, punctuated in 1946 when apostle Joseph Fielding Smith responded to a question from the Relief Society General Board. He wrote that while women's blessings were permissible in some circumstances, "it is far better for us to follow the plan the Lord has given us and send for the elders of the Church to come and administer to the sick and afflicted." His words were incorporated into the Relief Society handbook and served as the unofficial church policy on female ritual healing for decades.[34] Women continued to bless other women in the initiatory ordinance in LDS temples, and some women across ideological lines continued to bless loved ones in times of need. But without institutional support and instruction, the regular practice had nearly faded from living memory by the mid-1980s. Through new, widely read publications, more Mormon women were learning about this practice that reached back to the church's founding.[35]

Though retreat blessings most often took place in cabins with small groups of women, on at least one occasion, a blessing was held during the Sunday morning Quaker meeting. Knowing that Sue Paxman was in the midst of traumatic challenges, a group of women offered to bless her in proxy for all Mormon women. "They sang to me, and individuals spoke," Paxman recalled. "There was a slight breeze, just wafting over me like silk. It was incredible, and it was made incredible by the genuine, authentic way these various powerful, wonderful women spoke from their hearts."[36] For women whose connection to their shared faith first brought them together, the retreat allowed them to reclaim a sense of spiritual authority. Women conducted, preached, and owned their gifts in the all-female space. Many would go home feeling that they had the strength to continue in a patriarchal church that did not always recognize women's power.

---

33. Diaries of Emmeline B. Wells, Church Historians Press, churchhistorianspress.org.

34. Jonathan A. Stapley and Kristine Wright, "Female Ritual Healing in Mormonism," *Journal of Mormon History* 37, no. 1 (Winter 2011): 80–82.

35. See Linda King Newell, "A Gift Given, A Gift Taken: Washing, Anointing, and Blessing the Sick among Mormon Women," *Sunstone*, September/October 1981, 16–25; Derr et al., *Women of Covenant*, 219–23.

36. Booth-Forbes interview.

# 6 "Dangerous History"

By the early 1990s, the United States was enjoying some of the fruits of the women's movement. Women had closed the education attainment gap and slowly increased their ranks in legislatures and business boards. But backlash from the religious right mounted, and rain clouds gathered on the horizon for the Mormon intellectual community. In May 1993, LDS apostle Boyd K. Packer gave a speech to the All-Church Coordinating Council that oversaw teaching and standardization. He outlined what he saw as the three greatest threats to the church: intellectualism, feminism, and the gay-lesbian rights movement.[1] The new Strengthening Church Members Committee scoured LDS-related publications to evaluate orthodoxy, and they sometimes sent their findings to local leaders to use in church discipline proceedings. Historian Sara M. Patterson argues that, in this era of retrenchment, "church leadership clashed with church members over what the faith and the meaning of the Restoration would be."[2] While some apologists defended the action of church leaders in this period as necessary to create unity after a period of rapid global growth—tripling its membership since the early 1970s[3]—its methods included pushing out several progressive scholars from its universities and directing the excommunication of some writers and historians whose work clashed with the church's preferred public image. The retrenchment impacted writers and scholars differently based on where they lived, the response of their local church leaders, and whether their employment depended on the church. *Exponent II*'s staff avoided the most punitive aspects of the era, but the paper's subscription numbers were not left unscathed.

## "Challenging the Mormon Church"

In a church where male leaders seek to correlate a singular narrative, can women's history be dangerous? What if it calls into question the church's

---

1. Sara M. Patterson, *The September Six and the Struggle for the Soul of Mormonism* (Signature Books: Salt Lake City, 2023), 1.
2. Patterson, xxvi.
3. Lowell C. Bennion and Lawrence A. Young, "The Uncertain Dynamics of LDS Expansion, 1950–2000," *Dialogue: A Journal of Mormon Thought* 29, no. 1 (Spring 1996): 8–32.

conservative stance on women's roles or undermines patriarchal doctrine or theology? According to historian Jan Shipps, the sense of danger extends even to active, faithful historians writing women's history unrelated to the church if that historian identifies as a feminist and achieves national prominence.[4] At least, that seems to be the case for Laurel Thatcher Ulrich after she won the Pulitzer and Bancroft Prizes for her groundbreaking 1990 book, *A Midwife's Tale: The Life of Martha Ballard, Based on Her Diary, 1785–1812*. Through eight years of research, Ulrich used Ballard's diary to illuminate Maine's Kennebec Valley's social and economic relationships. "This is the untold story of eighteenth-century rural female culture," Claudia Bushman wrote of the book. "This is not a work of theory and analysis, but of grassroots narrative and description, showing the value of ordinary life."[5] Editor Sue Paxman conveyed *Exponent II*'s immense pride at their friend and co-founder's achievements: "The recognition that Laurel's interpretation of Martha Ballard's diary has received goes a long way in validating not only the *dailiness* of their lives but that *dailiness* in all our lives."[6] The book demonstrated that the details of women's lives matter and are meaningful to history and the present.

*A Midwife's Tale* brought Ulrich significant media attention, and one interview turned the spotlight to *Exponent II*. After reporter Suzanne Gordon published a feature story on Ulrich for the *Boston Sunday Globe Magazine*, she wrote a second feature story about the small Mormon feminist paper Ulrich had co-founded.[7] The article, published in March 1993, captures Exponent's struggle to produce a paper that makes room for the women's intersecting but often dueling identities as Mormons and feminists. The article considers the risk of exile that Mormon feminists face, citing examples of the excommunications of historian Fawn Brodie and activist Sonia Johnson. Connecting the risk to the paper's staff, Gordon touches on an issue that had recently been made public: the Brigham Young University Board of Trustees had barred Ulrich from speaking at BYU.[8]

In November 1992, months before the news was public, Ulrich learned from a friend that her name was "on the list"—the private, unofficial, shadowy list of people banned from speaking at BYU.[9] The BYU Women's Conference

---

4. Jan Shipps, "Dangerous History," in *Sojourner in the Promised Land: Forty Years among the Mormons* (Chicago: University of Illinois Press, 2000), 195.

5. Bushman, "The Tale of the Midwife's Tale," *Exponent II* 15, no. 4 (1990): 18–19.

6. Paxman, "Exponent II Founding Mother Wins Pulitzer Prize," *Exponent II* 16, no. 2 (1991): 2.

7. Exponent II Minutes, February 25, 1993, Exponent II records.

8. Suzanne Gordon, "Challenging the Mormon Church: Feminism Cautiously Tries to Find Its Place in a Conservative Faith," *Boston Globe*, March 25, 1993.

9. Ulrich, November 22, 1992, diary entry, transcribed and shared with authors.

Laurel Thatcher Ulrich at University Hall, standing in front of portraits of Harvard's past presidents. After winning the Bancroft and Pulitzer Prizes for her book, *A Midwife's Tale*, Ulrich became the James Duncan Phillips Professor of Early American History at Harvard University in 1995. *Used by permission, Jim Harrison Photography, all rights reserved*

committee had sought approval to invite Ulrich to speak at the 1993 conference, and BYU's Board of Trustees—consisting of the First Presidency, seven apostles, the church's Commissioner of Education, and the heads of the Relief Society and Young Women's organization—rejected Ulrich's name during a meeting when the women on the board were out of town.[10] Ulrich found the news odd as she had spoken to students at BYU the prior February, followed by lunch with the General Relief Society Presidency. Ulrich called her bishop, a good friend and neighbor, to ask if he had any reason to believe she had been banned from speaking at BYU. She recorded his response in her diary: "He gasped. Then told me some guy named Hafen had called from BYU to inquire about my status & [the bishop] had been rather cool—wondered why such a question [was being asked] outside of ecclesiastical procedures—but said I was a pillar of the Ward & they'd be lucky to get me because I was so busy."[11] Ulrich was indeed busy, partly because she

---

10. Peggy Fletcher Stack, "LDS Pulitzer Prize Winner Puzzled by Rejection as Speaker at BYU," *Salt Lake Tribune*, February 6, 1992.
11. Ulrich, November 22, 1992, diary entry. Bracketed words added by Ulrich.

was collaborating with producers from PBS on a documentary about the life of Martha Ballard and the making of her book. In February 1993, *Salt Lake Tribune* religion reporter Peggy Fletcher Stack called Ulrich to share that she was writing an article about the issue. Afterward, Ulrich called BYU's Provost, Bruce Hafen, to ask him about the reports she'd been hearing. He didn't deny calling her bishop but he conveyed his respect for her. Ulrich recorded that "he wished he could explain it all to me. He hoped that 'very soon' he could."[12] Hafen never did explain the decision to Ulrich.

The now-public news that BYU's Board of Trustees had rejected without comment the church's first female Pulitzer Prize winner deeply bothered many Utah-based Mormon feminists. The day after Stack's article came out, nearly 1,000 people gathered to hear feminist icon Gloria Steinem speak at an event sponsored by A Woman's Place Bookstore in Salt Lake City. According to Lavina Fielding Anderson, BYU student Kody Partridge expressed at the gathering her sadness that BYU wouldn't allow Ulrich to speak. Lynne Kanavel Whitesides, a University of Utah student with experience organizing Sunstone symposia, offered to help organize a conference. Planning efforts soon began in Anderson's living room.[13] The result was the first Counterpoint Conference—an independent women's conference that would stand as a counterpoint to the BYU Women's Conference, whose oversight had been wrested from female organizers by male church leaders.

Participating in the first Counterpoint Conference was complicated for some who were disturbed by the events happening at BYU but were personally connected to the church or university. Though the Counterpoint Conference was an independent venture, the Mormon Women's Forum—a Utah-based organization and newsletter founded in 1989 and largely considered to be a more radical arm of Mormon feminism—offered to subsume the conference as an independent subcommittee in order to extend their nonprofit bulk mailing discounts. When flyers associated the Counterpoint Conference with the Mormon Women's Forum, some scheduled participants feared repercussions. Seventeen BYU faculty and students named on the program met and unanimously decided to withdraw from the conference.[14] Two Exponent board members, Sue Paxman and Judy Dushku, had been slated to speak but withdrew due to the conference's changes in focus and sponsorship. Exponent II minutes indicate that, despite their withdrawal, "[Paxman and Dushku] support the conference and the Mormon Women's Forum." In a phone call during a board meeting, Ulrich encouraged her friends at

---

12. Ulrich, diary entries February and July 1993, transcribed and shared with authors.
13. Anderson, "Counterpoint 1993," *Exponent II* 18, no. 1 (1993): 4.
14. Anderson.

Exponent to "try to bring women together by writing to our Relief Society leaders, showing them our support, and asking them to lead us."[15] Seeking to maintain a balanced perspective, *Exponent II* published reports about both the Counterpoint Conference and the BYU Women's Conference. However, Exponent found additional events at BYU concerning. In "Voices from BYU," they published a collection of summaries and excerpts from *Salt Lake Tribune* articles, including one signed by eighteen BYU professors claiming that BYU was indeed hostile to feminism, despite the university president Rex E. Lee's op-ed saying otherwise. One example the professors gave was that the university allowed the Honors Program to advertise Richard Bushman's name, but not Claudia's, as speakers at a faculty seminar.

While some speculated that Ulrich's association with *Exponent II* was the reason for her being barred from speaking at BYU, Ulrich privately learned more details over the coming months. A friend revealed that a church bureaucrat had marked up her East/West article "Revising Mormonism" and that his highlighted version had been shared with some apostles.[16] In that article, Ulrich writes about encountering an example of "womanless history" in the church's magazine for children, the *Friend*. She describes the five phases of revising history curriculum to move from a male-centric, "womanless" history to one that makes room for the full human experience. She imagines a revised *Friend* article, where "sisters would teach and heal and even ordain one another, and they would pray for inspiration to create Primaries and Primary hospitals for their children."[17] This would not be a false history, but one that showed Mormon women's past actions. No church leader who objected to Ulrich's writing reached out to her directly, but some must have considered even imagining a history that showed women acting with power and authority to be dangerous. Ulrich reflected decades later, "Over and over again, the men refused to talk. But the women *talked*, and when they talked to each other, they taught people how to be responsible for themselves."[18] Ulrich's life and career did not rest on the goodwill of BYU's Board of Trustees. In 1995, she accepted a position at Harvard University as the James Duncan Phillips Professor of Early American History and Professor of Women's Studies. Ulrich being barred from speaking at BYU is a small piece of a large, complicated puzzle of the church's retrenchment, but it highlights how the personal, informal connections among Mormon feminists empowered some to act and think for themselves without waiting for the church to grant them institutional power.

---

15. Exponent II Minutes, March 25, 1993, Exponent II records.
16. Ulrich diary entries July 19–20, 1993, transcribed and shared with authors.
17. Ulrich, "Revising Mormonism," *Exponent II* 13, no. 3 (Spring 1987): 4.
18. Ulrich, email to the authors, December 8, 2023.

## Boston Stake Meeting on Women

While some male church bureaucrats in Salt Lake hid behind anonymity in making decisions about feminist women, the sometimes tense relationship between Exponent II and church leaders in Boston benefited from in-person communication. Nearly all of Exponent's staff were active church members, and many held prominent callings in their wards and stakes. Reportedly, both the Boston Mission President David Gillette and Boston Stake President Mitt Romney were displeased with the *Globe* article on *Exponent II*, fearing it would hurt the church's local missionary efforts.[19] However, while Romney did "not believe [Exponent] is helpful either to the church or to Exponent's members," he wrote that he "did not want to let my feelings about Exponent blind me in any way to the needs of the many sisters in our stake."[20] In 1990, Romney organized a stake task force to consider how to better meet the needs of women. He was not alone. Stakes in the California Bay Area had similar task forces, suggesting that the local culture of an area impacted how leaders responded to women asking for change.[21] In November 1992, Romney attended a regional training from the apostle M. Russell Ballard, who encouraged stakes not to treat women as "servants at the table" but to allow them to make meaningful contributions. In response, Romney increased the frequency of mixed-gender stake council meetings so he could hear more from women leaders. Helen Claire Sievers, Stake Activity Committee Chairman and Exponent volunteer, knew that Romney disliked Exponent. Appealing to his pragmatic nature, Sievers told him, "These conversations [about women in the church] can either happen in Judy Dushku's living room or at the church."[22] He saw the opportunity and invited stake members to attend an April 1993 meeting at the church to provide suggestions on better utilizing women in the stake. Stake Relief Society President Lucille Darley led the meeting, and nearly 250 people attended, including dozens of Exponent participants.

Both Exponent women and Romney felt that the stake meeting was a success. The open-mic format allowed for a wide range of suggestions, but Romney encouraged speakers to focus on areas where the stake had some control to make a difference.[23] Comments ranged from requests to include women on church disciplinary courts to ideas for improving gender equity

---

19. Exponent II Minutes, April 22, 1993.
20. Mitt Romney to Elder Cree-L Kofford, May 11, 1993. Letter shared with the authors by Helen Claire Sievers.
21. "Notes from the Field: Bay Area Task Force on Women," *Exponent II* 17, no. 2 (1993): 19–20. Task force meeting took place in July 1991.
22. Helen Claire Sievers, interview with the authors, January 20, 2023.
23. In his recent biography of Mitt Romney, McKay Coppins mischaracterized Exponent II as an organization "agitating for women to receive the priesthood" (pg. 39). That was neither Exponent II's position nor the concern that women brought to the 1993 Boston Stake Meeting on

in extending church callings.²⁴ Sievers, who helped organize the meeting, felt "the women and men there really tried to say things that President Romney could hear, and President Romney tried to remove any barriers to this communication." She heard from a bishop who attended that he had wept on the drive home because it had never occurred to him that there were things in the church that caused women pain.²⁵ Dushku, who had one of the tensest relationships with Romney and would go on to clash with him in local and national news outlets during his various campaigns for political office,²⁶ wrote that "it was a beautiful and constructive meeting." She encouraged readers to write in if their wards or stakes held similar events.²⁷ Romney sent a report along with a list of sixty-five suggestions that emerged from the meeting to a general authority so that the brethren in Salt Lake could be aware of these concerns.²⁸ Though Romney and the Exponent staff did not always reconcile their clashes so smoothly, in this instance, he provided a model of directly listening to and making changes to meet the needs of people in his stake.

### The September Six Excommunications

Fall 1993 was a dark time for progressive members. Though the era of church retrenchment began years earlier and extended for years to follow, September 1993 stands out. Six feminists and intellectuals—later known as "the September Six"—each faced disciplinary councils for public speeches or writing about church history and doctrine. One of the offending sources, Maxine Hanks' 1992 collection *Women and Authority: Re-emerging Mormon Feminism,* raised questions and offered possibilities for Mormon women to reconnect with the priesthood heritage they had been cut off from in the nineteenth century.²⁹ And while Exponent II women in Boston were able to advocate for resources for victims of abuse, church leaders considered Lavina Fielding Anderson's chronology of ecclesiastical abuse published in *Dialogue* an unforgivable overreach.³⁰ Church leaders restricted Lynne Kanavel

---

Women. Heather Sundahl and Katie Ludlow Rich, "In 'Romney a Reckoning,' McKay Coppins Misses the Mark on Mormon Feminism," op-ed, *Salt Lake Tribune*, November 2, 2023.

24. Sievers, notes from April 18, 1993, Boston Stake Meeting on Women, copy shared with the authors.

25. Sievers to Beverly Campbell, May 21, 1993, shared with the authors.

26. For one of several examples, see Ben Bradlee Jr., "Romney Seeks New Chapter in Success," *Boston Sunday Globe*, August 7, 1994.

27. "Sisters Speak," *Exponent II* 17, no. 4 (1993): 17.

28. Romney to Kofford.

29. Maxine Hanks, ed., *Women and Authority: Re-emerging Mormon Feminism* (Salt Lake City: Signature Books, 1992).

30. Lavina Fielding Anderson, "The LDS Intellectual Community and Church Leadership: A Contemporary Chronology," *Dialogue: A Journal of Mormon Thought* 26, no. 1 (Spring 1993): 7–64.

Carrel Sheldon presents Lavina Fielding Anderson with a boutonnière at the final Exponent Day Dinner in 1982. Anderson was excommunicated in September 1993. *Courtesy, L. Tom Perry Special Collections, BYU Library, Brigham Young University*

Whitesides's membership through disfellowshipment and excommunicated Avraham Gileadi, Paul Toscano, Hanks, Anderson, and D. Michael Quinn.[31]

Word of the disciplinary councils spread, and many of Exponent's staff were deeply troubled by the news. The board met on September 23, 1993, the day Anderson was excommunicated. Paxman recalls crying for a long time when she heard the news. "I went to college with Lavina and some of [the six] were people that I knew, and part of my angst about it was I knew them to be really good people. Why would they be called on the docket for anything?"[32] The board discussed the meaning of apostasy, what it means to sustain the brethren, and the effects of excommunication on family and friends. They closed the meeting at 11:30 p.m. with a prayer for "everyone involved on both sides of the current excommunications and disfellowships in Utah." Dushku wanted them to meet at a later time to reflect further on the happenings.[33]

The paper's next issue included Paxman's editorial, "Where Shall We Turn for Peace?" She reports on what was called the White Roses Campaign.

---

31. Patterson, *September Six*. Disfellowshipment meant a temporary restriction of a person's church membership until their priesthood leaders had determined that they had repented. Excommunication meant the permanent severing of a person's church membership unless that person was deemed repentant and only then could they be rebaptized.
32. Booth-Forbes interview.
33. Exponent II Minutes, September 23, 1993, Exponent II records.

During the October 1993 general conference, Shirley B. Paxman and Irene Bates delivered 1,000 white roses tied with white ribbons to LDS general authorities at the Church Office Building, paid for by donations from around the world and the Boston area. The accompanying letter entreats, "In the spirit of peace, we make this appeal: let the fear and reprisals end."[34] *Exponent II* published several heartfelt responses to the events, including one by Vanda Goodfellow from Fresno, California: "I am sure that the good people who were caught in the 'purge' will survive quite nicely without official, recognized membership in the Church. I am not sure about the health and survival of the Church without them and others who think and question."[35] The paper's general response was heartbreak and longing for a unity that included the voices of people outside of the priesthood hierarchy.

### A Perfect Storm

The fear engendered by the excommunications and retrenchment coincided with financial and organizational struggles within Exponent II to create a perfect storm that led to plummeting subscription numbers. Tracking the exact trajectory of subscriptions is challenging, as Exponent minutes and available financial records rarely state the number explicitly. An undated mailing list likely from the 1980s identifies 4,300 subscribers, but cleaning up the list was a perpetual task, and not all of those were current.[36] Board members came to refer to 2,500 subscribers as "the usual." Between 1992 and 1994, Exponent lost hundreds of subscribers, getting down to a circulation of around 1,900.[37] Their friends at *Sunstone* and *Dialogue* were experiencing similar challenges—the disciplinary councils led some readers to worry that subscribing to these progressive publications would compromise their standing in the church. Lower subscription numbers meant a drop in income, which made printing and shipping costs harder to meet. With paste-up parties gone and so much of the production reliant on Sue Paxman and Eileen Lambert, who were also balancing family and work responsibilities, the paper did not always meet its quarterly deadlines. If issues of the paper did not arrive when expected, it was harder for readers to know when to renew or whether they would get what they paid for in their annual subscriptions. *Exponent II* had also reached a crucial juncture in the demographics of their readers. After two decades, some of their original readers and contributors were no longer as personally anxious about the women's movement. Empowered by their education and careers or

---

34. Paxman, "Where Shall We Turn for Peace?" *Exponent II* 18, no. 1 (1993): 2.
35. Vanda L. Goodfellow, "Reader's Response," *Exponent II* 18, no. 3 (1994): 4.
36. Subscription mailing list, undated, Susan L. Paxman Collection of Exponent II records, MSS 6192, BYUSC.
37. Exponent II Minutes, October 27, 1994, Exponent II records.

confidently reconciled with their own lives, they moved on from the paper and feminist retreats and put their energy elsewhere.

The Exponent board started new initiatives to sustain the organization to varying degrees of success. One effort included improving the paper's production quality. The paper was printed on cheap newsprint for years and sent via fourth-class mail. While this was less costly, some subscribers reported that their mail carriers were throwing the paper out rather than delivering it because they assumed it was junk mail or, as some suspected about at least one Utah mail carrier, because he didn't think people should read its content. For the paper's twentieth year, they decided to update the look with smaller dimensions on thicker paper while retaining their distinct cottage industry look.[38] The new design, however, cost more to print and ship and required raising subscription prices, which was a difficult call to make when they were already bleeding subscriptions. As few staff members had personal computers, the organization needed to purchase and maintain computers, scanners, and printers. They carefully considered whether spending an additional $600 to print and mail a fundraising letter would pay off. They took the risk and the generous response of supporters brought in more than $13,000.[39]

With the influx of donations, the paper's production could continue for a time, but board president Robin Baker became increasingly concerned about subscription rates. In January 1996, she sent out a survey to lapsed subscribers to understand why the numbers continued declining. Some responses were as expected, citing the irregular delivery of the paper. Other responses ranged from a BYU professor who couldn't risk being seen subscribing, to individuals who had left the church and were no longer interested in Mormon topics, to some who felt the paper was too conservative, to others who felt it was too critical. Some readers wanted shorter articles and more variety. Aware they could not satisfy all readers, the board considered options such as hosting a poetry contest and adding a "Sunday Sampler" column to provide a more upbeat tone.[40] And as Paxman's life and family circumstances changed, the board discussed the need for a new editor.

---

38. Exponent II Minutes, July 29, 1993, Exponent II records.
39. Minutes, July 29, 1993.
40. Exponent II Minutes, March 28, 1996, Exponent II records.

# 7 "Mormonism's Stealth Alternative"

Previously, editor transitions had occurred relatively smoothly, but that was not the case as Sue Paxman neared the end of her thirteen-year tenure. Paxman had modernized the paper's production and explored essential topics, including abuse, abortion, and homosexuality. But Paxman's personal life became increasingly complicated by a painful, messy divorce; her divorce coincided with a time when she was troubled by what she viewed as the church's systemic silencing of women. Paxman's 1996 editorial, "First Hands and Backs, Now Feet and Voices," was a turning point for some board members. She called out church members who made "light, slightly ironic, comical references to Mormon women playing such roles as the backs and hands with which the work of the Church is accomplished or the neck that turns the head [of the house—her husband]." She believed that the age of behind-the-scenes, soft power needed to end. "We want to use our voices to help make the organizational and cultural decisions that create and influence the 'dailiness' of our lives in the Church structure." She wrote that women's voices were getting stronger, and women were voting with their feet, leaving a church unwilling to hear them. Paxman believed the church needed to make room for people who question or think differently.[1] Though perhaps tame in retrospect, some board members felt that both the impatient tenor of the editorial and its express directives to church leaders went beyond Exponent's carefully staked ground.

Because Exponent ran on relationships, working through competing visions for the paper's future was painful. Incidentally, the paper's new digital production methods led to a more substantial separation between the paper's work and the board's work, and the organization struggled with formalizing positions and voting procedures. Robin Baker knew that Exponent II could be polarizing for some Mormon women, so she had been nervous about taking on the role of board president. She sought reassurance from her bishop that

---

1. Paxman, "First Hands and Backs, Now Feet and Voices," *Exponent II* 19, no. 4 (1996): 2. Bracketed words in original. Find the full version of this editorial on pages 191–94.

accepting the position wouldn't jeopardize her church standing. As president, Baker leaned on experience from her PhD in organizational behavior to navigate the tricky path forward.[2] In May 1996, the board met at Paxman's house and talked through some of the pain of recent months that included "side talking" about board issues outside of official meetings and the difficulty of striking a balance between friendship and professionalism.[3] By the following month, Baker decided to lead the board through the vote for the next editor and then step down as president. Knowing that there would be a transition period after the vote, she did not want her role in the decision to distract from the work, and Karen Haglund was willing to take her place.[4] Simultaneously, Paxman was in the early stages of making post-divorce life plans that took her out of Boston: within a couple of years, she would move to Ireland and open the Anam Cara Writer's and Artist's Retreat. The board, including Paxman, decided that Paxman would retire as editor by the following summer.

Two strong candidates for editor emerged: Linda Hoffman Kimball and Jenny Atkinson. A married mother in her forties, Kimball had been with Exponent since its early days. Kimball joined the church as an undergraduate at Wellesley College and, upon reflection, believes she had naïvely assumed that all Mormon women were like the Exponent founding mothers who became her mentors. Though time had disabused her of that notion, she planned to present the board with her vision of a paper that could continue to publish on the dual platforms of Mormonism and feminism.[5] Atkinson, a single professional in her mid-twenties, had begun volunteering with Exponent as an undergraduate student and had worked closely with Paxman on the paper's production for several years. She was enthusiastic about the paper and desired to bring in new voices and perspectives.[6]

Fiercely divided, board members took months deliberating. Exponent's longevity would require bringing in younger leaders but, as Judy Dushku reflected, the decision between two "dichotomous symbolic alternatives" brushed up against the "core of most Mormon women's culture wars" between stay-at-home mothers and career-path women.[7] The board was also divided on how to make the decision—certain officers of the board were

---

2. Robin Baker, interview with the authors, September 26, 2022. Baker became president of Exponent II in October 1992.
3. Exponent II minutes, May 29, 1996, Exponent II records.
4. Exponent II minutes, June 27, 1996, Exponent II records.
5. Linda Hoffman Kimball, interview with the authors, September 23, 2022. Also, Kimball, "Editorial suggestions for *Exponent II*," 1996, Exponent II records.
6. Jenny Atkinson interview, July 7, 2022, and "Open letter as nominee for Editor of Exponent," 1996, Exponent II records.
7. Dushku, "Negotiating Controversy over Forty Years," *Dialogue: A Journal of Mormon Thought* 49, no. 2 (2016): 143–52.

elected, but the larger membership of the board was less formal, complicating who had a say. At a post-retreat meeting at Hillsboro Camp in July, they discussed the possibility of co-editors or having the women alternate editing issues. Undecided, they paused the conversation to spend time in the sun by the lake.[8] In September, each candidate submitted her vision for the paper, and the board came to a vote. The first vote returned an even split. The women stayed up late into the night debating until one person changed their vote and broke the gridlock. The board selected Jenny Atkinson as the next editor of *Exponent II*.[9]

### Blessing the New Editor

In 1997, Atkinson worked full-time at the Charlestown Boys and Girls Club. She was the same age her mother was when *Exponent II* began, but her mother already had several children by that age. It was from her mother's subscription—read in small scraps of time—that Atkinson first learned about the paper.[10] When Atkinson moved to Cambridge after high school to attend Harvard University, she found she lived a short distance from Paxman's house, where Exponent sometimes held paste-up parties. As a college freshman, she entered this sisterhood of hand-producing a feminist Mormon newspaper. Nine years later, Atkinson became editor in chief.

In Sue Paxman's—now Sue Booth-Forbes—final issue as editor, she gathered advice and well-wishes from the Exponent community to symbolically bring Atkinson into a women's blessing circle. Marti Lythgoe wrote from Salt Lake City, "I wasn't a 'founding mother'; the Exponent women found me—and helped me find myself." Working on the paper when she lived near Boston had given Lythgoe an identity beyond wife and mother. Longtime contributing writer RevaBeth Russell from Springville, Utah, wrote that while many things had improved for women in society, she didn't think that was the case for her daughters in the church: "The windmills we have tilted are still there. The battles are not over; the gentle persuasion continues." Founding editor Claudia Bushman marveled at the projects she and her friends accomplished and how they had felt "there was nothing we could not do." However, she added a caution that *Exponent II* needed to give "some serious attention to circulation problems.... The paper's message is wonderful, but its impact is lost if it does not arrive where it should be directed." These responses demonstrated that a vibrant community still loved and wanted the paper. The staff had to work to reestablish a consistent publication schedule and turn around lagging subscriptions.

---

8. Exponent II Minutes, July 21–22, 1996, Exponent II records.
9. Baker interview.
10. Atkinson, *Exponent II* 20, no. 4 (Summer 1997): 2.

Booth-Forbes and Eileen Lambert mentored Atkinson in the production process. Though most submissions still came through the mail, Atkinson inherited the Exponent fax machine and set it up in her bedroom. Much to her dismay, faxes would arrive any time of day or night, at times waking her up as writers in other time zones rushed to submit to the contest issue before the "midnight" deadline.[11] Atkinson hosted reader committee meetings in her living room where staff would discuss the essays. Typically, each submission was read by three committee members, with an attached form providing space for comments. Comments might include praise of the writing, recommendations for other publishing venues, or personal asides such as Atkinson's note, "read while watching *Melrose Place*."[12] Initially, Sarah Bush took on the role of design editor, Kristen Graves became managing editor, and Barbara Taylor moved to the role of database manager to clean up the subscription and mailing records.[13]

### Exponent's Offering to History

As the paper navigated its transition between editors, historian Jan Shipps visited Boston and spoke at an Exponent event. From Margaret Lazenby's home in Belmont, Laurel Thatcher Ulrich introduced Shipps as "an intellectual and spiritual light of Mormon history." Shipps, a non-LDS scholar who began her career when the Mormon Studies field was almost exclusively male, had experience as an outsider/insider. Shipps offered her perspective on *Exponent II*'s unique offering to history. Like the original *Woman's Exponent*, which "came into existence when feminist currents were stirring, so *Exponent II* began as feminism was again very much a part of American thinking." However, in the 1970s, *Exponent II* emerged after a correlated, streamlined church had stripped the Relief Society of much of its institutional power and decision-making. *Exponent II* was interested in this history, but even as it reprinted articles from the pioneer-era paper, it did not set out to reconstruct the past or get at the truth of the past. Primarily, it offered experiential stories that added to the body of evidence of what it was like to be a Mormon woman in the last quarter of the twentieth century. She said, "In reviewing the content of *Exponent II*, what I discovered instead [of arguments or historical truth claims] are direct and candid accounts of experience. They are of great value both to those who read them and, perhaps even more, to those who wrote them." She encouraged the new editor to continue in this vital work producing "Mormonism's stealth alternative."[14]

---

11. Atkinson interview.
12. Atkinson, Readers Committee Form, Exponent II records.
13. Exponent II Minutes, March 8, 1997, Exponent II records.
14. Shipps, "*Exponent II*: Mormonism's Stealth Alternative."

Historian Jan Shipps speaks with incoming editor Jenny Atkinson and outgoing editor Sue Booth-Forbes at an Exponent II event in Belmont, Massachusetts, October 1997.

Exponent received fewer submissions in the aftermath of that decade's excommunications and the paper's changing demographics, but personal voices continued to be the heartbeat of the paper. A crop of new writers, including Heather Sundahl, Pandora Brewer, Sylvia Cabus, and Karen Rosenbaum, mingled with longtime contributors such as Emma Lou Thayne and Mary Bradford. After moving to Chicago, Linda Hoffman Kimball wrote a regular column, "Goodness Gracious," employing her trademark blend of spirituality and reflections on everyday life. Though it appeared less regularly than in previous years, Judy Dushku continued to edit the "Sisters Speak" column, including the important topics of family planning,[15] date rape,[16] and returning early from an LDS mission.[17] Under Atkinson's leadership, the paper published an issue about body image and eating disorders[18]—crucial topics in '90s American diet culture—and focused more on single women's experience in the church. As the board sought ways to increase the paper's reach, the occasional board retreats and the annual national retreat were essential to help the women connect.

15. Sisters Speak: Family Planning, *Exponent II* 21, no. 4 (Summer 1998): 18–19.
16. Sisters Speak: Date Rape, *Exponent II* 22, no. 2 (Winter 1999): 16–17.
17. Sisters Speak: Missionary Return Responses, *Exponent II* 22, no. 3 (Spring 1999): 16–17.
18. *Exponent II* 22, no. 1 (Fall 1998).

Linda Andrews, Jenny Atkinson, Sarah Farmer, Carrel Sheldon, Sylvia Russell, Barbara Taylor, Lynn Matthews Anderson, Cheryl Howard (DiVito) at an Exponent II staff retreat in Martha's Vineyard, May 1999. *Courtesy, L. Tom Perry Special Collections, BYU Library, Brigham Young University*

## Changes Big and Small

The late '90s brought two significant updates to the organization and paper: Exponent II's first web page and a print size and format change. Sarah Farmer built the paper's first website.[19] The site included information on how to subscribe to the paper and hosted a private discussion board where the Exponent community could ask questions and seek advice from one another. While adding a website required a learning curve for people not used to spending time online, changing the paper from a newspaper to a magazine format fostered robust debate. Harvard Divinity School student Kate Holbrook first came on as design editor and led the charge: an 8 ½ x 11 magazine would be cheaper to print and mail, easier for readers to hold, and more convenient for storing on a bookshelf.[20] The magazine style made practical sense, but it was a hard decision for some board members who knew how beloved the old look and feel of a hand-produced paper was to some readers. Board President Karen Haglund mourned that this change would be part of her legacy as president, though she understood the need for progress and accepted the board's vote.[21] Just shy of the organization's twenty-fifth year, the Spring 1999

---

19. Exponent II Minutes, January 13, 1998, Exponent II records.
20. Exponent II Minutes, November 7, 1998, Exponent II records.
21. Exponent II Minutes, January 28, 1999, Exponent II records.

issue was the first with the new magazine size. But for most of the old guard, the quarterly will be forever known as "the paper."

After just over two years as editor, Atkinson told the board that she would soon be stepping down. Part of her reason was that she had stopped attending church. She wrote to the board that she admired the women who struggled to stay and make the church a better place. However, she felt "*Exponent II* deserved an editor who was more enthusiastic about the details of how to do that than I currently am." The organization already understood that it held a unique position in both helping people who felt marginalized stay in the church and helping those who left keep a connection to their heritage and each other—expanding what "Mormon" meant for its community—but it was still generally expected that Exponent staff be active church members. Atkinson also felt that the workload was too concentrated on the editor with too few volunteers to help lighten the load.[22] Initially, she planned to stay on for three more issues to allow for a smooth handoff to the next editor, but an out-of-state job opportunity thwarted that plan. Atkinson asked former editor Nancy Dredge to take over as interim editor. Believing it would be for just a few issues, Dredge accepted.

---

22. Minutes, January 28, 1999.

Exponent participants and friends of Bonnie Horne created for her a quilt with a "sunshine and shadow" pattern to speed her recuperation from breast cancer. Diane McKinney Kellogg, Bonnie Horne, Cheryl Howard (DiVito), Carrel Sheldon, Jo Maitland, Jan Braithwaite, Karen Haglund. 1999. *Courtesy, L. Tom Perry Special Collections, BYU Library, Brigham Young University*

Editor Jenny Atkinson teaches a belly dancing lesson to board members Sarah Farmer, Barbara Taylor, and Carrel Sheldon. Costume made for Jenny by Eileen Lambert. Circa 1998. *Courtesy, L. Tom Perry Special Collections, BYU Library, Brigham Young University*

# 8  *Exponent II* Goes Digital

In October 2003, *Salt Lake Tribune* religion reporter Peggy Fletcher Stack wrote, "Where have all the Mormon feminists gone?" A decade after the September Six excommunications, she noted that Mormon feminist activism seemed "awfully quiet." The Mormon Women's Forum's annual Counterpoint Conference in Utah could scarcely draw a crowd, and *Exponent II* still published from Boston, but she remarked, "It is more likely to take up issues of grief, aging and being single in a married church than the question of priesthood power."[1] Stack accurately noted that Exponent's focus had turned inward. The paper devoted less attention to institutional sexism or abuse while continuing to center women's voices about their lives. In these quieter years, however, foundational leaders of Exponent were forging relationships and mentoring younger women who would soon lead the organization. Stack's article also galvanized Mormon feminists in Southern California who would bring Exponent II into the online conversations of the "bloggernacle" and the next era of Mormon feminist activism.

### "Something Old, Something New"

When Nancy Dredge took over as interim editor in 2000, she did not anticipate leading the paper for the next nine years. She had served as *Exponent II*'s second editor in chief from late 1975 to 1981. In the intervening decades, she remained a mainstay of the organization, serving on the editorial board and on reader committees, hosting events at her home, and assisting with the annual retreats. In line with the board's goal to engage younger women in positions of responsibility for the paper, Dredge recruited associate editors, including Heather Sundahl and Kate Holbrook, who had been involved in Exponent since their arrivals in Boston in '96. The editorial team alternated taking the lead on issues, drawing from a pool of submissions that came in via email or paper mail, and soliciting work to fill in gaps. They addressed a blend of evergreen topics such as motherhood and women at work, along

---

1. Stack, "Where Have All the Mormon Feminists Gone?" *Salt Lake Tribune*, October 4, 2003.

The Exponent II board at Emily Clyde Curtis's apartment in Watertown, Massachusetts, 2002. Back row: Heather Sundahl, Evelyn Harvill, Kimberly Burnett, Emily Clyde Curtis, Aimee Evans Hickman, Michelle Martin. Front row: Nancy Dredge, Barbara Taylor, Judy Dushku, Cheryl Howard (DiVito), Robin Baker, Karen Haglund.

with specific historical events—such as gathering at the Exponent retreat just weeks after the September 11, 2001 attacks[2] and participants' experiences with the Winter 2002 Olympics held in Salt Lake City.[3] While the church increasingly turned its focus to its 1995 Proclamation on the Family that left many people outside of its stated ideal, Exponent discussed blended families,[4] and as Stack noted, being single in a married church.[5] Lynne Matthews Anderson, Connie Chow, and Evelyn Harvill served as design editors, and Harvill also revamped the website.

Now adults, the first generation of "Exponent babies" who had been on their mothers' laps while working on the paper had the opportunity to engage in the organization personally. Sundahl and Holbrook brought their babies to board meetings as Dredge had once done, while Dredge's now adult daughters, Margaret and Annie, attended the retreats or took on volunteer positions (in 2023, Elizabeth joined her sisters and mother at the retreat, completing the set of Dredge women). Anna Haglund, who came to her first mailing party as an infant strapped to her mother's back, served as board secretary for a time while her mother, Karen, was president. Long-time

---

2. Kimball, "Christmas in a Changed World," *Exponent II* 25, no. 1 (Fall 2001): 12–13.
3. *Exponent II* 25, no. 3 (Spring 2002).
4. *Exponent II* 25, no. 4 (Summer 2002).
5. *Exponent II* 27, no. 2 (2004).

contributing writer Gladys Farmer saw all three of her children—Sarah, Deborah, and Ray—participate in various capacities. Emily Clyde Curtis' first Exponent event came when her grandmother, Aileen Clyde, recently released as a counselor in the general Relief Society presidency, gave the retreat keynote address.

Reflecting another generational change, Clyde Curtis and her husband had just moved to Belmont for *her* to study at Harvard Divinity School. And while Clyde Curtis grew up in a household that subscribed to *Exponent II*, she had yet to envision having the opportunity to be tangibly involved with the organization. Clyde Curtis was quickly brought into the fold by Sundahl, who had become a friend when they worked together in Phoenix, Arizona, and both participated in the popular Mormon feminist listserv, ELWC (Electronic Latter-day Women's Caucus started by Lynne Matthews Anderson). "The first board meeting I attended was in October 2000, and I got put on the board ... as president," Clyde Curtis laughed, believing that the board recruited her only because she was too shell-shocked to say no.[6] Only twenty-four years old, she felt out of her depth being surrounded by so many veterans of Mormon feminism, but the board recognized in her an insightful and compassionate leader who would grow with the organization.

Attendees of that 2000 retreat were blissfully unaware that it would be their last at the rustic and magical Hillsboro Camp. The fall issue of the paper focused on Mormon feminist gatherings—the Exponent retreat in New Hampshire, the Rocky Mountain retreat in Colorado, the Provo Canyon retreat, and the Midwest Pilgrims retreat held at various locations in Illinois, Indiana, and Wisconsin. Dredge wrote about the wonderful "home again" feeling of Hillsboro—a sensory Eden with the "scent of pine needles mingled with those of cinnamon, rhubarb pies, or chicken" and the sounds of the "lodge screen door banging and canoes being plunked into the lake." Yet, as they were preparing that issue, Exponent got word that Hillsboro Camp was closing. Patricia "Puffy" Nissen had lost her sister and co-director, Harriet, to cancer a few years prior and was unable to continue running the camp. Exponent could never replace Hillsboro and their beloved camp directors, but they were determined to find a new venue.[7] It took work to find options that allowed them to keep registration costs low while also providing meal services so the women would not have to plan meals and cook.

Over the next decade, Exponent held its annual retreat at various locations in New England with mixed results. In 2001, they stayed at a camp in Plymouth, Massachusetts. The camp included flushing toilets and showers in

---

6. Emily Clyde Curtis, interview with the authors, March 30, 2023.
7. Dredge, "Something Old, Something New," *Exponent II* 24, no. 2 (Winter 2001): 3.

the cabins—an upgrade from Hillsboro—and also allowed for a September date, which became the schedule moving forward.⁸ Sadly, the smell of Boy Scouts lingered in the rooms and the food was disappointing. They tried locations in the Connecticut Berkshires, Southern New Hampshire, Cape Cod, and Western Massachusetts, but each venue left something to be desired. In 2010, after nine years of what Robin Baker described as "finding frogs while in search of our prince," Exponent found a new retreat home at the Barbara C. Harris Episcopal Camp and Conference Center along the shores of Otter Lake in Greenfield, New Hampshire. Even as venues changed, the retreat created a sense of belonging and engagement. That was the case for Aimee Evans Hickman who attended her first retreat in 2002. A couple of years prior, her husband had participated in a summer seminar at BYU run by Claudia and Richard Bushman; Claudia encouraged Aimee to seek out the retreat, and a month after the Hickmans moved to Boston, she did so. For her, the retreat felt like "an answer to a million different soul cravings." There she met Emily Clyde Curtis, who invited her to join the Exponent board as secretary, and before long, as co-president.⁹

### Creative Opportunities and Financial Challenges

Hearkening back to its founding, Exponent II co-sponsored two women speaker series with the Boston LDS Institute of Religion. The organization could not have copies of *Exponent II* present at the events or solicit subscriptions, but they brought in interesting speakers to the events held in LDS chapels. The spring 2004 series, organized by Clyde Curtis, included talks from New Hampshire congressional candidate Katrina Swett, internationally renowned cellist Allison Eldridge, Emmy Award-winning journalist Jane Clayson Johnson, Pulitzer Prize-winning historian and Exponent co-founder Laurel Thatcher Ulrich, and a graduate student panel. For fall 2005, Holbrook coordinated an interfaith series. Along with comparative politics professor and Exponent co-founder Judy Dushku, speakers included Gloria White-Hammond, a pediatrician and co-pastor of Bethel African American Methodist Episcopal Church; Debbie Little, an Episcopal minister at Ecclesia Ministries; Salma Kazmi, assistant director of the Islamic Society of Boston; Stephanie Wellen Levine, author of *Mystics, Mavericks, and Merrymakers: An Intimate Journey among Hasidic Girls*; Ann Braude, director of the Women's Studies in Religion program at Harvard Divinity School; and Wendy Cadge, author of *Heartwood: the First Generation of Theravada Buddhism in America*. These events reflected creative cooperation between Boston-area church leaders and Exponent II in a church that seldom highlighted women's

---

8. Exponent II Minutes, June 5, 2001.
9. Aimee Evans Hickman, interview with the authors, August 25, 2023.

Co-editors Emily Clyde Curtis and Aimee Evans Hickman at the end of their tenure, 2015.

voices or engaged with other faiths. This refreshing platform showcased the talent and divinity of diverse women and connected feminist scholars and Mormon churchgoers as like-minded seekers.

While the annual retreat and local events kept the organization strong for in-person participants, the paper struggled financially. Subscriptions took a big hit in the '90s and had not recovered as the digital era drove a decline of print periodicals across the country. The cost of printing and mailing the paper began to exceed the revenue coming in through subscriptions, and the organization's savings were dwindling. In November 2005, the writing was on the wall: "At a board retreat in May, Barbara [Taylor] warned us that we could be in serious financial trouble if we fell under 500 [subscriptions]—we are now in trouble."[10] Though the board considered options to raise funds and increase subscriptions, the financial outlook seemed bleak. Something would need to change for the paper to continue. Change came knocking on their door.

### The Southern California Issue

Caroline Kline, fresh off her master's degrees in classics and education, moved to Irvine, California, in 2002. She taught high school Latin classes while her husband began his job as a professor at the University of California,

---

10. Exponent II Minutes, November 9, 2005, Exponent II records.

Irvine (UCI). She was assigned to visit teach Jana Remy, a woman six years her senior who had two young children and was in the process of entering UCI's history PhD program. Remy had long been connected to the Mormon intellectual and feminist scene and had read Mormon literature and history widely. Sensing that Remy would be understanding, Kline opened up about some of her challenges as a feminist in the church. Remy responded by handing Kline a stack of her mother's *Exponent II*s to take home. "This was the first moment in my life where I had met another person who actually understood having issues with gender in the Mormon church," Kline reflected. Reading articles written decades previously by women who shared many of her present-day concerns blew her mind. New possibilities emerged. With their shared love for *Exponent II* and enthusiasm for engaging in conversations about Mormon feminism, Remy and Kline reached out to the women in Boston and pitched guest editing a Southern California issue of the paper. Dredge accepted.

To inspire content for the 2005 Southern California issue, Remy and Kline organized a gathering at UCI to open up an intergenerational dialogue about Mormon women's lives. Sixteen Mormon feminists from Southern California attended the event. Following a panel of speakers, Kline led a roundtable discussion, asking questions about how the older generation handled the church's response to the ERA, the gap between the church's teaching on gender roles and the lives of modern women, and what partnership looked like in their homes. The publication that emerged included excerpts from the event and additional essays by women such as novelist Lael Littke, who had guest edited Exponent's first Southern California issue in 1979, and Ruth Hathaway Mauss, one of the paper's original subscribers.[11]

Guest editing naturally requires negotiation and compromise during the collaborative process, and this was no exception. However, for the editors in Boston, the Southern California issue raised behind-the-scenes discussions about how to address certain controversial topics that had contributed to the excommunication of some feminist scholars and theologians, including Janice Allred in 1995 and her sister, Margaret Toscano, as recently as 2000. For Dredge, discussing women's priesthood ordination remained a line that the paper would not cross. During the UCI panel, Lorie Winder Stromberg argued in favor of women's ordination in a talk titled, "Power Hungry." When *Exponent II* published excerpts of Stromberg's presentation, they left out the portion on women's ordination.[12] Though disappointed by this decision, the

---

11. *Exponent II* 27, no. 3 (2005).
12. Stromberg went on to publish the full version of her essay in *Sunstone*. "Power Hungry," *Sunstone*, December 2004, 60–61.

tension over content did not dissuade the guest editors from seeking further collaboration. Remy and Kline attended the Exponent retreat in Connecticut in fall 2005. There they offered to create an Exponent II blog. The board had discussed the idea before, but Remy and Kline were willing to take on the labor to make it happen.

### Launching the Exponent II Blog

Remy and Kline keenly felt the importance of Exponent II starting a blog to engage in online conversations about Mormonism from a feminist perspective. Much of the Mormon intellectual community congregated at the network of blogs that collectively made up the "bloggernacle," a reference to the Salt Lake Tabernacle at Temple Square. Blogs such as *Times and Season*, *By Common Consent*, and *Feminist Mormon Housewives (fMh)* led the charge and often had thousands of daily visitors. Rather than join an existing blog or start an entirely independent one, Remy and Kline wanted to connect to the legacy of *Exponent II*. "We had this rich, fabulous history of women who were incredible thinkers, who had grappled with similar issues as we were," said Kline. "We also saw the blog as a way to archive some of these amazing articles from the '70s, '80s, '90s by retyping them in blog form, thereby giving readers access to the recent past of Mormon feminism."[13] A usable past required content that could be found via search engines.

The idea of a blog received a mixed reception from the board, largely divided by age. Some board members had already been thinking in that direction, while others were not as drawn to online conversations. A key challenge centered on protecting Exponent II's name and reputation—there weren't mechanisms to pre-approve the content on the blog, which felt risky. "Once you open up a blog, you're not editing people," Dredge reflected. "We've always wanted people to have their own voices. So it's been this dichotomy of we want people to have their voices, but we want to stay in business, and how to do that." Dredge simultaneously worried about potential blog content that might alienate some of the paper's dedicated readers while understanding that change was both necessary and inevitable.[14] Similar conversations were happening in newsrooms around the globe. How could a publication navigate both quality control and the immediacy of online conversations? As board president, Aimee Evans Hickman liaised between the women in Boston and Irvine. She understood the concerns of the women who had shaped and protected the organization for decades. She also understood the needs of younger women who felt an urgency to discuss topics that many long-time Exponent participants had worked out for themselves years ago. Mormon

---

13. Caroline Kline, interview with the authors, March 31, 2023.
14. Nancy Dredge, interview with the authors, August 17, 2022.

Five of the Exponent II blog's founders at a retreat: Deborah Farmer Kris, Sandra Lee, Caroline Kline, Brooke Jones, Jana Remy.

feminists encountering these issues for the first time still wanted a place to discuss ideas, and the blog could be a way to do that in real time.[15]

As they worked through tension points with the board, Remy and Kline went forward in building the blog and assembling a team. Remy managed the technical side. She built her first web page in 1995 and continued to grow her skills. Through connections made via the Association for Mormon Letters listserv (AML-List), she participated in the founding of AML's magazine, *Irreantum*, where she served as the book review editor. *Irreantum's* team was fully dispersed and communicated primarily through email. Remy was confident that the model could work for Exponent. By 2005, content management systems like Google's Blogger made building a blog possible with little custom coding, though the project still required significant time to maintain. They soon had a handful of bloggers signed on to the project. Deborah Farmer Kris (as "Deborah") in Boston saw the potential of the blog to expand Exponent's reach, a place that could be "vital to drawing in new voices—and sustaining older ones."[16] For Emily Clyde Curtis (as "EmilyCC"), whose family moved back to Phoenix in December 2005, blogging allowed her to stay connected to Exponent while living away from her once in-person feminist community.[17] Southern California women Sandra Lee

---

15. Hickman, interview with the authors, March 10, 2023.
16. Deborah, "10 Years of Exponent: If You Built It, They Will Come," *The Exponent* (blog), February 29, 2016, exponentii.org. Blog monikers added in quotation marks.
17. Curtis interview.

(as "Dora"), Amelia Parkin (as "Amelia"), and Brooke Jones (as "Brooke"), who had each participated in the roundtable at UCI, joined the effort. Linda Hoffman Kimball (as "Linda") in Chicago came on shortly after the blog's January 2006 launch. More permabloggers with a regular posting schedule followed, along with many guest writers.

Bloggers sought to balance privacy with openness. Many bloggers used pseudonyms or only part of their real names. They did not necessarily fear the excommunications of prior years, but they understood that writing about Mormonism online may risk their connections to ward and family members or interfere with their professional lives. However, a blog rule required writers to include a picture of themselves, even if partial or obscured, along with a brief bio. "Personal authorship was really important," Remy recalled. "When someone posted, it was representing their opinion. It was their post, not the Exponent's post." Semi-anonymity paired with personal authorship allowed bloggers greater freedom to tell their own stories.[18] While the relationship between the blog and the board would take time to smooth out—including years when the blog renamed itself from *Exponent II* to *The Exponent* to suggest greater distance—the initial report from the board was positive.[19]

The blog offered Exponent a way to engage with current events and provide time-sensitive content. One of its largest ongoing efforts, initially led by Kris, was making lesson plans for church use. Between 1998 and 2017, the church primarily used the series *Teachings of the Presidents of the Church* as lesson manuals for weekly Relief Society and adult priesthood meetings. Each manual focused on a particular church president and largely excluded substantive content about women. *The Exponent* lesson plans offered quotes from women leaders, insights about the scriptures, and stories that fit with that week's theme from a feminist perspective. Producing the lesson plans was time-consuming, and Exponent collaborated with guest writers from other blogs, particularly *Zelophehad's Daughters*. Over time, the blog provided lesson plans for Young Women's, the Sunday School, and other courses. Lesson plans attracted new readers and provided a way for the blog to influence how the curriculum was taught at church.

Through writing and commenting, bloggernacle participants got to know each other and formed friendships—or even feuds—that sometimes led to forming new groups or in-person gatherings. After winning an *Exponent II* essay contest, Kathryn Lynard Soper came to feel that Exponent was not a "faithful" enough space. She joined with friends to create *Segullah*, first as

---

18. Jana Remy, interview with the authors, May 5, 2023.
19. Exponent II Minutes, February 13, 2006. The Exponent II blog was known as *The Exponent* for roughly fifteen years. To avoid confusion with the magazine, it will be referred to here as *The Exponent*.

a print journal in 2005 and then as a blog in 2007. They wanted to make a space for Mormon women's writing that would not "lament policy, criticize leaders, or spin doctrine."[20] While the readership of *The Exponent, Mormon Feminist Housewives,* and *Segullah* often overlapped, some writers felt more comfortable in one space or the other. Wanting a geographically closer retreat, Exponent bloggers Jessica Steed, Caroline Kline, and Emily Clyde Curtis coordinated with other Mormon feminists to organize the Sofia Gathering for the Southwest. Then, in 2010, some Exponent bloggers and other Mormon feminists created the site *LDS Wave* (Women Advocating for Voice and Equality) as a space for specific calls to action for Mormon feminist advocacy.[21] The speed of online communication made it easier to innovate and carve out space to define for oneself what it meant to be a Mormon feminist.

### The Paper Moves Exclusively Online

While the blog engaged readers, page views didn't necessarily translate to paper subscriptions. With the paper's financial constraints, Dredge and associate editors Heather Sundahl and Kimberly Burnett made the difficult call to move the paper to an online-only publication. For their final print issue in 2006, they reused the cover of the July 1974 inaugural issue. Dredge wrote about coming full circle: "We hope to spread our tree of knowledge of the lives of Mormon women everywhere to a whole new generation of women who are computer savvy."[22] Between 2007 and 2009, they produced one online issue per year. The 2007 issue was open-themed, 2008 discussed online pornography use, and 2009 published a compilation of the "best of the blog." However, an annual pdf was not a sustainable model to attract subscribers. The editors felt burned out, and it seemed that the pool of potential new editors living in Boston had dried up. However, their commitment to the work kept the paper going until technological advancements allowed for a dispersed team to coordinate from outside of Boston.

---

20. Kathryn Lynard Soper, "Coming Home," *Times and Seasons* (blog), July 26, 2007.

21. *LDS Wave* founders include Jessica Steed, Meghan Raynes, Chelsea Shields Strayer, Susan Christiansen, Emily Clyde Curtis, Tresa Edmunds, Jenne Alderks, Stephanie Snyder, Elisabeth Calvert Smith, Kaimi Wenger, and Caroline Kline. See Joanna Brooks, Rachel Hunt Steenblik, and Hannah Wheelwright, eds., *Mormon Feminism: Essential Writings* (New York: Oxford University Press, 2015), 31.

22. Dredge, "Coming Full Circle," *Exponent II* 28, no. 2 (2006): 3.

# 9  Expanding Geographically and Thematically

In 2009, the magazine was on life support. Entering its third year as an annual online-only publication, the editors and board feared they would have to shutter the paper without someone who had the energy to bring it back into print. As board members considered their options, Judy Dushku began conversations with Aimee Evans Hickman about the possibility of continuing her work with Exponent in a new way. Hickman had served as board president in Boston before her family moved to Baltimore, Maryland, in 2008. The paper's production had previously been constrained to the Boston area, but nearly ubiquitous access to the internet provided new options. The blog's success demonstrated how fruitful online collaboration could be. Might Hickman consider taking on the editor role and building a dispersed team? She was interested. Dushku put forth Hickman's name at the board meeting following the 2009 retreat, and someone seconded the nomination. As Hickman held her six-month-old daughter—the youngest of three children—the board voted to approve her appointment.

Emily Clyde Curtis learned that her friend was to lead the paper and reached out from Arizona to offer her support. Hickman and Clyde Curtis had worked together on the board for nearly a decade and held shared hopes for Exponent's future. Hickman suggested they have a conversation, and over a long phone call, they envisioned a co-editorship that spanned the country. It wouldn't be paste-up parties with their soon-to-be six babes and toddlers underfoot or production meetings in cozy living rooms, but it would allow for an equally invested co-editor with whom to share ideas, frustrations, and successes. The next day, they collectively sent out nearly 150 emails. Within a month, they had assembled a volunteer editorial board and staff of over two dozen women from coast to coast. *Exponent II* would continue to reflect a shared purpose between deeply engaged collaborators.[1]

## *Exponent II* Returns as a Full-Color Magazine

Bringing the paper back into print required much of the same start-up energy

---

1. Aimee Evans Hickman, interview with the authors, March 10, 2023.

as the paper's founding. However, this time, the editors could lean on Exponent's national network for content and staff positions. Several bloggers volunteered as feature editors: Caroline Kline revived Dushku's "Sisters Speak" column, selecting comments from the blog; Deborah Farmer Kris compiled "Exponent Generations," republishing similarly themed pieces from the original *Woman's Exponent*, *Exponent II*, and *The Exponent*; and Jessica Steed led "Awakenings," focused on theology. More volunteers joined the geographically dispersed team while Hickman tapped her local friend, Margaret Olsen Hemming, as design editor. The women lived in the same ward in Baltimore, but they first met at the 2008 Exponent retreat when Hemming attended with her sister-in-law, Julie Hemming Savage. Hickman shared in a meeting about the struggle it had been to leave her friends in Boston and move to Baltimore, and Hemming perked up at the mention of her own new hometown. The women connected, realizing that not only was Hemming teaching Hickman's children in Primary, but that Hemming had worked on her high school's newspaper staff with Hickman's younger sister. Now, Hemming would lean on the InDesign experience she gained in high school for *Exponent II*'s layout. Perhaps more significantly, with the magazine being printed in full color for the first time, Hemming conceptualized expanding the paper's use of art as storytelling.[2]

Decentralizing production allowed the organization to innovate but also took away some of the joys of the work. Instead of gathering together at someone's home, staff and board meetings took place via conference calls. "Only one person could talk at a time," Hickman recalled, "and there was no way to queue up, so it was clunky. It wasn't ideal, but between conference calls and emails, we got the work done." Reader committees no longer passed along printed copies of essays, but instead collaborated over Google Docs.[3] Could online communication and handwritten thank-you notes from the editors build the relationships needed to sustain a volunteer team? The annual retreat took on added importance as a place where staff could meet in person. Soon, the board likewise expanded outside of Boston, looking to retreat regulars to fill needed roles. In late 2011, Kirsten Campbell in Indiana joined as board president and Suzette Smith in Virginia as treasurer. In previous years, the board had a level of informality that often allowed dedicated staff to vote on board decisions. With their professional backgrounds in nonprofit organizations, Margaret Dredge Moore and Anja Shafer pushed the board to contract so that only people with specific board roles would join the conference calls and vote on organization-wide decisions.

---

2. Margaret Olsen Hemming, interview with the authors, April 13, 2023.
3. Hickman interview.

Exponent II board members reprise the photo of the Founding Mothers at the John Harvard statue in 2014 (see page 16 for original). Top: Heather Sundahl, Linda Andrews. Back row: Anja Shafer, Kirsten Campbell, Linda Hoffman Kimball, Emily Fisher Gray, Suzette Smith. Front row: Caroline Kline, Emily Clyde Curtis, Margaret Olsen Hemming, Aimee Evans Hickman, Denise Kelly, Margaret Dredge Moore.

In a joint editorial, Hickman and Clyde Curtis explained the decision to return to print: "Both longtime readers and women new to Mormon feminism have expressed a longing for a reading experience beyond those available on the Internet: the chance to read longer pieces, to look at a wider historical context and most importantly, perhaps, to take the time for the quiet reflection of sitting with someone else's experience without the ability or expectation to immediately fire back a response in the form of a comment thread."[4] In the digital age, where so much seemed to get lost in the ether, the paper took on a feeling of presence and history that online writing sometimes lacked. With a print magazine and a thriving blog, Exponent was poised to participate in the new wave of Mormon feminism.

## Mormon Feminism and the "Mormon Moment"

In June 2011, *Newsweek* magazine ran a special double issue titled "The Mormon Moment." Its cover image transposed Mitt Romney's head onto the body of a leaping Mormon missionary from the Broadway musical, *The Book of Mormon*, which had premiered a few months earlier. Romney had just announced his bid for the 2012 presidential election. That same month, the LDS Church launched its "I'm a Mormon" campaign that included billboards in Times Square and a website that hosted thousands of profiles of church members from around the world.[5] The eyes of the nation were on Mormons, and with *Exponent II*'s long and at times rocky relationship with Romney, reporters came calling. *Salon*, *Vanity Fair*, the *Washington Post*, and more interviewed Exponent's past and current leaders, seeking a Mormon feminist view. Barbara Taylor, then board president, had worked as Romney's executive assistant when he was governor of Massachusetts; she believed he had evolved on women's issues over the years. Judy Dushku, however, was unconvinced and spoke frequently with media outlets about her concerns.[6] But the election dealt with more than one candidate's religion, and politics became the theme for the Fall 2012 issue. "In this historic political moment," Hickman wrote, "*Exponent II* is focused on putting to rest the notion that Latter-day Saints are one monolithic, Christian Conservative voting bloc." They sought to highlight the political diversity even within their progressive-leaning community. In subsequent issues, they invited broader views by again hosting guest editors, including Lisa Butterworth of *Feminist Mormon Housewives*, Neylan McBaine of the Mormon Women Project, and Nancy Harward and Linda Hoffman Kimball of Midwest Pilgrims.

---

4. Hickman and Curtis, "Rebirth," *Exponent II* 30, no. 1 (2010): 3.

5. "Mormon.org 'I'm a Mormon' Effort Launches in New York City," Mormon Newsroom, June 16, 2011, newsroom.churchofjesuschrist.org. For more analysis, see Benjamin E. Park, *American Zion: A New History of Mormonism* (New York: Liveright Publishing, 2024), 364–69.

6. Irin Carmon, "Can Mitt talk to Women?" *Salon*, April 19, 2012, salon.com.

The convergence of blogs, social media, and a new generation of Mormon feminists changed the nature of the conversations that Mormons were having with one another. If national media outlets could debate the church's position on LGBTQ issues and LDS politicians' temple covenants, then certainly Mormons themselves could enter the public discourse. Exponent's Spring 2012 issue, "Zion's Frontier: LGBTQ Journeys of Faith," was the paper's first to focus on the topic in sixteen years. They shared stories and art by several queer Mormons, and Hickman and Clyde Curtis called on the church to do better: "As a Church culture, we can't continue to force people into the closet by saying, 'Be quiet. Be celibate.'... We believe that the Gospel of Jesus Christ is more expansive and merciful than is currently being practiced."[7] The editors acknowledged the lack of trans voices—the organization had room to grow—but this issue served as a stake in the ground to widen its tent toward inclusion. The Summer 2012 issue centered on women and the temple. Fiona Givens wrote how in the endowment ceremony, she felt she had "walked out of the wilderness and into the light"; Margaret M. Toscano analyzed how myth and ritual function in temple ceremonies; and Amy McPhie Allebest shared "A Letter to the Brethren" expressing her heartache at having her concerns about sexism in the temple routinely dismissed.[8] Mormon women did not have a singular experience with the temple, and opening the conversation to a broader spectrum of experiences increased the possibility that future conversations could be met with empathy.

### A New Wave of Mormon Feminist Activism

Mormon feminists seized on the national interest in their faith. Increasingly, Mormon feminists harnessed digital tools to organize and advocate for greater equality in the church. Scholars Nancy Ross and Jessica Finnigan noted that the term "Mormon feminist" required more than just feminist views, but a willingness to self-identify with that label because of its associated social and religious risks.[9] For this self-identifying group, ideas spread quickly on social media. In 2012, Stephanie Lauritzen created the Facebook group "All Enlisted" and organized "Wear Pants to Church Day." On December 16, 2012, participating women would wear pants instead of the typical dresses or skirts to church, and supportive men were encouraged to wear purple ties. *The Exponent* and other blogs publicized and discussed the event, which drew national media attention. Historian Colleen McDannell argues

---

7. Hickman and Curtis, "Letter from the Editors," *Exponent II* 31, no. 4 (Spring 2012): 3.
8. Allebest's letter is included on pages 256–60.
9. Nancy Ross and Jessica Finnigan, "Mormon Feminist Perspectives on the Mormon Digital Awakening: A Study of Identity and Personal Narratives," *Dialogue: A Journal of Mormon Thought* 47, no. 4 (Winter 2014): 48.

that the group found its success less in the number of women who wore pants to church that day, but rather in demonstrating the ability to move from digital criticism to in-person activism.[10]

The next major Mormon feminist movement came from Ordain Women. Its website launched on March 17, 2013, as a forum to advocate for LDS women's ordination and full integration into the decision-making councils of the church. Months previously, human rights attorney Kate Kelly approached long-time Mormon feminist activist Lorie Winder Stromberg on how to organize; they assembled a board and decided on a measured approach that they hoped would help church leaders listen to their plea.[11] Following the format of the church's "I'm a Mormon" campaign, individuals in favor of ordination submitted their own profiles. Several well-known *The Exponent* bloggers were among the earliest profiles. The group's advocacy efforts escalated beyond profiles later that year. Ahead of the October 2013 general conference, Ordain Women requested 150 tickets for the Saturday evening priesthood session, which was traditionally only attended by men. The church denied their request. Hundreds of women stood in the standby line to request admission to watch the session from the historic Tabernacle in Salt Lake City. One by one, conference ushers denied the women entrance. The denials were largely symbolic, as ahead of the Ordain Women action, the church made the priesthood sessions available on broadcast television and online for the first time.[12] However, the events on Temple Square both garnered significant media attention and allowed supporters of Ordain Women to gather in person. Lori LeVar Pierce flew in from Mississippi, and with one exception, only knew other participants from online interactions. "And yet," LeVar Pierce recalls, "I walked in and felt like I was attending a reunion."[13] Online connections became personal friendships. In April 2014, the church again denied Ordain Women's request for tickets. An even larger group gathered at Temple Square and were refused entrance to the Tabernacle.[14]

In previous decades, discussing women's ordination in print was a line that Exponent would not cross. After Ordain Women emerged, the conversation could not be ignored. Exponent's Spring 2014 issue focused on Mormon women and the priesthood. In Sisters Speak, Kline selected responses that reflected how the topic was complicated even within the Exponent community.

---

10. Colleen McDannell, *Sister Saints: Mormon Women since the End of Polygamy* (New York: Oxford University Press, 2019), 184–85.

11. Lorie Winder Stromberg, interview with the authors, May 17, 2023.

12. Kristen Moulton, "Mormon Women Shut Out of All-Male Priesthood Meeting," *Salt Lake Tribune*, October 18, 2013.

13. Lori LeVar Pierce, interview with the authors, June 23, 2023.

14. Kristen Moulton, "Mormon Women Again Turned Away from Priesthood Meetings," *Salt Lake Tribune*, April 11, 2014.

Some were in full support of women's ordination, some suggested broader restructuring of the institutional church, while others wanted stronger partnership and greater visibility for girls and women without ordination as a goal. In June 2014, echoing Sonia Johnson's excommunication in 1979, Kate Kelly's bishop excommunicated her on grounds of apostasy.[15]

While church leaders sought to make a public example of Kelly, excommunication was not their only tool of punishment. Months later, *The Exponent* blogger April Young-Bennett shared that, as a condition to renew her temple recommend and therefore be able to attend her brother's upcoming temple wedding, her stake president required that she resign from the Ordain Women board and remove her blog posts advocating for women's ordination. She did so and committed to keeping her posts down so long as her temple recommend remained active.[16] Reflecting the grief that many of Exponent's readers felt at the time, Kristine Haglund, *Dialogue* editor and Karen Haglund's niece, wrote, "This moment of my life as a Christian, as a Mormon, as a woman, feels fraught and discordant. My friends are hurting on all sides of the political and theological chasms that have opened between us. I can't hear the melodies I have sought to comfort me in the past. And still I am sure they are there, beneath and above the discord, waiting to be sung in a new key, a deeper rhythm, a joyful transposition."[17]

With Ordain Women representing the extreme side of Mormon feminist activism, other voices appeared moderate in comparison. In the following years, the church made symbolic moves toward gender equality, including inviting women to pray in general conference for the first time,[18] permitting female church employees and sister missionaries to wear slacks,[19] and updating some aspects of temple ceremonies to make them appear more egalitarian.[20] Efforts fell far short of women's ordination.

### Fortieth Anniversary Celebrations

As *Exponent II* approached its fortieth anniversary in 2014, the board planned ways to celebrate the milestone. Events included a speaker series

---

15. Kristen Moulton, "Kelly on Excommunication from Mormon Church: 'I've Done Nothing Wrong,'" *Salt Lake Tribune,* June 24, 2014.

16. April Young-Bennett, "An Announcement from April Young-Bennett," *The Exponent* (blog), January 15, 2015, exponentii.org.

17. Kristine Haglund, "Leitmotifs," *Exponent II* 34, no. 1 (Summer 2014): 22–23.

18. Peggy Fletcher Stack, "First Prayer by Woman Offered at Mormon Conference," *Salt Lake Tribune,* April 12, 2013. The prayer followed the "Let Women Pray in General Conference" campaign that generated about 1,600 letters to general authorities from about 300 participants.

19. Taylor Stevens, "Latter-day Saint Women Rejoice: They Can Now Wear Slacks on Their Missions, and NOT Just to Dodge Mosquitos," *Salt Lake Tribune,* December 20, 2018.

20. Peggy Fletcher Stack and David Noyce, "LDS Church Changes Temple Ceremony," *Salt Lake Tribune,* January 2, 2019.

Foundational leaders at Exponent II's fortieth-anniversary gala in Cambridge, Massachusetts, 2014. Back Row: Carolyn Person, Susan Kohler, Marti Lythgoe, Bonnie Brackett Canfield, Jeannie Decker Griffiths, Mimmu Hartiala-Sloan, Barbara Taylor, Kate Holbrook, Susan Howe, Diane McKinney Kellogg, Heather Cannon, Helen Claire Sievers, Laurel Thatcher Ulrich, Cheryl Howard DiVito, Renee Tietjen, Linda Andrews. Front Row: Linda Hoffman Kimball, Claudia Bushman, Nancy Dredge, Sue Booth-Forbes, Judy Dushku, Carrel Sheldon, Roslyn (Roz) Udall

held across five states, a special double-issue of the magazine, and a gala the evening before the annual retreat, helmed by Anja Shafer. Stefanie Carson, a professional graphic designer, beautifully upgraded the look of the magazine and designed a new "Tree of Knowledge" symbol to roll out for the anniversary. Ahead of the gala, board members gathered at the John Harvard statue on Harvard University campus to recreate the iconic 1974 photo of the founding mothers—before being chased off by campus security.[21] The gala in Cambridge included singing, a brass band called "Hornography," and a large gathering of current and former volunteers. Laurel Thatcher Ulrich gave the gala's keynote address: "One of the most difficult tasks for any organization is to survive its founders. Very few do that successfully, and we have a serious task as we begin a process of understanding our place in a larger history of Mormon feminism and Latter-day Saint women." For her part, she believed the founders chose well where to place their efforts.[22]

---

21. Original John Harvard statue photo on page 16. Updated photo on page 81.

22. Ulrich, "Have We Made a Difference?" *Exponent II* 34, no. 2 & 3 (Fall 2014/Winter 2015): 60–64.

With the anniversary, the 2014 retreat had its largest attendance to date. Heather Sundahl, then board president, had traditionally performed comedic parodies for the retreat variety show. This year, she penned a heartfelt and somber hymn, sung to the tune of "How Firm a Foundation," that captured the heaviness that many Mormon feminists felt after the church's punitive actions: "A place at the table, a seat at the stand / Where sisters and brothers preside hand in hand. / Upon the Lord's altar we lay our broken heart. / Oh listen to our voices, Oh listen to our voices, Oh listen to our voices and we will do our part."[23] Joanna Brooks, then working on the book *Mormon Feminism: Essential Writings* with co-editors Rachel Hunt Steenblik and Hannah Wheelwright, gave the retreat's keynote address. She looked ahead to the next forty years of Mormon feminism, arguing that Mormon women and their organizations needed greater individual and collective financial independence. She considered that the too-white field of Mormon feminism must do more to address racial differences and build alliances with women of color.[24]

## Claiming Power

Mormon feminists were not united on the question of women's ordination, but Mormon women had a long history of exercising faith and gifts of the spirit without ordination. As discussed in chapter five, the practice of Mormon women giving blessings by the laying on of hands quietly continued after institutional support withdrew in the mid-twentieth century.[25] Many Mormon women had stories like the one Diane Pritchett shared in *Exponent II*:

> A woman in our ward was struggling with postpartum depression. The Relief Society had been arranging meals, caring for her children, and monitoring the family round the clock, but it became clear that we were working beyond our level of expertise. Hospitalization was essential. We knew that this was not news she would want to hear. Her husband, her visiting teachers, a member of the bishopric, and I gathered to discuss our options. As we prayed, it became clear to everyone in the room that before taking her to the hospital she needed a blessing and that this blessing must come from women.
>
> This answer to our prayers distilled gently and clearly throughout the room. It was not a revolutionary or radical statement. We did not ask permission. We did not consult the handbook. Apart from deciding how we would proceed and that I would speak the words, we didn't even discuss it much. We took action.

---

23. Sundahl, "A Seat at the Table," *Exponent II* 34, no. 2 & 3 (Fall 2014/Winter 2015): 32–33. See pages 308–9 for one of her comedic parodies, "Persisters in Zion/Daughter of Exponent: A Medley."

24. Brooks, "The Next 40 Years of Mormon Feminism," *Exponent II* 34, no. 2 & 3 (Fall 2014/Winter 2015): 15–20.

25. See pages 49–50 for earlier discussion of women's blessings.

We gathered in her living room. Her husband and the member of the bishopric sat quietly in the background while the women embraced her in a circle.[26]

For decades, feminist retreats allowed women to privately and quietly participate in giving or receiving blessings. As the 2014 retreat ended, divergent threads coalesced for some women to reclaim the beloved tradition more publicly.

At the start of the Sunday morning Quaker meeting, Annie Dredge Kuntz stood with her six-month-old baby. She invited a small circle of women to join her in blessing her son. A midwife by trade, Kuntz taught a retreat workshop on midwifery and feminism in 2013. Afterward, Kuntz had a vision of blessing the baby with whom she was then pregnant at a later retreat.[27] In 2014, Fara Sneddon led a retreat workshop on the history of Latter-day Saint women's blessings. Sneddon began researching the topic in earnest the previous year with encouragement from friends at the Midwest Pilgrims retreat.[28] In Sneddon's session, Kuntz learned that Mormon women had been called as midwives in their wards and would bless expectant mothers. Buoyed by this legacy, Kuntz blessed her baby surrounded by women she loved. From the audience, Rachel Hunt Steenblik held her infant daughter and watched in awe. Before Hunt Steenblik's daughter had been blessed at church, she asked her bishop if she could hold her baby in the blessing circle, and as many Mormon mothers have experienced, the bishop denied her request. Inspired by Kuntz, Hunt Steenblik stood as the final speaker of the Quaker meeting and closed the service by inviting a small circle to join her in blessing her baby.[29] Women for whom this tradition has been lost report witnessing or participating in a woman-led blessing to be a powerful spiritual experience. After the retreat, Kyra Krakos felt this tradition had been opened to her. She wrote in *Dialogue* about claiming this power to bless her own mother and produced a small leaflet asserting a woman's right and authority to bless along with some basic "how-tos."[30]

Without the constraints of church instruction manuals, women's blessings may be highly individualized. In the epilogue to her award-winning essay, "Lightwork," Dayna Patterson offers a glimpse into potential

---

26. Diane Pritchett, "So Many Words," *Exponent II* 33, no. 4 (Spring 2014): 4–6. Included in full on pages 266–69.

27. Annie Dredge Kuntz, "A Mother's Blessing," unpublished essay shared with authors, used with permission.

28. Fara Sneddon, conversation with Katie Ludlow Rich, October 5, 2023. Sneddon's book on Mormon women's history of blessings is forthcoming.

29. Rachel Hunt Steenblik, email to Exponent blogger backlist, September 16, 2014, used with permission.

30. Kyra Krakos, "The Order of Eve: A Matriarchal Priesthood," *Dialogue: A Journal of Mormon Thought* 53, no. 1 (Spring 2000): 99–107. Instructional leaflet shared with authors.

Annie Dredge Kuntz blesses her baby, Toby, at the 2014 Exponent II retreat Quaker meeting, surrounded by women she loves.

pre-blessing questions: "Do you want to sit or stand? Are you comfortable with others joining the circle? Are you comfortable being touched? Head or shoulders okay? Could others who feel moved join the circle and touch the shoulders of those touching you? Do you just want me to speak, or do you want the others in the circle to speak, if they want to? How would you like us to address you in the prayer? Are there terms you're more comfortable with addressing deity?"[31] For artist Page Turner, images come much more easily than words. When she was invited at a retreat to help bless a friend struggling with deep depression, she joined the circle and, instead of speaking, used a finger to draw the shapes that came to her mind onto the recipient's shoulder. On a stop during her train ride home, she walked through the nearby woods and collected small objects. Back on the train, she arranged the objects on the tray, took a picture, and sent it to that friend as a visual representation of the blessing. Her practice of visual blessings has grown as friends reach out with individualized requests. Recipients have reported using the images as part of a calming meditative practice.[32] Retreat blessings are a small part of a long tradition of Mormon women ministering through this spiritual gift.

---

31. Dayna Patterson, "Lightwork," *Exponent II* 41, no. 3 (Winter 2022): 42.
32. Page Turner, interview with the authors, September 27, 2023. A visual blessing by Turner, "Strands of Sisterhood Secured," is the cover art for the fiftieth anniversary issue, *Exponent II* 43, no. 4 (Spring 2024).

Linda Hoffman Kimball, Sharon Gray, and Stefanie Carson at the 2013 retreat holding the temple issue (Summer 2013, vol. 33, no. 1) to which they were contributors.

Kirsten Campbell, Cheryl Howard DiVito, and Pandora Brewer at the 2013 retreat with the quilt that Campbell and Brewer made and presented to DiVito. For more on the retreat quilt tradition, see page 95.

# 10  Implementing Sustainable Processes and Financial Safeguards

One of the first changes made by the new editors was to institute term limits. Early in their tenure, Aimee Evans Hickman and Emily Clyde Curtis decided to serve as editors for five years (twenty magazine issues) and then step down. They hoped to be able to hand over a beautiful, thriving publication to a new editor, but if not, they believed a clear end time would help them maintain the energy and focus they needed for this time-intensive volunteer labor.[1] As 2014 neared an end, they zeroed in on art editor Margaret Olsen Hemming as their replacement. She was interested in the role but hesitant. She had a master's degree in international peace and conflict resolution but didn't have formal training in editing. She was pregnant with her third baby, and her husband had a demanding medical residency schedule. Hemming worried that she lacked the Exponent community standing that the role required because she would be the first editor who had never lived in Boston. But the outgoing editors saw Hemming's maturity, dedication, and passion for the work.[2] And Hemming had ideas on how she could build the paper. Seeking a partner who had the skills she felt she lacked, Hemming asked Pandora Brewer to join as managing editor.

Editing a Mormon feminist paper-turned-magazine made no practical sense in Brewer's life. Brewer left Cambridge and Mormonism when she and her family moved to Chicago. There, she had an intensive career with Crate & Barrel, managing systems implementation at their corporate headquarters. But her Cambridge experiences left an indelible mark on her. She had moved many times while growing up before she and her husband landed in Cambridge in 1988, where they had their two children and stayed for nearly fifteen years. Through Exponent II and her Cambridge ward study group, she developed strong female friendships for the first time; the value she placed in these relationships and communities stayed with her.[3] Brewer went on a long walk after Hemming approached her with the managing editor position. She

---

1. Emily Clyde Curtis, interview with the authors, March 30, 2023.
2. Aimee Evans Hickman, interview with the authors, August 25, 2023.
3. See Pandora Brewer's essay, "Known to Your Bones: Living in the Company of Women," on pages 207–12.

returned feeling that the universe wanted her to accept this role. "I needed the extra revelatory push," she said, "because [saying yes] was illogical—absolutely absurd. I was working 65–70 hours a week, and I had not been in the church for a long time. But I felt certain it's the right thing to do."[4] Brewer knew that Hemming had worked closely with Hickman and Clyde Curtis to bring the magazine back into print and that she understood the paper and the board well. Because *Exponent II* was already a beautiful, quality product, Brewer felt she could apply her professional experience to create a sustainable workflow.

Before considering content for their first issue, Hemming and Brewer developed their process. "We built a machine," Brewer said. "The beauty of a good process is that if you build the right machine, it keeps running." They planned the production calendar and consistently met on Saturday mornings to keep everything on track. They implemented a system of Google Drive folders where everything would go and clear processes around art and review. Too often, the magazine's weight had fallen on the shoulders of one or two editors when volunteers—already giving time to family, church, work, and community—could not direct their energy to the paper. They recruited a deep bench of volunteers to protect against burnout and provide flexibility. "On any given issue, we had ten to fifteen people doing different things. We would wrangle them, but there was a lot of calm," Brewer recalled. If one volunteer wasn't available, someone else could step in. Most significantly, they created the role of author-editor, a position that worked individually with writers. The author-editors helped distribute the burden of content editing and allowed the magazine to invest more time with new and emerging writers to develop pieces for publication.[5] Emily Fisher Gray, a board member who later served as co-managing editor, encouraged the team to attract a more diverse pool of submissions by selecting topics and asking questions that might speak to a broader lived experience.[6] They hosted an ongoing series on global Mormonism, "Women's Work" interviews highlighting a range of careers, and published issues on feminist midrash,[7] poverty,[8] women's activism,[9] and new perspectives on family history.[10]

The magazine's growing emphasis on art allowed them to include broader perspectives through visual storytelling. When Hemming took on the role

---

4. Pandora Brewer, interview with the authors, May 5, 2023.
5. Brewer interview.
6. Margaret Olsen Hemming, interview with the authors, April 13, 2023.
7. *Exponent II* 35, no. 3 (Winter 2016). Midrash is a Jewish tradition of exploring and interpreting scripture that may include retelling stories from new perspectives. Feminist midrash specifically focuses on the stories of women in scripture, seeking to give them greater depth.
8. *Exponent II* 39, no. 1 (Summer 2019).
9. *Exponent II* 40, no. 1 (Summer 2020).
10. *Exponent II* 40, no. 4 (Spring 2021).

Margaret Olsen Hemming and Pandora Brewer display their first issue of *Exponent II* as editor and managing editor (Summer 2015).

of design editor in 2010 and then art editor in 2012, the vibrant community of Mormon-adjacent artists that emerged on social media did not yet exist. Cultivating a network required groundwork. Hemming initially leaned on her mother-in-law, artist Alice Hemming's, connections and wrote to artists asking if they would be willing to publish in the magazine. Slowly, the network grew, aided at times when established artists like Cassandra Barney and Rose Datac Dall were willing to publish in the magazine and share about it on their Facebook pages.[11] Initially, the art was a way to distinguish the print magazine from online content. "How can we make this something that people want to hold in their hands? Make it beautiful," Hemming reflected. But in time, the art became significant to her in its own right. "Not everyone is a writer, but these artists could share their experiences, their thoughts, how they had created theology—all the things that Exponent wanted to share—in an alternative way to the written word."[12] As editor in chief, Hemming brought on Page Turner as art editor and Rosie Gochnour Serago as layout editor.[13] Together, Turner and Serago worked to pair essays with art

---

11. Hemming interview.
12. Hemming interview.
13. Turner and Serago continue serving on the magazine team as of this writing. For more on Turner, see "The Sacred History of Remnants" on pages 263–66. For an essay by Serago about her process as layout editor, see "Exponent Wrapped" on pages 312–14. Serago also became *Exponent II*'s marketing director in 2024.

that provided multiple perspectives on coordinating themes. They carved out room to include artist statements that described the process and intentions behind the artist's work.[14]

### Engaging in the Reinvigorated Women's Movement

Though the "Mormon Moment" had passed, Mormon feminists actively participated in the reemerging women's movement. Much of feminist activism in the 2010s focused on more substantial LGBTQIA rights and sought to end sexual harassment, abuse, and the objectification of women. Many Mormon feminists increasingly found their values to be in direct conflict with LDS church leaders and policies. One of the starkest examples was what became known as the "Policy of Exclusion" (POX). In June 2015, the US Supreme Court ruled in *Obergefell v. Hodges* that the fundamental right to marry is guaranteed to same-sex couples. On November 5, 2015, an update to the LDS Church's general "Handbook 1" for leaders leaked on the internet. In what many consider to be the church's reaction to the legalization of same-sex marriage, the handbook update included new policies that classified people in same-sex marriages as "apostates" requiring disciplinary councils. It further stipulated that the children of same-sex couples would not be permitted to receive formal blessings or ordinances—including baptism—until the child had turned eighteen and had disavowed the practice of same-sex cohabitation and marriage.[15]

The Policy of Exclusion devastated many church members. Outrage at the policy extended beyond the typically progressive Mormon groups, and Exponent II became one of several platforms advocating for change. On the day the policy was leaked, blogger Libby Potter Boss (as "Libby") wrote that this was the least Christian thing she had seen come from the LDS Church: "Our leaders must—*must*—do better. We cannot call ourselves Christian—in fact, we cannot call ourselves Mormon—if we forbid Church participation and ordinances to children."[16] The Fall 2015 issue was nearly off to print when the POX leaked. Hemming and Brewer rewrote the editorial to acknowledge the pain and confusion the policy brought to so many of their readers. That issue already included an essay from longtime Exponent volunteer, Anne Wunderli, about learning to advocate for her daughter who came out as queer and joining the group Mama Dragons, which worked to empower mothers

---

14. Page Turner, interview with the authors, September 27, 2023.
15. Sarah Pulliam Bailey, "Mormon Church to Exclude Children of Same-Sex Couples from Getting Blessed and Baptized until They Are 18," *Washington Post*, November 6, 2015.
16. Libby Potter Boss, "Wherein We See Proof That Mormons Aren't Christian," *The Exponent* (blog), November 5, 2015, exponentii.org.

of LGBTQIA children to create healthy, loving, and supportive environments.[17] Then in the Spring 2016 issue, the editors made the unusual move of taking a stand in the magazine against the POX. "We chose a side, but there are not really sides," Brewer wrote of their decision to oppose the policy and share the voices of people directly affected. "This collective narrative takes on the strength to persevere and the power to change."[18] They wanted to promote love and connection, *and* they wanted the church to change its policy.

Sensing a great need for community, retreat directors Denise Kelly and Emily Fisher Gray opened more spaces than usual for the 2016 retreat.[19] By this point, it had become a retreat tradition for Kirsten Campbell, who had recently served as Exponent president, and Brewer to make a custom quilt together. They would select the quilt's recipient in recognition of a big life event or to extend comfort in a time of need. After the retreat variety show, they would present the quilt to its recipient. In 2016, Campbell and Brewer veered from tradition. Campbell's daughter had recently come out as queer and had begun dating the love of their life. Brewer's children were both queer. They knew the heartache that the POX caused for so many in the Exponent community. Instead of a single large quilt, they made rainbow heart quilt blocks to give to each person in attendance. "We chose the heart because our greatest blessing and responsibility is to love," Campbell reflected, "and the policy was the opposite of love."[20] Three years later, in April 2019, the church modified and partially rescinded the POX. Children of same-sex couples would no longer be barred from receiving ordinances, and same-sex marriage and cohabitation would no longer be automatically classified as apostasy, though it was still considered a "serious transgression."[21] However, the policy's lasting damage was not so easily rescinded. For many who had fought to stay active, the POX was a death blow to their relationship with the church.[22]

Later in 2016, many Mormon feminists found themselves horrified at the presidential election of Donald Trump, a known misogynist who openly bragged about sexually assaulting women. Many were disappointed at the support he received from members of their faith and that the church sent the Mormon Tabernacle Choir to sing at his inauguration. Mormon feminists gathered in cities across the United States to participate in the January 2017

---

17. Anne Wunderli, "Like Dragons Did They Fight," *Exponent II* 35, no. 2 (Fall 2015): 10.
18. Brewer, "Letter from the Editor," *Exponent II* 35, no. 4 (Spring 2016): 2.
19. Emily Fisher Gray, interview with the authors, September 21, 2023.
20. Kirsten Campbell, phone call with the authors, November 10, 2023.
21. Peggy Fletcher Stack, "LDS Church Dumps Its Controversial LGBTQ Policy, Cites 'Continuing Revelation' From God," *Salt Lake Tribune*, April 4, 2019.
22. Jana Riess and Benjamin Knoll, "Commentary: Did the 2015 LGBTQ Policy Drive a Mass Exodus from the LDS Church? No, But for Many It Was the 'Last Straw,'" Religion News Service, *Salt Lake Tribune*, May 29, 2019, sltrib.com.

Women's March. That month, Sharlee Mullins Glenn launched the Mormon Women for Ethical Government (MWEG) Facebook group, which quickly garnered over 4,000 members. With co-founders Linda Hoffman Kimball, Diana Bate Hardy, and Melissa Dalton-Bradford, the nonpartisan MWEG became a 501(c)(4) nonprofit with a 501(c)(3) sister arm and laid out its commitment to using the principles of peacemaking to advocate for the safeguarding of democratic institutions and to protect fundamental human rights.[23] Several Exponent volunteers joined the efforts of this group as it became a significant force for Mormon women's political activism in the United States.

More than a decade after its founding, Exponent II's blog maintained a strong readership and allowed the organization to respond quickly to major issues inside and outside of the church. For instance, in late 2017, actress Alyssa Milano reignited the hashtag #MeToo, coined by activist Tarana Burke, for sharing stories of sexual assault and harassment, and created a moment of national reckoning. In March 2018, blogger Morgen Willis (as "Adela-Hope") launched the #MormonMeToo blog series with an open letter to LDS Church President Russell M. Nelson, inviting him to listen to the stories of Mormon women.[24] As eyes turned to social media and many sites in the bloggernacle waned, *The Exponent* remained a place that readers could count on to discuss Mormon feminist issues in greater depth than social media posts typically allowed; as of this writing, the *Salt Lake Tribune*'s Mormon Land news coverage continues to quote Exponent II blog posts frequently.

## Betrayal Revealed

While Exponent was thriving by some measures, funds were perpetually lacking. In late 2016, Suzette Smith informed the board that she would step down as treasurer. Susan Christiansen would take her place, but Smith requested that Christiansen shadow her for a year before fully taking over. Over the following months, Christiansen and other board members picked up on indications that all was not right with Exponent II's finances. They noted Smith's seemingly evasive behavior, including denying Christiansen access to the organization's bank accounts. In September 2017, the dam broke. Smith revealed that Exponent II no longer had its nonprofit status, as she had not filed the necessary paperwork for years. This dealt a significant blow to the organization's ability to fundraise. Alerted to additional concerns, board president Heather Sundahl opened a paper bank statement and found

---

23. *The Little Purple Book: MWEG Essentials* (Salt Lake City: By Common Consent Press, 2018).

24. AdelaHope, "An Open Letter to President Nelson #MormonMeToo," *The Exponent* (blog), March 21, 2018, exponentii.org.

that, contrary to Smith's reports at board meetings, Exponent's account was overdrawn.[25] When asked to explain, Smith wrote in an email that she had "taken money and co-mingled money—and have run out of time to make it right."[26] Board members began consulting with lawyers and accountants. Initially believing the deception to be relatively small, they hoped to reach a private agreement for financial restitution.[27] That hope was dashed as Exponent gained a more comprehensive understanding of Smith's actions. After hundreds of hours of forensic accounting work by Christiansen—completed at great cost to her personal life and graduate studies[28]—the board concluded that it was necessary to bring in law enforcement. They called the Federal Bureau of Investigation.[29]

It was heartbreaking and humiliating for the organization to come to grips with this level of duplicity. Like the Parent Teacher Association and other small nonprofits, Exponent II relied on a volunteer model based on trust with few checks and balances. No one was paid for their time, and there was little accountability in place for each person's job.[30] Exponent's treasurer was expected to present financial spreadsheets at monthly board meetings; however, the reports were more often than not glossed over and assumed accurate as long as the printer was paid and the retreat center got their deposit. Board members were so used to the organization being broke that, despite their frustration at the lack of funds, they did not assume fraud until faced with overwhelming evidence. Sundahl bemoans that she learned too late that "with finances, like sex, multilayered protections are a girl's best friend."[31] While the gift of trust is essential for creating connection at a retreat, a nonprofit's business is different and requires safeguards.

The embezzlement case made its way to federal court in the *United States of America v. Suzette M. Smith*. The Statement of Facts signed by Smith as true and accurate concluded that over six years, Smith embezzled $191,674.91 and transferred or paid back $84,319.70, for a total amount stolen of approximately $107,451.21. In or about February 2012, shortly after Smith assumed the role of treasurer for Exponent II (referred to as Nonprofit #1), Smith "began to steal checks, cash, and other funds intended for or present

---

25. Heather Sundahl, interview with Katie Rich, July 27, 2022.
26. "Statement of Facts," *United States v. Suzette M. Smith* 1:18-cr-00393, E.D. Virginia, November 16, 2018.
27. Sundahl interview.
28. "Transcript of Sentencing," *United States v. Suzette M. Smith* 1:18-cr-00393, E.D. Virginia, February 22, 2019.
29. Gray interview.
30. Magazine editors were offered a small honorarium at this time, but they did not always accept the funds.
31. Sundahl interview.

in the bank accounts of Nonprofit #1 for her own personal use." Eventually, Smith's primary method of embezzlement became a direct wire transfer from Nonprofit #1's bank accounts to Smith's personal accounts. To avoid detection from other board members, Smith sometimes "transferred funds back to Nonprofit #1 in a variety of ways." Furthermore, Smith's actions were not done because of "accident, mistake, or innocent reason."[32] Through her attorney, Smith pleaded guilty to the charge of wire fraud. The judge sentenced Smith to prison for fifteen months, followed by a three-year supervised release. The court also required that she pay restitution in monthly installments following her release from prison.[33] At the rate of Smith's payments as of this writing, it will take decades for her to complete financial restitution.

Exponent II had several immediate financial concerns upon discovering the embezzlement. Its accounts held insufficient funds to pay for the printing and mailing of the Fall 2017 issue, the upcoming deposit for the 2018 retreat, and website and blog hosting fees. The organization undertook painstaking efforts over the previous six years to raise money. From handwritten fundraising letters to handmade quilts and jam sold at the retreat silent auctions, Exponent raised funds in small amounts by an all-volunteer staff. Despite frequent subscription drives, magazine subscriptions remained near their historic low. Exponent learned that Smith sometimes had pocketed money from subscribers without inputting their mailing information, causing an unknown number of subscribers to never receive their magazine and not renew their subscriptions. Smith's actions crushed the morale of volunteers who did not see the fruits of their labors and who had to divert massive amounts of time and energy to recover the financial and legal standing of the organization. News of the embezzlement damaged its community's trust in the organization, and Exponent had to indefinitely delay its goal to pay market-rate stipends to volunteers for their professional services, a feminist effort they had been working toward.[34]

### Moving Forward with Financial Safeguards

Upon discovering Smith's embezzlement, the Exponent board met regularly to develop a careful plan to implement financial safeguards and right the ship. They called founding mothers, former board members, and select donors to notify them of the issue. The board released a public statement on the blog and shared it in its Facebook discussion group to inform the Exponent community.[35] Messages of support flooded their inbox and comment section. In

---

32. "Statement of Facts."
33. "Transcript of Sentencing."
34. Victim Impact Statement, Exponent II Board, draft dated January 17, 2019.
35. "Exponent II Misappropriation of Funds Announcement," *The Exponent* (blog), September 24, 2017, exponentii.org.

Board members Susan Christiansen, Margaret Olsen Hemming, Heather Sundahl, Pandora Brewer, and Kirsten Campbell get glamorous at a TJ Maxx in New Hampshire on their way to the retreat. *Photo by Barbara Christiansen*

the following months, Sundahl transitioned to historian on the board, and Barbara Christiansen stepped in as president to spearhead the years-long process of restoring Exponent II's nonprofit status. Sisters Barbara Christiansen and Susan Christiansen took on the labor of coordinating with lawyers, accountants, banks, and government agencies to bring Exponent to a place of legal and financial solvency. They set up dozens of safeguards to prevent future embezzlement. The complicated process included refiling twelve years of tax returns and filling out hundreds of pages of applications to the state of Massachusetts and the US government.[36] On February 13, 2020, the IRS issued a letter stating that Exponent II had been reinstated as a 501(c)(3) with a back date that effectively made its 501(c)(3) status continuous since its founding.[37] In fall 2017, an anonymous donor gave the money necessary to print and mail the magazine's Fall 2017 and Winter 2018 issues.[38] Hemming and Brewer's

---

36. Susan Christiansen, notes provided to the authors, December 5, 2023.
37. Internal Revenue Service letter to Exponent II Corporation, February 13, 2020.
38. Hemming interview, April 27, 2023.

production systems allowed the magazine to continue publishing without missing an issue.[39] With an influx of small donations from individual donors and other organizations in the broader Mormon community, and with subscriptions and renewals appropriately making it into the bank account, they were soon able to cover continuing production costs. Despite forgoing typical fundraising activities between late 2017 and 2020, Exponent slowly climbed to basic financial stability.

For her part, Hemming refused to let money be the reason that Exponent folded. She had begun working with Rev. Dr. Fatimah Salleh on their three-volume series, *The Book of Mormon for the Least of These*, published by BCC Press. In their early discussions, Hemming and Salleh considered how, in the Book of Mormon, the Nephites' downfall was a lust for wealth, which led them to create social hierarchies, divisions, and conflicts that ultimately escalated to war and violence. Though she felt personally betrayed by Smith, who had participated in fundraising letter-stuffing parties at Hemming's house, Hemming thought that the best way to counteract the betrayal was to prioritize the Exponent staff and community's relationships over the loss of money. In an echo of past support, Michael Austin, then board president of *Dialogue*, approached Hemming and offered for *Dialogue* to pay Exponent II for her to guest edit their Spring 2020 issue. With the opportunity to connect to the history of *Dialogue*'s 1971 women's issue and the financial boon this would be to the organization, Hemming accepted. Throughout 2019, Hemming edited the magazine, the issue of *Dialogue*, and wrote her books with Salleh. She hoped that 2020 would be a rest year.[40]

### Global Shutdowns and Grappling with Intersectionality

In March 2020, governments across the globe initiated shutdowns to prevent the spread of the COVID-19 virus. In response to the emergency, the LDS Church suspended church meetings and temple worship worldwide.[41] The multifaceted devastation of the pandemic was far greater than can be addressed here, but like all organizations, the pandemic impacted Exponent II. Exponent's blog responded quickly, sharing dozens of posts with the hashtag #CopingWithCOVID19. The series ranged from discussing the challenges of a "home-centered church" for women who are denied the priesthood authority to bless the sacrament at home, to loneliness, to the strains on caregivers suddenly managing online homeschooling. Retreat director Katrina Vinck Baker, Robin Baker's daughter-in-law, monitored COVID conditions

---

39. Brewer interview.
40. Hemming interview, April 13, 2023.
41. Sydney Walker, "Timeline: How the Church Has Responded to the COVID-19 Pandemic," *Deseret News*, January 6, 2022, thechurchnews.com.

and how local regulations impacted the retreat center in New Hampshire; Vinck Baker led the board in its 2020 and 2021 agonizing decisions to cancel the retreat until the situation improved.

Simultaneously, Exponent II sought ways to refine its mission to better live its values—an ideal that would soon be tested. Implementing a 2019 decision, the Spring 2020 issue dropped the magazine's long-used tagline "Sharing Mormon Women's Voices since 1974" from the front cover as a move toward including gender minorities. They also published a revised mission statement that identified the organization as "a feminist space for women and gender minorities across the Mormon spectrum" and said it was "building an intersectional community that amplifies marginalized voices and advocates for equality."[42] In 2018, LDS Church President Russell M. Nelson asked both church members and the media to cease using the nickname "Mormon" in favor of using the church's full name. In using the term "Mormon spectrum," Exponent II sought to recognize that its community included both temple recommend-holding church members and those who were neither active nor believing; for many, the term "Mormon" felt as much like a cultural heritage as a religion. Through building an "intersectional" community, Exponent sought to recognize better how identity impacts Mormon feminists' experiences with systemic oppression. The term "intersectional," coined in 1989 by critical legal race scholar Kimberlé Williams Crenshaw, considers how systems of power affect people differently according to their overlapping identities of race, gender identity, class, sexuality, and ability.[43] Exponent brought its values to action in various ways, but its desire to be intersectional was more aspirational than descriptive.

The absence of in-person community gatherings due to COVID-19 protocols and a firestorm of political division drove people online. Social media algorithms promoted conflict in an already tense atmosphere. The police murders of George Floyd and Breonna Taylor sparked national Black Lives Matter protests against police brutality of Black bodies. After a grueling, inflammatory campaign, Donald Trump refused to concede defeat to former Vice President Joe Biden in the 2020 presidential election; Trump allegedly incited an insurrection at the US Capitol on January 6, 2021, when Congress met to certify the election results. For millions at home, these were some of

---

42. *Exponent II* 39, no. 4 (Spring 2020): back cover. In 2018, LDS Church President Russell M. Nelson asked both church members and the media to cease using the term "Mormon" in favor of using the full name of the church. "'Mormon' Is out: Church Releases Statement on How to Refer to the Organization," *Church News*, August 16, 2018, churchofjesuschrist.org.

43. Kimberlé Crenshaw, "Demarginalizing the Intersection of Race and Sex: A Black Feminist Critique of Antidiscrimination Doctrine, Feminist Theory, and Antiracist Politics," *University of Chicago Legal Forum* (1989): 139–67.

the issues that led them to engage in conversations about social justice for the first time. Exponent II's Facebook discussion group grew rapidly during the pandemic, adding thousands of people to reach a height of nearly 5,300 members. Though many found the group to be a supportive place to discuss topics related to their lives and church experience, conflicts arose as group members were increasingly unable to hold space for varying perspectives and experiences. Too often, ignorant or malicious comments hurt the group's most marginalized members.

The Exponent board had long discussed the challenge of hosting wide-ranging conversations online and the speed at which conversations could turn hostile. Group moderators consisted of unpaid volunteer bloggers on the social media committee who attempted to mediate conflict and enforce group rules. Blogger and board member Caroline Salisbury sought to address the growing issues with efforts such as a campaign to encourage group members to "call in" rather than "call out" other commenters. However, in February 2021, when a group member sought to hold Exponent accountable for its failure to provide a genuinely intersectional space, the group devolved as some members insisted on immediate sweeping changes that exceeded the organization's ability to meet. The board "paused" the group to prevent new content, initially planning a temporary halt. Board members and moderators sought solutions to reopen the space and host the connection and community the group sought while providing the structure and accountability that supported marginalized folks. Ultimately, in a decision that disappointed many, the board concluded that the organization did not have the resources and volunteer power to host the space and voted to keep the Facebook group paused indefinitely. They were not alone. In March 2021, the *New York Times* abandoned moderating its 77,000-member Cooking Community Facebook Group, reportedly due to concerns about staffing and how the group had been "riddled with controversies and debates involving class, race, and privilege."[44] Exponent II had often served as a bridge between Mormon feminists across the political spectrum, but a year into shutdowns and political upheaval, they found Facebook a river too wide to span.

---

44. Lauren Strapagiel, "The *New York Times* Is Giving Up Its Cooking Community Facebook Group with Over 77,000 Members," *BuzzFeed*, March 18, 2021, buzzfeednews.com.

# 11 Looking to the Future

In September 2022, after a two-year hiatus due to the pandemic, the return to New Hampshire felt more like a reunion than a retreat. On Friday night, Judy Dushku followed the precedent the late Carrel Sheldon established by inviting participants to set their intentions, let go of unmeetable expectations, and offer trust as a gift.[1] The retreaters attended Saturday workshops and small group discussions that led up to a keynote address by Allison Hong Merrill, who shared insights from her award-winning memoir, *Ninety-Nine Fire Hoops*.[2] On Sunday morning, Exponent's new president, Lori LeVar Pierce, presented her spiritual autobiography. Then, as she had many times since 1983, Nancy Dredge opened the Quaker meeting, where attendees stood to speak when moved. Retreat director Andee Bowden expanded practices from past years—such as encouraging pronouns on name tags and inviting participants to adapt routines to meet their physical, emotional, or neurodivergent needs throughout the weekend—as a way to create belonging through recognizing differences. Participants ranged from their twenties to eighties, from first-time attendees to foundational leaders. Many considered the retreat a particularly "sunny" year, with participants simply grateful to hug their friends in person. Despite recent challenges, the heart of the organization—deeper friendships through personal storytelling—maintained its strong beat.

## Building on Exponent II's Strengths

Some recent changes included new board members and magazine editors. After their immense efforts to get the organization back to financial safety and restore its nonprofit status, Barbara Christiansen and Susan Christiansen completed their three-year terms as president and treasurer, respectively. As LeVar Pierce and incoming treasurer Jeanine Bean took over these positions, Exponent II's financial security remained a top priority. Following Barbara's recommendation, the board hired a law firm and an accountant specializing

---

1. See pages 48–49 for more on Sheldon's Friday night ritual.
2. Allison Hong Merrill's essay, "The Trench Coat of Multiple Colors," is included on pages 330–33.

Rachel Rueckert and Carol Ann Litster Young in 2015 at the MIT Sailing Pavilion in Cambridge, Massachusetts, after a sail on the Charles River skippered by Carol Ann. In 2021, they became editor and managing editor of *Exponent II*, respectively.

in nonprofits to keep up on the vital work of compliance with state and federal agencies. Bean continued to uphold and further deepen the organization's financial safeguards with practices that included sharing monthly line-by-line transaction summaries and quarterly financial reports with the board. Bean also recruited a volunteer, non-board member to audit accounts regularly, ensured a second set of eyes observed all in-person transactions at the retreat, and provided a transparent annual financial report to share on the organization's website.[3] With these protections in place, LeVar Pierce committed that Exponent II's fiftieth anniversary would be the year to begin building a financial endowment to sustain the organization long into the future. She also worked to strengthen the board's communication and unity by adopting a consensus decision-making model; rather than a simple majority vote, the board would only move forward when they reached a decision each member could accept.[4]

As editors, Margaret Olsen Hemming and Pandora Brewer anticipated that finding their replacements would be one of their most important responsibilities. Always looking to create sustainable systems, they formalized the selection process: for the first time, *Exponent II* publicly advertised the opening for an editor. Hemming and Brewer worked with the outgoing

---

3. Email exchange between Jeanine Bean, Lori LeVar Pierce, and Katie Ludlow Rich, September 18, 2023.

4. Lori LeVar Pierce, interview with the authors, June 23, 2023.

president to narrow the pool of applicants to three strong candidates. They gave each candidate two essays that represented opposite ends of the spectrum of belief and orthodoxy that the paper received and asked them how they would handle the submissions. Rather than reject one or both options, candidate Rachel Rueckert returned having marked up both essays with her recommendations for revisions before publication. "It was so clear that she understood the organization's mission," Hemming recalled. "She wasn't going to be about imposing her voice on everybody else, but strengthening everyone's writing so that it was the best that it could be."[5] Rueckert, who had served as a volunteer author-editor for the magazine, was then completing an MFA at Columbia University, splitting time between New York City and Cambridge, Massachusetts. The search committee was impressed with her writing and editing skills, her vision for harnessing new technology to expand the paper's reach, and her commitment to supporting emerging writers. The board selected Rueckert as the next editor in chief.[6]

The magazine's production center temporarily moved back to Cambridge after more than a decade away. Rueckert asked Carol Ann Litster Young and Sam Layco to join her as managing editors. Rueckert and Litster Young both lived in what residents called "Mormon Big House," an old building divided into six apartments; over the years, up to four apartments at a time housed members of the LDS Church. Other residents included Lisa Van Orman Hadley, a former *Exponent II* feature editor, and Courtney Toiaivao, a former blogger. Rueckert and Litster Young met when they moved to Cambridge in 2012 for teaching jobs. Through friendships with the women in "Mormon Big House," they began attending retreats and volunteering with the paper. Both left secondary teaching—Rueckert making her way to a career as a memoirist and novelist, and Litster Young working to address housing equity and discrimination. Layco, who lived across the street and was new to Exponent with this role, brought a fresh perspective from their work in the theater industry. Although the magazine's production occurred through coordinating online with a larger team, the editors experienced echoes of years past, going in and out of each other's homes and attending church together.

As the new editors prepared their first issue, Layco believed it was essential for *Exponent II* to begin paying contributing writers and artists.[7] With the magazine's tight budget, the editors pooled and donated from their modest stipends and asked the board for additional funds to pay honorariums. The contributors could then accept the honorarium or donate it to one of the new community funds. The funds included the BIPOC Artist and Writer

---

5. Margaret Olsen Hemming, interview with the authors, April 27, 2023.
6. Hemming interview.
7. Carol Ann Litster Young, interview with the authors, June 9, 2023.

Scholarship (an expansion of the LDS Women of Color Artist scholarship that Hemming announced in 2019); collaborative art commissions; retreat scholarships to support attendees who identify as BIPOC, queer, or experiencing financial need; and editor back pay. The retreat's annual silent auction also became dedicated to supporting retreat scholarships. In fall 2022, recognizing that Exponent's commitment to becoming a genuinely intersectional space remains a work in progress, the board updated its mission statement: "Exponent II provides feminist forums for women and gender minorities across the Mormon spectrum to share their diverse life experiences in an atmosphere of trust and acceptance. Through these exchanges, we strive to create a community to better understand and support each other."

### Harnessing Technology to Nurture Community

Having inherited robust production systems, the editors worked to strengthen their geographically dispersed community. Their efforts included virtual magazine "launch parties," a new podcast, and a free online writing workshop series. Litster Young led the quarterly launch parties that celebrated the upcoming release of each issue, inviting writers and artists to talk about their work and interact with each other and subscribers. Litster Young, whose family had moved from Cambridge to Minnesota, joined with co-hosts Heather Sundahl, now in Utah, and Ramona Morris in Barbados, to produce the first season of the Exponent II podcast in 2023.[8] They interviewed Mormon feminists, discussed popular culture, and chatted about current events. The podcast captured the sometimes irreverent spirit of Exponent and sought to find the sacred and the profane in the mundane.

Rueckert hosted bi-monthly online workshops to democratize writing skills and increase writing confidence.[9] The first meeting of the month focused on craft instruction. Rueckert prioritized rotating between leading the instruction herself and inviting guest writers, such as novelist Rosalyn Collings Eves and *Exponent II*'s poetry editor Abby Parcell, to teach their specialties. The second meeting of the month focused on generative writing, meaning participants generated new material based on a prompt and then shared their work with others in the group. The workshops drew in a mix of writers, from undergraduate students to stay-at-home parents to seasoned authors, who participated from multiple states and foreign countries. One workshop regular, Allison Pingree, began attending Exponent retreats in the late '80s while getting a doctorate from Harvard before she moved to Nashville for work. When she returned to Cambridge years later, much with

---

8. From 2017 to 2019, blogger April Young-Bennett hosted an Exponent blog series in podcast format called the "Religious Feminism Podcast."

9. The workshops continue as of the time of this writing.

Katrina Vinck Baker, Lori LeVar Pierce, Heather Sundahl, and Kirsten Campbell pose following a Barbie-themed skit at the 2023 retreat variety show.

Exponent had changed. "Everyone was talking about the 'bloggernacle.' I'm not a blogger, and I'm not on social media, so I felt alien, like an outsider," Pingree said. With the writing workshops, "I feel like I belong again. I'm writing, I'm in the mix, I know the new editor." The workshops encouraged her to do more of the personal writing she longed to do. A prompt in a generative session led her to write the flash essay, "A Place That Doesn't Exist," about her husband's Alzheimer's.[10] For Rueckert, the workshops brought together her identities as a writer, editor, and teacher. "It's easy for me to see the good in any piece that comes in, especially if it's from an emerging writer," she said. In these online meetings, she could support writers, and they could encourage each other with peer feedback.[11] Cynthia W. Connell, Kate Bennion, Alma Frances Pellett, and Alixa Brobbey are some of the many writers who have published pieces from the workshops.

In January 2023, Exponent II launched an updated website that brought the organization and the blog under the same digital roof for the first time. Since its founding in 2006, the blog produced over 5,000 posts and 70,000 comments—all of which had to be migrated from the-exponent.com to exponentii.org. The website visually united the organization and updated the magazine's subscription and payment systems. The board had discussed the

---

10. Allison Pingree, interview with the authors, September 16, 2023. Her essay, "A Place That Doesn't Exist," is included in this volume on pages 328–29.

11. Rachel Rueckert, interview with the authors, June 2, 2023.

Lori LeVar Pierce and her daughter, Sarah, wave from the front row at an Exponent II Women's History Month event at Writ and Vision in Provo, Utah, 2024.

project for years but hit roadblocks including cost, project bloat, and ideological differences, with some wanting tech support to remain in-house. The board decided that the technology upgrades were essential to the organization's future and hired a digital agency to perform the work. Rueckert spearheaded the website overhaul, with Rosie Gochnour Serago designing the new look, LeVar Pierce representing the board on the frequent conference calls, and Katie Ludlow Rich acting as a liaison for the blog, which she had joined in early 2021. With the website upgrades and the magazine staff's subscription drive efforts, *Exponent II*'s subscriptions doubled in about fifteen months.

# Epilogue
*Exponent II*'s Legacy

Years before becoming editor, Rachel Rueckert was called to co-teach Sunday School with Laurel Thatcher Ulrich in the Cambridge First Ward. Rueckert was initially intimidated by the prospect but found the experience transformative. They taught from the Doctrine and Covenants, a book of scripture in the LDS canon that primarily contains revelations received by the church's founding prophet. Rueckert and Ulrich used the church-produced book *Revelations in Context: The Stories Behind the Sections of the Doctrine and Covenants* in their lessons. Rueckert recalled that as they would teach, Ulrich would often slip up on the title and refer to the book as "Revolutions *in Context*," which made Rueckert smile each time. "That's what Laurel is, a revolution in context," Rueckert said, reflecting on the award-winning historian whose career was partly inspired by her conversations about the women's movement with her Relief Society friends and the projects they worked on together. She continued, "And we all are, or we can be if we step up to that, though we can't know what impact we will have."[1] Both women came to Boston from the Intermountain West, Ulrich having been raised in Sugar City, Idaho, and Rueckert in Davis County, Utah. While many women in Ulrich's generation initially went East by following their husbands, Rueckert's generation was just as likely to enter careers or graduate school themselves, with or without a spouse in tow. In Boston, Rueckert would get to know many of the paper's foundational leaders who, over fifty years, created a body of work that reveals much about the modern Mormon feminist experience.

While revolutionary for its participants, *Exponent II*'s founders did not consider the paper a protest against the LDS Church. When Susan Kohler found copies of the *Woman's Exponent* in the stacks of Harvard's Widener Library and took them to her friends, they saw in their pioneer foremothers a path of faithful exploration of the tensions within Mormonism, feminism, and gender expectations. More than a thought exercise, the work of the paper built skills that launched careers as writers, editors, scholars, artists, and

---

1. Rachel Rueckert, interview with the authors, June 2, 2023.

more. It gave Mormon feminists a place to find themselves in the women's movement, reconcile their dual/dueling identities, and make agentive decisions about their lives. It provided a haven for those who felt isolated and marginalized in the church and broader culture. Though it is the longest-running independent Mormon women's publication, *Exponent II* is now one of several places where Mormon feminists can connect. The community can help meet its needs through numerous blogs, social media channels, podcasts, conferences, and other nonprofit organizations. Demographic trends indicate that younger generations of Americans are leaving their religious traditions at higher rates than their parents or grandparents, and it is increasingly the trend for Mormon feminists to leave rather than stay and advocate for greater equality from inside the church. All pillars of Exponent II—the magazine, blog, and retreat—have become a place for those who stay and those who leave to connect to their heritage and each other.

*Exponent II* still arrives quarterly in mailboxes "like a long letter from a dear friend,"[2] but it also arrives in inboxes and RSS feeds, via earbuds and online workshops. Whether in person at the annual retreat, on the page, or on a screen, Exponent helps individuals find their voices and witness one another's lives and stories. It continues, as former editor Aimee Evans Hickman said, "to act as a living history of the current moment." The organization rejects ideological purity and shares a broad range of perspectives in word and art. Hickman wrote that while this may not appear radical, "the quiet voices that are often lost to history may be where the biggest cultural shifts are manifested in the end."[3] The challenge of Exponent II is to continue to adapt as the LDS Church's demographics shift and technology changes to provide an independent platform and nurture a vibrant community where Mormon feminists can bring their whole selves in a spirit of trust and belonging.

---

2. Claudia Bushman, "*Exponent II*: Why?" *Exponent II* 1, no. 2 (October 1974).

3. Hickman, "The Radical Mission of Exponent II: 40th Anniversary Gala Address," *Exponent II* 34, no. 2 & 3 (Fall 2014/Winter 2015): 25–27.

# UNIT 1: 1974–1984

## Introduction by Heather Sundahl

Just as the first ten years of a person's life are filled with more growth and change than perhaps any other period, the same was true for the first decade of *Exponent II*. Unlike the highly curated magazine we have today, "the paper," as it was called, was initially seen as disposable, albeit informative. "Poised on the dual platforms of Mormonism and Feminism," founding editor Claudia Bushman wrote that the paper's purpose was to give Mormon women status, share useful information, and provide a place to connect through open sharing of "news and life views." She asked readers to consider it "like a long letter from a dear friend."[1] The paper presented some light and satirical material but planted kernels of weightier matters, too. As the decade progressed, subsequent editors Nancy Dredge and Susan Howe took on controversial topics like sexuality, the Equal Rights Amendment, and depression head-on.[2] Perhaps because church leaders had made it clear that *Exponent II* did not represent the church, it freed the editors to explore the issues of the day and perennial topics like marriage and motherhood. The paper demonstrated how Mormon feminists rejected attempts to label their dual identities as oxymoronic as they explored a range of spiritual, social, intellectual, and domestic topics with insight, humor, and faith.

Through personal essays, writers explored a broad range of Mormon womanhood. Kathleen Flake illustrates some of the challenges of being a "sister" missionary—how their particular needs are often ignored—and outlines ten basic suggestions that could transform the mission experience for men and women, some of which the church has since implemented. The satirical piece "Patti Perfect," by Margaret B. Black and Midge W. Nielsen, presents the mythical Mormon Mother who has and does it all, leaving the reader entertained but exhausted at what it takes to exemplify womanhood. The removal of the LDS Church's racial temple/priesthood ban in 1978 prompted much reaction in the *Exponent II* community. At a time when many church members focused on the impact of Black men now receiving the priesthood, Chris Rigby Arrington considers the implications for and reactions of Black women.

In "Line Upon Line," Susan Arrington Hill beautifully illustrates what *Exponent II* does so well, taking simple snapshots of life and revealing depth and complexity in the ordinary: getting children ready to play in the snow, packing an overnight bag for the hospital, late night nursing. The Frugal Housewife column provided practical tips for running a home and raising a family. Yet,

---

1. Claudia Bushman, "*Exponent II* is Born," *Exponent II* 1, no. 1 (July 1974), and "*Exponent II*: Why?" *Exponent II* 1, no. 2 (October 1974). More on Bushman's tenure as editor in Chapter 2.

2. More on Nancy Dredge's first tenure as editor in Chapter 3. More on Susan Howe's tenure as editor in Chapter 4.

despite its Betty Crocker-veneer, submissions like the one by Helen Candland Stark (who later funded an annual essay contest) often took on a satirical tone. In this instance, Stark warns of the dangers of frugality gone too far, of canning things that ought not to be canned, and the road to hell being paved with store-bought food. She openly wonders if she can ever measure up to the overabundant expectations of a third-generation pioneer woman. Can one both extoll and question the virtue of seventeen jars of cantaloupe butter? You bet.

As a women's periodical, the paper strived to be a safe place to share intimate reflections about the body's intersection with identity. We see this most prominently in its poetry. Margaret Munk's poem "Mother's Day" explores the hope and fear inherent in trying to conceive and conveys the pain when biology won't cooperate. In "Coming Apart Together," Mary Bradford describes her ongoing passion for her spouse despite the physical tolls of aging. In Vernice Wineera Pere's poem "Heritage," the speaker describes using sharp natural objects to tattoo themself so that their body reflects their Māori cultural legacy.

The paper's poetry further explores varied facets of relationships. Linda Sillitoe tries to rock a fussy newborn to sleep in "Lullaby in the New Year." In "Scouting," RevaBeth Russell offers a short but powerful observation about gender bias and labor imbalance in families. In Susan Howe's poem "Wind," a traveler describes the drought-desiccated Wyoming desert—their road trip partner's nonchalant response intimating the erosion of their relationship. Playing on the idea of "earth as mother," Kristine Barrett looks to evidence of the feminine divine in her poem "To Mother."

As discussed in Chapter 3, when the paper started, the church had yet to take an official stance on the Equal Rights Amendment (ERA). Two years later, in 1976, the First Presidency issued a formal statement against ratification, warning that the ERA would "stifle God-given feminine instincts."[3] The church began directing its members to engage in covert anti-ERA lobbying efforts. This was most dramatically seen at Utah's 1977 International Women's Year (IWY) conference, part of the series of state conferences leading up to the national IWY conference intended to promote the need for legislation on equality. Nearly 14,000 Utah women, most sent by their local LDS leaders, showed up to vote down any and all proposals.[4] *Exponent II* published many responses to the events. We include excerpts from two selections here. In the first, "Mormon Denial," Rebecca Cornwall outlines the frustration she felt when an overwhelming group of Mormon women denied the need for any

---

3. D. Michael Quinn, *The Mormon Hierarchy: Extension of Power* (Salt Lake City: Signature Book, 1997), 376–77.

4. Martha Sonntag Bradley, *Pedestals & Podiums: Utah Women, Religious Authority, and Equal Rights* (Salt Lake City: Signature Books, 2005), 175–76.

change regarding the treatment of women. In the second, "From Vanguard to Rearguard," W. & M. Woodworth lament the shift in Mormon women from early advocates for women's rights and suffrage to aligning themselves with "Klansmen, Birchers, and the American Nazi party."

Though produced in Boston—a hub of the Mormon diaspora—*Exponent II* was a national platform that connected dispersed pockets of Mormon feminists and intellectuals. Women writers and historians in Salt Lake City, some of whom had attended school in Boston, were frequent contributors to the paper and speakers at events like the Exponent Day Dinners held to celebrate the original *Woman's Exponent*.[5] In "One Woman's Perspective: Eliza R. Snow," historian Jill Mulvay Derr explores Mormon women's fluctuations of institutional power, generally lost in times of transition, including recent actions from the church's correlation movement that eroded some of the Relief Society's power. Lavina Fielding Anderson spoke at the final Exponent Day Dinner, held in 1982. In her talk entitled, "On Being Happy: An Exercise in Spiritual Autobiography," Anderson posits that there is spiritual power awaiting the women who will claim it: "Our birthright is joy not weariness, courage not caution, and faith not fear. By covenant and consecration, may we claim it." In the ensuing years, Exponent adopted Anderson's focus on "spiritual autobiography" at their annual retreat, encouraging participants to grapple with their dual and sometimes dueling identities by examining their lives, their relationship with the divine, and how they have claimed their power.[6]

The beloved "East/West" column featured Laurel Thatcher Ulrich (East) and Emma Lou Thayne (West), each writing about her life from their respective locations. In "Ode to Autumn," we see Ulrich wrestling with unstructured summer vacations and how to get kids—and herself—to buckle down. In Thayne's essay, "Milk and Honey Motherhood," she shares that, despite the passage of time, many aspects of mothering never change. She suggests that perhaps "it's the ongoingness of it that continues to be so compelling." Ulrich and Thayne later published a collection of their essays, mainly from this column, in the book *All God's Critters Got a Place in the Choir*.[7]

The paper's longest-running column was Sisters Speak, conceived and managed by Judy Dushku for approximately three decades. Dushku would pose a question in one issue and publish readers' responses in the next. As a political science professor and activist, Dushku was never afraid to ask hard questions while allowing women to share their truths in a judgment-free

---

5. More about the Exponent Day Dinners on pages xi, 7–8, and 36.
6. More on the 1982 Nauvoo Pilgrimage and the development of the first Exponent II national retreat on pages 34–36.
7. Ulrich and Thayne, *All God's Critters Got a Place in the Choir* (Salt Lake City: Aspen Books, 1995).

zone. In this sample, we include opinions from Lorie Winder (Stromberg) on community involvement, Heather Cannon on depression, and Cindy Barlow on her response to Sonia Johnson's excommunication.

The first annual national retreat, held in the fall of 1983, was called a "reunion" as part of *Exponent II*'s tenth-anniversary celebrations. It was a time for reflection. In "The Founding Foremothers," readers sit in on a retreat workshop conversation between several of the paper's founders: Laurel Thatcher Ulrich, Mimmu Haritala-Sloan, Judy Dushku, Susan Kohler, Bonnie Horne, and Carrel Sheldon. Like any event witnessed by multiple people, *Exponent II*'s origins already had slightly different versions. From the success of the guidebook *A Beginners Boston*, to consciousness-raising meetings, to Susan Kohler's discovery of the *Woman's Exponent* at Harvard's Widener library, to starting a paper, these reminiscences reflect the founder's communal spirit and the brilliant determination of a group of (semi) well-behaved women who made history.

*Unless otherwise indicated, editorial insertions and footnotes are the editors and are not original to the publication.*

## Exponent II: Why?
Claudia L. Bushman
October 1974 (vol. 1, no. 2)

We have been asked what we are doing publishing a newspaper for Mormon Women. What purpose is served? What do we hope to accomplish? Of course, there are many reasons for the paper, not the least of which is it gives us something to think about while doing the dishes. However, for this issue we will isolate three major purposes:

1. To give our sisters a little status.

No one thinks of Mormon women today as exploited slaves but few people realize what extraordinary people they are. Is there another group that can touch them for service to others, efficiency, devotion, imagination, intelligence, education, beauty? Yet modest and supportive by long training, they limit their aspirations. Experienced teachers, speakers, and executives, our women could rise like the cream in community organizations, yet they often hide their talents under bushels. *Exponent II* wants to shed light on the achievements of the sisters. Our readers are urged to share the triumphs of others, if not their own, as inspiration to all.

2. To disseminate useful information.

We encourage our sisters to submit articles on subjects relating to or of particular interest to Mormon women. Two to six typewritten pages, double spaced, will do very well. Share your special expertise, or those long thoughts that finally solved your problem. Seeing your name in print is good for the soul.

3. To keep in touch.

*Exponent II* aims to be entertaining and friendly, like a long letter from a dear friend. That some people need this friend is evident from the letters we receive. Let us hear from you.

## In the Mission but Not of the Mission (excerpts)
Kathleen Flake
September 1976 (vol. 3, no. 1)

One of the social changes of the last five years has been women's increasing awareness of their need to talk to each other about their feelings, experiences, and ideas, as well as about their canning, cooking, and children. I hope this change means we will also see more women willing to talk about the why-fors and the how-tos of missions. Again, let me stress this point: while the central aspects of mission activity are directed by revelation, obviously much in the mission environment is determined by its social structure. This male-directed, largely male-oriented structure can present real problems for women trying to operate within it. This distinction between the spiritual and the social dynamics of missionary work having been made, I would like now to turn to some of the weaknesses of the social structure, as far as women are concerned, and to suggest possible solutions....

The typical missionary conference is a good example of how the mission social structure fails the woman missionary. Conferences are designed to make the missionaries more effective through receiving instruction and encouragement from mission leaders and to strengthen their conviction of the truthfulness of the gospel and of the importance of missionary work by bearing testimony to each other. Imagine yourself arriving at conference with your companion and taking your place with the other sisters in a specially designated section of the chapel. You know there is a reason for this segregated seating arrangement, though no one has ever really explained it to you. You then open your hymnbook to sing "Come All Ye Sons of God" and the program begins.

The program is always an inspiring one: The president and the young men who assist him in the mission home and the young men who conduct the music and the young men who are chosen to represent their zones and districts assure you that it is through the priesthood you hold that you are able to experience success in the Lord's work and your future success depends on your magnifying this gift.

It is a nice break to hear the president's wife speak. She takes five minutes to encourage you not to think about your girl back home and to cook nutritious meals. Finally, the time comes for testimonies. You rise to your feet and try to relate what the mission experience means to you, careful to omit any remarks which may cause you to be misunderstood as sentimental or less than professional. Sometimes you even find yourself manipulating your vocabulary to imitate theirs: talking about "winning," "team effort," "keeping your eye on the ball," "keeping your guard up," "not dropping the ball," and on and on. Before sitting down, you make sure they understand that you owe your success to the elders in your district; without them, you couldn't do a thing. And then it is time for the conference to close with a rousing chorus of "Ye Elders of Israel."

Although there are countless other, more subtle ways of communicating it, the message is essentially the same: "You are guests; you are different, not one of us." Similarly, you may occasionally receive an acknowledgment not unlike an apology: "We know you're here, but we don't exactly know what to do with you." There is kindness; there is courtesy; there is even chivalry. But there is rarely comradery, and almost never the respect accorded true equals.

The problem is complicated by the fact that the sisters themselves are not always consciously aware of the dynamics of their relationship to the mission, its people and system. However, this does not mean that they do not, at some level of awareness, feel and respond to the message the system gives them.

I am convinced that much of the depression and physical illness experienced by women during their missions is a consequence of these dynamics. If we accept the clinical view that depression is caused by repressed anger, then there can be few situations more catalytic to depression than the mission field. Here a woman, who believes she is able to do the work and also has the conviction that she has responded to a call from God to serve in the mission field, is constantly being told (indirectly) that she is, by virtue of her sex, not as capable or as committed as the young men she is serving with. This message, coupled with an atmosphere which prohibits expression of her sense of injustice, would naturally cause the anger to be repressed. Depression, of one degree or another, is not a surprising consequence.

Could this depression be the cause of the frequency of sickness among women on missions, making the real rigors of the mission field for women the emotional, not the physical, demands? Could emotionally-induced illness be the reality behind the stereotype of the hypochondriacal sister missionary? I believe these questions deserve serious study....

Please make no mistake: What I have been talking about is the social order of the mission field, not the spiritual. It is the spiritual rewards of the mission field which enable a woman to pay such a high price to serve, and it is her spiritual contribution to the work which makes her truly an integral and necessary part of the mission....

A mission is a suitable goal for all worthy members of the Church. It is a demanding and rewarding experience. It is my hope that the rigors of the mission will be only the necessary ones. Let us not add unnecessary burdens to an already overwhelming commission that "ye that embark in the service of God, see that ye serve him with all your heart, might, mind, and strength" (D&C 4:2). Let us not sap the strength of those worthy women who desire to honor this commission. To that end, I offer the following suggestions as a place to start:

1. Treat the gospel training of young women (ages 12–18) with the same seriousness given to teaching the Aaronic Priesthood.

2. Be slow to accept most generalizations and stereotypes about sister missionaries.

3. Do not tell jokes or stories which degrade the calling of a woman missionary or the woman herself.

4. Evaluate missionary materials—rule books, manuals, cultural training packets—for sexist language and attitudes.

5. Avoid segregating missionaries by sex whenever appropriately possible.

6. Emphasize to both men and women that the gifts of the spirit are available to all righteous members of the Church.

7. Allow women to function in all leadership positions possible.

8. Invite sisters to participate in teaching and preaching whenever possible.

9. Take care that mission parents function as a team, the wife being a dynamic, spiritual role model for the sisters. Encourage her to exercise her spiritual gifts on their behalf and to give doctrinal addresses to assembled missionaries when appropriate.

10. Encourage further dialogue between returned missionary sisters to discover affirmative ways of restructuring the social climate of missions so as to take full advantage of what women have to contribute.

This article is by no means definitive. Hopefully, it will encourage others to contribute their experience and insight to the growing dialogue among women in the Church.

## "Line Upon Line" (excerpts)
Susan Arrington Hill
St. Cloud, Minnesota
Winter 1978 (vol. 4, no. 2)

*August 24*: Today was the first day of school in our neighborhood. My preschoolers were still pajamaed while all the neighborhood schoolers popped out of their houses with crispy new clothes and undented lunch pails. Everybody looked washed and fresh and eager. As I washed the breakfast dishes, I watched the yellow bus roll off to a new year, and I had a lump inside me. It wasn't in a particular place like my heart or my throat, but it was a general lump of "left out-ness."

Why am I not at school too? Oh … that's right, I'm a mother of two and one fourth and I'm no longer a school music teacher. I'm an at-home teacher with unwritten lesson plans. I love the September excitement of new pencils and new students, but this seems to be a larger curriculum. Currently I suppose I am riding the "life" bus; I'd better pack a big lunch. It's a forever journey. The bus doesn't stop.

*September 30*: Happy birthday to me! I'm twenty-nine; it must be a mistake—the real me is only twenty-two.

And a mother? Horrors … no, wonder of wonders. Remember me? I'm the one who never longed to babysit … who never rushed up in church and begged, "Please let me hold your baby." Let them hold their own. And now I do. I love Erica and Mandy—they must be mine, even though they look just like Frank. Am I really their mother? Maybe it's just someone in my name and clothing.

*October 12: I suddenly realized the magnitude of parenthood, Lord.* If I am patient and helpful when they are good, that is commendable. But if I turn into a tiger when they are disobedient and I am exhausted, all the good is negated. It frightens me. *Please … I can't do this alone.*

*October 19*: After a rousing morning of puzzles and Fisher-Price people and PlayDoh on my shag rug, I am impressed again by my discovery that my ambivalent feelings toward motherhood are shared by many others. By this ambivalence, I mean we know we should be doing what we are doing, but we don't always like it. Marge and Dawn both—separately—shared similar feelings with me. I don't feel imprisoned often—just on those days I am unable to have even thirty minutes alone. Actually, I feel demeaned when I meet other mothers at the playground and we chat around the sandbox. I don't want to feel demeaned, but I do. That's my ambivalence. I feel like a nanny and a non-contributor to my society. My light is under a giant bushel. I don't want it to go out before our home no longer stocks diapers. We must each solve this with our husbands individually, I guess.

*November 2*: I am enjoying my new home study course in literature. It's hard to sandwich chunks of study time between naps and dinner, but I somehow hunger for this small achievement. I spent my own "giving-music-lessons" dollars for this course and I feel independent financially. Naps are a bore, but my new cargo demands it. Also, 9:30 bedtime. Yuk!

*November 5*: It's good to stay home out of the rain and know the applesauce is canned for winter, Lord. My joys are prevalent here, but will You also help me determine my personal equation for fulfillment? I know You expect more of me than babysitting or Tupperware parties. I want to study, to ponder, to create... as well as complete my genealogy and keep the house clean. Help me—guide me.

*November 14*: I'm supposed to teach them to work, Lord, but I can't even get them to set the table. I'm sure you never shouted or threatened. How much can I raise my voice? How early can I expect results? I'm not always sure that free agency is the way I would choose. I love them always, Lord, but the liking is tedious sometimes. I am responsible for their faith, too. Lord, guide me in verbally sharing my testimony.

*November 17*: No, I don't need a date with Frank. Just a time to talk with him. We don't talk at movies; I hunger for talk with my dear husband—current events, his studies, his projects. Our daily phone call is now set up for that and sometimes evening reading time. It makes me real. I hope we can be intellectually together more when he is out of school.

*November 23*: The snow is imminent. The kids are inside all day long—summer, where are you? I am busy with our book discussion group and a sextet for the Christmas program. Added on is, of course, presidency of our youth group and choir organist—oh, and organist for Sunday School. Sometimes my franticness is ridiculous, but some power in me says, "Life, don't pass me by!" Why can't I relax and enjoy and be slower?

*December 15*: Lord, motherhood is stone grinding me. I'm not the rough diamond but rather a small brown kernel of wheat. I am forced to share as I'm ground finer by dailiness. Shall I ever be smooth and fine enough?

*January 15*: We are snowed in. Boots, snowsuits, mittens—in and out. It is hard to bend with my watermelon tummy. The days are an Olympic competition. Who can get up the earliest? To date, I'm the winner, but I must rise at 5:45 to accomplish this feat. I feel compelled to journalize then, and besides, my scriptures are meaningful to me only at dawn. They become incomprehensible in the jumble of later.

*February 15*: I made a huge batch of bread which leavened us all. The kids have their own little pans and they love to spank the bread. I am like bread, I think. Punched and kneaded. Will I be smooth and shiny and rise to succulence, or will I crumble and be dry? Love will be the oil. I want to be love.

*February 27*: My suitcase isn't packed for the hospital yet, but I know the end is near as insomnia sets in. I feel like a Sherman tank, although Frank says I'm beautiful. It takes a crane to get me out of the recliner chair. My skin is shiny tight on my tummy, and we watch my clothes jump during church.

*March 16: Who am I, Lord? Who am I supposed to be? Am I far afield from the blueprint you had for me, or am I near target?*

*March 20*: I'm at the hospital. We met our newest daughter. It was time: I had the windows washed and the house ready for Grandma, and I could no longer turn over in bed. Our littlest angel arrived in 45 minutes—from start to finish. Good thing we live close to the hospital. Frank was there this time, and the Dr. said I was very brave. No yelling anyway. Lots of deep breathing. I feel good. Frank says the girls keep asking where baby Gary is. Still in heaven, I guess—but they'll love Cristi. She looks like they did, with a turned up nose and no hair.

*March 25*: Night nursing is noxious to a day-lighter like me. No danger of insomnia now. I'm willing to wake up but can't seem to break through consciousness. I can't determine which end of the baby goes which way except for the sogginess. However, I'm sure this is better than heating bottles.

*April 2*: Grandma's gone but spring is here. Our schedule creakily adjusts. I suddenly realize I'm not as mobile as before three little ones. Our triple trio still makes it to the library and the store, just not as often.

*April 30*: School is out for the year. The kids are back with old clothes and dented lunch buckets. No more bus to watch as I wash the dishes. My school goes on. I like summer term. We will blossom outside with trikes and training wheels and our stroller.

*May 2: May I have patience in battle, Lord, and remember to capitalize on the daily portion of my joy. It is right for me ... for now ... this life. I gain line upon line, but I am progressing toward my potential. Thank thee.*

*The following two selections come from reader responses to the church-directed anti-Equal Rights Amendment activity at Utah's International Women's Year convention in 1977.*

## Mormon Denial (excerpts)
Rebecca Cornwall
Salt Lake City, Utah
Fall 1977 (vol. 4, no. 1)

I believe denial is a pattern among Mormons, especially Mormon women, individually, but also as a group. We do not want to admit that historically we've been denied opportunities and considered weaker, less able than men, not really adults, and that this is just as true in Mormon history as in American society, although in early Mormonism there were more active opposing vectors than in society at large. Mormon women as a body deny this. They concoct elaborate rationales to avoid it—fascinating womanhood, subordinate but equal, queens in our homes, men-are-more-carnal, the hand that rocks the cradle rules—and they become very defensive with people who bring up the subject.

National women's groups keep bringing up the subject. And the IWY meetings brought it up. On Mormon territory. So Mormon women did in mass what they've been doing individually in wards throughout the Church. It is to their credit that they did it only when prodded.

What surprised me about the Utah IWY meeting was the intensity of the hostility. For Mormons really are a peaceable, mild people. But at this meeting, outside of an outward general decorum, there was no mercy shown, even though Mormons were by far the majority and were assured every decision. Had it not been for the almost unbelievable restraint of the IWY organizers, feelings would have run much higher. When toward the end of the Saturday afternoon sessions somebody received an ovation for moving that funds be vetoed for all future IWY activities in Utah, I lost my equanimity and went home crying. They wanted the last ounce of vengeance.

But vengeance for what?

I am not of the school that wants to accentuate the positive and shuffle the unpleasant under the rug. Although very good things can come out of traumatic experience, it was a frightening event which elicited strong feelings in nearly everybody concerned. Talking about feelings is very important, or they go underground. Probably the vengeance Mormon women wreaked on the IWY people was the accumulated festerings of many, many feelings they cannot vent or even admit because the feelings touch on untouchables: working, birth control, patriarchal authority, polygamy, evolution of the Relief Society from a publicly significant force to a women's auxiliary, and a number of private, personal conflicts. Such things cannot be discussed honestly in a Church setting and often not at home except in small measure....

I fully believe that when Mormons are more concerned with the actual condition of women and girls, than with theories, chains of command, and justifying ourselves, that answers will begin to come about the problem of women in our culture. Presently the overwhelming trend is to deny that a problem exists.

## From Vanguard to Rearguard (excerpts)
M. and W. Woodworth
Provo, Utah
Winter 1978 (vol. 4, no. 2)

Not since the suffrage struggle at the turn of the century has there been such a deep-cut polarization among Utah women. It occurs to us that what is unique about Mormon women then as opposed to now is a difference in the way the women's movement itself is perceived. The attitude of early Mormon spokeswomen toward the feminist movement was essentially positive. They viewed it as part of the great political and economic revolution of the world as it moved toward a more just society in which all people would enjoy a sense of dignity....

So intense was this positive feeling that Eliza R. Snow called Bathsheba Smith and other sisters on political missions to travel throughout the territory preaching women's rights. She and others, such as Emmeline B. Wells, met and/or wrote frequently to other feminists of the day to consult on problems and devise strategies for overcoming the resistance to change. Feminists, such as Susan B. Anthony, like today's feminists, were denounced by many as crude, masculine females who had somehow lost their femininity in their fanatic cause of women's rights. Yet Mormon sisters respected and agreed with them.

Leading Utah women today differ from their forebearers with respect to how they see the feminist movement. Rather than see it in its 200-year historical context, the contemporary view often dates back only to Betty Friedan's *The Feminine Mystique*. Their tone describes feminism as something sinister, evil, and of the devil. Indeed, as a Church we witness strange new bedfellows. Who would have predicted the day would come when leading sisters of the Church would attend political rallies alongside such company as Klansmen, Birchers, and the American Nazi party? George Q. Cannon argued, "There are no people who need and who can find use for education to the extent the Latter-day Saints can." In contrast to this aspect of our heritage, the proud position of one LDS woman who rose in the Salt Palace was revealing of not only herself but many Utah sisters: "We are not educated. We don't want to be educated. And you can't make us be educated!" Her brilliant declaration was rewarded with a standing ovation.

In outlining what seems to be a 180-degree turnabout with rather dramatic and traumatic consequences for Utah women, one may question the need to get all these events and contradictions out in the open. Why resurface wounds already months old? Our intent is not so much to blame, but to question and seek better resolutions....

For instance, we question whether the Utah IWY really speaks for the majority of Utah women in spite of the thousands who attended the Salt Palace. It was largely a middle class affair. Most working women could not be there to represent the realities they experience. Those with either political positions or status within the Church or community have assumed that they speak for "Utah women" or "Mormon women" universally, while in fact only a small portion of Church members ever give feedback to their leaders. It is our contention that much of this feedback is extremist, communicated by people with very strong feelings. Moderates, by definition, are more inclined to live and let live, and have less need to voice their positions. Thus their influence is less in impacting the politics of change. What may be needed in the Church is a broadening of participation so that the one side will be more clearly perceived for what it is—unbalanced fanaticism. Unless alternative views are also articulated and seen as legitimate, the extremist stance becomes embedded in the popular mythology known as "the Church position."

Ultimately we would hope for an increased appreciation for the diversity in the Kingdom and for the value of uniqueness and individuality which result in stronger unity, but not necessarily uniformity. How we handle differences is one of the great challenges facing the Church between now and the end of the century as it grows in size and cultural differentiation.

**Mother's Day**
Margaret Munk
Silver Spring, Maryland
Summer 1978 (vol. 4, no. 4)

I am afraid
To plant this seed.

The sun is warm,
The earth is rich and ready,
But the days go by,
And still no planting.
Why?

The springtime of my life
Is passing, too,
And ten years' plantings
In a willing soil
Have borne no living fruit.
So many times I've waited,
Hoped,
Believed.
That God and nature
Would perform
A miracle
Incredible but common.

Nothing grew.
And often times I feel
The mystery of life and growth

Is known to all but me,
Or that reality
Is not as it appears to be.

I have a choice:
To put aside this seed,
Leaving the planting
To the proven growers,
Pretending not to care
For gardening,
And knowing,
If I do not try,
I cannot fail.

Or plant,
And risk again
The well-known pain
Of watching
For the first brave green
And seeing only
Barren ground.

He also spoke
About a seed,
The mustard's tiny grain,
Almost too small to see,
But, oh—the possibilities!
Those who doubt,
Who fear,
Are not inclined to cultivate it;
But it was to them He spoke.

And God remembered Sarah …
Rachel …
Hannah …
Elizabeth …

The seed is in my hand,
The trowel in the other;
I am going to the garden,
And the Gardener,
Once more.

## Blacks, Priesthood and Sisterhood
Chris Rigby Arrington
New York, New York
Fall 1978 (vol. 5, no. 1)

"I think that we are getting close to the end of time, because I think that we, perhaps, have reached a state of brotherhood." —Ruffin Bridgeforth

Along with the brotherhood, a new sisterhood has begun to grow in the wake of the revelation opening the priesthood to worthy black men. While the priesthood restriction fell directly on black men, it affected the lives of black women as well. Now those women can be sealed to their husbands and families in the temple, can see their sons ordained to the priesthood, can share even more deeply in the sisterhood of Mormon women.

A white woman in Tooele, Utah, cried with joy when she heard of the revelation—even though she had never met a black person in her life. A white woman called a black member of the Tabernacle Choir, Marilyn Y. Smith, to tell her the news, and Marilyn said, "After she told me, we both had a good cry." Michigan teenagers Valerie Hermann and Stephanie Burton, one white and one black, were taken together into their Mormon boss's office to learn the news; back home after a year as BYU roommates, they hugged each other and cried.

For these women, learning about the revelation was an experience of joy and deepening love. It was a second beginning.

The first beginning for black women in the church came shortly after the restoration of the gospel. Among the early black sisters was Jane Elizabeth Manning James, who traveled to Nauvoo, Illinois, during the time the saints were headquartered there.

"We walked until our shoes were worn out," she wrote, "and our feet became sore and cracked open and bled until you could see the whole print of our feet with blood on the ground. We stopped and united in prayer to the Lord; we asked God the Eternal Father to heal our feet, and our prayers were answered and our feet were healed forthwith."

In Nauvoo, Jane and the other members of her party lived with the Prophet Joseph Smith in his home until he was martyred. Then Jane stayed at the home of Brigham Young, later crossing the plains and remaining active in the church for the rest of her life.

A latter-day descendant of those early pioneers, seventy-six-year-old Lucille Bankhead, is proud that her grandfather was a member of the Mormon Battalion. "I was born in the church," she said emphatically. "I have been active all of my life. I went to the primary, Beehive girls, and I sang in the choir."

Today she is Relief Society president for a group of black Mormons called Genesis that meets in Salt Lake.

"It's not easy to suddenly get something you've been denied all these years," she said. "A lot of our people will have to learn to crawl before they can walk, to live worthy of the blessings."

Sister Bankhead has expressed again and again her joy for the young black members of the church. "I know how the young boys who will become deacons feel," she said. "I have a grandson who last Sunday was to go in with the deacon's quorum. I know the heartbreak of not being able to."

Nineteen-year-old Stephanie Bulger is a member of the church because of her mother, Dollie. "When the missionaries came, my mother was living in an apartment with me and my brother, and my father had just had his leg amputated in Vietnam and was in the hospital."

Dollie listened to the missionaries' message and "just loved it. It was a process she could believe in," according to her daughter. The whole family joined the Church, Dollie first, and they have been stalwarts in the Detroit First Ward for many years.

Stephanie is now in her second year at BYU, majoring in foreign affairs and studying French. She wants to graduate and work for the government in Washington, D.C. She plays the piano well and is a very mature, poised young woman.

Her first year at BYU was not easy, and she turned for counsel to Alan Cherry, author and former member of the BYU Young Ambassadors, and to Judy Dunsson, a Centerville social worker. Judy, a black woman, had gone to BYU and knew what Stephanie was experiencing. Stephanie said she found strength in twice-yearly gatherings of black Mormons at Judy's house. Always held at conference time, the meetings were forums for religious and intellectual discussions.

While Stephanie had dated in high school, she was not asked out at BYU. She was constantly stared at, and people she didn't know would say hello. These things bothered her the first year, but this year she says they don't. She has turned her attention more seriously to her career goals.

When Tabernacle Choir member Marilyn Smith heard of the revelation, she said, "My first thought was for my child [Robb McNiel Smith, 21 months old]. When he is twelve years old, he can hold the priesthood and be ordained a deacon. Now he won't have to live through the ridicule and downgrading that others of us have."

Marilyn did not have an easy time deciding to marry her returned-missionary husband Robert Smith, whom she met in the Tabernacle Choir. She was worried about the position of the church and the future of their children.

"I called Elder Howard W. Hunter of the Quorum of the Twelve," she said. "He told me that not only would the church give permission, but that it would also give its blessing. Bob and I were married August 2, 1972, by my bishop, David S. Hatch."

The day of the revelation, Marilyn found herself "deluged by affection" and flooded with calls from friends and well-wishers.

To Clydia M. Kelley, a black woman who joined the church in 1962, the revelation is a blessing for her and her ancestors. She had done more than 200 baptisms in the Washington Temple for her family members who have died.

Sister Kelley traveled from her home in Jacksonville, Florida, to see the Washington Temple before it was dedicated. "I saw the bride's room and fell in love with it," she said. "My niece was with me and said how wonderful it would be to be married in the temple. I explained that only worthy priesthood holders and their brides could be married there."

"I always felt that the barrier would someday be lifted," she said, "and that my people would have the full benefits of the temple ordinances."

Mrs. Shirley Frazier and her five children were baptized in Phoenix, Arizona, about four years ago. "There are a lot of blacks in Phoenix, but not a lot of black Mormons," she said. "We always had the 'Uncle Tom' stigma. We only felt secure when we were with members."

Shirley had faith that a revelation would come, but she never thought she'd see it in her life. She said she has long yearned for a temple marriage. Her husband, John, a white man, "will be able to give the boys the priesthood soon," she said. "He's been so good with helping us be familiar with the priesthood."

Of the church's 4.2 million members, fewer than 1,000 are black, according to *Time* magazine. *Newsweek* said estimates range from 1,000 to 5,000 (there is no way of knowing for sure since church records don't indicate race).

Their numbers are small, but the testimonies of these women are firm, strengthened by their own resolve to eliminate hidden discrimination, and by sincere love from other church members. As a renewed sisterhood grows up around these black women, it will help bind all Mormon sisters together.

## Patti Perfect
Margaret B. Black and Midge W. Nielsen
Orem, Utah
Spring 1979 (vol. 5, no. 3)

*Many LDS women unconsciously compete with an idealized image of the already-perfect wife and mother who successfully incorporates all the demands of family, church, and society into her life. Although we have never met such a woman, we persist in believing she's out there somewhere. We can just imagine what she must accomplish in a day...*[8]

Patti gets up very early and says her personal prayers. She zips her slim, vigorous body into her warmup suit and tiptoes outside to run her usual five miles (on Saturday she does ten). Returning home all aglow, she showers and dresses for the day in a tailored skirt and freshly starched and ironed blouse. She settles down for quiet meditation and scripture reading, before preparing the family breakfast. The morning's menu calls for whole wheat pancakes, homemade syrup, freshly squeezed orange juice, and powdered milk (the whole family loves it).

With classical music wafting through the air, Patti awakens her husband and ten children. She spends a quiet moment with each and helps them plan a happy day. The children quickly dress in clothes that were laid out the night before. They cheerfully make their beds, clean their rooms, and do the individual chores assigned to them on the Family Work Wheel Chart. They assemble for breakfast the minute mother calls.

After family prayer and scripture study, the children all practice their different musical instruments, Father leaves for work on a happy note. All too soon it is time for the children to leave for school. Having brushed (and flossed) their teeth, the children pick up coats, book bags, and lunches which were prepared the night before and arrive at school five minutes early.

With things more quiet, Patti has storytime with her pre-schoolers and teaches them a cognitive reading skill. She feeds, bathes, and rocks the baby before putting him down for his morning nap. With baby sleeping peacefully and the three-year-old twins absorbed in creative play, Patti tackles the laundry and housework. In less than an hour, everything is in order. Thanks to wise scheduling and children who are trained to work, her house never really gets dirty.

Proceeding to the kitchen, Patti sets out tonight's dinner: frozen veal parmigiana that she made in quantity from her home-grown tomatoes and peppers. She then mixes and kneads twelve loaves of bread. While the bread rises, Patti dips a batch of candles to supplement her food storage. As the bread bakes, she writes in her personal journal and dashes off a few quick letters: one to her Congressman and a couple of genealogy inquiries to distant cousins. Patti then prepares her mini-class lesson on organic gardening. She also inserts two pictures and a certificate in little Paul's scrapbook, noting with satisfaction that all family albums are attractive and up-to-date. Checking the mail, Patti sees that their income tax refund has arrived—a result of

---

8. This editorial note is part of the original publication.

having filed in January. It is earmarked for mission and college savings accounts. Although Patti's hardworking husband earns only a modest salary, her careful budgeting has kept the family debt-free.

After lunch, Patti drops the children off at Grandma's for their weekly visit. Grandma enjoys babysitting and appreciates the warm loaf of bread. Making an extra call, Patti takes a second loaf to one of the sisters she is assigned to visit teach. A third loaf goes to the non-member neighbor on the corner.

Patti arrives at the elementary school where she directs a special education program. A clinical psychologist, Patti finds this an excellent way to stay abreast of her field while raising her family. Before picking up her little ones, Patti finishes collecting for the charity fund drive.

Home again, Patti settles the children down for their afternoon naps. She spends some quiet time catching up on her reading and filing. As she mists her luxuriant house plants, the school children come through the door. Patti listens attentively to each one as they tell her about their day. The children start right in on their homework, with mother supervising and encouraging them. When all schoolwork is done, Patti and the children enjoy working on one of their projects. Today they work on the quilt stretched on frames in a corner of the family room.

Dinnertime and father arrive, and it is a special hour for the whole family. They enjoy Patti's well-balanced, tasty meal, along with stimulating conversation. After dinner, father and the children pitch in to clean up so that mom can relax. She enjoys listening to the sounds of laughter and affection that come from the kitchen.

With the teenaged children in charge at home, mother and father attend an evening session at the Temple. During the return trip, they sit close together as in courting days. "Well dear," says Paul Perfect, "did you have a good day?" Pat reflectively answers, "Yes, I really did. But I feel I need more challenge in my life. I think I'll contact our Family Organization and volunteer to head up a reunion for August."

## To Mother
Kristine Barrett
Sterling Park, Virginia
Winter 1981 (vol. 7, no. 2)

The flowers you left for me
I found and pinned them to
my hair upon my wedding
day. And under a mountain

in Africa was found
the diamond you buried. Of
the gold of South America
was pressed the band I wear.

I think of you often.

I walk along the beach
and do not find your footprints.
But the shards of sun
you sowed, I follow towards
the veiled horizon.

I drove once through Wyoming
and saw how you had matched
the sage and mustard flowers
pretty little violet
wilds. It was lovely.

Your letters haven't yet
been found and bound. Whenever
black seeds lie upon
white snow or flocks aflight
embroider dawn, I look
for your writing.

At pollinating time
last year, close by the honey-
suckle, I breathed the air
of your perfume and wondered
if you had come perhaps
and I had missed you.

I try to remember what you
look like. Some nights through my
reflection in our high window
I see the stars and think
I see strung diamonds plaited
in your hair. I think
if I could look into
the sun, I'd see your picture.

I want to know your name.
I know it is lovelier than Mary

or Sarah or Eve. Can you please whisper it to me? What is your name?

## One Woman's Perspective: Eliza R. Snow
Jill Mulvay Derr
Alpine, Utah
Spring 1981 (vol. 7, no. 3)

> *The following remarks were given at the University of Utah women's conference, "Mormon Women: Three Perspectives," in October 1979. The other participants were Marilyn Warenski and Sonia Johnson.*[9]

As a believing and practicing Latter-day Saint, I cannot claim to be a dispassionate student of Mormon women's history. The facts do not speak the same way to all of us, but I will share with you how they have spoken to me. In studying Mormon women I personally have rejoiced to find a great diversity of role models. I don't think of myself as typical and it's been a delight to find women in Mormon history with whom I can identify at different stages in my life: single, sometimes frustrated school teachers, twenty-nine-year-old brides, women who married divorced men, stepmothers, employed mothers and at-home mothers. I feel as a Mormon woman that I have a rich heritage of diversity and I find myself living at present among a wide diversity of women—so diverse, in fact, that I feel I can only speak for myself as one individual person and not for any group of women, although some may share my perspective.

My emphasis here is not on the individual Mormon woman but on Mormon women as a collective group. I want to take a look at them as a force within the Mormon Church and what has happened in their organizations. When we talk about women's power within the Mormon Church, we need to look at where women have been powerful: the Relief Society, the Mutual Improvement Association and the Primary. My experience is not dissimilar from others who have studied Mormon women and have found some disconcerting things in their institutional life.

The 1870s was such an exciting period for Mormon women that it is hard not to idealize it. It has captured the attention of scholars because of women's sudden visibility and their new responsibilities—both economic and political. Their participation in the institution became direct and overt rather than indirect and covert. My studies have led me to conclude that Eliza R. Snow was, in some respects, the leader of a female hierarchy that almost paralleled

---

9. This editorial note is part of the original publication.

the male hierarchy. She was tremendously influential. Ten years after her death the *Instructor* wrote that young children ought to honor "the Prophet Joseph Smith, Eliza R. Snow and the holy priesthood." I'm not sure that was taught as doctrine anywhere, but the quote suggests the tremendous influence that this woman had.

For women the 1870s was a time of great spiritual awakening. For the first time, in significant numbers and over an extended period, they operated their own organizations. They did not just meet with men in meetings; they had their own spiritual gatherings and they exercised spiritual gifts. During this period Mormon women seem, to us from our present perspective, to have been very powerful. And it is disconcerting that we don't see that power continuing to the present. In fact, it dropped off long before the present period; by about 1920 it had diminished substantially.

However, further studies show that there have been periods in the twentieth century when Mormon women have gained similar visibility and responsibility, the conditions we equate with power. The most outstanding examples in the twentieth century were women's involvement in social services, and the control they exercised over the Primary Children's Hospital and the substantial money in the wheat fund. Those who are familiar with the coming of correlation in 1970 know that at that time the *Relief Society Magazine* and the *Children's Friend* were lost; women's organizational funds were turned over to the Church; the social services and hospital that women had run so successfully were also put under priesthood, or male, leadership. Again there was a rise and fall of women's power.

As a student of Mormon women, I have seen this gain and loss of power happen twice in the space of a century (1870s to 1970s), and this has been painful for me to perceive. I have had to ask myself: Why is this happening? What has happened?

Applying some theory from organizational behavior has helped me to better understand. It is easy to say that Mormon women have never in fact had any power. That is one way of looking at it, the approach summarized with "Let's not kid ourselves. We are not talking about something that was gained and lost. Women have always obeyed the priesthood." It is true that Mormon women leaders have not gone outside the limits prescribed by the priesthood, but I think we have to be honest about how organizations work. The Church isn't different from most corporations and institutions where people who want to survive usually do not go directly against hierarchical wishes. Otherwise they may eventually find themselves outside the organization. Certainly they would forfeit possibilities of becoming part of its leadership. So we see Mormon women, through the years, "playing" essentially the same organizational "games" that most people play: that is, abiding by the rules and respecting authority in order to gain the maximum possible power. (Perhaps calling it "game playing" downgrades the process, since at its best this is the means whereby relationships of trust and reciprocity are established.)

There was not a better expert at winning the confidence of those in authority than Eliza R. Snow. She can be talked about as a puppet of the hierarchy because she didn't rebel against them, but in fact no woman before or since has had greater power. She knew the rules and was committed to abiding by them because she believed they were part of a system that would ultimately benefit everyone, including women.

Mormon women have never had the priesthood. They have never held the sort of power usually termed authority. But authority isn't the only kind of power there is within an organization. Mormon women have frequently managed to gain informal influence, the kind of power that comes from associating with and having access to people who are in positions of authority. Eliza R. Snow had that kind of power; Belle Spafford and Florence Jacobsen and many women through the years have had that kind of power. They have been able to get many things done because they had access to members of the Twelve and the First Presidency, the people in authority in the Mormon Church.

One of the problems of informal influence is that it is usually lost in times of transition. This seems, in fact, to be what happened both in the 1920s and in the 1970s to women's influence in the Church. During both these eras, systems of informal access to those in authority were replaced by formal systems. In the 1870s and 1880s Eliza R. Snow had access to church presidents Brigham Young and John Taylor, so it was very easy for her to get things done. In the period of turmoil that began in the late 1880s—the Manifesto, Utah's bid for statehood, a quick succession of Church leaders—women lost this informal influence. The networks were simply no longer there because of the ongoing transition. By 1890 and 1900 sisters in the Primary were saying, "We just cannot make our leaders understand." That is because they no longer had access to the leaders. Access was not systematically denied; it was just lost in that time of transition. A formal system was set up to replace the informal system, but formal systems emphasize superior/subordinate relationships, and women therefore lost their power, their informal influence.

A parallel thing happened with the correlation movement. Correlation was implemented in the midst of a quick succession of Church presidents. Those informal networks that had been established over a long period of time—Belle Spafford was Relief Society president for thirty years—broke down. When that kind of network is swept away, those dependent upon it inevitably lose a lot of ground. Women lost their informal access, and it was replaced by a very formal system which again emphasized the superior/subordinate relationship.

One other way women have been able to hold power in the Church parallels the role of the professional or the expert in other organizations. The grain storage program in the nineteenth century and the Relief Society Social Services in the twentieth century are good examples of women gaining power because they held expertise in given areas. Women in the Mormon Church do not have any exclusive areas of expertise now, and that is another reason why they may feel a great loss.

For me, watching women's power rise and fall institutionally has been frustrating and painful. We live in an age that values and demands equality. It is disconcerting to see any one group losing power on a regular basis. Informal influence and expertise always lose out in times of transition. Women do not hold the priesthood; therefore they do not have the long-term authority men have. I think this fact sometimes makes us feel that half of the Church, the male half, has the power and half of the Church, the female half, has no power. This is not entirely true since the Church is a hierarchy where very few people have ultimate decision-making power.

Within a hierarchy everybody is unequal; dealing with a hierarchy in an age which stresses equality is very painful. Ideally in a religious hierarchy power is arbitrary—and God is the Arbiter. Authority is not merited; it is distributed by divine decree: "a man must be called of God by prophecy." Certainly Mormon doctrine holds the promise that in spite of the hierarchy people can be valued as individuals. Ideally, we are unequal within the hierarchy of Church society but equally valued as individuals. Often, however, since it is run by humans, the Church does not function ideally—although I have been in situations where it has.

At most levels of the Mormon hierarchy—from the upper echelons down to the families—there are abuses of hierarchical privilege or power, abuses that hurt people. I have seen some of these abuses and know people who have been hurt by them. But I believe that it is possible to get people to reevaluate how the hierarchy should function and move it toward functioning more perfectly. I believe that President Kimball's addresses to women in the women's conference and to men in the general priesthood meeting were examples of a Church leader stressing equality, explaining that people can function as equals within an ordered system.

My personal conception is that, as the New Testament promises, the offices of the ecclesiastical priesthood are given to us only until "we all come in the unity of the faith, and of the knowledge of the Son of God." I look forward to the time when there will be such a unity and we, having come "unto the measure of the stature of the fulness of Christ" may no longer be given apostles, prophets, evangelists, pastors and teachers. (Ephesians 4:11–13)

Before concluding my remarks about power, I must refer to one kind I have not mentioned. It is the sort of power that students of organizations are writing about today, the sort of power that Christians have always advocated. That is personal power. Organizational behavioralists say that it is difficult, if not impossible, to change hierarchical organizations from the bottom up—at least in the short run. If one wants to remain in the organization, one must raise one's personal consciousness to an understanding of her or his relationship with the institution, and then undertake a self-directed resocialization to the organization. This has been true for me personally. Though I feel considerable pain at how the Church functions, particularly with regard to women, I know I can choose how I will relate to the organization. I choose to perceive it as both human and divine, knowing I can quibble with and sorrow at that which is human and rejoice in that which is divine. The gospel of Jesus Christ teaches me that I have the personal spiritual power—personal revelation—to distinguish the human from the divine. This personal power is not subject to the institution's fluctuations, but it can have some impact—however minute—on some corner of the institution—however far removed. In the midst of pain, that knowledge brings me a modicum of peace.

## Wind
Susan Howe
Cambridge, Massachusetts
Summer 1981 (vol. 7, no. 4)

It is a dry year.
You and I have seen it,
Traveling Wyoming desert
In the same car.

You say it doesn't matter—
A temporary drought,
No permanent damage;
One wet storm will heal the dying land.

But I tell you, you lie.

The wind is harsh and brittle
Falling through the canyon,
And the pines,
Trunks stiff like pride,
Burn copper on the mountains,
Their needles scorching in the
Relentless wind.

The land shrivels around us,
Barren and hot.
It is being destroyed.
You and I can feel it:

Riding Wyoming desert
In silence
In the same car.

**Heritage**
Vernice Wineera Pere
Hawaii
Spring 1982 (vol. 8, no. 2)

Take the sharpened pipi shell,
piece of paua, bird-bone,
razor-blade if you like.
Carve upon my face the marks
of Maoritanga. Let the blood spurt
and dribble down my chin
like the moko of the old women
wrapped in blankets round the cooking-fire.
Rub the juices in the wounds,
charcoal, vegetable dye, India Ink.
Make beautiful the design, like
the young fern curled across the moon,
or the kiwi feathers in grandfather's proud cloak.
Seek the patterns of the paua's inner shell,
the curl of kumara vine.
Trace the call of the karanga across the marae,
the nose-flute in the night.
Slice the flesh like the teko-teko's stare.
The soft flesh, lip, membrane, skin.
Cut statistics on my face:
name, age, place of birth, race,
village, tribe, canoe.
Carve deeply, erase doubt
as to who
I am.
Use the sharpened pipi shell,
bird-bone, razor-blade.

Use them harshly, lacerate
my legacy upon me
where all who can read
will perceive that I am
taking my place on this vast marae
that is the Pacific.

## On Being Happy: An Exercise in Spiritual Autobiography (excerpts)
Lavina Fielding Anderson
Salt Lake City, Utah
Summer 1982 (vol. 8, no. 4)

I think there are periods in most members' lives where they find the Church sustaining and nourishing. I think there are also times in most members' lives where Church involvement is at least as demanding and draining as it is rewarding. These cycles are natural; to weigh the down side with guilt makes it harder, in my opinion, to accept the upswings joyously and naturally.

I feel that my spiritual life is my own responsibility—that the Church, the scriptures, and the Holy Ghost offer a smorgasbord of opportunities from which I select what my spiritual diet requires right now. I find myself attracted to the ideas of personal spiritual power because now, particularly in contrast with certain other periods of Church history, the contributions of women seem circumscribed to carefully defined areas, and the very thoroughness of the organization of the Church means that there are few areas not covered by some rule, policy, or the need for someone's permission to act. Yet I feel that the Church cannot indefinitely continue to afford the sheer waste of restricting women and their talents to the spheres in which they are most commonly exercised at present.

I do not want to imply that I think the work of women in the Church is trivial or unnecessary. Quite the contrary, I do, however, want to suggest that there are some limitations built into the current roles for women in the Church that may be limiting in ways that the gospel itself is not....

I feel very strongly that the relationship between spiritual authority and institutional authority has become lopsided in recent generations—that we are given callings and then we seek for the spiritual skills and gifts we need to fulfill those callings, experiencing genuine growth but frequently losing the new talents when we are released from the calling. I believe, however, that if women were spiritually equipped to serve, opportunities would be created to match capabilities and that we could offer the Lord our strengths as well as our inadequacies. People I know who have sought and received the gift of charity do not need an assignment to exercise it, for it overflows any calling they receive. But these people are also likely to receive callings.

One of the women who has become a spiritual mentor for me has been Elmina S. Taylor, a convert who, during the first four years of her marriage, never lost faith in the promise made to her through the gift of tongues that she would have a family. She bore seven children and was later called to become the first General President of the Young Women's Mutual Improvement Association. When she died, Joseph F. Smith preached the main sermon. He had been associated with Elmina since 1880 when he had become first assistant to the general YMMIA superintendent. He was now not only its general superintendent but President of the Church as well. Announcing rather tartly that "it is not my custom to speak praise of our departed loved ones," he made an exception to his own rule and characterized Elmina as "one of the few in the world who walked by the light within her" instead of by "borrowed light.... Therefore," he said, "she had power among her associates and her sisters. She was legitimately the head of the organization over which she was called to preside. She borrowed no influence from others. She bore her own influence upon the minds of those with whom she was associated."

A great deal has been said in recent years about women and power. I suggest that we follow Elmina's example and seek the power of personal righteousness, power from on high, power in testimony, and power in the Lord Jesus Christ. I was impressed by the Lord's commandment to Oliver Cowdery when he was experimenting with translation to "trifle not with these things; do not ask for that which you ought not." This warning could be a frightening one, but the next sentence urges, "Ask that you may know the mysteries of God" (D&C 8:10–11).

The Lord promised Joseph and Oliver that they should "both have according to your desires, for ye have both joy in that which ye have desired" (D&C 7:8). It is significant to me that their joy confirmed the righteousness of their desire, that their joy was the reason the Lord granted them their desire. It reinforces my idea that the seeking of happiness is a spiritually healthy thing to do and corroborates my experience that happiness characterizes righteousness.

I feel that we may have circumscribed our limits too narrowly. Our birthright is joy not weariness, courage not caution, and faith not fear. By covenant and consecration, may we claim it.

## Coming Apart Together
Mary L. Bradford
Arlington, Virginia
Fall 1982 (vol. 9, no. 1)

We exchange in great detail the weather report
We describe our coming decay and dissolution
Your sight has considerably worsened in one eye
Your dentist is into your mouth for five hundred
Your little finger reacts unfavorably to the cold
and a close friend only four years older died.

I allow as how I'm hiding out from my gynecologist
since he removed certain valuable organs
and my neuritis is still making a grand tour
of my body. My skin, it seems,
is deteriorating, my hair congealing,
and a childhood sweetheart died only last month.

And yet, we fall upon each other
in springtime lust just as if we still had
all our teeth, hair, eyesight, and internal organs
just as if we had been created brand new this year
just as if we ourselves had invented
the weather, our bodies, and love itself.

## Scouting
RevaBeth L. Russell
Springville, Utah
Summer 1983 (vol. 9, no. 4)

"Scouting is for families."
I sat, watched and heard
Applauding through the years as
Four brothers received their awards.

I learned how to set tables
Fold party napkins
And wash dishes
Used on scouting trips.

I learned a lot about families and life through scouting.

## Ode to Autumn
Laurel Thatcher Ulrich
Durham, New Hampshire
Fall 1981 (vol. 8, no. 1)

With every fiber of my obsessive-compulsive soul, I resist summer. I resent being lifted from my well-defined path and dropped into the underbrush of June. Some college professors look forward to a summer of research and recuperation. I look forward to a season of reluctant domesticity. Summer brings to the surface my deepest conflicts. All winter I store away domestic guilts which pop out of my cupboards in June, forcing me into a role I do not like but have not yet escaped. Determined to be Earth Mother, I become a shrew.

Home with no schedule and the children underfoot, I struggle for definition. I make lists. I call family councils. I schedule dentist appointments and answer forgotten mail. Fighting the blossoming anarchy, I try without success to mobilize my offspring, who, being creatures of nature, only wish to be left alone.

June passes. Under heavy skies, I pick my way through a year's accumulation of unsorted drawers toward the decadent wilderness of July, a morass of watermelon rinds, dropped bathing suits, sweating toilets, and declining expectations. August will be more bearable, I think, because, despite the heat, I can begin my countdown to September. Slowly I begin to bend with the season. As popsicle sticks continue to accumulate on window sills, I sleep late. I read Family Circle. I forget for a day at a time to look at the calendar, though somewhere inside me a time bomb is ticking, waiting to explode.

Summer is for children or for childlike spirits who soak up sun in blissful ignorance of the week after next. I remember the day I had my hair cut really short for the first time. I must have been about to enter the sixth grade. I was standing under the maple tree in our front yard when a neighbor walked by and complimented me on my hairdo. I cautiously replied that I liked it well enough for summer but planned to let it grow out for school. "You'll have to hurry then," she said. "You've only got two weeks." I still remember how her words intruded on my paradise.

In summer, mothers and children shout at each other across an unbridgeable chasm of perception. Some days I feel like a backpacker carrying Grim Duty up the Himalayas of my children's timelessness. I see the boys sprawled on the living room floor, their knees and elbows bent at dizzying angles above the glacial moraine of their science fiction novels. Through the fog, I glimpse a summer day when I was about thirteen. My parents were away, and I spent eight hours curled in a raspberry-colored chair with a stack of chocolate-frosted cookies reading a novel which my father, in his role as superintendent of schools, later sent back to the Book of the Month Club as unfit for a high school library.

One of the curses of middle-age is becoming one's own parent. I hear myself repeating my mother's words, "The book will be better after the work is done." My children ignore me as I ignored her. And so, I slog through summer as through a long, hot pregnancy, knowing that in September I will be delivered. On the Wednesday after Labor Day, with the children back in school, I will be reborn a scholar.

## Milk and Honey Motherhood
Emma Lou Thayne
Salt Lake City, Utah
Spring 1984 (vol. 10, no. 3)

Over a decade ago our writing committee on the General Board of the M.I.A., (a not-bad name, Mutual Improvement Association!) rewrote the manuals for all six age groups—two years each of Beehive, Mia Maid, and Laurel lessons. I remember writing one for Mia Maids based on Erich Fromm's concept of mother love in *The Art of Loving*. When it came to a mother teaching a daughter about sex, he said, lucky was the daughter whose mother had a sense of self. In that case, he claimed, it wouldn't matter if the mother said babies came from the moon—everything would be all right.

That mother with a sense of self was a milk-and-honey mother. Milk is food at the table, clothes for the back, shelter for sleep and growth, but honey is the marveling at spring, a bird, a snowflake, being ready to laugh as well as cry, being a respondent to the miracles of being alive.

I loved writing that into a lesson for young girls on what to look forward to in motherhood. Thinking about it now, I love having had that as subliminal masterminding for whatever happened in subsequent years with my own five daughters and me. Goodness knows how hectic were those years of having four teenagers at once, two telephone lines: for them, for a realtor/bishop husband, and for me—being in graduate school, on the General Board, teaching part-time in the university English Department, and coaching the University of Utah women's tennis team. The phones were simply symbolic of what in the world was buzzing in and out of our home in those hectic but wildly satisfying years. Beneath, around, and above it all, I loved mothering, felt authentic in it, longed mostly for more time to indulge it.

But time was not, happily, the only index of our finding each other when we needed to. And by then it probably had a lot more to do with honey than with milk. Being what we were for each other was a matter of letting the honey flow—laughing with each other over recitals, crying over break-ups, talking ideas while stirring gravy, rehashing a night out at 2 A.M., planning on a ski lift or on the boat, complaining to each other during a work party, or cleaning up after a trip. Never out of touch—literally—much of our honey flowed between hugs and goodnight kisses and xoxoxo's on letters to and from Brighton Camp, an exchange student in Haddonfield, New Jersey, later a missionary in France, very soon, brides becoming mothers in Dallas, Portland, and L.A.

When my own mother died (the grandmother with whom they had all lived for fifteen years after we built a house with a wing on it for her), the *Ensign* asked me to write about mother/daughter relationships. What a joke. Whoever could come up with anything even close to definitive about that elusive and always challenging connection? But I tried—two days after my mother died, because I could use her as my beacon. The piece concluded with, "May my five girls grow up as I did, with love, Mother."

That was twelve years ago. They have grown up, married, three have babies of their own. But the mothering, the pouring out of milk and mixing in of honey never changes. Maybe it's the ongoingness of it that continues to be so compelling. This winter the storms that my mother prayed away as she tapped the pioneer barometer on the front wall have been raging—for one three months in bed with a precarious pregnancy, for another a struggle with novitiate teaching of English in an eighty-percent minority intermediate school, for another the healing of a child in a disfiguring accident, for another the displacement of new homes and new jobs, and for another—hardest of all—the ending of a marriage while love still lasts.

One week, fifteen of eighteen in the family were sick; my husband was rushed to the emergency room, dehydrated and maybe with hepatitis. The rest of the winter continued the same theme: swinging back and forth between sickbeds, from Salt Lake to Portland; trying to teach our Institute class with Carlisle Hunsaker on Thursday nights, "Mormon Doctrine and Philosophy for Women"; and for sanity, trying to sandwich in a national senior tennis tournament on my home courts.

Then the well ran dry. The flu took over, and I was the one in the hospital. My daughters covered for me. They canceled my ridiculous commitments, smoothed my pillow, and held my hand. In my dim and not happy days of submission, too drained to care about much, I realized what honey those girls had been for me forever—that laughing, crazy, reaching, finding, holding, yes, sometimes crying connection to what must surely lie under all that ugly black snow on the ground since November—Spring. They are my source as women even as they were when they were little girls. And now I have those sons-in-law as well "to liven like a barrage of salt / these years trembling with passing."

To say nothing of another generation buzzing with sweetness and challenge.

As I return to a world I have scarcely looked at in three weeks of post-viral exhaustion and the most I have ever known of depression, I come to this page thinking of mothers and daughters, and I know where the bounty lies. Not in easy flow, which goodness knows has sometimes been hilariously fun. But in the wrenching and floundering. The covering for each other, the knowing that whenever and whatever, the other will be there—the sisters, the daughters, the finally and forever friends who once occupied my womb, always my life, and someday will occupy whatever waits where Mother is.

In all of it, I recognize more than I ever have the ongoing power of love between generations, between a Father and Mother in Heaven and me—faltering or flourishing—least able or most deserving of milk and honey anything.

## The Good Woman Syndrome: Or, When is Enough, Enough?
Helen Candland Stark
Salem, Utah
December 1976 (vol. 3, no. 2)

When a third big kettle of beets boiled over, I stared at the bloody mess and asked myself if this were mere happenstance. Perhaps here was a Freudian slip trying to tell me something. Perhaps I had better sort out a few feelings, the one uppermost being: When is enough, enough? I also wondered if I am a solitary case or whether other women find themselves in a similar bind.

It goes back, of course, to childhood. I learned early that grandmothers differ. The culinary skill of my paternal grandmother never rose much beyond a cooked glob of flour and milk known as Mother's Mush. On the other hand, my maternal grandmother had a flair for everything from herbed dumplings to delicate Swiss pastry. Since my mother proved to be a dutiful daughter, I also strove to follow the tradition. So it was understandable that when I first read *Silas Marner*, I took note that in the Lammeter household they "never suffered a pinch of salt to be wasted, yet everybody had of the best, according to his place." Food in our home, too, was regarded thankfully, expertly, and above all, providently.

Since I was the eldest of nine children, with no sisters until after four brothers, I naturally fell into the role of Mama's little helper. In addition, Mama had a legitimate escape hatch—she liked to work in the garden. So I manned, or rather womanned, the kitchen. Third-generation girls in my day were well-indoctrinated into the virtues of waste not, want not. Potato water and a little sugar zinged the yeast start in a two-quart jar. Our "drippers" filled the oven with cheek-by-jowl loaves. There was the separator to wash, the cream to churn, the astrachan apples to strain through a jelly bag, and always, supper to serve when the men came in from the evening chores, famished and tired, and usually after dark.

Perhaps it was this last round of dishes that sowed a small rebellious seed. To the long day, was there no end except bed? Something in me cried for some time of my own. Especially at dusk. In an adolescent burst of self-pity, I scribbled, "The canyon breeze comes floating down, / A perfume-laden stream. / The tired housewife only knows / It's time to skim the cream." Needless to say, someone quickly pointed out how lucky I was to have cream to skim.

So we fed thrashers, tried out fat for soap, made headcheese, dried corn, processed in a three-quart old pressure cooker croakers from Utah Lake (the bones softened admirably), and dunked the old hen into boiling water, the better to de-feather it. I pondered with awe the unlaid eggs in its viscera.

Pending the subsequent arrival of the clan from the ranch back to Provo, in the fall I was sent ahead to "take care of the fruit." Five bushels of peaches, eight bushels of tomatoes, three bushels of pears. A copper boiler with a wooden rack in the bottom yielded up dozens of quarts toward the goal of an ultimate 800. One autumn, I flunked the wood-chopping test, almost severing a finger. But one learns to make do with splint and bandage when the kitchen floor is strewn with bushel baskets.

And I did collect brownie points. When she checked the laden shelves, Mama always said I had done well. She died young, and we tried to carry on as we had been taught. We couldn't have done otherwise.

Eventually, belatedly, and gratefully, I married and went East to live. I was determined to be the best wife known to man. During the honeymoon, simply heating up a can of beans was unthinkable. I had to do intricate and tedious things to it. This zealous kitchen activity was taken in stride by my husband, reared in the same pioneer tradition....

But my specialty lay in salvaging borderline produce. Seventeen split cantaloupes in the morning became seventeen jars of cantaloupe butter by night. The celery that could not freeze but did became quarts of puree for soup. A blender and assorted ingredients turned overripe corn into pudding. Salt water routed the bugs in broccoli. And the cat found no comfort in our turkey bones, long simmered for every calorie.

And again, all this was not without recognition. The grand tour of the house ended in the basement where our astonished eastern friends were expected to make appropriate cluckings over the marvel of row on row of filled jars. Guests at dinner were regaled with how much of it we had grown ourselves. And always, at the end of a hard day's canning, the output was counted and approval bestowed. If someone in the community fell heir to a lug of kumquats, I was the expert to call. I wore the good woman halo so well polished that why should I think about writing poems? Hence, the summer that I had my fancy heart operation, I dared not admit my secret relief that a drought had curtailed production, and there could be a respite while I got my second wind.

So year after year, plied with goodies, my men remained svelte, but not the purveyor thereof. There came a time when my doctor, on call at the slightest emergency, wondered sadly what more she could do for me if my weight continued to climb. I was suddenly ashamed. I had expected medical science to keep me alive, although I was not willing to do my self-disciplining part. Now I faced two equally gruesome alternatives: On the one hand, I could die; on the other hand, I would become a nobody, a non-person, a cipher. My entire image as a good woman was tied up with food. Without a canning lid in my hand, would anyone even like me any more?

Guilt-ridden, I remembered an article in the *Ensign*, in which the author said virtuously that there had been a benighted time, when, for their travels, "I used to stow in anything easy, ready-made and grabbable." However, she repented, and now has learned to spend "as much time and imagination on our portable meals as I would at home." This concept prompts her to deep-fried chicken wings, to be served with a whipped-cream dip ("if you don't mind a bit of a mess"). There is no mere opening of a can to toss salmon together with a little celery, mayonnaise, and pickle. She begins by rolling a crust of defrosted patty shells to surround a complex filling using a dozen ingredients.

Or consider the advice in the *Era* on "How to be a mother ten feet tall." You bake cookies every day; even, presumably, on Sunday, for seven recipes follow. "Mothers and grandmothers," admonishes the author, "have cookies for their medals of honor. So for Mother's Day, and for the other 365 days of the year, fill up the cookie jar and receive acclaim."

To stay alive, I must abandon this highly esteemed cultural pattern?

Men do not deliberately keep women over a hot stove, although this adds to their image as good Providers. In their defense, I do not think they consciously plan that women be so busy with food that they have no time for bridge, shopping, politics or other forms of mischief. In fact, I don't think they object if a woman has assorted strings to her bow, so long as she can keep her priorities straight and can rev up to fulfill the exacting requirements of Superwoman. What they basically want is a continuity of mothering. No break in the comfort of chewing at the breast. When one of my more sophisticated students brought his bride to call, he said, "I want you to meet the women who bakes the best bread in the state." Thud! Here I had thought he valued me for our deep literary discussions, and that he found me wise and witty. Instead, I was just another earth-mother.

I am pushing this too far, I know, but as a third-generation pioneer woman is there a legitimate way out? ...

Ultimately, it is my option whether I shall rise obese on Judgment Day, so addicted to squirreling away food that I can be at home only in the terrestrial sphere. According to my cultural lights, I have tried to be a good woman. But only I live inside my too-tight skin. I must decide when enough is enough.

*The following three selections come from the reader responses printed in the Sisters Speak column*

## Community Involvement (excerpts)
Lorie Winder
Boston, Massachusetts
Winter 1979 (vol. 5, no. 2)

I recently discovered a rather unsettling malady which a friend of mine identified as "livingroom liberalism." "Livingroom liberalism" is a curious phenomenon in which the guilt for neglecting our social and Christian responsibilities is effectively resolved, not by charitable acts, but by the mere discussion of pressing social issues and needs. Thus, the more vehemently, intensively, and frequently we talk about what ought to be done, the less we actually have to do to soothe an aching conscience.

I had become quite a master of this self-deceptive craft until my ward Relief Society presidency called my bluff and asked me to serve as their Community Affairs director. This calling forced me to recognize how infrequently my charitable thoughts, even those more eloquently expressed, are translated into action.

Soon after my call, I received a letter from our Relief Society president. She wrote of the importance of this new program, which at that time was particular to the Boston Stake, and enclosed a letter from the Relief Society General Board. It said, "In the founding period of Relief Society, the prophet Joseph Smith admonished women to 'assist by correcting the morals and strengthening the virtues of their communities.' Each woman should realize that she can be an effective, concerned citizen. One vote, a phone call to a local TV station, a letter to one's local or national legislator—any of these by an informed person can have a positive effect in the community."

For me, the key word in this statement is *informed*—informed as to basic political and social issues, problems and activities within the local community, and the mechanisms whereby change can be effected on an individual and group or organizational level. I discussed these ideas with my ward and stake leaders, and we decided that my role would be that of a resource person who would sponsor discussion groups on various issues led by qualified local sisters and gather information on community organizations according to the individual expressed interests of the sisters in the ward.

A simple survey distributed in Relief Society helped to identify these interests....

Being careful not to abuse my position by pushing personal interests and viewpoints, I began collecting material, using the survey as a reference to meet individual needs. Soon my mailbox was stuffed with pamphlets and letters from interest groups and organizations within our immediate area. These were, in turn, passed to waiting hands in the foyer between Sunday meetings.

My ward Relief Society presidency set aside meetings dedicated to community involvement as well as time for once-a-month fifteen-minute presentations to be given in conjunction with the social relations lesson. So far, with the help of other sisters in the area, we have demonstrated how relatively easy it is to write a letter to a local paper or legislator, and how influential such an action can be, especially if a bit of time is taken to learn a few letter-writing techniques and to become informed on an issue, so that one can back up statements with facts.... After one such presentation on writing letters to local and national television stations ... many sisters felt much more comfortable, and thus more motivated to write that long-overdue, foam-flecked or favorable letter we so often talk about writing, but never do.

We're still trying new approaches and learning about the community of which we can be a much more influential part. Personally, I find I am still a chronic "livingroom liberal," with many of my good intentions remaining unactualized. Yet, I have appreciated this chance to experience some "Christian consciousness-raising."

Boy, do I feel better for having written this letter!

## Depression (excerpts)
Heather Cannon
Arlington, Massachusetts
Spring 1979 (vol. 5, no. 3)

If someone close to you is depressed, what can you do to help him or her? We tend to want to make someone's pain go away, to want to do anything to bring her relief. But it is important to remember that you can't make someone else's depression go away, as you can't eliminate her grief or loss. You *can* comfort her and love her and let her know that you care. For this reason, offering advice isn't very helpful, even though it is a very normal and common response. *Listening* is what you need to do, and listening can be hard. We don't want to hear of someone's pain or sorrow. We don't want pain and sorrow to exist. When we listen, we are forced to face suffering, and it hurts. It is also hard to know what to say to a depressed person—speaking is what she needs; nods and murmured responses are enough from you....

Don't be frightened if a friend expresses anger with the Lord when she is depressed. It really doesn't mean she has necessarily lost her testimony, and it shouldn't threaten yours. Unfortunately, one aspect of severe depression or grief is a feeling of being cut off from the Lord. He's promised comfort, and you've prayed for it and the pain and sorrow still hurt unbearably. In Gethsemane, even Christ repeated, "Oh my Father, if it be possible, let this cup pass from me." I know what He meant. My cup is less bitter, but still more than I want. It is very hard for me to identify as strongly with the rest of this quote: "Nevertheless not as I will, but as thou wilt." I don't have Christ's fullness of understanding about what God's will implies. I'm afraid it includes more pain, and I don't *want* it. Therefore, it's hard for me to say, "All right, I'll *accept* it." If I can't be spared pain, at least I want the Lord to soothe me and make it easier. There are many interpretations of Christ's words from the cross, "My God, my God, why hast thou forsaken me?" To me, this says God won't do it for us. We must work through our sorrows. Why we need this experience, I don't begin to truly understand. But Christ's example says to me, "That's the way it is." I do know that when I am at a point where the Lord has not made my way clear and is not giving me the light I've prayed for, it has helped to have a friend who's not been threatened by my raving that I don't understand the Lord offer to pray with and for me. My pain has not been lessened, but somehow the pressure has. I guess I feel, "You haven't listened to me, but maybe You'll listen to someone else in my behalf." That kernel of hope allows me to function and break out of the feeling of being totally locked in despair....

## Some Positive Repercussions
Cindy L. Barlow
Cambridge, Massachusetts
Winter 1980 (vol. 6, no. 2)

The Sonia Johnson dilemma has aroused much turmoil within me. I have felt confused as to where I should stand. I started out categorizing the affair as "justified retribution." Then, after talking with Sonia herself, I did a turnabout and called it "bitter injustice." After further thought and discussion I labeled it an "unfortunate occurrence," and if I were asked my view today, I'm not sure I'd feel comfortable with any stance. As a whole, this affair is a very perplexing incident.

Although the episode has caused much dispute and pain for many, it may also have had some positive repercussions. I know it has had in my life.

It awakened within me the need to be closer to my Heavenly Father. As my head spun with unanswerable questions and ambiguous answers, I realized that no one but the Lord could bring peace to my mind. I soon found myself praying earnestly and with determination.

I have not received answers to all my questions, but I have since experienced a deep quietude, a sense that Heavenly Father is aware of my problems, that the Church is true, that I, myself, am responsible for my salvation, and that if I am constant with my prayers I will be blessed with the assurance of knowing right from wrong, good from evil. Had the situation never occurred, my spiritual complacency might have never been disturbed and the blessing of inspiration that comes from building a closer relationship with my Father in Heaven would still lie dormant.

## The Founding Foremothers
Comments from a retreat workshop
Fall 1983 (vol. 10, no. 1)

The story of *Exponent II*'s beginnings is important because it says so much about the women of the Church—where we are, the attitude of the Church toward women, the attitude of the women themselves, and where we need to be going. The first formal discussion of the Reunion focused on these beginnings. We were fortunate to have several of the founding mothers with us. Participating in this reminiscence were Laurel Ulrich, Mimmu Sloan, Judy Dushku, Susan Kohler, Bonnie Horne, and Carrel Sheldon.

*Carrel*: Why did it happen to work? Because there was an incredible commitment to make it work! Nobody said, "I need some sleep," or "I can't have twenty children mess up my house." We were completely committed to doing it once we started, and we worked incredibly hard to make it happen. Whatever it took we did, and we never heard anything like "You have to take care of yourself; you have to get your rest." It was that kind of a commitment; we would just do it.

*Judy*: I think there were many times when some people said they were tired. I wasn't reminded of this actually until we were driving up here, and Bonnie and I were talking about how we did the Sonia Johnson issue. We were remembering the many, many meetings that we had to have to plan that issue. It has taken me until now to recognize one of the really lovely things that I think is symbolic of the *Exponent*—the collective process.

I had my feelings hurt during that series of discussions. I disagreed with some other people—which didn't bother me—but some of my friends on the board felt that they couldn't tell me about their disagreeing with me on issues that went beyond those of the newspaper. After working through all of this, what I prized most was what we had established over the years—a truly collective process. I felt good about that process because I knew it was something that we had all participated in from the beginning. You hear a lot of ideals about collective organizations, but I don't know many that have worked as well, especially with so many people being so different.

One of the long-standing jokes was that I used to invite people to my house and at ten o'clock I'd say "good night" and go to bed. Everybody would stay. ["And get breakfast for themselves in the morning," interjected Laurel.] My feeling was that it was truly an organization that didn't just say that it accepted everyone's differences; it really did.

*Susan*: I was not involved at all with any of the writing of *Exponent II*, but I was certainly very involved in the discovery of the *Woman's Exponent*. I just lit up when I came across it at Widener Library. Its discovery was like the opening of the heavens, and I shared it with everybody. Because I had found it, they said, "Why don't you pull out some excerpts from the *Woman's Exponent* that you think might be interesting to the readers of *Exponent II*. It was one of the things that I did very early on.

I also kept track of who might be interested in receiving our first issue. That whole process was kind of interesting. We were dealing with the names of the people that the fifteen of us knew. Before long we had quite a substantial list of people. How were we going to address all those papers? Carrel Sheldon's husband was very well connected with the MIT computer. Because this was back in the dark ages when not all of us had word processors at home, we weren't exactly sure how a computer could help us. We went down to the MIT computer center late at night—that was the only time we could get free use of the equipment—and we learned to keypunch. Each of us had been given slips of paper on which to write a list of twenty names; these were the ones that we keypunched into the computer.

The other thing I remember with some fondness is the first night the papers were delivered. They came to my house, and I had no idea how much room 5000 papers took up. There we were on the floor attaching the labels that, I believe, had come in some sort of zip-coded order. Then we had to sort and bundle them and deliver them to the post office. These are marvelous memories—the most mundane mechanical tasks—but the fellowship there was as warm as when we were talking about issues.

*Bonnie*: I guess that we discussed this dream—the idea of a paper—for about a year. Finally one day Sue Kohler said, "Let's quit fooling around and get going." Carrel Sheldon called a meeting and said that this was what we're going to do. I see Sue and Carrel as the real motivators. Without them, we would still be sitting around thinking about it.

*Susan*: I had some very strong feelings about the need to communicate. I knew that there were lots of people out there who would be just as excited about the things we were talking about among ourselves. I looked upon myself as an "everywoman" person. I just knew that if I was excited, others would be. My feeling was to get the paper out there. Let's make it look as nice as we can with our limited talents; let's put it on newsprint; let's make it cheap; let's just do it. Actually I think in our enthusiasm that first year we printed five issues. That's not bad!

*Laurel*: Maybe I should explain how it all happened. It started in 1966 with *Beginner's Boston*. Bonnie Horne was the Relief Society president in our ward, and we had a $200 welfare assignment. She had a friend who was having an identity crisis, someone who needed a project other than carrying food to the new mothers in the ward. I got assigned to organize the production of this guide book on which we all worked. All the Harvard Business School students said that it wouldn't work and that they didn't want to get involved. Neither did the elders quorum. Bonnie said that it would work, and so we did it. When we got our first copy, Bonnie said that we were taking it down to the *Boston Globe* for a review. That was typical of the attitude involved—we could do anything and, to our great astonishment, we did. We sold about 20,000 initially. We printed several editions.

*Bonnie*: The first edition sold out.

*Laurel*: We made lots of money. In fact it was a really bad thing for the ward spiritually. [Laughter] What a humorous affair. I mean we were this little group of housewives with lots of kids. We had outdone the business school and the elders quorum! [Clapping, laughter.]

We also had this Mormon attitude that you had to always have a product. We had started talking through consciousness raising, or whatever we were calling it then. I think Claudia Bushman had a lot to do with that. She was anguishing, and so was I. We started getting people together, but initially we would just fight and argue in these terribly draining discussions. Claudia's version is that it was because these discussions were so painful that we decided to turn them into a product that eventually became the pink issue of *Dialogue*. My version is that we never considered doing anything else but a product. It happened like this: We were meeting in this "We can do anything; we haven't figured it out yet, but we're going to tell the world about it; let's do an issue of *Dialogue*" mode. So the pink issue was the second stage.

Stage II was just as I was moving to New Hampshire. I missed the discovery of the *Woman's Exponent*. News would filter up to Durham, and I felt very bad that I wasn't near enough to work on the primary research and historical documents. Together we did some Institute lessons that winter and then started working on *Mormon Sisters*.

Now this is the anecdote I wanted to get to because it was important for me—I was a little on the fringes. I knew something very, very exciting was happening. I remember one night coming to Boston for one of the Institute sessions, and Claudia Bushman was just euphoric. She said something like, "We all know what is happening now. All we need to do is figure out what happened in 1912. That's the only missing piece." That's how good it felt to discover our history. I've been accused of exaggerating this. Of course everybody was doing this all over the Church, but I only knew what we were doing in our little enclave. All I knew was what was happening in Cambridge.

The reviewers who were reading the essays for *Mormon Sisters* said that there was nothing new. We also had some responses to the first Exponent dinner. At the second Exponent dinner, Juanita Brooks spoke. As we were leaving, we were discussing *Exponent II*. Should we or should we not do it? Claudia said to me, "So you see"—she had told me about some rejections of *Mormon Sisters* from various sources—"so you see why it is important. If it's going to be done, we have to do it ourselves." I think it was a gradual process; a lot of us thought we were just going to let people know what the needs of women were, then the people in charge would just fill those needs. A real transition point was reached when we suddenly realized that it is a wicked and slothful servant to have to be commanded or applauded or even accepted. We knew what we had to do. I think it was in that spirit that *Exponent II* was founded.

*Mimmu*: I really got involved at a time when I couldn't speak English very well. I couldn't write at all, so I stood in the background. I offered moral support more than anything else. When we were doing the Institute seminar on Mormon women, I found that in studying the old ladies (or early ladies I should say), I could relate to those women much better than I could the women in contemporary times. They were much closer to the kind of Mormons we were in Finland. Finland was still a rather new mission in Europe; in fact, it wasn't until 1947 that the mission opened. My parents were very involved from the beginning. There were only a hundred members when they joined the Church, and nobody could speak English. They were kind and wonderful people, but they couldn't really translate anything, and the songs were absolutely hideous. My parents immediately got involved and were translating the Book of Mormon and the Doctrine and Covenants, and so forth. My mother was very much involved; she had been a leader before she joined the Church, so I had never known that women weren't supposed to do some things. I felt very strongly about the way I had grown up in the Church. I was taught that women were supposed to do something and be something and be sure of themselves. I really believe that we're supposed to say what we think and think for ourselves. When I came here, I was so shocked because I felt like things were so far away and different. That was when Judy told me that I was a radical. I guess I could relate to those early ladies so easily because my parents were the early pioneers in the Finnish mission. I was a Sunday School teacher when I was eleven years old. I was in the mission Mutual presidency when I was fourteen. I grew up very fast, and I did many things that many people have not had an opportunity to do.

I never learned to type, so I put these little letters on the titles and a lot of other things. When I moved away from Boston, I had to come back for *Exponent* meetings and paste-up because they were a lifeline for me. So this whole experience has been very exciting but at the same time a testimony to me that we are individuals and we are supposed to be different. It is the difference in each of us that makes us rich. I felt that I could really share and be accepted. I did not feel like a foreigner with the *Exponent* group like I felt in other situations. That's the sisterhood that I believe *Exponent* is helping to create. It doesn't matter where you are from; we are all sisters. I think that is really the most important thing that the *Exponent* has done for me. It creates a sisterhood within the gospel that knows no boundaries.

*Carrel*: I'm going to report two stories. One is mine, so I'll tell it quickly. In the beginning we had all these talented people who knew they could create this great paper, but they didn't believe they could sell it or that it would work. I was the one who said it would work. I called the printers; I called Connie Cannon's husband, who became our lawyer; I did detailed financial analyses. I proved that we could do it over and over again to them. I was sure that if we had 500 subscribers we could pay our bills. What is incredible to me is that we printed 5000 copies of the first issue, even though before it came out we had just a few more than 500 subscribers. But still we printed 5000 copies; that's why there are some still here tonight. The subscription list is now between two and three thousand, and it has been right around that from the first year.

The other story is Stephanie Goodson's. We were at a retreat when we decided, "This is it; we're going to do it. Who's going to do what?" Stephanie said, "I'm going to be the editor." She had a degree in journalism, and she had worked many years on newspapers. She wanted to be the editor. She was Relief Society president at the time, and she felt that she had to be released. She couldn't do both. She went to her bishop and literally begged him to release her. She felt that she had been called to do this other work, to be editor of *Exponent II*. He refused to release her. She went back again and again and wept many tears. He still refused by saying, "I know you are supposed to be Relief Society president." So she had to decline the editorship. Claudia very ably became our first editor.

*Bonnie*: It was Claudia's idea to produce the paper. She had that dream, and she had been dreaming about it constantly.

*Judy*: I think one of the other things that we learned from Claudia was to keep complete records. She always said that we should write down what we did because someday people would want to know what was going on in this living room. That was an anathema, but it was part of her spirit, as an historian—to write down what we were doing, to save our correspondence with each other, to send it all to the BYU library as a gift. [Laughter] We did it. It's there. You can read our letters to one another. That's the historian's spirit; that's something Claudia believed in, and that's part of why she believed in the paper. There have really been some high spots, but there have been some emotional struggles, too. Some of them have had nothing to do with spirituality. I think that part of the strength of the experience for us is that it has been professionally, personally, and emotionally gratifying. It has been a very great effort, but there have been times that have lifted me to spiritual heights and saved me during times in my life when I needed support.

*Carrel*: In those early days, we worked like sisters. We loved each other; we hated each other; we fought; we struggled; we supported one another. It was incredible. I really didn't have those kinds of relationships anywhere else in my life, except in my family. I did not feel free to get even a little angry with other women. We could do that. But whether we would work things out or we wouldn't work things out, we still hung together. That was great!

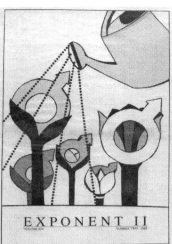

# UNIT 2: 1984–1997

## Introduction by Katie Ludlow Rich

Sue Paxman—later Booth-Forbes—led *Exponent II* into its second decade and served as editor in chief for thirteen years from 1984 to 1997.[1] No longer a fledgling, *Exponent II* spread its wings and helped expand the Mormon feminist landscape. The paper provided a place for Mormon women to wrestle with challenging parts of their history, seek resources for victims of abuse through grassroots organizing, and find openings to discuss complex topics like abortion and homosexuality. As the church increasingly used disciplinary councils to silence outspoken writers, scholars, and advocates, *Exponent II* leveraged its emphasis on personal voices to address evergreen and overtly controversial topics.

Women's history was a driving force of second-wave feminism, and Mormon women were no exception. The two poems included here exemplify how women grappled with the faith and pain of their ancestors even outside of professional scholarship on Mormon women's history. In "Substance of Things Unseen," Helen Mar Cook considers how she sits under the "shade of heavy branches" of trees that her great-grandmother carefully tended and brought across the plains as saplings. In "Wife #3," Violet Tew Kimball puts to verse the heartache of Emmeline B. Wells, who at seventeen became the third wife of a much older man and "learned to stand alone." The poem supposes that Heavenly Mother could not have imposed the "burden" of plural marriage.

At the core of *Exponent II*'s style, personal essays allowed writers to share experiences and life lessons. In the award-winning piece "Don't Look to Me for Direction," Claudia W. Harris presents a two-part essay—part one about settling into middle age and taking comfort in her personal roadmap, and part two after a series of family tragedies shifted her perspective. Now a widow in uncharted territory, Harris has fewer answers, more empathy for suffering, and a desire to live in the present with less judgment. Cheryl Davis Howard (later DiVito) writes about a modern urban legend in "Cheese and Crackers." While the idea that a woman would diligently save for a cruise and frugally eat cheese and crackers in her room is laudable, it is tragic that ignorance kept her from knowing until the final evening that meals in the dining room were included in the price of her trip. Howard wonders if there are blessings and privileges she is already entitled to but missing for want of asking. In "Looking Back: Reflections on President Benson's Talk," Margaret Blair Young considers how Benson's infamous 1987 talk "To the Mothers in Zion" brought her closer to her own mother as they discussed what "joy" means to each of them. Unsurprisingly, their greatest joys are not constrained to the "making of beds, doing of dishes, and fixing of meals."

---

1. More on Booth-Forbes's tenure in Chapters 5 and 6.

After Paxman organized the 1983 "reunion" at Hillsboro Camp in New Hampshire, Exponent II's national retreat became a beloved annual tradition. At the July 1986 retreat, former editor Susan Howe offered the keynote address. In "Creativity: A Constant Renewal," Howe considers how humans are innately creative, which is part of learning to become like their Heavenly Parents. Creativity, however, requires humility and takes the shape of practice, a willingness to do something poorly, and respect for masters of the craft. The retreat served as a microcosm of the paper's larger project of allowing participants to listen deeply to each other's experiences and allow individuals to integrate their sometimes dueling identities as Mormons and feminists.

Though *Exponent II* was decades behind trailblazing feminist publications in discussing family planning and abortion, they found paths to move the conversation forward. In "Birth Control: My Choice, Your Choice," Diane McKinney Kellogg recognizes how moral judgment surrounding the topic divides Mormon women from one another. She argues that recognizing personal choice and offering one another "our non-critical love and support" would do more to encourage sisterhood. Religious stigma made abortion a fraught topic for Mormon women, so in their issues on abortion and adoption, Exponent asked women to "speak from experience" about their own tough decisions to continue or terminate pregnancies. The paper hoped to create room for empathy over ideology. In "Unheard," Carrel Sheldon considers the weight of moral judgment and the threat of excommunication when she faced the decision to abort an unwanted pregnancy paired with a life-threatening blood clot. Though she was already a mother to five children, her bishop and Relief Society president brought preaching and shame rather than the support and care she needed. Robin Zenger Baker writes that in reading the stories from the "Abortion" issue, she sees how complex and individual the decision to have an abortion can be. While honoring each individual's right to choose, Baker shares her experience with adopting her daughter in "The Adoptive Mother." She hopes that people in the position to do so will consider adoption as an alternative to abortion.

Not forgetting the lessons from the Vietnam War, which ended one year after *Exponent II* began, the paper repeatedly turned to the topic of peace. When the Gulf War broke out in August 1990, Exponent women gathered to share their mutual concerns and light candles. In "The Light's Still On— Spring 1991," Claudia Knight-Zimmer writes of the anxiety of waiting for her youngest son to return from war months after the fighting was declared over. She longs for the sacrifice of military service to be better acknowledged by ward members. In her award-winning essay "Women's War," Shari Siebers Crall writes of opening her local paper on Memorial Day and finding the usual photo of war veterans along with memorials of warriors of a different sort—stories of women and children killed or sexually assaulted by men. "Maybe someday," she wonders, "we'll build a memorial to the women whose lives were lost before we won the battle to make the world safe for our daughters to grow up in."

The abuse of women became a rallying cry that pushed Exponent II into direct advocacy in support of victims both on and off the page.[2] Following their Spring 1987 issue on "Unequal Power and Control," Paxman was overwhelmed by the volume of stories the paper received. Abuse became the paper's central theme for years. Included here are excerpts from "The Abuse of Women: An Interview with 'Jane,'" wherein a woman discusses the physical, sexual, and emotional abuse she suffered from her priesthood-holding husband and the social and structural barriers that made many church members unwilling to believe her. From publishing editorials, essays, and articles by experts to hosting convocations at Brandeis University and speaking to local LDS wards, Exponent sought to raise awareness and bring resources to victims. Locally, they saw some positive results from their effort. For instance, in a letter included here, Bishop Dennis Lythoge writes about attending an Exponent event with a guest speaker who helped him recognize the signs of abuse with people he counseled as bishop and opened his eyes to the need to do more.

Judy Dushku's long-running Sisters Speak and Sisters Help columns exemplify how sharing women's voices allowed *Exponent II* to address big topics in a non-threatening way.[3] In "Living with Disabilities," Joan D. Groesbeck writes about her experience with lupus, an inflammatory auto-immune disease. She hopes to raise awareness so someone else might get a diagnosis sooner than the ten years she had to wait. Sisters Speak provided the paper's first opportunity to discuss homosexuality openly. Ina Mae Murri, a former international coordinator for Affirmation/Gay & Lesbian Mormons, writes about her experience trying to organize a support group for lesbians, who are often overlooked in the church. She says, "It is a great struggle to be called sinners when what we want is to love and be loved; to have our love out in the open; to have acceptance from our families, friends and, yes, from the Church." Then in 1996, one year after the LDS Church released its "The Family: A Proclamation to the World," *Exponent II* published its first issue dedicated to homosexuality. In her editorial "Embracing All of Our Sisters and Brothers," Dushku writes that the rejection and hostility of the church

---

2. More on Exponent II's advocacy for victims of abuse on pages 41–44.

3. In Sisters Speak, Dushku would pose a question, and in Sisters Help, she would share a letter from a reader asking the Exponent community for non-preachy, sympathetic advice. For both columns, reader responses to the question or letter would be published in the following issue.

toward its gay members causes harm and suffering to individuals and families as well as damages the image of the church.

Public advocacy and more open scholarship about complicated aspects of church history and theology was met by a wave of anti-feminist, anti-intellectual, anti-homosexual retrenchment at LDS Church headquarters. The retrenchment crested with the excommunication or disfellowshipment of six writers and scholars in September 1993.[4] Writing from their respective ages of twenty-five and fifty, Jenny Atkinson and Sue Paxman responded to news of the excommunications in a joint editorial, "Annus Horribilis." Finding discomfort and unease widespread among church members across the political and religious spectrum, they argue that sharing personal feelings is essential for moving toward a place of healing. Then in 1996, after decades of women's roles in the church becoming increasingly proscriptive and small via the priesthood correlation movement, Paxman wrote "First Hands and Backs, Now Feet and Voices." She argues that the time had come for Mormon women "to use our voices to help make the organizational and cultural decisions that create and influence the 'dailiness' of our lives in the Church structure." Though *Exponent II* was spared the harshest aspect of the church's retrenchment—none of its staff faced church disciplinary councils for their work—the publication's subscriptions plummeted partly due to church members becoming fearful of reading or affiliating with unsponsored LDS publications. But as the pieces in this unit and the units to follow demonstrate, *Exponent II* persisted in its work of carving out space for Mormon feminists to integrate their identities.

### Substance of Things Unseen
Helen Mar Cook
Ogden, Utah
Fall 1984 (vol. 11, no. 1)

To make room for three wagon loads of saplings,
my great grandmother, suntired, sixteen,
walked across the plains.

When time came to rest
she searched for the nearest stream,
a muddy river or a stagnant pool
to carry brimming pails for thirsty roots
as any woman drawing water from a well.

---

4. For more on Exponent's response to the church disciplinary councils, read pages 57–59.

When dust filtered through her eyelashes,
and dry winds scraped her cheeks, she
tended carefully the covering of rags
to keep the young trees moist.

Ascending, descending western mountains
she finally reached the place for planting.

As summers waned and autumns wasted,
saplings grew.
She thirsted with the parched leaf,
prayed away all pestilence.
When winter came, she waited out the storms.
In springtime, she listened for rain
and watched for buds.

On the other end of generations
I sit in the shade of heavy branches,
feel her presence in multitudes of leaves.

## Wife #3
Violet Tew Kimball
Spring 1987 (vol. 13, no. 3)

"I have no one to go to for
comfort or shelter..."
Emmeline B. Wells

Someone else calls you husband.
Father is also one of your titles.
Some bind by law,
some by love.

I would not want to
usurp rights or privileges
of the others,
or impinge on your measured time.
I have learned to stand alone.

But sometimes...
sometimes when cold,
sickness and sorrow
sap my spirit and strength

and I yearn for unproffered comfort,
I feel betrayed.

Would it be a sin
if my load were lifted?
Would nature be wounded
if I could have this craving stilled,
and the love and desire I feel
be returned?

Mother
I cannot believe
this burden was imposed
by Your decree.

## Birth Control: My Choice, Your Choice (excerpts)
Diane McKinney Kellogg
Lexington, Massachusetts
Winter 1985 (vol. 11, no. 2)

Many LDS women today still have questions about the use of birth control. Would God want us to limit our families? Use standards of convenience and income to determine the spacing and number of children? Delay children for reasons of education or simply to have more time as a couple?

Personally, I am less plagued by the questions themselves than I am plagued by the need I feel to support my sisters in whatever issues they face. I have longed for ways of supporting those women who feel awkward about announcing their sixth pregnancy; for ways of helping women feel less "guilty" about using birth control; for ways of helping others feel more free to consider birth control instead of either abstinence or perpetual pregnancy. Women should not have to feel either defensive or guilty about their choices. At the same time I think it is useful for sisters who do not want to use birth control to have ways of thinking about it that leave them less likely to judge other sisters as "unrighteous" for planning their families through the use of birth control....

Far from increasing the sisterhood and bonds of love hoped for in the stakes of Zion, these attitudes serve to distance sisters from one another and keep us actively judging rather than actively loving one another. I have found that the Christian appeal of "please don't judge each other," isn't enough. We need to think about the issues more specifically. Some historical tidbits have contributed new perspectives to my own thinking on the subject.

The first was provided by Ida Smith, the former Director of the Women's Resource Center at BYU, in an address to the BYU Honors Society. She reports that in the 1800s upper-class women wanted freedom from perpetual pregnancy but had no reliable contraceptives available. The medical knowledge of the time simply didn't tell us enough about the ovulation cycle and the process of conception to be helpful. These women often sent their husbands to prostitutes to have their sexual needs fulfilled, feigning ignorance of their spouses' whereabouts on certain evenings. In any case, in 1870 two-thirds of the Chinese women in California were prostitutes, many of them having been recruited to come to this country for that purpose. In 1856 there were five thousand known prostitutes in New York City alone. Prostitution was becoming recognized as a method of birth control, at least for the non-prostitutes. Had reliable birth control been available, would it not have been more moral for these women to keep their husbands home?

In the 1930s, when Margaret Sanger advocated the use of the diaphragm as a "moral alternative for women," those who knew the immoral alternative (prostitutes) supported her cause. This medical revolution made it possible for couples to choose to separate love-making from baby-making, or to make the two synonymous by choice rather than fate.

It had only been a few years prior when one mother of eleven children (none well-clothed, fed, or educated) had asked her doctor how she could prevent further pregnancies. He told her, "Tell Jake to sleep on the roof." And so she anticipated the inevitable twelfth child, not with joy but with dread.

Sanger's education process was aimed at making child-bearing and rearing a joy: a happy choice rather than a fateful consequence of marriage.

I wondered how Jake and his wife would have felt about abstinence. Abstinence certainly can't be evaluated as either moral or immoral; neither seem to be appropriate categories. Instead, one must look at the positive and negative impact on the marriage relationship. I find it almost as easy to find cases where abstinence would help a relationship as cases where complete abstinence would damage the quality of intimacy between husband and wife.

Each choice—from abstinence to having one's tubes tied—has positive, negative, and neutral consequences. To label any option either "moral" or "immoral" is too simplistic a way of thinking about the issues. Further, each person or couple will view the costs and benefits differently.

As responsible free agents, we must make thoughtful choices that will bring peace, rather than guilt. And as sisters in the gospel we must not only allow, but encourage, others to do the same, offering our sisters not our own point of view, but our non-critical love and support.

## Cheese and Crackers (excerpts)
Cheryl Davis Howard (DiVito)
Medford, Massachusetts
Summer 1985 (vol. 11, no. 4)

When I was growing up and had to give two-and-a-half minute talks, I sometimes resorted to padding my own brief ideas with stories or poems from one of those compact little books called something like *Golden Nuggets of Thought* or *Thoughts for Talks*. Their tables of contents promised anecdotes for everything from anger to zeal. The books themselves were small enough that in my youthful naivete I thought that I could mask one with a few loose papers so that the congregation wouldn't necessarily have to know that most of the talk came prefabricated from one quick source—just add tears.

And I did shed many a sincere tear over those tender stories that were geared to strum the heartstrings. But as the years pass and I hear these stories time and again—usually from teenagers who distrust the notion that the best experience is one's own—familiarity breeds contempt. I squirm in my foreknowledge of what happened to the second pair of footsteps in the sand, or I wish that the violin strings were missing in "The Touch of the Master's Hand."

I have to admit, however, that there is one story that continues to haunt me. A woman allegedly scrimps and saves for years and is finally able to go on a cruise. She calculates that if she limits herself to cheese and crackers in her cabin on the ship she will even have enough money to pay for one meal in the main dining room. After indulging in this dinner on the last night of the cruise, she inquires of the steward where she should pay the bill. Somewhat confused, he replies, "But, madam, the price of the meals is included in your ticket." The woman has focused so hard on scrimping and saving that she is unaware that she had the right to so much more.

At sixteen or seventeen, I trembled to think that I, too, was leading a cheese-and-crackers existence. Even now, I take stock to see if I have my nose stuck in *Life on $5 a Day* while the more knowledgeable are reading *Feodor's Guide to Luxury*.

I have reason for my suspicions; I recognized the symptoms early. I recall a steak fry up Provo Canyon to celebrate high school graduation. I brought a tuna fish sandwich. Actually, many people thought that I showed foresight because no one brought charcoal fluid, but I knew that premonition wasn't my real motivation. I could well afford the steak, but a steak seemed rather ostentatious when a sandwich would do.

And the scrimp-and-save mentality has continued. Even with a good teaching job and money in the bank, I still live in the bargain basement. When shopping for clothes, I find myself muttering, "Ha! I could make that for less than half." Then, with my adrenalin high, I spend two hours in the fabric store, three hours scheming how to lay and cut out the pattern (I always buy less fabric than what is called for—everybody knows that the pattern companies are in cahoots with the fabric mills), and two nights sewing the dress. One of my non-sewing friends once pointed out to me that if I had to pay myself for the time that I spend sewing, the dress would probably cost less if I bought it. I pushed back what hair I had left, squinted at her through bloodshot eyes, and told her that my sewing was purely recreational, an artistic outlet....

I suppose that I wouldn't feel that this frame of mind was so insidious if it ended with shopping. I could label it "being frugal" or "shopping smart" and pat myself on the back for getting the best of a bargain, but my scrimp-and-save mania even pervades vacations....

Last summer, I became bent on proving that I was not a "cheese-and-crackers" person, that I could indulge in life. I signed us up for a trip to Greece, including a three-day cruise. Admittedly I chose the cheapest tour available, but I figured that a tour was a step in the right direction. At least I wouldn't miss half the countryside trying to figure out how to by-pass toll roads, and I could avoid the shoulderbag droop that comes from carrying extra rations because I knew that most meals were furnished. The basics were taken care of....

Then I received the *sign*. I haven't quite figured out the interpretation yet; I just know that it is significant. It came on our last night aboard the cruise ship. We had usually dined on deck at the smorgasbord. That night, though, everyone was expected to attend the captain's formal farewell dinner. Late that afternoon, however, it became evident that many guests would opt to forego the festivities because of the increasingly rough seas. Bob and I lay on our bunks for about an hour before we decided not to attend. We didn't feel sick, but neither were we willing to risk feeling really awful later by going to the dinner. I was lying there trying to reconstruct the rescue scene from "The Poseidon Adventure" when I heard a knock at the door. I'm sure that the staff thought that they were doing us a kindness by sending a steward around with snacks for those of us not at dinner, but what he proffered drew me up short—cheese and crackers.

At this point, I get muddled trying to ascertain the exact significance of this incident. Does it indicate that I will always be cursed with this pinch-penny mentality? Or is it a curse? Maybe the incident emphasizes the fact that a cheese-and-crackers existence is a firm foundation that will provide strength in times of stress. Maybe I have cut through the excesses of life to find a Truth.

In my more lucid moments, I realize that I have shied away from the more obvious interpretation of the original story. Frugality is irrelevant; ignorance is the focus. The story of the woman saving for the cruise is unsettling because the woman does not realize that she is entitled to more. Her scrimping to pay for the trip is laudatory; her ignorance of her rights is painful. This story haunts me because this woman is a victim of ignorance. She gets less than what was already paid for. Now if anything could upset a scrimp-and-saver like me, that's it. And no matter how much sympathy I want to give to that woman, I cannot forgive her for not knowing. Why didn't she read the brochures more carefully? Why didn't she ask?

It's even worse when I try to deal with the spiritual interpretation. How much enlightenment and how many spiritual blessings have I missed because of my own ignorance? The admonitions are there: "Ask, and ye shall receive; knock, and it shall be opened unto you." We have been promised ". . . line upon line, precept upon precept," based on our readiness and our *asking*.

I can only judge my spiritual awareness by noticing how many blessings come as complete surprises. The prime example is when the priesthood was given to Black members. Even though I counted a black woman among my best friends, I am ashamed to think how little asking of the Lord I did.

The price for salvation has already been paid. It's the price of ignorance that appalls me. I may be dining on cheese and crackers while others are eating steak.

## Creativity: A Constant Renewal (excerpts)
Susan Howe
Denver, Colorado
Winter 1987 (vol. 13, no. 2)

*In July 1986, Susan Howe gave the keynote address at the Exponent II retreat. At the beginning of her speech, she gives an expansive view of creativity.*

We need only to look around us to realize how women are creative—and how many ways there are to be creative. There are as many examples as there are individuals; we are all creative. And we continue to learn about creativity throughout our lives. Because creativity is an attribute of God, the more we create, the more we can learn to be like our Heavenly Parents—if we create as they create.

*Howe then goes on to explore various implications for us. For example, what stops us from being creative and what are the potential costs? And how can we explore and expand the creative process? Howe asserts that humility is key:*

Everything about creating requires humility.

First of all, one must serve an apprenticeship. Simply wanting to create is not doing it. When one begins, one is a beginner, and pride is exacted before one improves.... In order to be able to create, then, we must accept the ignorance and dispossession that are a part of learning to create. We have to give up everything that is safe and well-known and comfortable and move to experiences that are not easily predictable, experiences at which we may fail. It takes courage to try when it is possible to fail, and only humility can help us to accept these conditions of creating.

Do you remember, from your childhood, how terrifying it was to try something new for the first time—to jump into the deep end of the swimming pool, to ride a bike, to perform in a dance or piano recital, or to speak in church? As adults, we don't do things that are entirely new as often, so we forget what it is to experience that kind of fear. But that same, exquisite fear is always there as one begins to create, and somehow one has to accept and yet surpass that fear, knowing that it never goes away, that it is always a part of creating. Flannery O'Connor, near the end of her career, wrote: "I've been writing eighteen years and I've reached the point where I can't do again what I know I can do well, and the larger things I need to do now, I doubt my capacity for doing." To create is to attempt to surpass what one has done before, and there is always fear in that.

What helps me to deal with that fear is a statement made by Bin Ramke, a fine contemporary poet, in a poetry workshop I attended last year. One day in class he said, "Anything that is worth doing is worth doing poorly." That helped me realize several things: that it is usually the case that we have to do something poorly before we can learn to do it well, that if one doesn't risk doing something poorly one will never improve, and that practice—often excruciating practice—is required to succeed.

Anything that is worth doing must be done poorly and then must be done again and again and again. One should never underestimate the work that is required to improve. A friend of mine, an artist who is concentrating on figure drawing, told me of trying to copy two Degas figures. He said that they look simple—as if they were hurriedly drawn, and perhaps they were—but are really very complex. The bodies in Degas drawings are always in unusual positions that are very hard to duplicate. My friend took three hours to complete these Degas copies, and then he read the introduction of the book he was working from. It stated that Degas did eight figure drawings a day throughout his career, just for practice!

When I asked Emma Lou Thayne if she would write the "West" column for the "East and West" section of *Exponent II*, she said that she would enjoy it—in fact, that she wrote an essay every morning to warm up as she began her day's writing! It is astonishing to realize how hard creative people work to achieve what they achieve. Nothing is simply given; it is—as are most worthwhile things in life—earned by incredible effort. As Flannery O'Connor said about writing: "... all writing is painful and ... if it is not painful then it is not worth doing." The same is true of any endeavor: If it is not painful, it is not stretching you and making you grow, and therefore it is not worth doing.

Another aspect of the humility required to create is that one must respect, learn from, and master what has been done before by others. We have two ways to learn in this life—by trial and error and by studying what others have learned. There simply isn't time for us to make all the mistakes that have already been made. It is such a shortcut in terms of possible accomplishment, though not in terms of effort, to study what others have learned. It is vital that a writer read constantly; I have been told that I should read at least one novel a week. We have all seen artists in galleries attempting to copy masterpieces. Trying to move from the position of novice to that of master, one has to learn what it is to be a master. Then, too, in terms of craft and style, by studying in this way, one learns what one accepts and what one rejects as a basis to work from.

Once one has mastered the craft of one's art, it is essential to be true to oneself.... "A just assessment of one's own worth" is key. We should always respect ourselves and our creative ideas and ask ourselves, when advice or criticism is offered, "Will this advice subvert my work from the goals I see for it or will it help me achieve those goals more fully?" That requires a deep understanding of oneself that can only be achieved through humility. Flannery O'Connor had that humility. One of her finest stories is "Good Country People." She wrote it in just a few days and sent it off to her editor, Robert Giroux. He suggested that she reintroduce two of the characters from the story at the end to diffuse the tension and provide a sense of denouement. She wrote a new ending right away and sent it to him. Ms. O'Connor was open to suggestions and comments, but she had to be—first of all—true to her own vision....

There is in each of us that which is individual, true, and unique, that which we must finally trust.... Not even this trust in one's own vision is enough. Besides being true to oneself, a greater humility is required: to recognize that our most valuable creations will always be beyond our actual capabilities. There are powers beyond us that influence what we can do—the power of the human spirit, as Matisse calls it, and the power of the Holy Ghost. In any ultimately creative effort—art, fiction, music, or the more important work of creating ourselves—both must be involved. To quote Matisse:

A musician once said: In art, truth and reality begin when one no longer understands what one is doing or what one knows, and when there remains an energy that is all the stronger for being constrained, controlled, and compressed. It is therefore necessary to present oneself with the greatest humility: white, pure, and candid with a mind as if empty, in a spiritual state analogous to that of a communicant approaching the Lord's Table. Obviously it is necessary to have all of one's experience behind one, but to preserve the freshness of one's instincts.

Do I believe in God? Yes, when I am working. When I am submissive and modest, I feel myself to be greatly helped by someone who causes me to do things which exceed my capabilities.

This quotation tells us that we are important in creating. We are not nothing. To create we must have our experiences behind us, and we must preserve the freshness of our instincts. But we are not all. We must have a contact with and respect for the human spirit and the depth and height possible to it, and with that firmly in mind, we must respect the power of inspiration that is the actual muse and that will help us create what is true and worthwhile—of a dance, a poem, or anything else we choose to create.

To accept the fear and hard work of creating, to learn from others, to be true to one's own vision, and to realize, humbly, that one must work beyond oneself and trust the power of the human spirit and the power of the Holy Ghost for assistance are necessary aspects of the greatest creations. They result in works that ring true to those who experience them....

Humility must be remembered and accepted again and again and again if one hopes to create with integrity. The experience of creating is always new and always difficult, because if one repeats what one has done before, one is following a pattern and no longer creating. T.S. Eliot, in "East Coker" of the Four Quartets, explains:

> There is, it seems to us,
> At best, only a limited value
> In the knowledge derived from experience.
> The knowledge imposes a pattern, falsifies,
> For the pattern is new in every moment
> And every moment is a new and shocking
> Valuation of all we have been....
> The only wisdom we can hope to acquire
> Is the wisdom of humility; humility is endless.

Like life, creating is painful, terrifying, exhilarating, demanding, and of inestimable value. But it does exact its costs, costs that must be accepted in order to progress....

To create beauty and goodness in things that are of lasting value to us is an essential part of becoming like our Heavenly Father and our Heavenly Mother. As we begin a new creation, we can never know what it will finally be, even though we have a certain vision in mind. As we work, however, we find that inspiration gives variety and depth to the creation that we could never anticipate, that the creation finally becomes itself and only in a secondary capacity something we have made. But the making is vital, for in doing it, we learn a little more about who we are, about what matters, about truth.

## The Abuse of Women: An Interview with "Jane" (excerpts)
1987 (vol. 14, no. 1)

*Exponent II*: Jane, why did you agree to be interviewed about your life as an LDS woman who has been abused by her husband?

*Jane*: Because I live with the hope that somebody out there will listen and, more importantly, hear. I also hope that people in the Church will believe what I say. If they can hear and believe what I say, maybe they will listen to other abused women and believe them. And then I also hope, of course, that readers will give abused women the kind of support that they need for getting on with their lives.

*Exponent II*: Your tone suggests that you think what you hope for will be hard to obtain. Is that true?

*Jane*: I find it really quite easy to understand why people in the Church have a difficult time hearing what I and others like me have to say. We are saying that even here—in this "families are forever" community—cruelty is a reality. Many fathers and husbands routinely abuse and batter their wives and children, verbally and physically. It is horrible, and it is happening in most wards in our Church.

We are beginning to understand that such awful things go on "in the world," but we believe that we in the Church are safe from such things. We believe that the gospel makes us significantly different from those in the world who abuse others and protects us from the horrors of abuse.

These beliefs are often so central to our love of the gospel and the Church, it seems, that we will go to great lengths to protect our beliefs from being challenged. Simply put, when we hear accounts or stories that challenge our beliefs we either block them out, or we decide that the people who are challenging our beliefs are telling lies (in this case, abused women), or we change the stories that we hear from abused women just enough so that they will still fit into our belief system, allowing that system to stand.

For example, some people in the Church will accept a story of abuse from a woman if the abuse has ended or if the woman's husband is inactive or a nonmember, however, if her husband is an active, priesthood-holding member, most Mormons whom I know simply cannot hear her when she tells them that he abuses her and or his children. I have even heard that there are men in authority in the Church who think that the abuse of women is "a fad," that a lot of women think they are abused because it's the "in" thing to be, and that the "fad" will soon pass.

*Exponent II*: You sound like you have had experience.

*Jane*: Of course I have, and there are other abused women whom I know in the Church who have had identical experiences. They tell members, visiting and home teachers, Relief Society presidents, and bishops what is going on in their lives and find that they are simply not believed. One woman whom I know was admitted to the hospital after one particularly awful attack by her husband. She called the bishop, who had always been her friend and who knew something of the situation, to tell him that she was in the hospital. He did not come to see her, and he didn't ever ask her what had happened to put her there. Later, she said that she believed that the bishop was so unresponsive because he simply could not face her and acknowledge that her husband, a counselor in his bishopric at the time, was beating his wife....

*Exponent II*: What can people do for you and for other women who are abused?

*Jane*: First of all, listen and believe us. Tell us that you believe us and be willing to use our words to describe what has happened to us. My therapist is good at that. She is not morbid, but she calls things by their names, which helps me trust her and trust myself. People can do that, and they should. Also, be willing to listen for as long as it takes for the victim to work through the years of abuse to a position of self-esteem once again. Each of us responds differently to different situations; help us find our own way to recovery.

*Exponent II*: Because there are fewer observable scars, how can an outsider or, for that matter, the victim herself recognize her emotional abuse?

*Jane*: It's difficult. I recognized the ways that Jim abused me sexually—I never felt that I could say no to him—and physically first. It took me longer to see the emotional battering, and those scars are the deepest, by far. Because I am a Mormon woman and one of my temple covenants was to submit to my husband, I found it difficult to tell the difference between the kind of righteous submission to a righteous goal that was for both of us and the kind of damaging submission that Jim required of me. In fact, that dilemma kept me in my temple marriage for a long time. How could I continue to work toward righteous obedience to inspired priesthood authority and free myself from the awful tyranny that Jim held me with? It was tough; I had to sort that out alone.

*Exponent II*: What helped you in that process?

*Jane*: At that time, I was not aware of many role models, but the few that were there seemed to be sent from the Lord. My therapist helped me recognize the cycle or pattern of abuse that I was suffering. He once recommended that I watch a made-for-television movie about an abused woman. I felt such joy when I saw this woman break free from the cycle that I had learned to recognize in my own life. I remember wondering if my joy was inspired.

Watching another woman break free from what you know is a kind of hell helped me. I guess that is why I agreed to go through with this interview. It hurts to go over this sometimes, but I keep hoping that someone, somewhere will read this and gain courage from knowing that somewhere there is a middle-aged, mother of six, active Mormon housewife who, after twenty years of repeated abuse at the hands and words of an active, priesthood-holding, leader husband, left and became free. I am broke, often lonely, often suffering from old wounds, but I am happier than I have ever been in my life. I am healing, and I stand free and tall, facing the world with a sense of my own worth and the power to control my life and channel my new energy to achieve really good things for me and my family.

## Don't Look to Me for Direction (excerpts)
Claudia W. Harris
Atlanta, Georgia
Winter 1988 (vol. 14, no. 3)

*In part one of her winning essay for the Helen C. Stark Personal Essay Contest, "Don't look to me for direction," Claudia Harris wrestles with finding herself on the "downhill side" of her 40s and the conflict she experiences. While those around her seem to assume she is an "elder statesman" full of wisdom and council, she sees roads not taken and opportunities lost.*

People are always asking me for directions. This morning when I was out for my morning walk, three drivers stopped to use me for a road map. I suppose, because I'm out there on the street moving along at a determined clip, they assume that I know where I'm going, but it's probably not good for them to also assume that I know where they're going. In fact, it's not wise to assume that I know where I'm going in any but the most literal sense. I can tell you where I've been, and I can tell you what my big goal is, what my eternal aspirations are, but bogged down as I frequently am in the mundane, I sometimes miss the signposts that would tell me where I'm headed.

For that reason, I feel like a sham when I become aware that others are looking to me for direction. And the older I get, the oftener I find myself in that role. Here I think of myself as still thoroughly involved in the process of becoming, and others see me as having already become. Perhaps I'm too sensitive, but I find myself less ready to contribute in Relief Society because I suspect what I say is given more importance than it merits, I'm resisting, and resenting a little, this elder-statesman role that has come to me much too soon....

So despite how much I might resist the uncomfortable realization, I probably am more at the point of having become. The older I get the more limited my possibilities appear to be. One choice precludes another, and soon a path has been set that I did not anticipate....

I have always felt on the brink—still able to live out any possibility. But now my honesty, or cynicism perhaps, forces me to admit that if I haven't committed myself to something by now I probably won't do it. It is this strong dose of midlife reality that chips away at that youthful inner center I try to maintain. For instance, I don't believe I'll ever learn to ride a bicycle despite the training wheels my husband put on my daughter's old bike for me. The whole prospect is just too frightening; the ground looks so far down and falls hurt more now. Besides, I did feel a little silly with the whole family running along, encouraging me. So now I say that I am going to wait until I am old enough to ride a tricycle again; thus, I have become someone who doesn't ride a bicycle and probably never will.... I like what I am; I just don't like closing out all the possibilities of what I might have become.

And so, what is the answer? When people ask, I really do try to send them in the best direction, even though I sometimes resent being interrupted in my own struggle along difficult terrain. But I also try to be much more open about my unsureness and the details of my struggle.... I am also relieved that I have arrived at this point with only a few regrets. So look to me for direction at your own risk, but join me on the walk any time you'd like.

*Part two of her essay comes with a giant asterisk. A few years after writing the initial piece, Harris experienced devastating losses that upended her world and shifted her perspective.*

Soon after writing this piece, my life fell apart. My sister, her husband, and two sons died in an automobile accident in Spanish Fork canyon. I suffered a nine-month illness that, when it was finally diagnosed, led me to think briefly that my own death was imminent. This frustrating period was immediately followed by my husband's diagnosis of cancer. His predicted six months blessedly stretched to eighteen. Just before his death, my nephew's twenty-year-old bride died after a six-week bout with recurring cancer. After her four cancer-free years, we were totally unprepared. Interspersed in all this were biopsies and successful cancer operations of several other loved ones.

Because I have now become that most dreaded of all things—a widow—I decided to see if this essay on my discomfort with having almost become still expresses my feelings. I laugh as I read of my desire to stay on the brink of possibility because I'm now perched uneasily on an abyss of confusion. Anything is possible except what I spent thirty years building. What were comfortable givens are now all open questions. Too much choice is hell. My life then seemed clearly mapped out compared to the uncharted territory opening up before me now. I find that I don't delight in change quite as much as I indicated.

While my husband was recovering from his first operation, I taught his Gospel Doctrine class. Word of the dismal prognosis had spread quickly, so when a sister came up to me one Sunday after class, I expected her either to express sympathy or say something about the lesson. Instead she looked at me hard and said, "I've got my eye on you; everyone has their eye on you." She then told me angrily of her own husband's poor health and of her fear that she might one day be in my position. "Women all over are watching to see how you handle it," she said. I'm sure she had no clue how devastated and alone she left me standing. At that time, I remembered this essay and wanted to shout: "Don't look to me for direction!"

I'll probably always feel uncomfortable if I think someone is using me as a guide. Being responsible for my own actions consumes enough of my energy. But there's a paradox here. Why write about it if I'm not willing to be judged? My husband hated bumper stickers and shirts that advertised. So one Christmas I had a sweatshirt silk-screened for him, "I REFUSE TO FLAUNT MY OPINIONS," followed by his signature. My point to him was that the refusal itself was an opinion. My point to myself is that teaching was the wrong career choice if I really didn't want to be a model. I say that I don't like being watched, and yet I put it out here for all to see.

But there's still the difference between who I am and who people think I am. I wish I had a dollar for every time these last few years someone has told me that I'm strong. However kind, the remark robs me of my emotion; it tells me what's expected. Recently, I was with a group of women, and one was sharing some lovely memories of Chet. Tears began to well up in my eyes; I so love knowing others appreciated him and miss him, too. But when I realized a particular sister was carefully watching my reaction, I involuntarily closed down. My tears dried, and I felt my face take on the pleasant mask that I usually wear in public. This sister has told me repeatedly how well I'm doing and that she would never be able to manage. I'm sure she doesn't believe me when I tell her that she could do whatever she had to do and that all I've managed to do is put one foot in front of another....

In no other period of my life have I learned as much, but although I'm blessed by the knowledge, I'll probably never delight in it. I'll always curse the circumstances. This is one experience I could have done without. I'm tired of growing. But my life is not unpleasant when I remember what I've learned about being happy despite my situation. As long as I stay in the present, I can take pleasure in the moment—a step back in time, I feel regret; a step forward, fear. And I've begun to recapture my zest for living. The time stretching before me seems more like a gift now than a burden. I've also begun to appreciate some of the new possibilities open to me. When I keep my eyes on the present scene—not on the ground but also not straining to see the distant horizon—I can even smell a rose or two....

And so, what is the answer now? I certainly value the knowledge I've gained. Working so hard to be joyous has chipped away at my cynical shell and given me renewed innocence. Just learning to appreciate the intrinsic value of each moment of life has itself been a blessing. This path I'm on is one I would never have chosen, but nonetheless, I'm determined to make it a memorable journey. I get a funny kind of comfort standing in the cemetery looking at my name hammered deeply into that beautiful pink granite. Despite where this unexplored path might lead me, at least I know where I'm going to end up.

On the last walk my husband felt strong enough to make, I put my hand in the center of his back to give him a boost up a particularly steep hill. He let me leave it there only for a moment; although the support felt good, he was afraid someone might see. But, hey! I'm not proud. Give me a push if you're so inclined. I'd welcome the feel of your hand in the middle of my back. What I'm saying is that not only are you welcome to join me on the walk as I once said, but please come. The path seems less steep with a friend by my side.

## Looking Back: Reflections on President Benson's Talk (excerpts)
Margaret Blair Young
Provo, Utah
1989 (vol. 15, no. 1)

I will say this for President Benson's talk (yes, *the* talk): It brought my mother and me closer together....[5]

After President Benson's talk, Mom phoned me. "So what did you think of it?" she said—a little gingerly.

And I—a little gingerly, too—said, "I had problems with it."

Then we talked. Talked for maybe an hour, and the next day talked some

---
5. Ezra Taft Benson, "To the Mothers in Zion," Fireside Address, February 22, 1987.

more, and the next day some more. The Prophet had turned the heart of at least one daughter to her mother.

Now we didn't hate the talk. We even agreed with much of it.... The biggie—the sentence that made us want to paint a little mustache on that lovely old photo of the ideal woman—was the one about a woman's greatest joy being the making of beds, the doing of dishes, the fixing of meals for her beloved husband and children.

Joy was something I didn't sense from Mom when she was making the beds or doing the dishes of her beloved family.... I knew there were cockroaches in our apartment and that the summer days in Indiana made everyone sweat. And I knew that Mom was not joyful. There was one night when I lay on the top bunk and she came into the room, dropped onto the bottom bunk, and started crying. I asked her what was wrong. She said she wished I would make my bed better and more often. I started crying, too, pitying things I couldn't fathom....

Of course, I wonder sometimes what kind of chaos I am sowing when I choose to write a short story while my baby naps, instead of dusting the piano or doing the breakfast dishes. Certainly I could give up that precious time and make my house spotless, and many would think it noble to do so.

I choose what I love, and what really does bring me joy. I find that I am my own best doctor in preparing the prescription for this precious commodity. Joy. The thing for which men—and women—were created. I have not always found it where others have.

I have chosen, for example, to work part time. Because it is from choice and not need, I am no longer a secretary. I teach one section of Freshman English. My teaching time is self-verification and service. I find it refreshing, invigorating. I wish that my mother had had some kind of a meaningful career—perhaps something that would have taken her out of the house for only one or two hours a day—and that she had farmed us kids out to babysitters during that time. Actually, she wishes it too. She and I agree that she probably would have been a better mother and a happier person. She needed something more for her self-esteem and personal growth than a white carnation on Mother's Day and a speech about self-sacrifice....

So, after all our discussions of motherhood and patriarchy, of making beds, doing dishes, fixing meals, and of where these chores really do fit into a definition of joy, I sit here looking back on my life and trying to understand Mom's. If through some miracle I could give her a great gift, it would be time for herself. I would say, "Leave home, leave home, leave home. Do something you love to do. Spend a few hours a day in an adult world where Robert Frost, not Mother Goose, is quoted. Write a poem. Make a song. Become more than a plan maker for next week's clean house." And maybe I would add a blessing on her head—not for being perfect, but for giving her daughters so much that's good and interesting to live for and to love.

## Unheard
Carrel Sheldon
Initially published under "Name Withheld"
1990 (vol. 15, no. 4)

After five children, I decided that I had had my last. When I became pregnant for the sixth time, I felt that it was too late for me, and I became very depressed. I couldn't stand the thought of being a mother again. I went to bed for two weeks, contemplating abortion. I told one of my friends that I couldn't face this pregnancy and that I was going to have an abortion. She became quite hysterical, quoting all kinds of odd, Mormon-related references, assuring me that I would be excommunicated. She called me regularly with new arguments with which to try to dissuade me. She was sure that my eternal salvation was hanging on my decision and that I was going to make the wrong one.

Although I believed that it was nobody else's business whether I had an abortion, I thought a lot about excommunication. Up to this point, my whole life had revolved around the Church; I couldn't bear the thought of being cut off from it. I loved working in the Church; I loved all my Church friends—as a matter of fact, all of my friends were Church members. Outside of my family, my involvement with the Church and the women of the Church were the only things that mattered to me. The fact that my Church might excommunicate me for doing something that felt so necessary depressed me even more.

After going through two weeks of what felt like hell, my doctors discovered that I had a serious blood clot in my pelvis. I was frightened, but I also felt tremendous relief. Surely this meant that I could have an abortion and be saved from excommunication and an unwanted child. I spent the next two weeks in the hospital being pumped dangerously full of blood thinners, dealing with all the concerned people in my life, and scheduling the abortion.

After much discussion and consultation, the doctors decided that an abortion wasn't absolutely necessary to save my life. They told me that with a great deal of care and some certain risk to my life and health I could deliver a full-term child who would have a fifty-percent chance of living. I had hoped that the blood clot would make it absolutely necessary, that there would be no question any longer for those people who were against it and thought they had some say in my life. However, various concerned people tried desperately to convince me not to have an abortion.

One day, my bishop came to visit me. I was alone in my hospital room, unable to move, with blood thinner dripping into my body. He regaled me with stories of his sister and her [intellectually disabled] child and what a blessing that child had been to the family. He told me that "as your bishop, my concern is with the child."

Here I—a baptized, endowed, dedicated worker, and tithe-payer in the Church—lay helpless, hurt, and frightened, trying to maintain my psychological and physiological equilibrium, and his concern was for the eight-week possibility in my uterus—not for me!

I told him that I had seen our stake president, a doctor who had been on rounds in the hospital the day before, and that he had laughed at the thought of my carrying this pregnancy to full term. He had said, "Of course, you should have this abortion and then recover from the blood clot and take care of the healthy children you already have. This is a risk you don't need to take."

My bishop retorted, "I don't believe you. He wouldn't say that. I'm going to call him." Then he left.

Sounding a bit hysterical, I asked my husband to call this man and tell him not to come see me again.

When my Relief Society president came to see me, she told me that she thought what I was planning to do was wrong. As she left, she said that she would be watching me. If I later had spiritual problems it would prove that she had been right about the wrongness of my decision to have an abortion. I have often thought of her watching and judging me.

Although a few of my friends listened helpfully, the entire decision-making process was, for the most part, a horrible ordeal. The abortion itself was nothing, and I've never felt bad about having it. What I do feel bad about is that at a time when I would have appreciated nurturing and support from spiritual leaders and friends, I got judgment, criticism, prejudicial advice, and rejection.

## The Adoptive Mother (excerpts)
Robin Zenger Baker
Boston, Massachusetts
1991 (vol. 16, no. 1)

Lately, I've been waking in the middle of the night thinking about—of all things—my feelings on abortion. The articles in the Fall 1990 issue of *Exponent II* on abortion (15.4) were enlightening, gripping, compelling, and have motivated me to analyze and commit my beliefs on the subject to paper. Part of my reason for writing is that my daughter, my sweet three-year-old adopted daughter, is a part of our family because someone had some serious qualms about abortion. Luckily for us, our daughter's birth parents or birth grandparents felt strongly enough that abortion was not the best option to be willing to endure social stigma, the physical rigors of pregnancy and birth, the mental and emotional heartache of bringing a baby into the world, who would not become an intimate part of their family.

I suppose if anyone should be anti-choice, I should be. And yet, after reading a number of descriptions written by women anguishing over whether they should abort a pregnancy, it is clear that many feel that they simply have no choice. They were willing to go to great lengths to terminate a pregnancy because, if they hadn't, they felt that they would lose something unbelievably precious to them: life as they had known it, the respect of others, the ability to cope with their future, a continuation of important relationships....

Having been pregnant once myself (eight months after our adopted daughter was born), I know that even when you're as delighted as you can possibly be to be expecting a baby, being pregnant is no small physical and emotional challenge. As excited as I was, I still felt moments of panic at the thought of raising two small babies only sixteen months apart while trying to finish the schooling that I was so close to completing. I felt trapped in a sense—even though I desperately wanted the child that was creating my "trap."

It's horrifying to imagine how women physically and emotionally unprepared to give birth or to raise a child must feel if forced to carry an unwanted child to term. Stories abound of women who feel so strongly that they must abort a baby that they are willing to pursue illegal, dangerous, traumatic medical avenues. It seems tragic to deny women so desperate to end a pregnancy the right to a safe, legal, affordable abortion. In fact, women's circumstances vary so drastically, it's difficult to see how a blanket policy can cover all contingencies....

What I have experienced, however, is that adoption doesn't have to feel like a cruel punishment. It doesn't have to occur with all the secrecy and mystery that would cause someone to feel like her flesh and blood were lost in the world, never to be seen or heard of again.... To some extent, I am advocating that people in a tough situation be willing to turn their pain into someone else's joy. That's clearly a lot to ask, but in the end, it may also bring a measure of satisfaction to those giving as well as those receiving. Hearing our story may help illustrate why I want to champion the cause of adoption.

I've been married nearly ten years now. We always wanted children, but after a few years, it became apparent that becoming pregnant was not going to occur in an automatic "wish it and it is" fashion. After four years of doctors and prayers and trying, we received a life-changing phone call one day. A friend knew of a child soon to be born.... About a month later, we learned that the baby could be ours if we wanted her to be. The birth mother, Lisa, had selected us for a number of reasons, including the fact that we were also LDS. We received a phone call from Lisa's attorney who wanted to know as much about us as we could tell him. Lisa called us next. She was excited to have found a good home for the baby and wanted us to know how glad she was that we would be taking the child. We chatted for a while about how thrilled we were. She told us a little bit about herself and shared her expectations that she would be having a little girl.

Two weeks later, we received a phone call to tell us that Lisa was in labor, four weeks earlier than we had expected. We took the first airplane we could catch to her state—loaded down with bottles, baby clothes, diapers, blankets, even a toy.

We arrived at the hospital just a few hours after Shannon was born. Our first stop was to meet Lisa, to hug her and thank her for this unbelievably precious gift. She was physically exhausted, doubtless feeling emotionally precarious, but looked glad to meet us. She was particularly impressed with my husband Rich and told us, the next day, how happy she was to be able to give her little baby a father, something she couldn't give Shannon herself.

Our next stop was to go see the baby in the nursery. We dressed in green hospital gowns, put masks over our faces; then the nurses brought us the most adorable baby anyone has ever seen.... The next day, we spent time with baby Shannon, Lisa, Lisa's sister, and some of the friends whom Lisa had made at the high school she had attended while she was living with foster parents. We heard about her pregnancy, all of us taking turns holding the baby and taking an album's worth of pictures.

We said goodbye to Lisa that afternoon, with hugs and tears. We thanked each other. She left the hospital with her sister—to continue her youth, to pursue her dreams, to try to return to normal life, to go to college eventually. She left that day, perhaps sadder than she'd ever been before, but perhaps also happy because she had met us and had been able to see what a miraculous thing she had done for us. We left the hospital that day with a new life—in more ways than one.

That was three years ago. Now our little Shannon is a feisty, delightful preschooler. We feel daily the blessing of what we call our "miracle child" in our lives. I wish I could fully describe Shannon's delightful personality—complete with perfect pitch; an uncanny ability to remember songs, names, events in her past; a dedication to all things beautiful and frilly, especially clothes; a vast heart that she shares by bestowing smiles and hugs with many whom she's befriended.

Of course, Shannon is also a normal three-year-old—obstinate and ornery at times. She does her share of whining to get what she wants, would eat only butterscotch for all meals if she could, and can get the most wide-eyed, gritty look on her face when she feels her brother needs greater discipline in his life. But every night at bedtime, she is reminded and clearly knows that she is our very favorite girl.

Since the day Shannon was born, we have kept in regular contact with her birth mother. We have written to each other many times. We nearly always include photographs of Shannon and describe how she's growing and the new funny things she's doing. In response, Lisa has sent letters and small gifts—a necklace, a stuffed animal, a book, a poem. She has expressed gratitude for knowing how Shannon is doing. When Shannon was two years old, we happened to be visiting the state where Lisa was living, and we suggested getting together. We wound up going to the zoo with Lisa and her brother one afternoon. I'll admit I was nervous about how that would work out, but it was clear that Lisa was more like a long-lost aunt than parent to Shannon. When Shannon's tummy hurt, she cried for Mommy—and reached for me....

I doubt that anyone would choose to put themselves in a position where they feel that they need to have an abortion. Unfortunately, it happens, in many circumstances, by accident. Because I can't know all of the circumstances in which people will find themselves, I echo the opinion of Linda Ellerbee: "I've said over and over that I am not for abortion, that no one is for abortion. I am for a woman's right and a man's right—I'm for your right to make your own hard choices in this world." But I desperately want those facing this tough choice to know that giving a child up for adoption doesn't need to be as terrible as might be imagined. The choice made by one young mother not to abort has blessed our lives immeasurably, and I believe that it has also blessed her life. Perhaps other lives will also be blessed by a choice for adoption rather than abortion.

## The Light's Still On—Spring 1991
Claudia Knight-Zimmer
Brockton, Massachusetts
1992 (vol. 17, no. 2)

Yellow ribbons, once tied into crisp bows, hang in dirty tatters from the antenna; the Christmas tree sits forlorn on the china cabinet, its needles, sparse and brown, sport bright yellow ornaments that look out of place; but three white candles still shine brightly every night on the sill of my living room window. Now that the newspapers and TV anchormen have declared the war over, I suppose that I should untie the ribbons, toss the tree, and turn out the lights, but for me the war isn't over yet. Jon Paul is still in Saudi Arabia.

I believe that our country needs to be militarily strong for peace. The military has been a part of my life from a very early age. The first memory I have of my father is the day we drove to Amarillo, Texas, to meet him when he returned from Germany after the occupation following World War II. As I was growing up, our home was home-away-from-home for local GIs.

GIs were considered the cream of the crop by my parents... men who were giving their time, talent, and energies so that I might grow up in freedom. I was taught that a military career was as high a calling as a doctor, a lawyer, or even a minister.

My children's father served in the Marines, and I was proud to be a military wife. When Dan, my oldest son, and later Jim, the middle of the three boys, decided to enter the Marine Corps, I felt that they had made good decisions. Jobs were hard to come by in northern Idaho, and the Marines offered them a way out. Several years ago, Jon Paul, my youngest, decided that his only hope of getting away from the drug scene was to join the Army. My husband, Tom, and I both encouraged him to enlist. We felt that the regimentation would be good for him. It was also a chance for him to finish school, to rebuild his self-esteem, and to get back on the right side of things. Even though I was very much aware of what had happened in Grenada and Panama, I still felt that, overall, military life was good.

On the other hand, I am peace loving... and very much anti-war. I pushed the two older boys in their stroller as I took part in walks for peace. Jon Paul grew up in a home where he was taught that we should work for peace, and that there is no place in our lives or our world for aggression and war. I made separate compartments in my mind for the military as a way of maintaining peace and for the military as a war machine.

From the time Bush started sending American troops into the Middle East, I knew that Dan would have to go. I did not like the idea but accepted his deployment as a given: He is a career Marine and a weapons specialist. Jim had been out of the Marines for several months and was living in Arizona with his wife and daughter; I wouldn't have to worry about him. Jon Paul was stationed in Germany, working in communications with the MPs; so I felt he was safe, too. On November 11, the whole situation changed. Jon Paul called to say that he was being sent to Saudi, and I was scared.

As more and more troops were sent in and the rumblings of war grew louder, the UN chose an ominous deadline for Iraq's withdrawal—January 15, Jon Paul's twenty-third birthday. I somehow muddled through the holidays; no Christmas spirit prevailed in our house, just a heavy feeling of impending doom. As the 15th drew near, I struggled with my fears, fears that Jon Paul would never get past his birthday. We talked several times as he was installing phones in bunkers and needed to test the lines. He laughed and teased me but let me know that he, too, was concerned. He said that he had two prayers: One was that he would come home safely, and the second was that he would not have to fire his weapon at anyone. The 15th passed quietly, but tension mounted as I waited for the proverbial other shoe to drop.

The evening of January 16 brought the news that the war was raging. The phone rang: It was Jim calling to say that he was going to re-enlist; he felt that he could not sit back while his two brothers were putting their lives on the line. I spent the night in front of the TV, crying and praying. Never had I felt so alone. Over the next few days, I lived with nightmares, afraid to watch TV, but also afraid not to. When I slept, it was with the lights on. The phone rang constantly, friends from across the country wanting to know if we had heard from the boys and to let us know that they cared.

The war wasn't even mentioned in the opening prayer of our sacrament meeting on Sunday, and when the high councilor spoke about how hard it is to have your children go off to college or on a mission, I had to leave the chapel. I felt that "alone" feeling all over again. As the war progressed, however, I found a wonderful network of support. There was a group of eight Quaker men and women who stood out on a corner in Newton, a town near where I work, every evening with their candles lit in prayer for peace. It did not matter what the weather was; their only concession was to change from candles to flashlights if it were raining. Several times, I stopped and talked with them; these eight caring people prayed for my sons while they stood out in the sleet, rain, and snow. There were the staff and students at the school where I work—yellow ribbons abounded and notes and calls reminded me how much they cared. There was my family who surrounded me with love.

But, there were some big silences that hurt—from my husband's family and our ward. One ward family called on a regular basis; my best friend in the ward also called, listened to my fears, and made sure that I did not sit around wallowing in self-pity. Other than that, *silence*.

A month after the war started, I was asked to speak in sacrament meeting and to talk about how I felt with two sons in Saudi. I interrupted a weekend retreat with my *Exponent* sisters in Maine to tell my ward of my fears, my faith, and my network of support that was so important. After the service, several people spoke with me or with Tom about the boys. Then, once again, absolute silence.

One of the worst times for me came when the eleven young Marines were killed near Khafji by "friendly fire." The uncertainty was horrible. About 3:30 A.M. the following morning, I stood in front of the TV as a CNN newscaster read off the names, finishing with "... and Daniel Walker," my oldest son's name. I thought my heart would stop. I managed to yell for Tom, and then the newscast cut to Dan's mother. The young Marine was Daniel B., not Daniel G. I felt as though a scud had landed in my backyard; this was much too close. As the day went on, many people called to see if I was O.K., to see how I was feeling. There was no sense of relief; I was glad it wasn't my Dan, but my heart ached for the other mother.

On the Wednesday before the ground war started, I got a call from Jon

Paul. "Mom, they said I need to make final arrangements. I don't want to be in Arlington or Massachusetts; will you take me home to Idaho? I want to be buried by Pop." Stark reality. Later that evening, Jim called. He had received a telegram telling him to report the next day to Camp Lejeune. All three boys were now involved. The ground war moved swiftly and, in just days, was declared a success.

For several weeks, we heard nothing from any of them. Then one by one the calls came; they were all O.K. Jon Paul said his prayers had been answered; he was dirty and tired but didn't get a scratch. Much more importantly, he had not even had to aim his weapon at anyone. What a contrast to Dan who told of no longer seeing enemy targets but of seeing the faces of those that were his targets.

Looking back over the past few months, I see the many changes that this war has brought into our lives. Jim and his wife Crissy have separated over his decision to re-enlist. Dan says that he feels much older than his twenty-seven years. I have some real resentment over a bishop, a home teacher, almost an entire ward that did not care enough to even call. I have put walls up with Tom's family.

But I have rediscovered old friends, developed new friendships, and realized how very precious my children are to me. I get a bit impatient with people who keep telling me that the war is over, that I need to put it behind me and get on with my life. Yes, Dan and Jim are home. For that I am extremely grateful, but ... Jon Paul, haven't you heard that the war is over? It is time to come home. I am leaving the light on for you.

## Editorial: Annus Horribilis
Sue Paxman and Jenny Atkinson
1994 (vol. 18, no. 3)

In her annual Christmas Day address to the Commonwealth in 1992, Queen Elizabeth II said, "Like many other families, we have lived through some difficult days this year; the prayers, understanding, and sympathy given to us by so many of you in good times and bad have lent us great support and encouragement ... as some of you may have heard me observe, it has indeed been a somber year." In fact, things got so bad for them that she referred to 1992 as *annus horribilis*.

Well, Sister Windsor, we now know how you must feel; 1993 was somber at best and *annus horribilis* at the worst for our Mormon family. And, if the difficulty that we have faced as we attempted to write this editorial is any indication, talking about the events of the past year is no easy task either. To avoid doing the writing, we cleaned the *Exponent* office, had lunch, read articles from the past to inspire us, read the excerpt from Gloria Steinem's latest book in the March issue of *Ms. Magazine*, sat around laughing over her essay exploring what Freudian psychology would have been if Freud's first name had been Phyllis, and finally decided to meet again to write when Jenny got back from Utah.

Jenny's back, our deadline is here, and we must somehow convey our view of this momentous year from where we sit as the group of women who, as Aileen Clyde puts it, "take care of *Exponent*." Part of the difficulty is caused by the fact that *Exponent* is often a barometer for how women in the Church are feeling, and we must find a way to reflect the spectrum of voices that we hear. Another part is that we here on the staff have had difficulty in sorting out how we feel, individually and collectively.

As the stories of disfellowshipment and excommunication began to circulate in the fall of 1993, it seemed that the first reaction by both *Exponent*'s readers and staff was to turn inward, to wonder what all of this activity meant in terms of our own individual relationships with our Church. As we started to speak, often tentatively, with friends about our personal reactions, we each learned that we were not the only ones who felt confused or worried or paranoid. In fact, these feelings of discomfort and dis-ease seemed to be reflected, on some level, throughout the political and religious spectrum of the Church. Recognizing that similarity of reaction though, we also realize that we must talk about our own experience in order to come to any place or kind of healing.

**From Jenny's perspective at almost twenty-five:** I grew up in a family of people who are committed to the Mormon Church. I remember feeling safe when I asked my parents questions about religious things that did not make sense to me. I knew that my questions did not imply that I was not committed in a larger sense to what the Church stood for the honesty, integrity, and love that our family read about in the life of Jesus throughout the New Testament and the Book of Mormon. On the contrary, I knew that they knew that my questions grew out of my desire to become more committed to a church that I loved. I grew up in a church that taught me that actions speak louder than words and that truth sets us free.

This fall, though, as I read what Church leaders as well as those who had been called in for courts had to say about the excommunications, I began to wonder. Suddenly, I did not feel safe speaking what I thought was truth, I felt that I might be judged on something I was thinking about in speech or in print rather than on my actions, my attempts to follow the example of Jesus by serving and loving others.

During this same time, a smart and feisty friend at BYU told me, "I'm not going to talk about what I think until after I've graduated. I can't take the risk of being kicked out of school." At that time and now, I understand her choice, but it saddens me to think of the lost conversations and discovery because of her need to censor herself in order to preserve herself. I have had time to think about the risks that she and I both perceive in light of our church's actions, and I have concluded, for the time being, that I face a greater risk by becoming part of the community of people who censor their thoughts, speech, and writing. So, I choose to face, with faith, whatever risk there is in doing what my family and my church have taught me.

**From Sue's perspective at almost fifty:** I had a friend in high school who said that he liked to bang his head against a wall, which he did on occasion, because it felt so good when he stopped. That, coupled with the grounded, solid feeling of having made it through almost half a century, pretty much sums up what I'm feeling at this moment—some relief because the pain-inducing activity has stopped, some anxiety that the lack of pain may lull me into apathy, and a strong sense that we will endure and that right will prevail. My heart and my support is with our sisters and brothers—dear friends—who were disfellowshipped or excommunicated last fall in Utah and the two more recently disciplined in Virginia and Massachusetts, and I feel some relief that, to my knowledge, those actions are not continuing to be taken. But I don't want anyone to begin the "banging of heads" again just to feel the relief when it stops.

I want—and somehow it is easier for menopausal, near-fifty women to say out loud what they want—the Church to be the "place of safety" spoken of in D&C 45:66. I also want more of us to follow Christ's example and be "full of patience, mercy, and long-suffering, quick to hear the cries" (Alma 9:26) of those around us.

I wish I could articulate fully how much I want these things and how certain that I am that if I work hard enough and talk long enough I will get them. You see, as Judy Duskhu pointed out to me a long time ago, this is my church, too. And because it is my church, I want the fear that grips the hearts of some of my sisters and brothers eliminated. I want each of us to use our free agency to build strong enough relationships with our Heavenly Father and Mother and our brother Jesus Christ to feel confident in our decision making powers. I want to follow the teachings and example of Christ and help to build His kingdom here on Earth without having to look over my shoulder to see who might be watching. And that's just what I'm going to do.

So, we agree, and in the words of a Baptist friend, we're just going to "keep on keepin' on." We plan to continue to use our God-given power as women in His church to: Do what is right; let the consequence follow.

*Postscript: On Tuesday, June 7, 1994, the* Boston Globe *ran an article under the headline "New Mormon Church leader urging reconciliation." Included in the story was a quote from President Howard W. Hunter: "To those who are hurt and struggling and afraid, we say let us stand with you and dry your tears.... To those who have transgressed or been offended, we say come back ... we offer comfort, hope, and encouragement to keep up the good fight." We join our new prophet in pleading for more compassion, forgiveness, and understanding within the Church.*[6]

## Women's War[7]
Shari Siebers Crall
Temecula, California
1995 (vol. 19, no. 1)

On Memorial Day, I unroll the paper and gaze at the usual photo of war veterans marching in parade on a sunny Southern California day. As I read on, it is not until I finish all twenty minutes of my small town newspaper that it hits me. On this Memorial Day, the paper is not filled with reminiscences of traditional soldiers, but warriors of a different sort.

Next to the front page photo, a story reports that an ex-wife and her five-year-old daughter have been shot and killed by their ex-husband/father. Turning the page, I read of a bride, shot dead in her white gown on her wedding day by a jealous ex-lover. It came as no surprise that a restraining order against him proved useless. Next, I read of "Sweething Barnard," age eighteen. Since she was five, her father had molested her sexually. Running away from home at sixteen, she attempted suicide several times and used alcohol and marijuana to numb the pain. The news release stated that she had finally checked herself into a mental institution and found seven other personalities residing within her.

There is more. Another page tells of Charles Campbell who is awaiting execution for three murders of revenge. The paper reports that he slashed the throats of Renae Wicklund, Barbara Hendrickson, and eight-year-old Shannah Wicklund, whom he nearly decapitated. He was mad at Wicklund about serving time for raping her and at Hendrickson for her testimony against him on that charge.

All in one paper, all in one day, Memorial Day. I sit and wonder, where are their memorials?

All of this has hit hard because our small town of 28,000 is mourning the loss of our first police officer killed in the line of duty. In the early hours

---

6. This editorial postscript was part of the original publication.
7. This essay won the Helen Candland Stark Essay Contest.

following Mother's Day, Officer Kent Hintergardt came into harm's way responding to neighbors' calls of a disturbance at an apartment building. Hintergardt arrived at the building and stopped a man in the parking lot. The man, Mark Kamaka, had his twelve-year-old son in the car. In front of his son, Kamaka shot the officer point blank in the head, killing Hintergardt, a young father whose wife was pregnant with their second child.

During the resulting commotion, a neighbor saw a little girl wandering in her pajamas. He approached her and the breathless six-year-old told him that her mommy was upstairs and wasn't moving. The neighbor followed and found that Officer Hintergardt was Kamaka's second victim. On her bedroom floor lay Allison Jacobs, single mother to little Brittany, her struggle futile against her one-time boyfriend's strangling hands.

There are more incidents, of course. We all know battle stories. Our neighbor down the street, our sister, ourselves. That is the point. I know a few veterans; I can think of two who saw combat; yet, in the same circle of my acquaintance, I know scores of women who have suffered violence at the hands of men, regular men who hold jobs and don't serve time unless they finally kill one of us. In my suburban, almost rural, setting, I know only two people who have been robbed and one whose car was stolen; yet, I have three women friends who have been raped.

As I read the paper that day, I thought back to another incident. After shopping at our local department store one day, I loaded three of my kids into our van. I noticed a couple parked directly in front of me, chatting, I thought. I saw nothing strange as I put my key into the ignition, although he was leaning in particularly close to her. We prepared to pull away when the woman opened her car door to get out. The man grabbed her belt and flung her back into the seat. As if in slow motion, I watched as the expression on her face turned from normal to surprise to oh-so-much humiliation. Stunned, I sat there. Eventually, both of them lit cigarettes and looked toward me. If nothing else, I was determined to remain a witness. They both mouthed,

"It's okay; it's okay."

It's okay? What's going on?

The bus stop where I and my neighboring housewives bring our kindergartners seems innocuous enough. In fact, it is lined with old soldiers. Four of the six suburban mothers waiting there are recovering from violence—physical, sexual, verbal—by fathers, stepfathers, uncles, teenage boys, fathers of friends, and a man whose children one of them babysat; all four of those women are Mormon. Some days, long-hidden landmines explode as we walk through the minefields laid in our youth.

At this daily gathering, we check on each other. If someone begins to cry or we realize that Bea is wearing the same thing she wore yesterday, and the day before, one of us goes over later with a flower or a poem. Chatting in the poignant dignity of survivors watching the parade pass on, like old soldiers in uniform, we wave to our smiling five-year-olds as the bus lurches forward.

Of course, there are no parades or uniforms for veterans of women's war. Not even a rally saying, "Give peace a chance."

Where I live gangs have yet to make a dent. You can go for a walk at 9:00 P.M., and ranchers, who never did, still don't lock their doors. Yet, it seems violence to women is inescapable. Besides Allison Jacobs, our lively town hall receptionist, Sally Gilbert, was shot dead by her boyfriend who then turned the gun on himself. Her memorial service was the first public gathering held at our brand new community recreation center. The same week, thirty-seven-year-old Sharon Maxwell was beaten to death with a hammer by a former boyfriend while her two small children slept in their nearby bedrooms.

I want to stop listing story after story, but I am compelled to tell their names, determined that somewhere their deaths will be counted. Surely these women have sacrificed their lives in as senseless a quagmire as any found on a battlefield.

Don't think it won't touch you. Don't think it isn't touching you now. Statistics claim one in three women is sexually abused by the time she is eighteen. Think of three women you know: count down three women in the row in front of you at church; your daughter and her two best friends; or three female co-workers. Chances are, no matter how sheltered their circumstances, one of them has fought this war.

Maybe someday we'll build a memorial to the women whose lives were lost before we won the battle to make the world safe for our daughters to grow up in. Last Memorial Day, the body count in my local paper stood at six dead and Sweething Barnard, who just wishes she was.

## Editorial: First Hands and Backs, Now Feet and Voices
Sue Paxman
Lexington, Massachusetts
1996 (vol. 19, no. 4)

During my years in the Church, I have often heard light, slightly ironic, comical references to Mormon women playing such roles as the backs and hands with which the work of the Church is accomplished or the neck that turns the head [of the house—her husband]. And I know that, at times, I have even participated in the almost conspiratorial smiling and nodding of heads that sometimes accompanies such references to jokes based on our common experience. I believe that the time is here for this joke to be over.

We women of the Mormon Church have much more to contribute than just our behind-the-scenes support. We want to use our voices to help make the organizational and cultural decisions that create and influence the "dailiness" of our lives in the Church structure. To participate fully in the building of the Kingdom of God, we need to strengthen our voices as we speak truth and bear witness, and then our voices need to be accepted and our experience incorporated into the fabric of our culture.

I have just reread the editorials of *Exponent II*'s former editors from the last three issues (19.1, Claudia Bushman; 19.2, Nancy T. Dredge; and 19.3, Susan Howe). By reading them one right after the other, I came to understand the evolution and progression of the women of the Church in a new way. Our voices are getting stronger; however, the acceptance of and respect for what we have to say is not increasing at the same rate.

*Exponent II* began as a place where Mormon women could exchange everything from their latest insights and recipes to their testimonies and spiritual experiences. Over the years and under the nurturing guidance of the editors and staff, the publication has developed a stronger voice in its Mormon world as the voices of those who write have gotten stronger.

Together, we have supported each other through such difficult discussions as depression, emotional and physical/sexual abuse, drug and alcohol abuse, the effects of unrighteous dominion, abortion, being single in a married church, infertility. We have talked honestly and from our own experience about many topics that our culture has previously considered off limits, sometimes even a threat to testimonies.

What we have learned in the speaking is that we have ideas to contribute, experiences from which others can learn, opinions worth being heard, and spiritual gifts that bless others as well as ourselves. And, through it all, we continue to bear witness to the principles that sustain us and do all we can to shoulder each other's burdens by listening to and believing each other's stories.

For some of us, *Exponent II* has been the only place in our Mormon world in which we felt safe enough to be honest and open. For others of us, our culture's efforts to maintain the status quo as the only way to keep our Mormon world safe and comfortable has meant everything through the spectrum from ignoring us when we speak to excommunicating us so that we cannot speak.

But from what I am hearing and reading, particularly in a number of the essays in this issue, those days will soon be over. We are beginning to speak with strength and clarity wherever we find ourselves. We are exploring who we are, not just the roles that we are asked to play, and we are insisting that we be heard and recognized for who we are.

Unfortunately for our community, when we are not heard or recognized, some of us seem to have only one last option. In increasing numbers, we—particularly those of us in our late teens and twenties—are voting with our feet. We are leaving, choosing not to participate in a system that does not encourage us to participate fully, that does not validate us by respecting what we have to offer, or that does not extend to us the respect that we are finding elsewhere.

I believe that this movement away is a terrible loss, a loss that can be avoided. First, we need to recognize and respect the diversity and breadth of Mormon women's experience. Relegating us to one or two acceptable roles and refusing to allow us to participate in the decision-making bodies of the Church keeps us "as little children" in a humiliating—not a humble—way. How can we be expected to negate our own experiences, giving up our self-esteem and self-respect, by continually sitting and waiting to be told what to do and when by those "in authority" over us? There are times and places for all of the children of God to be His obedient servants, to be subservient to His authority; no one should expect that being woman means always being obedient and subservient to everyone else.

Second, to make a place for women's voices, we need to rid our culture of what appears to be the prevailing feeling about those who speak up, who ask questions, or who question a decision or policy: The Church is true; love it or leave it. Blind, arbitrary acceptance does not enhance personal growth or access to personal revelation; raising and resolving personal questions does. Our assuming that those who question are somehow less than faithful is destructive to each of us as well as to our community of Saints. I believe that by being willing to allow each other to ask the questions and seek the answers together we can make the Kingdom of God progress.

And last, we need to change our perspective and to listen. We have much to learn from the voices of Mormon women, lessons about—among many others—relationship building, the true love of Christ, the pain and rewards of solitude, the joys of repentance and forgiveness, the struggle that is compromise, the strength of collaboration, the exaltation in steadfastness. Asking so many of us to remain silent about the most important aspects of our lives is creating a sickness that can only be healed by moving away from the source. We cannot afford to lose these voices, the lessons that they teach, and the witnesses that they bear.

*Exponent II* will continue to make a place for us to share what we know and believe, to speak honestly from our own experience; however, I believe that we need to ask, even insist, that we be able to do the same in our Relief Society meetings, in our sacrament meeting talks, in our bishop's interviews, in our ward and stake councils. I believe that as Mormon women we understand that we are responsible for ourselves and our salvations, but we also understand that taking that responsibility requires that our voices be heard as we speak about how our lives are lived here on earth.

## Editorial: Embracing All of Our Sisters and Brothers
Judy Dushku
Watertown, Massachusetts
1996 (vol. 20, no. 1)

Last fall in testimony meeting, an otherwise lovely sister told three jokes about gay people, and most of the congregation laughed out loud. The man sitting next to me was gay. He had not been to church for several years, but that Sunday his sister and her family were visiting from California and they had apparently decided to come together. As the gay jokes were being told, this large family sat silently and solemnly, staring straight ahead. Gratefully, the bishop and his wife rushed up to them after the meeting to try to encourage each one, especially the teenagers, to stay for Sunday School and to try to help them find the right classes, but the visiting family explained that they had decided to leave. My daughter and I also tried to find words to make them know that they were welcome in our ward, but what had happened had already conveyed an entirely different message.

During that same meeting, I had been aware of four ward members with grown, gay children or siblings. One woman has spoken to me about her Salt Lake family trying to support her lesbian sister as she struggles to stay active in the Church; she is so frequently bombarded with hostile remarks made either directly to her or within her earshot or at or about someone else who is gay.

"It is so difficult," my friend says. "The whole family suffers every time someone says something unkind. My family has always been so active, but this cruelty is taking its toll on the level of involvement of several of my sisters and brothers. We are all very close, and my sister's unhappiness and people's rejection of her is killing them."

Another couple keeps their son's gayness a secret to all but a few and have shed many tears over his being rejected in his own ward in another part of the country. Another friend, whose son was excommunicated after serving a mission, is secretive and somber. Her son is gay and also lives far away and resents her staying active in the Church. The fourth ward member's sister divorced her gay husband, and the stories that he tells about their family's saga since the divorce and the revelation of the husband's gayness are ugly. It seems that the reactions in the congregations of each of his family members have also affected the whole family. They have gone from absolutely being a part of the mainstream of the Church for generations to feeling somehow on the outskirts . . . somehow lesser beings who are viewed with suspicion. He commented that "we have emphatically told other Mormon families whom we know who have gay members to lie because the information will take a terrible toll."

Now, because my ward is an average ward, I know that these stories are not unusual. In fact, there may be other members of my own ward with similar stories that I don't know about. The point is if this many people are hurting over these kinds of experiences in my ward, brothers and sisters in your wards are hurting, too, for the same reasons. To what end? Not one of my ward friends to whom I have talked believes that the hostility and rejection poured out by others on their gay family members has contributed anything positive to anyone's life—in or out of their family. In fact, they can't imagine a circumstance under which a good purpose could be served by such actions. They also all admit that they themselves held different views before they knew that someone in their family was gay but that now they are clear and firm—no good is served by rejection and hostility. No one changes; people only suffer.

Where I live people don't know a lot about Mormons. They know the Tabernacle Choir, the Utah Jazz, Laurel Thatcher Ulrich, and Mitt Romney. They have read recently in *The Wall Street Journal* that Mormons often do well in business because they speak many languages. They have also read that there was opposition to the proposed temple in Nashville. They have nearly all met a missionary. And now, they have seen the pictures of angry Utah Mormon demonstrators calling gay people in Utah names and have read about the Salt Lake community publicly debating the issue of gay/straight clubs in the local high schools. Some of my neighbors are telling me that now they know us for who we really are. I could cry.

They have forgotten all the tender TV spots about loving families and affectionate relationships and how impressed they were during the "Sixty Minutes" interviews by the genuineness of President Hinckley and others. They are now questioning the honesty of that program because of what has so recently been publicized about Utah's fight against gays. The beautiful messages so many people have tried so hard to get out to the world are being drowned out for the first time by the talk about this hate and meanness.

My neighbors are asking me about what they see as hypocrisy in the Church. In a way, the Utah school committee and legislative fights are not ours; Utah *is* far away. But, the actions in Utah affect the image of Mormons all over the world. These anti-gay demonstrations will set back our missionary work and community relations everywhere. It is sad; and, again, to what end?

Last month, the Boston newspapers carried a story about a gay teacher in the high school from which my son Ben graduated. Polly Attwood is a favorite and is an inspiration to many students, most of whom are now rallying in support of her and of the high school, both of which are being sued. A couple is claiming that because Polly is a lesbian their daughter suffered emotional damage because four years ago she was a student in Polly's class. The school administration has supported Polly. When she first complained, they had made every effort to place her in another class, but the family opted to take her out of school. No other student has made such a complaint about Polly; she has a fine reputation and has been a fine example of civic responsibility and community service for her students for years. My family knows her partner, as well, because she has been a pastor and a colleague of mine at the university where I teach.

Polly and her partner called me recently to say that their lawyers have discovered that the campaign against her is being organized outside the state by anti-gay groups who are targeting gay teachers all over the United States. Allegedly, some of the group leaders live in Utah. The women wanted to know if I knew anything about this. They asked me because I am the only Mormon they know. I explained to them that I am a locally active Mormon who, I assured them, plays no role in any anti-gay campaign to ruin careers of fine teachers. I also told them that I could speak for my women friends who are also active Mormons and who work on our newspaper, which tries to promote the kind of Mormonism that is love-based and committed to a policy of welcoming all who yearn to join with us in the worship of the Savior.

What else can we say when we are suddenly called to account for the excesses of people who appear to act in our name far away and without our consent or counsel? It seems quite simple, I guess, and probably personally strengthening in the long run: we must rely on our own light and the truth that we receive through our own relationship with the Lord. I will never defend any behaviors or actions of which I don't approve and that seemingly use the name of the Mormon Church, especially when those actions are nasty and violent and motivated by hateful rage.

From time to time our ward, like yours, fasts for the missionaries. This last two months that effort seems to be a contradiction: We fast for the missionaries; yet, the papers are filled with news of gay-bashing Mormons in Utah saying the kinds of things that would drive anyone seeking the gospel of peace and love away from us as fast as it takes a missionary to ring a doorbell. Whenever we are invited to fast for the missionaries, I have decided to fast and pray for an end to this kind of hatefulness; I am convinced that approach will be twice as effective.

At *Exponent's* annual summer reunions, sisters from all over the country have often unburdened themselves by telling their stories of being rejected by people in the wards where they have spent their lives in activity and service. The causes—a gay son or lesbian daughter; a gay husband; their own discovering that they themselves are gay. The reactions—no support, no embracing of their families; no expressions of love. And, to what end? These women come to the reunions hoping and expecting to be embraced. And they are, but they often have to go home to more judgment and recrimination. Some of us who are involved in the *Exponent* effort have developed a certain sensitivity to the issues of living with gay family members in the Mormon Church. Because we have hope that we have offered ourselves as supporters of members in all their diversity. It is now expected of us to be genuinely inclusive, and I feel that this embracing of any members who have struggles should be the normal role of home wards and visiting and home teachers.

And, of course, I feel that this embracing is best accomplished when people feel free to openly discuss their lives with each other. With that in mind, we print these articles about homosexuality in this issue of *Exponent*. We make no claim to have covered every experience of gayness in the Mormon community. As we reviewed the articles that have been submitted, we realized that there are obvious as well as less obvious gaps.... May these gaps not send a message that some things cannot be said, cannot be discussed. May they rather invite responses and more sharing.

*The following three selections come from the Sisters Speak and Sisters Help columns.*

## Affirmation and Supporting Mormon Lesbians
Ina Mae Murri
former international coordinator for Affirmation/Gay & Lesbian Mormons
San Francisco, CA
Winter 1987 (vol. 13, no. 2)

In the past eight years, I have been active in Affirmation, and I have also tried to organize a separate support group for Mormon lesbians. In that time, I have met, written to, and read of the experiences of hundreds of Mormon lesbians. When most people think of homosexuals, they think of gay men. Because women are often ignored or neglected, relegated to a role of mother and sexual partner of men, the problems they experience are not thought to be serious. When homosexuality is thought to be a problem in Mormonism, it is the men, the priesthood holders, who get the attention. The instructions to bishops for counseling homosexuals has one line about women.

Since Affirmation was established, we have dealt with gay men and lesbians, many of whom have been married. We have dealt with some who are still married trying to find a solution that will work for all. We've met and counseled with children, parents, siblings, friends. In recent years, we have had some dialogue with local bishops and stake presidents and some LDS professionals in counseling and psychology. Our experience has shown that there is a great deal of heartache but also a great deal of love in families. Many wish to stay in the Church, but there is also bitterness on the part of those who resent the treatment that they have received.

There are thousands of stories to be told.... Hopefully, with more discussions, more *Sunstone*s, more *Exponent II*s willing to address this subject, some of the fear, repulsion, and heartache will end. We will be found to be just like all the rest of Mormondom—some strong, some weak, some faithful, some lax, some spiritual, some active, some inactive. We cover the gamut of the membership of the Church.

As for myself, I am the eighth of nine children. My parents were married in the temple. I grew up in southern Idaho. I was very active as I grew up. I married an inactive, but we divorced after I rediscovered my love for women. I have one son. I have remained a Mormon in thought if not in activity. I have a great concern for my brothers and sisters who are struggling with their sexuality and the Church.

It is a great struggle to be called sinners when what we want is to love and be loved; to have our love out in the open; to have acceptance from our families, friends and, yes, from the Church. Maybe by telling our stories, by sharing our lives with you, our friends, all of us can come to a better understanding and can begin to really be brothers and sisters in the gospel.

## Living With Disabilities (excerpts)
Joan D. Groesbeck
Pasadena, California
1987 (vol. 14, no. 1)

I certainly appreciated the articles in the last *Exponent* (13.4) written by parents of handicapped children because I have a severely-disabled five-year-old granddaughter; however, I was disappointed that there were no responses to your request from people who were themselves disabled or handicapped. Perhaps many with disabilities feel that they might seem to be a "poor me" complainer. Perhaps they had neither the health nor energy to respond at that time. This is my own belated response to that request.

My personal disability is *systemic lupus erythematosus*, commonly known as *lupus* for obvious reasons! My chief reason for writing is that many know little or nothing about the disease, and as my own case of lupus went undiagnosed for ten years, I want to "spread the word" in hopes that other people with lupus may avoid a similar experience....

Lupus is an inflammatory disease caused by abnormal over-activity of the immune system. Antibodies that normally defend healthy body cells instead attack healthy body cells. The disease has been misdiagnosed and misunderstood for years. Its course is unpredictable and sometimes goes into remission, only to flare up again for no apparent reason. Extreme weakness, extreme fatigue, chronic low-grade fevers, achy or swollen joints, and painful muscles are common symptoms. Another symptom is a "butterfly rash" over the nose, similar to the rash of *discoid erythematosus* that affects only the skin. I myself originally thought that I was repeatedly coming down with the flu.

At present, there are only theories as to the cause of lupus, and there is no known cure. Treatment consists of confinement to bed, anti-inflammatory drugs, and—in some cases—doses of cortisone. A minimal cortisone dosage has helped me greatly with only minimal side effects.

As to the emotional effects of this disease, I must admit that I am not a "good" patient, and I sometimes feel great rage that my body, not my mind, ultimately controls my ability to function. I should also state that I am slowly, very slowly, learning more about such virtues as patience, faith, and humility. Living with this problem for nineteen years has found me growing into having more empathy and insight for other people, whatever their problems.

My biggest blessing is the total support that my husband, family, and friends give me. Emotional support for lupus patients is vital, and if one does not have this support, it must be sought....

## On Learning to Recognize Spousal Abuse (excerpts)
Dennis Lythgoe
A bishop for the second time in Hingham, Massachusetts
1988 (vol. 14, no. 3)

... But with all of my interest in women's issues and with my history of feeling like a real advocate for enhancing the influence in the Church and the respect for women, too—for some incredible reason, the thought barely surfaced in my mind that there might be, either in my ward or in the Church as a whole, cases of spouse abuse. Church leaders have occasionally given rather impressive sermons about the need for couples to cultivate loving relationships. One of the more notable talks was Gordon B. Hinckley's "Cornerstones of a Happy Home," delivered in 1984, in which he said to men: "If you are guilty of demeaning behavior towards your wife, if you are prone to dictate and exercise authority over her, if you are selfish and brutal in your actions in the home, then stop it! Repent!"

As direct as that advice sounds, it was not couched in terms like "spouse abuse," and bishops all over the Church were probably less likely to detect the ultimate meaning of "controlling relationships." At least that was my problem—until very recently. In my second tenure as a bishop, I observed disturbing signs of the need to control in several men as they related unsuccessfully to their wives. And yet, in none of these cases did the wife come to me and complain, nor did any of them suggest, even in veiled terms, that the husband might be guilty of abusive behavior. Nevertheless, I thought about the possibility for the first time.

Then I was invited to attend a session sponsored by *Exponent II* dealing with the topic of spouse abuse. Byron Ray was in attendance, representing the Church's Social Services program. The speaker was Sharon Fleishacher, who works with abused women through the Women's Protective Services program in Framingham, Massachusetts. She was very experienced and highly effective in presenting her message, which was that many more women suffer abuse than any of us would have suspected and that the signs visible to those outside the marriage are often subtle.

As she talked, I could picture several women whom I had counseled—women, for instance, who constantly looked at their watches and who will leave a meeting or a conversation abruptly in order to keep a deadline. This type of behavior illustrates one of the subtle signs that she is being controlled. It was important for me to learn that verbal abuse is, in fact, spouse abuse and that verbal abuse often leads to physical abuse and even more violent behavior. It was also evident that even men who subscribe to religious values may be victimized by their own family backgrounds and/or certain psychological problems that will lead them to spouse abuse.

I asked Sharon Fleishacher many questions that evening and stayed afterward to talk to her about specific but unnamed cases. I invited her to come and speak to the bishops and Relief Society presidents of our stake and share her expertise with a group of Mormon leaders. She was happy to oblige and gave an equally convincing presentation to them; they reacted much as I had as they focused in their minds on people they suspected of suffering spouse abuse in their own wards. Afterwards, the Relief Society president of my ward invited Sharon to come to an evening Relief Society meeting to discuss the same issue, and several women at that meeting remained following the meeting to discuss the problem in greater depth. It was evident that a nerve had been touched in our ward and stake.

Since then I have had occasion to assist some members of the Church in securing the type of counseling that we hope will help them with their problem relating to spouse abuse. It is still too early in the game to judge whether I or leaders in our stake will be more effective at dealing with this problem in the future, but at least we have been awakened to its existence, and we recognize its seriousness. All of us now see it as that great sleeping problem that may be present even if initial problems seem only superficial....

EXPONENT II VOL. 21, NO. 2

Exponent II Vol. 22, No. 2

# UNIT 3: 1997–2009

xponent II Vol. 22, No. 3

EXPONENT II
Vol. 24, No. 4   SUMMER 2001

## Introduction by Heather Sundahl

When I arrived in the Boston area in 1996, the first person to welcome me in my congregation was Judy Dushku. She had been tasked with writing short intros of the fall's new arrivals. Two minutes into the call, we connected. *You've been to Beijing?* I've *been to Beijing! You're a feminist?* I'm *a feminist!* Forty minutes later, when she asked if I wanted to be part of a locally founded Mormon feminist organization, I felt like a bachelorette being handed a rose. The next week, Linda Hoffman Kimball took me thrift shopping. Within the month, Robin Baker invited me to dinner. I met the board when I was invited to a mini retreat in Rhode Island—Linda Andrews driving me both ways. Shortly after, Jenny Atkinson asked me to join the reader's committee. These women were mentors and friends, tour guides, helping me find work and navigate being a grad school wife about to have her first baby. I was desperate for intellectual stimulation, connection, and an outlet for writing.

A year later, Atkinson became editor in chief. Though her tenure was short-lived, she made an impact. Having shadowed longtime editor Sue Booth-Forbes, she hit the ground running and focused energy on recruiting younger women to Exponent. Perhaps as the oldest of nine, or because she worked for a company that is all about mentoring, Atkinson knew how to gauge people's strengths and could give critical feedback in ways that instilled confidence while also expecting excellence. And though many of us said "yes" to Exponent because of Atkinson, she facilitated excitement that kept people committed, even after she left for an out-of-state job. In short, Atkinson was instrumental in altering the staff's age demographic at a time when growth was critical.

In March 2000, two weeks after I turned thirty—and six weeks after the birth of my second child—Nancy Dredge phoned to offer me an associate editor role.[1] I was shocked and flattered—I wasn't sure Dredge even knew who I was (fun fact: she didn't). I told her I had a nursing infant, Georgia, who I'd need to bring to meetings. "No problem," she replied. "We do some of our best work with babies in our laps." I had to accept, despite my overwhelm and general cluelessness. This was Exponent, and I was all in.

Dredge, who had served as *Exponent II*'s second editor from 1975–1981, took over "temporarily" for Atkinson ... and served for the next nine years. Dredge embraced Atkinson's push to recruit younger women, with twenty-somethings Kate Holbrook, Mikelle Fisher Eastley, and Kimberly Burnett also serving tenures as associate editors. One of Dredge's legacies is her emphasis on training a new generation of women to lead—"Generation Ex," if

---

1. Over the years, the editor job was often split into editor in chief and managing editor with clearly delineated roles, with the managing editor taking on more administrative tasks. Other editors like Dredge had "associate editors" who took turns curating issues at Dredge's request.

you will—to invest in and grow the organization. In her editorial, "Something Old, Something New," she celebrates that the paper had "not lost the Mary Bradfords, Claudia Bushmans, Karen Rosenbaums, Emma Lou Thaynes, and Sue Booth-Forbeses. However, their work has now been wonderfully 'added upon' by the Mary Johnstons, Linda Kimballs, Diane Browns, Victoria Grovers, Pandora Brewers, Heather Sundahls, Laurel Madsens, Kate Holbrooks, and Dana Haights, to name but a very few." Dredge celebrated the blend of old and new.

Like every *Exponent II* editor, Dredge got pushback for being both too bold and too timid. In a 2006 editorial, she wrote that an adult daughter of an Exponent board member observed that "Exponent has lost some of its old edginess. Her comment made me smile. For one thing, whether we have been too 'out there' or not 'out there enough' has been a debate from Day 1 of Exponent's existence." Topics were not chosen to shock or to placate. Most issues were an eclectic blend of submissions faxed, mailed, and emailed in. Sometimes, a theme emerged in the zeitgeist and coalesced naturally. Other times we (and I can now say "we," since I joined the magazine staff by this point) solicited essays, poetry, and art that focused on a topic, such as being single in a married church, pornography struggles, work and career, the art of quilting, global saints, blended families, and aging. Dredge also knew the power of guest-edited issues. Not only did it give us a respite from production, but it deepened ties to other Mormon women's groups, like the Midwest Pilgrims and the Beacon Heights Writer's Group in Salt Lake. And sometimes it created new bonds that would exponentially enhance the organization, such as the guest issue from Southern California that led to the creation of the blog in 2006.

An evergreen topic, *Exponent II* approached grappling with motherhood from many angles. Judith Curtis shares the wonder of gestation and childbirth in her poem, "Holding My Grandchild, Come to Land this Morning," capturing the otherworldliness of an infant and the love that awaits. In her heartbreaking and gorgeous poem "Encircling," Kylie Nielson Turley takes on what happens in miscarriage, a subject with which many women know deeply but few dare speak of publicly. Turley writes of bleeding on the floor and being embarrassed to call for help, "Unsure about this intimacy. So physical / This process. My body shared, then not." In my editorial "Cap of Many Colors," I explore what it means to be not just unexcited about a pregnancy but deeply depressed. I felt as if I had failed some ultimate test of my faith and sex, like I was in danger of losing my "motherhood card." If my crime was depression about an unexpected pregnancy, in her contest-winning essay, "Minus Motherhood," Karen Rosenbaum's was being happy about remaining child-free. She explores the benefits of not having children without judgment for herself or those who make different decisions. She embraces her life circumstances and pushes back against anyone who assumes she cannot possibly be happy about it. When it comes to processing motherhood, *Exponent II* has no prescriptions. Each writer presents and interprets her lived experience as she sees fit.

Like Rosenbaum, many of our selected essays not only explore but celebrate what it means to be "off script" from the typical narrative. An original blogger, Sandra Lee refuses to bemoan or apologize for being single. In her blog post, "Staking My Claim, Claiming My Stake: Mid-Singles," republished in the "Best of the Blog" magazine issue, Lee posits that "singlehood is not a punishment, a condemnation or a cruel joke. It's just a fact of some lives, and mine in particular at this point in time." Lee then explores how her stake seems unsure of how to best serve and utilize the mid-singles, with Lee coming up with practical and insightful solutions. In "The Stump's Last Stand: The Giving Tree," Julie Hemming Savage challenges the idea that endless sacrifice is woman's highest calling. She writes, "It is no coincidence that the giving tree is female." Savage advocates for healthy boundaries, equity in decision-making and resources, and sacrifice where all family members participate, not just mothers.

Fleshing out her Exponent retreat workshop, "Personal Revelation in an Authoritarian Church—Balance of Power or Detente," E. Victoria Grover provides a model for developing and leaning into one's personal authority. She gives specific questions we can ask ourselves that help us lean into our power without attempting to dismiss others when our belonging is questioned. When Linda Hoffman Kimball interviewed the legendary Cathy Stokes—a Chicago-based co-founder of Midwest Pilgrims—we also get glimpses into not "fitting in" regarding race, gender, and religious background and how one can claim space and assert belonging. Stokes says, "Let's stop for a minute to think about this whole question of 'do I fit?' Whether or not I fit has never been an issue. That's not a question that I ask myself. The issue is 'Do I want to be here?' and how do I help these people 'fit' with me?" For Stokes, there is power in claiming your place.

Sylvia Cabus is another woman pushing against the script. Long before "white feminism" was a label, Cabus, a Filipina-American, would gently but firmly draw attention to the lack of BIPOC representation at the retreat or on the board, causing us to acknowledge the ways we created space for differences in feminism, Mormonism, and even sexuality, but did so inadequately for race. True to form, in her essay, "From Victoria Secret to Beehive Clothing," Cabus tackles the previously taboo topic of LDS underwear, aka "garments"—a subject that Claudia Bushman forbade Carrel Sheldon from taking on back in the day. With her characteristic irreverence and insight, she writes of transitioning from zebra print bras and panties to the extremely modest garments worn by those who take on temple covenants. Cabus shows how she adopted her new religion, undies and all, while never surrendering herself. Her last line perfectly captures her devotion and humor: "I feel naked without them, I am naked without them."

The world shifted during the second year of Dredge's editorship on September 11, 2001. Linda Hoffman Kimball wrestles with the impact of 9/11 as she attempts to write about Christmas for her column "Goodness Gracious." While there is no escaping the sorrow that shrouded the US, Kimball observes this event has given us "rapt attention to one another's existence." That kind of connectedness is the hallmark of Ann Stone's writing. Stone was a founding member of the Midwest Pilgrims, a frequent *Exponent II* contributor, and a glorious keynote speaker. In her poem, "Period," she shares how her mother's quilting bee reacted to the news of her first menses, wrapping her in one of their creations: "Double wedding rings billow overhead as the women incant their secrets, cover and enfold me." After receiving a cancer diagnosis that would eventually claim her, Stone lays herself bare in the poem "Love Making." Her losses, physical and emotional, pile up like the hair collecting "in the sink enough to clog a sewer pipe."

Loss is also a theme in the poem "Dress," by blogger Brooke Jones. A woman unearths an old sewing project, only to discover that her memory of the carefully stitched collar and tucks do not correspond with the unfinished fabric in her hands. Past and present are misaligned; memory cannot be trusted. In "As Regards Touching," Kate Holbrook and her mother dress her grandmother Belle's body in preparation for the funeral. The essay tenderly explores how she and her grandmother cared for each other over the years, with Kate washing her grandmother's feet when she could not: "Not long into my task, I was embraced by a feeling of holiness. I felt that God was pleased with my small service and that this washing was, in some sense, outside of time, echoing through the ages." When Holbrook passed away in 2022, her mother once again took up the task of dressing the body and noted how her daughter's flesh looked so like Belle's as she came to die.

"In the Shadow of His Wings," blogger Deborah Farmer Kris recounts her interactions with a wounded fourth grader and the friendship that emerges from Kris's tender ministrations. Kris can sense the girl's divinity: "I felt a force from Elsewhere, felt more love than my body could hold, as if God wanted to touch her for a just moment in this lonely world and my lap was the nearest conduit." In "Known to Your Bones: Living in the Company of Women," Pandora Brewer unfolds her years-long initiation into female friendship. In the beginning, Brewer reflects that "community is a concept that I have circled cautiously through the years, sniffing at, wrinkling my nose, coming close and then backing off." And through the small transformations of shared vulnerabilities and radical acceptance, Brewer arrives at a place where she believes that however fulfilling marriage or mothering relationships may be, "there is no substitute for being known down to your bones, of standing by yourself, circled by women, visible, palpable, blessed."

Brewer's sentence captures perfectly the sensations I had when I was first welcomed into the Exponent circle, which I feel again and again at retreats, in long email chats on the blog backlist, in late-night Marco Polos, and on cross-country phone calls with founders now in their 80s—who I still can't quite believe know who I am. But they do. And because of these women, I know who I am, too.

## Known to Your Bones: Living in the Company of Women
Pandora Brewer
Winter 1999 (vol. 22, no. 2)

Last summer I went to the Exponent retreat as part of an entourage, five of us, each taking turns being the celebrity around which the others fussed. We decided on a cabin and immediately pushed our wobbly cots together so that all our voices were within earshot, piling duffels and sleeping bags and hanging towels to establish our territory. But it didn't seem enough of a mark so we created a shrine to ourselves in a grotto between cross beams: a flowered bikini top consisting of two tiny breastless triangles and some string, an X-files magazine, the first page of a screenplay, a cigarette, a black and white self-photograph from England, and a rainbow sticker with a metallic unicorn head. Quirks, scandals, triumphs—this collection represented something tangible about the depth of our intimacy, each of us knew the story behind the offerings, each of us knew the story behind the woman.

At dinner a young woman sat down at our table and asked us about our friendship. "I've never seen women like this," she marveled, "How did you meet? How did you become so close? How does a community like this happen?" We were boastful and silly and came up with some sort of dinner table answer, but her questions have echoed in my mind over the past months with exquisite irony. Surrounded by this group, this company of women I've known for years, I related to this earnest outsider with more empathy than she imagined. How did I get here? How did I find myself hypothesizing about gathering and sharing? What do I know about formulas and philosophies when it all still seems so miraculous and new? Inventing pen names at 3:00 AM, impersonating Joan Baez at night by the pond in front of an adoring audience of four, praying with joined hands, shining the flashlight beam along the path, noticing that every face in the firelight has the most beautiful features, having someone brush your hair. I see myself with these women from the inside out—that soul, heart, gut part of me that only hackneyed words can describe reaches out and grips their soul, heart, gut part with a chemical, catalytic connection that feels like sex and baptism and ice cream, only better.

How did I get here? If I had been able to steer her away from the panel theatrics of the dinner table last summer, I could have answered the young woman by showing her another shrine. This one also has relics: snapshots, bits of paper and odd objects. Community is a concept that I have circled cautiously through the years, sniffing at, wrinkling my nose, coming close and then backing off. But I have kept the loot from my forays into friendship and association—pictures and people I remember—and I gloat over them reverently, carefully delineating the details in the album of my imagination. I did not easily join the women that I love, it happened over time; a tiny need expressed and fulfilled, a minor insight blossoming to an epiphany.

The first image on display is expository, the caterpillar stage, the establishing shot. When I was about fifteen I was banished from Thanksgiving. I must have contradicted my mother or made a crack about the overcooked turkey because my dad reacted with characteristic indignation and sent me to my room for the rest of the day. I cried a little bit, slept, wrote a poem about how misunderstood I was and then after everyone was asleep, crept downstairs and watched old movies all night. I also ate an entire apple pie, crouched on the floor before the glowing light of the TV.

There was a duality in my life that was cinematic to extreme. I went through the motions of being a "new kid" or a "smart kid" at school or "the oldest" or "the teenager" at home, acting out any label I was dubbed in public and then harboring a vital and lush inner life when alone. I spoke elaborate stories aloud, heard music in the background when I walked, and lived everything worth living vicariously through books and film. My community was my insular family, one or two English class buddies, and a world of literary saints, heroes, and Woody Allen one-liners. I was arrogant and envious towards the gaggles of girls that hung close and giggled without my knowing why. They were obviously shallow and scared to be alone. I had the ultimate capacity for being by myself, observing every nuance, scribbling in my journal, dreaming in color.

I have a snapshot of my first day of college, Fall 1981, Brigham Young University. I was wearing a homemade granny skirt of calico with a matching triangle kerchief around my neck, Mary Jane shoes, and a mop of frizzy dark hair. I was greeted by preppie mania—pink and parrot green madras, Bass weejuns, and little plaid kilts. All the hair on campus blended into one blond, smooth bob and most everyone was either from California or pretended to be. I was from Iowa and had spent my summer detasseling corn, not shopping for clothes or style. I had expected my social life to improve at BYU. Considering my pristine Mormon ways had set me apart back in my rowdy high school, I imagined that I would finally fit into this 25,000 person club of which I was automatically a member.

But my outfit was only the beginning, a harbinger of all the wrong outfits to come. Everybody was indeed righteous, but they also seemed part of a distinctly Western culture, and they all brought friends from home. I never found other refugees from the mission field; I was battered silent by the realization that I was still a freak, only now a smaller freak in a bigger pond. I wasn't completely alone during the next four and half years, two colleges, and seven majors. I had a roommate that I had known from the fourth grade of one of my numerous elementary schools, a true Californian. She told me long rambling stories about beach parties and boys who teased her about "good vibrations" and asked her to dance. She had gold wavy hair and freckles, the kind of All American Girl who had lived her adolescence outside in front of everyone. She listened gamely to my longings for home, my mournful records, and she would wake me up from my naps in some carrel of the library and buy me French fries. I often felt suspicious and separate from her open warmth, but she would patiently dust off my complexities and tell me to get up and on with it. I did, though I attributed my tenacity to my own sense of martyrdom and not to her pragmatic affection. While my roommate went to see *Camelot* with the gang, I was smuggling a video of *Sophie's Choice* into the audio visual center at the library under some class assignment ruse.

After I graduated, I moved to Las Vegas for a job, a mundane retail job, considering the locale. I was basically in exile; I had no friends in a quiet, comforting sort of way. I trapped cockroaches in my seedy apartment with a toilet plunger and discovered Joni Mitchell. The significance of this city in my story of community was that I discovered a place where people were not trying to be perfect and had no interest in matching a template of behavior. I blended through a crowd of people who wore any and all emotions like neon signs across their faces. People cried at jackpots or losses right there in the open of the casino. They impulsively got married and gorged on prime rib for $6.95 for breakfast, lunch, and dinner. There was a lawlessness that relaxed the tense control I had clamped on my sadness and frustration and consequently it ebbed away with each garish sunset. The real world was so bright in Las Vegas that for once the movies paled in comparison, and I watched them a little less.

I went back to Utah to marry a man I had met several years before (not at BYU) and who had been out of the country for a year. During our long engagement, I took a class at the University of Utah. I was trying to build back my educational self-confidence after the college fiasco and decided to take what I thought was a literature-based mythology class. Having come from a school where Women's Studies meant Home Economics, I expected an English elective. I found my suddenly very sheltered self in a class full of women in flowing dresses or army fatigues talking about French intellectuals, Mexican painters, Earth Goddesses, and lesbian love. Amidst feelings of naiveté and awkwardness, I felt their passion provoke a dormant space that my exile had softened. I should have felt as alienated as ever, I should have felt like a stranger, but I felt the opposite, a sense of the acceptance that had always been so elusive. On some spiritual, intellectual level that I had never known existed, I discovered I had far more in common with these wild women than with my family, my fiancé, my friends, or even my God or religion up to that point. Although their interests and anger resonated, what was so compelling was being in a room full of women whose sole purpose was to connect as women first—all other comparisons simply added texture to this essential relationship. I was experiencing inclusion based on a part of my identity that I had never identified. I never thought of myself as a woman who could be open or honest with other women. In fact, I am not sure that I had ever defined myself as woman at all.

I left that class wanting to find women friends but was distracted by marriage and a cross-country move to Cambridge, Massachusetts. I blubbered most of Highway 80, terrified of leaving my family again, haunted by images of the granny skirt. But I discovered after just one Relief Society lesson that this new ward was more like my Women's Studies class than BYU. The women were all out of their established space and time—students, starting marriages, families, careers, and in some cases personal rebellions. I had no idea how to recreate the power I had felt in those heated class discussions so I began gathering for just ordinary rituals: baby showers, birthday luncheons, play dates, even a Tupperware party—stereotypical celebrations with crackers and cheese and Rice Crispy treats. I got better at it and one spring threw an elaborate tea party with handwritten invitations; rice paper layered on printed floral stationary with my loopy, 19th century longhand requesting that each woman bring a bouquet of flowers. The flowers were placed in ten waiting vases surrounding a white tablecloth, bone china, and glazed orange scones. At the end each woman carried home a different bouquet than the one she had brought with her.

The conversations at parties like this wandered through daily and situational anecdotes—why we chose the kinds of flowers we did, what we thought of a particular book. Eventually, over time, these meandering chats deepened, unlocking some common secret, something shared but hidden, something assumed too raw to articulate, something that certainly if anyone else knew, they would think less of us. Once loose, the stories spilled, tripped, overlapped—thick, loud, grating words that had waited so long to be heard and known. I served cheesecake and felt unnerved by what I had unwittingly initiated. I had expected a sort of cerebral synergy, a yeshiva school dialogue of ideas, and instead the sharing was so personal, the immersion into what I considered private pain so wrenching that I was unprepared to speak, it was too soon, too talk show.

As I struggled to find a place in these changing group experiences—trying to balance my skepticism and dismissal of them as cheap therapy with a growing closeness and familiarity to the women brave enough to reveal themselves—I was saved from utter confusion by a woman who taught me more about friendship than a hundred tea parties. We have both written that the metaphor for our relationship was the story of Mary and Martha and it is this page from the New Testament that reminds me of her. She embodies Mary's spiritual intensity and practical nonchalance with her own earthy, romantic intelligence. This woman would read Jane Austin with her six-month-old in a field of daisies and never notice the sagging diaper or that her daughter was eating beetles. It didn't matter because the words were poetry and the sun was penetrating her always tanned legs in the most delicious way. My Martha self would fret about in the same field, unwrapping sandwiches, watching the clock for nap time, measuring every dip and degree of the weather. Our one-on-one conversations imitated the group intimacy in safer ways, and I began to be known by this woman who I never tired of listening to—she was better than Las Vegas, better than any movie or book, she was real and fascinating and even as we tried to top one another with how erudite and insightful we could be, we both knew that the other was far smarter. We were inseparable and when she moved, I was lost. I had experienced a very daily community and for the first time realized how much I needed it. It wasn't just a way of recapturing an intellectual buzz, it was a way of being in the world that was integral and true. The more my friend knew me and the more I knew her, the less I had to live in my own head, and the more connected I began to feel with people in general.

We moved to Japan for a few years soon after and I met many different kinds of women. It surprised me to realize how much in common I had had with my Cambridge friends, how similarly we looked at things. In Japan, I knew Japanese, European, and American women as diverse as possible. I was drawn to a woman from Indiana, who had the magical gift of playing with children. She was receptive and unconditional and my sharp questions didn't scare her in the least. She and other women offered me a resting place to have conversations as light or heavy as I wanted, with no real expectations. I learned to have fun at zoos, museums, and eight-story toy stores. It wasn't all about disclosure and emotion; community was fun. The common link was a fondness, a lack of judgment, and a singular respect for the other's gifts. My friend from Japan had always assumed she had no talents until I convinced her that mothering was an art that she had mastered and that I still labored to understand.

I came back to Cambridge a new woman in a million ways that far exceed the scope of this essay. I came back a better friend. There were several groups still getting together, long gone were the structured reasons for gathering. I settled back into one of these with fresh energy and grew especially close to two women I had known for years. Our trio, each with a different hair color—blond, black, and red—became the most trusted confidants, The Witches of Eastwick, sharing secrets that I would have never dreamed of divulging before. It was this core and expanding circle that went to the Exponent retreat together last summer, and for all the exemplary bravura shown at the dinner table, we all knew that the moment was cosmic and fleeting. Within weeks, my two friends moved and I was left again.

How did I get here? A strange place that is alone but so changed from the alone I felt as a young woman. Somewhere, someone convinced me to stop wandering the peripheries of community and join in. Once you have felt the love of such an invitation, the precedent is hard to deny. I have come to believe that however fulfilling my married or mothering relationships, there is no substitute for being known down to your bones, of standing by yourself, circled by women, visible, palpable, blessed.

## Minus Motherhood
Karen Rosenbaum
Spring 1999 (vol. 22, no. 3)

*Winner of the Helen Candland Stark Personal Essay Contest.*

Ours is not the Home of the Empty Cradle and the Unoccupied Nursery. We have never shopped for a crib or a carseat. What had been the baby's room in the house we bought almost fourteen years ago is Ben's cluttered study. When I lean against the door jamb and look in, I do not imagine Winnie-the-Pooh wall borders; I see what you would see: an Oriental carpet, an office desk, a laptop computer, and innumerable file folders for taxes, insurance, and other adult affairs.

Childless Mormon couples are not common, and we are not typical of even that minority. We were not young when we married—I had just turned 43, and Ben was 47. I attended church and participated with some regularity; he had not been involved for 21 years, and he had no intention of resuming his post-mission activity. We lived—and live still—in the San Francisco Bay area, not a predominantly Mormon locale. Our neighbors, our work associates, and most of our friends have accepted our status without question. Even the Mormons who inquired usually nodded at our standard response ("we're too old").

In my 20s and 30s, I did not assume I would marry, but I did assume that *if* I married, I would have children. The children I knew well made me feel loved and important, made me want to have children of my own. I thought four sounded like a good number, but I wasn't counting on four. I wasn't counting on one. I wasn't counting on a husband, who, to my perhaps antiquated way of looking at things, seemed a prerequisite for children. Nine years in a singles' ward and a number of relationships made me leery of counting on things. I often felt isolated, sometimes unsettled, occasionally incomplete like the unmatched earrings in my jewelry box. But I did not feel the despair that my friend Elaine felt. "I weep inside," she told me, "when I see a woman nursing a baby."

When I turned 40, I knew that no matter what Maxine Hong Kingston's *Woman Warrior* Mother had done, I would not have four children. Then I met Ben. During our eleven-month courtship, I acknowledged that he would be a part of my life, but we were both jittery about day-to-day realities. Ben's previous (also childless) marriage had ended in divorce. If we gave ourselves two years to get to know each other before we tried to conceive, I would be 45, Ben almost 50. Aware of several mature friends' futile attempts to bear children, we discussed adoption of an older child. Ben had been orphaned at nine and raised by his grandparents. He had very strong feelings about adoption and older adoptive parents. I worried about raising a child in a home in which it was the more religious parent who felt so ambiguous about her faith. We made our decision well before our wedding. It has been the right decision for us.

Here we are, my young Relief Society friend, late on a Saturday night, just the two of us bent over the stainless steel sinks in the ward kitchen. The others have zipped up children's jackets and collected empty casseroles and trailed off to their cars. Your husband is stacking folding chairs onto a four-wheeled scooter while your sons chase each other in circles around him. My husband is reading a book to your three-year-old on a couch in the corner. The question to ask me as I plunge the silverware into the hot water is not "Why don't you have children?" The question to ask me is "Why aren't you more miserable about it?"

Why indeed? Might I qualify as one of the blameless barren who will be compensated in the hereafter? I doubt it. On the contrary, I am not miserable because I have never believed that the object of my existence is to bear and raise children and that I therefore have missed the major lessons and blessings and suffering that give life its meaning. Even had I married in my 20s, even had I married a man who had continued to affirm that Joseph Smith was a prophet, I would not have believed that a childless woman should be disconsolate, that she should apologize for the joys and wonder in her life.

Some of those joys are children. There are children in our life. Nieces, nephews, the children of friends. Their parents are almost always eager to loan them to or share them with us. We go to soccer games and baptisms and bat mitzvahs and recitals and play performances and graduations. We make dinners for picky eaters. Ben does sensational Donald Duck imitations. I've had Primary jobs. And when the small people have been buckled back into their car seats or seat belts and when we have righted the furniture and dust-busted the crumbs and returned the player piano rolls to their correct boxes, we smile and sigh and say, "We knew we were too old to have children," and we topple into bed.

Some of those momentous lessons of life can be learned by being a daughter, a niece, a friend. Sometimes, because we don't have children, we can be at a deathbed or a sickbed where we are needed. We can hear a catch in a voice, and we can fly across the country or drive across the bay to puree yam soup and walk dogs and rub backs and offer our gifts of love. Sometimes we have more hours to listen. Sometimes we have more money to lend or give.

My friend Christie died last summer. She had a long and difficult death, but she was able to spend almost all of her last year in the home she loved with the menagerie of mangey animals she had rescued from the streets. Her husband had divorced her before her final illness. Her children were affectionate and concerned, but one was away at school, one was in the military, and not until her last month were they able to return home. Christie was able to live in her own house and sleep in her own bed because of her two nephews—one gay, one straight, both childless. They arranged their lives to take care of her; one was always there. After the bones in her legs broke, they carried her up and down the front stairs when she had to have treatments or see a doctor. When she was nauseated, they found food that she could eat. When she was bed-bound, they cheerfully helped her onto a bedpan. They dusted and swept. They filled her bedroom with flowers.

Sometimes the childless are saints.

Creation can give life meaning. Those who have children may think of child-bearing and child-rearing as creative or productive processes. Those who do not have children can find other ways. I satisfy my creative urges by writing and by helping others, usually young adults in my classes, to write. I've taken shorter term pleasure in other creations—a garden of succulents, a sailboat quilt. But my writing and my teaching—however imperfect—have worth. As I work, I learn and I grow; sometimes my students learn and grow.

And even if they never write a sentence with grace and ease, they learn from me that they matter; they are important.

I cannot claim my work will save the world, but it saves me.

I want to make and leave the world a better place, not because there will be little Rosenbaum-McClintons running around in it, but because there will be human beings running around in it. In my transfer composition class last fall, I used as a text a moving book about the juvenile dependency court and the troubled children it serves. The authors' thesis is that we can only help these young people if we stop regarding them as "Somebody Else's Children."[2] Although the future residents of our planet will not be my literal and direct descendants, I do not consider them "Somebody Else's Grandchildren."

Ben and I do think about our own futures. We joke about adopting an engaging 25-year old with an MBA and a wife who is a nurse. They will be childless too, of course, so they can concentrate on taking care of us in our old age. We look around us. Not all children can or do take care of their elderly parents. Whom can one depend on? Ah, another question we can't yet answer.

We admit to selfish pleasures, pleasures that would be harder to come by if we were raising children. We sit in the front row of the War Memorial Opera House's balcony circle and shiver when Ruth Ann Swenson sings *Caro nome*. When a favorite local actress starts her own theater, we subscribe. Saturday mornings often find us, not at a soccer match, but with binoculars slung around our necks, tramping muddy trails behind the birding instructor of our adult school class. Although we keep resolving to patronize libraries instead of bookstores, our house teems with books; on the wider shelves, stacks of books lurk behind the upright volumes. We talk a lot about traveling to Alaska, New Zealand, the French Alps, Ukraine although most of our trips are to Salt Lake City to see family. But when we do travel, we travel light. Once we managed five weeks in England with one medium-sized carry-on apiece.

The ward silverware is back in the drawers. I dump the damp dishtowels into a plastic bag to take home to launder. Your husband has locked the last of the chairs into the storage closet and is heading towards the couch. What do I mean by this six-and-a-half-minute talk? There are many kinds of precious seeds to sow and many kinds of fruitful vines. Happy is the man whose quiver is full of love. Blessed is the woman whose womb is full of compassion.

*Listen*: Ben and I are driving home from the transit station where we meet after work. "Oops," I say. "I forgot to take my tapes back to the North Berkeley library."

"Uh oh," Ben says. "I think the Arizona travel books are overdue at Kensington."

---

2. This note was part of the original publication: John Hubner and Jill Wolfson, *Somebody Else's Children* (Three Rivers Press, 1996).

"Oh," I wail. "I was going to stop by the Triple A office!" We bite our bottom lips.

"And Karen?" says Ben. "Do you know what else we forgot?"

"Oh no," I think. "What else?" I ask.

"We forgot to have children!"

*Hear*: Peals of laughter. Because we didn't forget.

## From Victoria's Secret to Beehive Clothing
Sylvia Cabus
Fall 1999 (vol. 23, no. 1)

Garments.

I used to see them all the time, in a combination of voyeurism (on my part) and exhibitionism (on their part). They'd peek out from under too short Bermuda shorts; they'd flash under skirts when legs were crossed; they'd even show under collars when a handbag strap pulled the wrong way. They marked endowed members, distinguishing them from mere recent converts like myself.

Even as a baptized tithe-paying member, I did not feel like a "real Mormon." I hadn't served a mission, and seemed unlikely to, since my two years as a Peace Corps Volunteer probably counted as a secular mission for the U.S. Government. (Even as a tool of American foreign policy not much was expected from me; if I was often mistaken for a nun, it was because I had to adopt over the knee skirts in order not to be mistaken for a prostitute.)

I am an over-educated, single, bicoastal Mormon. I study gender and international development in graduate school. I don't have a perm. I am an alumna of UC Berkeley, the great Satan of Universities. My only time in Utah consists of one weekend trip. I don't have a Franklin Planner. I have never read Steven Covey. I have no experience with resin grapes, Minerva Teichert paintings, or green Jell-O. I turned down a full scholarship to BYU for graduate school even though I was told that I could get married there; that was before I was informed I'd already been priced out of the Utah marriage market. Admittedly, I have a collection of flowered dresses, some even with matching hair accessories. Then again, I was told that I couldn't wear pants to church.

I do now, however, wear garments.

My life as a convert followed the same basic pattern: baptism, patriarchal blessing, endowment, perhaps marriage and family to anticipate as well. I knew that I would be going to the temple upon my one-year anniversary as a Mormon, and, consequently, my lingerie days would be over. No more annual shopping trips to Victoria's Secret on Valentine's Day for me.

During the first year after my baptism I went through a major transition.

Summer in Montreal: I attend the French-speaking ward and take advantage of the exchange rate and the August sale to buy an impressive array of lingerie.

Autumn in Washington, D.C.: I get my first real look at garments in a shared dressing room at JCPenney with a friend from the ward. They look innocuous and sedate. I start taking the temple prep course and read a couple books on the subject. I experience my first encounter with the oblique discourse surrounding the temple. I remain confused.

To gain cross-cultural perspectives on social change, I read an essay on veiling practices of Muslim women in Bali. I think I am beginning to understand.

Winter: Not until the evening before, as my escort and I are chatting, am I informed of the game plan for the next day. She and I have the ceremonial laying away of the lingerie. As I take out each item she oohs and ahs in admiration. I fold them neatly into a Talbots bag, now relegated to closet Siberia.

Spring: The day of my endowment I wear my favorites—black and white zebra striped undies under the most Molly Mormon dress I own. I pray fervently that Mormons inside temples do not possess X-ray vision.

My first pair. Dri-silque. Baggy. I have a hard time pulling on my pantyhose afterward.

The distribution center. A madhouse on a Saturday afternoon. I hurriedly finger the fabric samples and decide on the poly-cottons. I am told to order more through the toll-free number.

I go home and try on all my questionable clothes. Most can stay; a couple of short skirts and dresses have to go. That evening I go to a dance party. I feel the extra layer keenly and wonder if anyone else notices.

While I had been taking the missionary discussions I'd bought a dress with the money I would have spent on the latest in reproductive technology. I can no longer wear this dress because of my garments.

In an attempt at bravery I wear thigh high stockings to work. They roll down as I walk down the hallway toward my boss and I expose myself as I tug them upwards again.

On the phone my mother mentions seeing Steve Young on TV and wondering if he wears the "funny underwear" he had talked about on *60 Minutes*. I miss a golden chance to explain.

I am now the proud owner of a two weeks' supply. I only wear white bras these days. I have a favorite fabric and style of garments. I still feel them, but in a more comfortable rather than constricting sense. I feel naked without them, I *am* naked without them.

**Love Making**
Ann Gardner Stone
Spring 2000 (vol. 23, no. 2)

My hair is dropping like
needles from a dying Christmas tree.
Clumps on my pillow every morning;
in the sink enough to clog a sewer pipe.
Remove my gay designer scarf and the hair follows.
Strands hang from the collar of my coat
Worse than a shedding dog.

I watch the wastebaskets fill like
the Sorcerer's buckets
carried out the door by a brigade
of dancing combs.

Soon I am brushing furiously
to finish what the drugs began.
But a few stubborn strands resist.
Such defiant tufts.

While I hold the mirror
he lathers my head with sweet-smelling soap
and shaves it clean
to kiss when he's through.

**Period**
Ann Gardner Stone
Spring 2000 (vol. 23, no. 2)

Mother, a keeper
of secrets, has warned
me with a booklet.
When my period arrives
I take the news to a quilting bee,
to six women hunched over frames,
my mother stitching scallops
along a spotless border.
Sweating, nauseated,
I whisper in her ear.
She lays me on the couch,

drapes a wet cloth
on my forehead, thimble
still on her finger.
Rhetta brings me peppermint tea.
Margaret eases my knees to my chest
then rubs the small of my back.
Josie says she started at eleven
and stopped at nineteen.
Leona remembers tearing rags to
hold the blood.
Mother tells how she fainted
the first time it happened to her.
Together they lift the edges
of a worn patchwork.
Double wedding rings billow overhead
as the women incant their secrets,
cover and enfold me.

## Personal Revelation in an Authoritarian Church—Balance of Power or Detente?
E. Victoria Grover
Fall 2000 (vol. 24, no. 1)

*Summary of a workshop held at the Summer 2000 Exponent Retreat.*[3]

Sooner or later, almost every Latter-day Saint experiences conflict within the framework of his or her religious community. That conflict is particularly challenging when it seems to involve differing interpretations of the will of the Lord. In a religious environment that places great value on both personal revelation and obedience to authority, what are we to do when these two principles clash?

The Church has clear structural and ideological answers to these conflicts when they occur: Either the hierarchy of authority or the principle of stewardship tells us which interpretation will prevail.

But what do we do as individuals when we feel the promptings of the spirit get overruled? When we seem to find ourselves ill-used by someone else's decision or perhaps even believe that we are victims of injustice within the Church? Whether it's a matter of how Church welfare resources will be distributed or where new ward boundaries will be drawn, hundreds of decisions are made by those in authority with which we may deeply disagree.

---

3. This editorial note is part of the original publication.

How do we deal with this when it happens? What is there for us to learn from these experiences, and where are the dangers? Finally, what is unique about the Mormon view of the dispersement of spiritual power and how can the implicit tension it creates enlighten us as individuals and as a larger community of wards and stakes in Zion?

These are the questions I asked during a recent retreat workshop, and I felt richly rewarded by the responses women shared within the group. I believe we were led to a consensus of faith in the power of the gospel to bind together diverse and unique individuals into a community striving to be at one with the Savior. What follows is my interpretation of the ideas expressed in that workshop.

About ten years ago, I had an interaction with a new bishop that changed the course of my spiritual life forever. In that short meeting, it became rapidly clear that he and I had very different views on fundamental principles of commitment and obligation. Over the next week, I struggled with a flood of feelings surrounding the bishop's decision and the implications it held for me and my children. I prayed for understanding, and when that didn't come, I prayed for relief. I felt a pressing weight of confusion, despair, and helplessness each time I thought about the difference between my conception of what was right and the bishop's and how his decision was now going to affect my life. I felt my anger slice like a hot blade through the very cords that bound me to my ward and to the whole Church. For the first time in my adult life, I could envision the Church going forward without me in it.

I can't remember at what point during that week I finally received an answer, but I remember the answer itself very clearly. Alone in my bedroom as I wept and poured out my story of injustice to the Lord yet one more time, I suddenly felt a piercing affirmation coming out of a place of emotional stillness that was not a part of me, telling me very simply, "You are right." Motionless, I listened for the rest of what I wanted to hear—the part about how the bishop was wrong and the wrath of a righteous God would soon fall on him like a thunderbolt! But that message never came. Instead, the Holy Ghost poured love out on me, and in those wonderful minutes of spiritual clarity the absence of any accusation against my bishop spoke volumes. The bishop, right or wrong, was not my concern. Instead, I saw the task of enlarging my heart and strengthening my soul lying before me, and with the assurance of God's love and the blessings of free agency won for me by Mother Eve, I knew I had all that I needed to move on.

When our ideas or opinions are overruled by others, the first and most natural reaction is to contend with those others on behalf of our heartfelt beliefs. But contention is extremely dangerous because it hardens our hearts and drives away the Holy Ghost. It is possible for people to hold different views of what is right without succumbing to contention. People can state their views, explain them, even point out possible flaws in another person's thinking, without invoking the spirit of contention.

One way to do this is to clarify in your own mind the purpose of the explanation in the light of unconditional respect for the free agency of the person with whom you are speaking. If the purpose of your explanation is tainted by a desire to overcome the other person with your words—to convince, to control, to win—you move into dangerous territory. If, while you are speaking, you feel your respect for the other's free agency draining out of you, watch for contempt to replace respect and any remnant of charity to disappear. You are now contending, and the purpose of your discussion has changed from explanation to defiance, from enlightenment to domination.

Contention comes not from having different ideas of what is right, but from the effort to prove another person wrong.

For all our talk about tolerance and diversity, contention as a way of sorting out our differences is both honored and glorified in America's culture. The world often asks us to fit people and their disagreements into the dichotomous arrangement of "right and wrong." While there certainly are important laws and principles that fit that arrangement—and knowing that we must guard against the danger of trying to rationalize away our very real sins—still, the rule of "right and wrong" serves us poorly in most disagreements with others. Even so, it is what we naturally fall back on whenever conflict occurs. As we start to fall, we grab onto contention to prop us up and support our need to be seen as "the right one" in a dispute. Even when we try to acknowledge valid issues on both sides of an argument, the very fact that we have taken sides pushes us into the "us/them" duality and its corollary, which says "they" are wrong and need to be stopped—or changed—by "we" who are right.

Christ asks his disciples to see conflict with different eyes—with our spiritual eyes—and get off the see-saw that says, "If I'm up, you must be down!" He wants us to look at our brothers and sisters as a part of ourselves and realize that contending with them is as foolish as the foot contending with the hand on the same body. I believe Christ would agree with the comic strip philosopher Pogo: "We have met the enemy, and he is us."

The Church asks us to gather ourselves together in communities of many different people. Different is difficult, and this gathering into communities has created challenges for members since Joseph Smith first restored the Gospel. The challenge is intensified by our belief in individual personal revelation. It is disciplined by asking our obedience to a hierarchical authority. The tension between personal revelation and authority keeps each of us vibrantly humming and engaged in both the workings of the Church and the pursuit of our own salvation. I believe the latter task is the more important one for each of us, from President Hinckley on down, and the Church organization serves us best when we keep that fact in mind. Then we realize that it doesn't really matter whose idea gets acted on in the day-to-day business of running the ward, the stake, or the Church itself.

What *is* important is how each of us uses the Church community to refine our souls, to come unto Christ, to make ourselves perfect and complete. When we come before him, Jesus will not ask us if we won in our disputes with others or even if we were on the right side. Instead, he will ask if we won our struggle with the natural man, the desire to control, the need to be essential, to feel powerful, to be right instead of righteous. If we are called upon to sacrifice on the altar of God our most tender and delicate parts—a piece of our ego—then truly in that act we become one with our Savior.

The philosopher/psychiatrist Sheldon Knopp said that all the significant battles are waged within the self. These are the only battles Christ is truly interested in.

## Editorial: Something Old, Something New
Nancy T. Dredge
Winter 2001 (vol. 24, no. 2)

One of my best friends got married last week. Cheryl Howard (née Davis, now DiVito) is a long-time writer, board member, historian, photographer, and retreat organizer extraordinaire for *Exponent II*. Her courtship with Michael culminated in one of the most fun weddings I have ever experienced.

It was nice to attend the wedding of a friend—not the wedding of a friend's son or daughter—for a change. Because Cheryl's family and friends live in Washington, D.C., suburban Boston, and Utah, and Michael's live in Philadelphia and on Cape Cod, Cheryl and Michael crafted a ceremony that would allow each other's friends and family to get to know the couple better. They chose to sit in the choir pews in front of us, which allowed their audience of well-wishers to see their reactions to the exquisite vocal duets and anecdotes about their lives from close friends and relatives. One of the duets, "The Prayer" from *Camelot*, was partly in English, partly Italian, a wonderful nod to Michael's heritage and the several Italian speakers in the crowd. Cheryl's sister got so teary sharing stories of Cheryl's many accomplishments and giving personality that she paused and said, "It sounds more like we're burying her than marrying her!" That remark brought down the house.

After a family luncheon, the new couple left three feet of New England snow behind for the sunny climes of southern Italy. They also left behind old friends and new, now joined to the couple as surely as they are to each other.

Cheryl's wedding started me musing on the old and the new in our lives. How hard it is sometimes for us to give up the old, and yet how welcome and refreshing the new can be.

It is ironic that while preparing the Fall issue of the paper on retreats, we learned that the beloved site of the Exponent retreat for eighteen years is closing down. Those of you who are retreat goers will no doubt be as shocked and decimated as we were to hear this news; non-retreaters who read that issue can osmose the sense of loss we feel to no longer have the "coming home" feeling that Hillsboro gave us. But, while Hillsboro can never be replaced, the retreat will certainly carry on in a new place.

When I took over the helm of *Exponent* from Jenny Atkinson last year, I came across a letter in the files from a disgruntled reader, who said she missed the "old guard" of writers and was therefore canceling her subscription.

Her comment made me re-read several past issues of the paper. I was amazed at the depth of insight and beautiful writing in the articles. I wanted to write back and say, But we haven't lost the Mary Bradfords, Claudia Bushmans, Karen Rosenbaums, Emma Lou Thaynes, and Sue Booth-Forbeses. However, their work has now been wonderfully "added upon" by the Mary Johnstons, Linda Kimballs, Diane Browns, Victoria Grovers, Pandora Brewers, Heather Sundahls, Laurel Madsens, Kate Holbrooks, and Dana Haights, to name but a very few.

I love it that Exponent is itself such a lovely combination of the old and the new. Thanks to Jenny for bringing new life to our board and staff. We are all enjoying each other, learning from each other, new skills and old.

It has been hard for some old-timers on the board to adapt to new ideas, such as putting *Exponent* online, adopting a new logo (we still don't have one), and altering our purpose statement. But, with the encouragement of new staff and board members, we are ever being led into the twenty-first century.

Happily, our readers also fall into categories of the old and the new. Thank you, long-time readers of the paper, for your support and loyalty. And welcome, new readers, as you join in our sisterhood—something old that is continually being renewed.

## Christmas in a Changed World
Linda Hoffman Kimball
Fall 2001 (vol. 25, no. 1)

It's a challenge to be jolly. I'm trying to think Christmas, to think mistletoe and holly. The assignment is here, and I am committed to it. But today—a beautiful autumn day less than a month past September 11th—I wonder how I will feel when Christmas arrives. Everything has changed.

To look at Central Street in my town of Evanston, Illinois, this October day you'd think it was the 4th of July. Banners and bunting festoon every building, every flagpole. You have to understand what the 4th of July is like in Evanston. It is huge, gaudy, and outrageous. People set out lawn chairs along the parade route a week in advance, and heaven help the soul who infringes on someone's staked out territory. Our parade has Klezmer bands and veterans and gay rights activists and Mothers of Multiples and the Jesse White Tumblers and costumed theatrical groups on stilts and some lone woman who dresses up in a red white and blue nightie with an enormous fake bald eagle on her head. Many parade watchers sport jiggling star headbands or some other goofy patriotic accouterment.

Today everyone's in the red-white-and-blue mood, but we steer clear of goofy. It would be like wearing a clown nose to a funeral. By the time Christmas comes, will we be fully back in the red and green mood? Will we have followed the counsel to boost the economy and buy, buy, buy? Will we have the stamina to sing "Grandma Got Run Over by a Reindeer" or will we stay mum until New Year's, when we can sing that melancholy Tennyson lyric, ". . . the year is dying in the night, ring out wild bells, and let him die."

But I will not write a gloomy piece about Christmas. I will sit and think about mistletoe and holly until something cheery strikes me.

And already it has. Holly. That's my sister's name. I see her smiling in photographs on my desk, and I celebrate our shared years of mischief and memory. Her name, Holly Lou, was the concoction of '50s parents who loved their dimpled daughter but who must not have foreseen all the "Holly Lou Ya" jokes she'd have to endure. Today, Holly (a flight attendant) is alive and well and a distinct Hallelujah in my life.

Let's try Christmas carols. What do they bring to mind? Angels we have heard on high goes one. I recall driving in the Boston area on my way to the Exponent retreat on September 21st. At the airport, I saw men in black uniforms toting rifles inside and dozens of state police cars parked outside. As I drove, I listened to National Public Radio with the fixated interest I had developed over the previous ten days. Weighed by the psychological debris, I sagged in the driver's seat until I rounded a turn on Route 2 near my old town of Belmont. There, up ahead, sparkling gold in the afternoon sun was none other than the angel Moroni! "Hello! Hello!" I yelled in my rental car. "How long have you been there!?"

As it turned out, Moroni had been put up that very afternoon. Legal battles behind it, the steeple and the angel went up on September 21st in commemoration of Moroni's first visit to Joseph Smith on September 21, 1823. (Steeples went up in Nauvoo and the Netherlands that day as well.)

A photographer for the Boston *Globe* captured the steeple dangling from a crane next to the Boston temple's boxy form. There it was in the paper the next day surrounded by articles about beefed up security and imminent anxieties. In the Metro section and on Route 2 amid grim present realities was a golden messenger of hope and eternity, the angel I had heard on high.

A phrase struck me deeply in one of the many conversations I heard in the aftermath of September 11th. Did I hear it at the retreat? Was it on Oprah? Was it Maya Angelou or Marianne Williamson ... or my friend Mary Anne Foley? The phrase I recall was that this event has given us "rapt attention to one another's existence."

I know exactly what that means! That, of course, is why Christmastide holly draws me to my sister. It is why I emailed so many friends and called loved ones in New York and spoke to my children at college several times a day. It is why I suddenly cared for all the strangers in line in front of me at the grocery store. No price on that item? No problem—take all the time you need to check it. I'm just so glad you're here, whoever you are.

It is why I felt a pang of remorse last week when some speeder cut me off from the right hand lane, and I snapped in my surliest tones that he was "an over-eager twit." I don't want that rapt and compassionate attention to fade. I don't want to fall back into old habits of annoyance and grumpiness toward the inevitable over-eager twits who will always be with us.

Being fond of wordplay, I hear a Christmas spin in that phrase. Christmas provides us an opportunity to demonstrate "wrapped attention to one another's existence." So yes, it is our patriotic duty to buy, buy, buy. To boost our economy, to carry on with our lifestyles—fine tuned and less innocent as they may now be. Our physical gifts are visible symbols of our deepest feelings. They can't convey it all, but they convey something.

And another Christmas connection. There He is in the manger in the hay in the Middle East, which even at that time was troubled and tortured. Bound in His swaddling bands, He was and is and is to come God's wrapped Attention to our existence.

I may not be in the mood for "Grandma Got Run Over by a Reindeer" this Christmas, but I will sing these lyrics:

*He came down to earth from heaven, who is God and Lord of all, and his shelter was a stable, and a cradle was a stall....*

And, the next week, moving from melancholy to its final major chord, I will sing these words with fresh and deeper meaning:

*Ring in the valiant ones and free, the larger heart, the kindlier hand. Ring out the darkness of the land; Ring in the Christ that is to be.*

## As Regards Touching
Kate Holbrook
Fall 2002 (vol. 26, no. 1)

My grandma's skin was cool and dry, her joints surprisingly supple as we pulled white clothing over her heavy limbs, stroking her arms and legs. I tried to be meticulous in the execution of my service. My grandma had firm opinions about clothing, appearance, funerals, and I didn't want to shame her. But despite our intentions, my aunts and I were awkward—I suspect the mortician tidied our work once we had finished. I stared and touched and smelled, trying to fill the giant void of her absence. But her physical presence only accentuated the impact of her spiritual absence, and the void engulfed my thoughts and speech. Only my emotions survived the vacuum of grief; they were screaming.

I remembered sitting on my grandma's lap as she told me the story of Billy Goats Gruff in our oversized orange chair. She had French-braided my hair with these still hands and taught me to knead fudge, to test for the softball stage. She had put sample pieces in my eager mouth. I mourned my absence at her deathbed and wished that I knew more clearly where she had gone and how she was responding to the transition. I prayed that she would not find it difficult. I understood for the first time why Chinese tradition includes prayers to ancestors; I didn't ask for blessings, but forgiveness.

I first attended to my grandma's physical needs during kindergarten. My mother and I had recently moved from California to live with Grandma in Utah, and Grandma had slipped on some twigs on a path in the Uintah woods, breaking her ankle.

I spent each school morning feeling misunderstood by my little peers and teacher as I focused on how I might present convincing symptoms of illness and return home early. It did not help that I had tried and failed to do so two days prior.

After those few unpleasant school hours each day, I was free to return home and make peanut butter sandwiches for Grandma and me (with too much jam and, she thought, too little peanut butter). In first grade, a potential friend made me a peanut butter, butter, and honey sandwich on store-bought white bread, which delighted my young palette. But I was not allowed to introduce this discovery into our family's culinary repertoire as 1) we ate homemade bread, but what we then thought more important, 2) two butters was simply too decadent for three women with figures to maintain.

After lunch, I would clear our plates to the kitchen, and my grandma and I would play checkers on a little tray balanced on the arms of our adjacent chairs. We played and talked and she told me how smart, able, and pretty I was (though, as she always reminded me, "pretty is as pretty does"). Home was not always conflict-free—there was piano practice to endure—but I could be sure there that I was loved and had worth. After checkers, my mom, a schoolteacher, returned home and recited the day's events.

Grandma's ankle healed, but leg and back problems plagued her remaining decades, and I learned never to leave her when stairs, ice, or a barbed-wire fence stood in our path.

Years of our deliciously inappropriate laughter (during sacrament meeting, at congregants' hair) intervened. My grandma taught me to measure flour, separate eggs, and disassemble the shower drain. We bought clothes and shoes for every occasion. We ate all kinds of candy. We went to the ballet, where I received a maternal reprimand for making too much noise with my Skittles. I attended BYU, and since my mom and grandma lived in Provo, I occasionally lived at home during college.

During one of those times, my grandma had back surgery in a fruitless attempt to ameliorate her chronic pain. One afternoon, my grandma was giving herself a sponge bath and wasn't able to reach her feet. She called to me and, full of apology, asked whether I could help her to wash her feet. My grandma hated to ask for help, but neither could she abide filth (one of her favorite words), so her loathing for a dirty body must have overwhelmed her reluctance to ask for help.

My memories don't have corners (even my unconscious revels in female roundness) but consist of portraits replete with smudges, blurs, and points of clarity. I don't remember the expression on my grandma's face or why I was home in the middle of the day. But I remember her calling to me and my entering her bathroom, which is still white and bright with scattered floral kisses of pink and blue. On that day the room was full of sunlight, and she sat at a stool near the sink with an orange plastic hospital tub at her feet. I remember feeling uncertain how I would react to helping her—I took special care of my own feet and harbored no special enthusiasm for encounters with those of others.

But I assured my grandma that I was glad to help and hoped she wouldn't sense any reluctance. She was probably too acutely aware of her own discomfiture to note any coming from me. As I knelt and placed her foot in the tub of soapy water, my hesitation dissipated and I set about my washing as carefully as I could.

Not long into my task, I was embraced by a feeling of holiness. I felt that God was pleased with my small service and that this washing was, in some sense, outside of time, echoing through the ages. I suddenly, with clarity, understood the many paintings I'd seen of Christ washing his disciples' feet. I felt poignantly, if infinitesimally, closer to a comprehension of Him. Sadly, foot-washing, however sacred, is a simple task, and I could not linger there for long. I wished for this communion to continue, but my grandma was tired of her stool.

More years passed, and I moved to New England, where I married and began to learn the unusual experience, for me, of living with a man. After six months living in St. Petersburg, Russia, and a first Christmas with in-laws instead of my mothers, I planned a January trip to Utah to compensate for the long separation.

My grandma was not herself. She didn't approach me with her usual stream of questions and news, and she spent too much time in her bedroom. She had even given up hiding the fact that she lay on the couch to rest in the middle of the day. I saw her longing for past intimacies. She often grew confused in the night and thought she was once again sleeping with her sister, Elithe, who had died several years before. She confessed, and my mother confirmed, that she often called out my name when she heard the house creak at night, thinking it was me returning from a late outing and creeping past her bedroom to the stairs. As she explained this, her eyes filled with tears because I no longer lived with her.

A few nights before returning to Boston, I gave myself a pedicure while watching a video with my mom and grandma. One of my mom's students had given her a selection of foot scrubs, washes, and lotions. From the initial soaking of my feet to the final waiting for the polish to dry, my conscience burned that I should do the same for my grandma. I recognized a message that I was meant to do so, that a pedicure would be a kind of ordinance, but I could not. The knowledge that my grandma's desire for life was fading had started to penetrate my staunchest efforts to remain ignorant. I wanted to show her my love, but I could think only of Mary anointing Christ's feet with spikenard and that Christ died not long afterward. I refused to prepare my grandma for burial.

The weightiest matters are beyond my control, and weeks later there were phone calls, heart attacks, and an agony that consumed me. In desperate attempts to make up for my sins of omission, I composed her long obituary, delivered her eulogy, wept, prayed, and did not sleep. And I dressed her body for burial.

I have a baby daughter, Amelia, now six months old. She has a range of coy, sometimes fetchingly wicked smiles, a few that she's borrowed from my grandma. Amelia seems to have my grandma's zeal for social interactions and, like my grandma, to take delight in laughter. When you look at Amelia in her stroller, her grin comes out and her enthusiasm struggles against the restraints of stroller seatbelts.

Three years after my grandma's death, I sometimes see her in dreams where she is often unwell, a faceless body that needs my care. Awake I still yearn for the vibrant woman I loved. And I care for Amelia. I wash, stroke, and dress her warm limbs. I bathe her little feet—with water and with my kisses.

**Encircling**
Kylie Nielson Turley
Fall 2002 (vol. 26, no. 1)

Miscarried late one night when I was groggy
Perhaps a skinny, laughing girl,
With soft blond hair and green eyes
As I dreamed the night before.
My almost-baby was gone before I understood
The cramping pains that buckled my knees
And sent me whimpering to the bathroom.
I would have called out for help or comfort
If I weren't embarrassed,
Unsure about this intimacy. So physical
This process. My body shared, then not.

In my mind, I call her Eden, a name
Without a mother or a child.
Still, I miss
Her head tucked into my neck, breathing softly,
Her warm-sleep body gathered in my arms—
Even after holding other children of my creation.
Like Eve, I suppose.

On a brisk December birthday
I would have swaddled
Her in a blanket or two to take her home.
Instead, an early birth-death: May,
So bright and shiny. Two days later
I sat in the sun by the pool—
Swimming suit taut over my empty stomach.

Every year now there's that circling,
The May, the December, the May.
She's a thought—brief—
I find myself thinking another without realizing
But the return
Is a comfort, a marking, a naming
Of Eden,
Mother of my mothering.

## The Stump's Last Stand
Julie Paige Hemming Savage
Winter 2003 (vol. 26, no. 2)

I just threw away my copy of *The Giving Tree* by Shel Silverstein. Do you remember it? It's a simple tale of a long-time friendship between a boy and a tree. The boy loves the tree and the tree loves the boy, but as the story progresses, their relationship becomes increasingly lopsided; the boy quits giving anything back to the tree, continuing to take—first the apples, then the branches, then the tree's very trunk. The boy often becomes discontented, but the tree is satisfied in her giving. It is not until her trunk is gone that she reveals any regret; the tree is happy, "but not really." When the self-centered boy returns as a weary old man, the tree stump says, "I wish that I could give you something… but I have nothing left. I am just an old stump. I am sorry." She then straightens herself "as much as she can" and offers the man a place to rest. The man sits and the tree "is happy."

I hate that story. I want to rewrite it. In my story, the tree gives to the boy and the boy gives in return. As the boy grows, he learns to water, nurture, and prune the tree; the tree shares her abundant, delicious apples with him year after year. Rather than hacking down her branches to build a house, he brings his children to keep her company and play in her branches. The boy learns about unselfish love and finds himself less downhearted. The tree delights in her own growth and explains her limits when the boy wants to mistreat her. In the end, the old man reclines not on a stump but in the shade of the tree, enjoying her fruit, and they again delight in each other's good company. My strong adverse reaction to Mr. Silverstein's story stems from the fact that his story line is repeated too often in the courtships and marriages that I see around me. It is no coincidence that the giving tree is female. In many budding relationships, there is a time when the boy and the girl both take care of each other and both are happy, but as time progresses, the girl's role changes to that of the self-sacrificing tree. The husband and children receive and thrive while the wife endlessly gives.

Imagine this: A young returned missionary kneels before a sweet young woman proposing marriage. He pleads ardently, "Will you marry me, my love? I will make you the happiest woman on earth. We'll share the housework and both go to college. As we run out of money, of course you won't mind dropping out to finish putting me through school with a minimum wage job. Then, while I go away to work with interesting people and play basketball in the evenings, you will do my laundry, make all the food and clean up, and enjoy the company of our many delightful children. I appreciate that you will want me to continue my hobbies and my time-consuming work as a volunteer fireman. I believe you'll find plenty of time for your hobbies after the children are in bed and the house is cleaned. Besides, you will have ample opportunities to go out: I will babysit the children each month so you can attend Enrichment Night. If you do decide to work, I hope you don't mind that the home will still be your primary responsibility. We will move, and often, when it seems my job could be more fulfilling elsewhere, and I will leave you with the blessed responsibility of short-term single parenting and selling and packing up the house. Oh, and the glorious nights when I will sleep contentedly while you get up with our screaming children. The bliss! I can hardly wait! Will you be mine, mine, mine? All mine?"

An absurd proposal, yes. A joke? No. If the truth were told during many a Mormon proposal, this would not be an exaggeration. Sadly, the dominant paradigm adopted by couples still demands that women give while men retain the power to take and give at will. In these families, the mother becomes the most self-sacrificing person in the family—praised on Mother's Day as the one who gives everything up for everyone else in the family to be fulfilled and happy. But what about her talents? And what about teaching other members in the family to sacrifice? Is it really okay to adopt a family model wherein primarily the mother is sanctified by serving and nurturing? Should she be the only one who learns ultimate patience and Christ-like love?

I am increasingly aware that feminism's gains are least likely to be experienced in women's relationships with their husbands. In this arena, for too many women, it is as though the women's movement of the last hundred and fifty years hasn't occurred. Despite the strides women have made politically and theoretically, in real relationships, behind the closed doors of homes across the country, many women have made minimal steps toward their own self-fulfillment. While it is rare for young couples to admit outwardly that major inequalities exist in their respective partner's ability to wield power, examining a household's division of labor along gender lines clearly shows that women almost always perform the majority of housework and attend to the daily needs of others in the family to a much greater degree. Many women have worked for women's right to live life fully; we need to continue to fight the good fight to bring about a greater degree of equity, not only in the world, but in our families.

As Elizabeth Cady Stanton so wisely stated in 1851, "We have had women enough befooled under the one system, pray let us try the other." In this vein, I propose that we examine our relationships and chosen family models to see how our family's resources and energy are flowing. With the complexities of demands on families in terms of money, time, and other resources, it is not enough for women to wonder why they are doing all the housework or going to all the PTA meetings alone. They know why—because no one else will do it and (not unimportantly) because there is a level of satisfaction in performing such labors. So, instead of attacking the problem in terms of "mother getting more out of her life" or "father 'helping out' with the housework," I believe a whole reshaping of the family model is in order.

The most equitable family model is one in which all members are responsible for sacrificing for each other's needs, knowing that simply ascribing roles to certain individuals will always fail given the flux of energy, time, and the surprising variety of needs in family life. We must constantly ask ourselves: Is each member of the family given the opportunity to sacrifice his or her wants and needs for other members of the family, or is it the mom who is doing all the giving? Are children taking all the lessons, or do they sometimes have to cut back on activities to accommodate a parent who wants to acquire or hone some skill? How much do husbands support their wives in new endeavors and sacrifice work and down time to make it possible for them to accomplish tasks or benefit from new experiences? Who has time to read the paper? Who is doing most of the housework? Does it shift and flow with each change in the family, or is the mom always left with holding everything together?

From personal experience, I have found that adopting a family model that sets out to fulfill everyone's needs, rather than only the husband and children's, turns out to be good for all involved. Children learn to be less self-centered and more flexible and giving. Husbands have the opportunity to be involved in their children's lives in meaningful ways. Everyone needs to be willing to sacrifice and shift the balance of power and dissolve their roles at different times and in different ways.

It is easy to fall into a rut. Consequently, it is imperative that we ask hard questions and seek what is best for each family member, including the mom. I firmly believe that everyone is better for having sacrificed for the others.

Women have made tremendous gains since the nineteenth century, but we have miles to go in figuring how to fully reap the gains in our own lives. A suggestion on where to start: Let's quit reading *The Giving Tree* to our children and pick up a copy of *The Paper Bag Princess* instead.

## Holding My Grandchild, Come to Land this Morning
Judith Curtis
Winter 2003 (vol. 26, no. 2)

I swaddle you tight to mimic the watery womb
of your metamorphosis
where you emerged, tugged by froggy legs
from your mother's belly
not two hours ago.

The doctor cut you free from the enchanted pond
of your gestation and laid you on her chest,
a lump of jelled flesh held together by waxed skin,
where you flopped and twisted, mired
in the glue of gravity.

Our pulses beat in and out of sync;
yours rushes, then slows,
the irregular breaths sighing minuscule protestations
at having to force the nothingness of air
into damp lungs.

Your amphibious eyes, liquid blue, squint and blink,
unused to light,
while your mouth works like a tadpole's on the side of
an aquarium;
you are hungry, hungry for milk,
the potion that will complete your transformation.

I cradle you, my hatchling child, and ponder
what your birth reveals about origins;
how water is our first world, then air, then earth,
and it is left for us to tell how we have tried
to solve the mystery of fiery flesh that welds us
to the ground and subtle spirit that lures us up to seek
what came before and
what is yet to come.

## Life is Good: An Interview with Cathy Stokes (excerpts)
Linda Hoffman Kimball
Spring 2003 (vol. 26, no. 2)

Cathy Stokes is a woman of smarts and spirit. The first black nurse in the U.S. to hold an administrative position in a state nurses association, Cathy is now a force to be reckoned with for infection control in health care for the State of Illinois Department of Public Health. A world traveler, Cathy leaves her home in Chicago for her work, for her assignments with Church Public Affairs, and for her love of the many people around the globe who "by mutual consent" are her relatives. She has been to such exotic ports of call as Ghana, Fiji, Japan, Ireland, Australia, New Zealand, and Monticello, Utah. She is as well known for her barbecued rib dinners as she is for her generosity of spirit, her commitment to the Gospel, and her sometimes saucy turn of phrase. In the following interview, Cathy shares some thoughts on her childhood, her education, her career, and her experience as a Mormon since 1979.

Ex2: Tell us about "Cathy Stokes: The Early Years."

CS: I am child of the rural South, born into severe poverty in 1936. I was the youngest of six children of a sharecropper family. We had a great aunt in Chicago who had just gotten married who was too old to have any children. She wanted someone to help her in her old age, so by virtue of birth order, I got to go. That turned out to be a blessing for me. For example, I was the only one of my siblings who got to go through school.

Ex2: Do you mean high school, college, elementary?

CS: All of the above. They may have had one or two or three years. Schooling was not a priority in the South then. There were no electric lights, no running water, no flushing toilets.... People are always asking me to go camping. I tell them I camped in my youth in that shack in Mississippi.

Ex2: Tell us about heading North.

CS. I remember very vividly that night we left. I must have been about three or four. I remember the moon casting shadows on the moss hanging off the trees. I remember riding in a car. I don't think I had been in a car before. We went to a place in Louisiana to visit some of my great-uncle's relatives, and we had supper there. They had fried fish and spaghetti for supper. In Mississippi, we were given our food on a tin pan and then we'd find a place on the floor to sit and eat. That night in Louisiana I was given a real plate. I remember the feel of this new thing in my hands. I looked around for a place to sit on the floor. I remember the feel of my great-aunt's hand on my arm lifting me up and hearing her say very tenderly, "We don't do that anymore."

Ex2: A new life for you.... Where did you go to school?

CS: I had all my schooling here in Chicago. I went to a Catholic grade school for a while until I got expelled.

Ex2: Expelled?! What did you do? How old were you?

CS: I was about eleven. I got expelled because the nun said that anybody who wasn't Catholic was going to hell. Yeah, they said that in those days. It was before we were all "friends" and "ecumenical" and all that. I raised my hand, not in defiance but rather in innocence and said, "No, that's not so, because my family isn't going to hell." She promptly took me out of the class and sent me home.

I remember walking home with fear and trepidation because school was very important in my life.... I just knew I was in deep trouble. Strangely enough, when I got home Papa looked at me and said, "It was time for you to leave that school anyway." There was a big sigh. That's probably the first time I realized that there is a God and He loves me.

Ex2: What a relief.

CS: Yeah. I was so innocent. I always thought if anything was true, you ought to say that and everybody would be happy. I still believe in saying what's true, but I know it doesn't always make people happy. You have to be careful how you say it.

Ex2: Where did you go after you were expelled?

CS: I went to a public school and then to Hyde Park High School, which at that time was the premiere public high school in Chicago. There were half a dozen black students. I did well in high school. As a matter of fact, I was the outstanding senior in my graduating class that year.

Ex2: So after high school?

CS: I went to nursing school and after I graduated, I got a job working in a hospital. Then I worked in a pediatrician's office—worked for the first black pediatrician in the city of Chicago.

Ex2: Somewhere in here you got married?

CS: I met my husband and got married on Valentine's Day, 1960, hoping that he'd always remember it.... In October 1962, my daughter Ardelia was born, my only daughter. (Well, the only daughter I gave birth to. I have some other "daughters" by what I call "mutual consent.")

By the beginning of the next year, the marriage had failed. I would always tell people I was widowed. I realized you get an entirely different reaction if you tell them you're a widow.... If you say you're divorced, people look at you with a raised eyebrow. That's when I learned that women have a hard time without a husband. I basically raised my daughter. She saw her father periodically, and he provided the support that was required by the court. Life went on. That was the start of my angry years. I wasn't going to take it. I learned to fight back, effectively if not kindly. I have repented. I continue to repent for all the harsh words I have inflicted upon people.

Ex2: You went back to work?

CS: I was working when I was pregnant with Ardelia. I believe in working until you can see the whites of the baby's eyes. Then I took off and hadn't planned to go back to work. Necessity prompted, and I had to. The two physicians I worked for were very kind. Grandma and Papa took care of the baby. After about a year, I decided to go back to school and get a degree so I could work in Public Health. I recall going back after work to give Ardelia her supper before going off to school. She'd cry and wail, and I would leave their house in tears myself. One day I forgot something and I went back. She was dancing and singing and having a great time. That taught me a valuable lesson. Don't think you're essential. Life goes on.

I was blessed to have those wonderful parents who helped me, and I had wonderful friends who also helped me. Life was expensive, but we managed to stay one step ahead of the sheriff. And the Lord provided.

Ex2: Now you're working in state government?

CS: After I got my degree, I worked for the local health department and then the Illinois Nurses Association.... I went from that job to state government. I'd gone to see the director of the agency. He wanted a public health nurse. He said, "My dear, let me just be candid. I want a public health nurse because I think they're smart. The women are raising hell because we don't have a woman on the staff. The blacks are raising hell because we don't have a black on the staff. You are all three. If you would consider taking this job, I guarantee we'll have fun." Indeed, he kept his word.

Ex2: Tell us how, in the midst of all this, you became a Mormon.

CS: In 1978, I got introduced to the church on an airplane to Hawaii. The pilot told us we should go see the Polynesian Cultural Center and the temple since we wouldn't have many opportunities to visit the temple in our life.... I went to the Polynesian Cultural Center. I saw the Joseph Smith story and inquired about what they had done with the golden plates. Did not feel I got an answer.... I did sign that little slip, expecting that I'd get a magazine and a request for a donation. Instead I got these two lovely white boys in their suits and ties who came to my house one evening in the fall. I asked them, "What in the hell are you doing out here this time of night?"

They told me they were elders. And I said, "Yeah, right." But their innocence and the spirit about them was such that I was comfortable to let them in. They were the first to open the predominantly black area where I live. One thing that struck me was how frightened the one from Idaho was. In 1978 and '79, it was very tense between black men and white men, as it continues to be. The tension is always between the men. You overlay that with the young militants, and you have two white boys—too young and too sweet to be cops, but that's what they look like. The thing that saved them is that they were easily identified as ministers. Ministers still move with ease in most communities. Ministers and nurses and EMTs.

I call mine a "backdoor conversion." I realized I didn't disbelieve anything.

Ex2: So you were okay with angels coming and all that....

CS: Absolutely. Absolutely. I believed in angels. I always wondered why God would leave us without prophets. Somehow it just stopped there? Is that all? Much of what they told me filled in some holes for me.

Ex2: You're a single black woman in the Mormon Church. You don't exactly fit most people's stereotype of a Mormon.

CS: Let's stop for a minute to think about this whole question of "do I fit." Whether or not I fit has never been an issue. That's not a question that I ask myself. The issue is "Do I want to be here?" and how do I help these people "fit" with me? We all fit in the church; we just sometimes have to work with folks to get them to understand how we fit. We belong here in this place together. The Lord has something for us to do with one another—to learn, to serve, and to move ahead in our lives....

I go wherever I go in the Church with the expectation that we share a commonality. I'm available to you and you to me based on that commonality. I'm glad to see you, and I'll just be shocked if you're not glad to see me.

Ex2: Can you share what you love about the Gospel or life in the Church?

CS: I love that if I have something worthwhile to do and I need help, my fellow saints are going to help me. I don't have to persuade them. I don't have to get a big stick. They come willingly to work together for a good cause. I love that we extend ourselves.

I love the emphasis on prayer and scripture and personal revelation. I love standing for something—to borrow a phrase. I love the people of the Church, even the ones who are a little grouchy, cause then I'm determined I'm going to bring 'em around....

I love the way the Church reaches out to the world. Good works are done privately, and our Father in Heaven rewards openly. Indeed, He has rewarded us as a community of saints, as individuals. The fact that we know God loves us is such a blessing. There are people who don't know that.

Are there things in the Church we need to work on? Yeah, yeah. The Church is the environment where we're supposed to work with each other and for each other and help each other come unto Christ. That's what it's all about—coming unto Christ.

## Cap of Many Colors
Heather Sundahl
Winter 2003 (vol. 26, no. 2)

It's hard to remember when the depression started. Was it on the seven-hour flight back from California when that nasty old lady refused to switch seats so that we could sit as a family? I ended up boxed in with my toddler asleep on my ever-growing belly, starving and nauseous but unable to eat because I could not access the tray and wondering how rude it would be if I asked the woman next to me to please hand me a barf bag. Was it wondering where on earth this unexpected third child's gear was supposed to go since I already shared a dresser with the toddler and we were on top of each other as it was?

Whenever it started, by fall I couldn't hide it anymore. I was falling apart all the time. One friend started bringing me dinner several times a week, saying she had made too much and I was doing her a favor by taking the extras. After a month of this, she and I both dropped the pretense and I'd arrive at her house after work, return her Tupperware, and leave with fresh containers filled with meals that felt consecrated. Other friends routinely took my kids, and I knew that while I felt unable to hear the promptings of the spirit, the women in my community certainly did.

I think the all-time low was my fast food meltdown. I was running late for work, trying to feed the kids at Burger King before taking them to the sitter's. The guy at the counter messed up my order, shrugged "It's not my problem," and went to help the next person. I exploded, called him a not-so-nice name, and burst into tears. At my booth I put my head on the sticky (ketchup? Sprite?) table and bawled as my four year old patted my back and the toddler offered me a soggy French fry.

I prayed hard for relief. I wanted to feel joy but couldn't. Instead, I was mired in a mixture of misery and guilt. What was wrong with me that I was less than elated? How could a Mormon woman not see pregnancy as a blessing? Even when things were going well, the depression could sneak up on me like the shark in *Jaws*. One minute I would seemingly be enjoying a nice swim, and the next minute I was literally drowning in pain and darkness. I prayed as I tucked the other two in bed at night that they would not be damaged by my foul moods. I prayed as I drove to work that I'd be able to stop crying long enough to teach the three-hour block. I prayed as my husband gave me blessings of comfort that I'd actually be able to feel the peace he promised. I prayed as the psychologist that my OB made me see told me that my depression would go away if I just ate more salmon.

I have never been a still-small-voice-hearing gal. My mother-in-law gets clearly articulated answers to prayers, and I think she thinks I'm a bit defective spiritually since I am unable to hear like she does. Perhaps I am spiritually challenged. This is not to say that I don't get answers to prayers. I do. Sometimes. It's just that it seems that when God does decide to respond to my pleas, he uses alternative means of communication. Even so, I was still surprised at what became the turning point in my pregnancy.

When I was six months pregnant, some girlfriends decided we should go to the outlets up in Maine. They thought a little retail therapy might help me. And if that failed, there was a Dairy Queen nearby. Salmon was not going to relieve my hormonal upheaval, but a Peanut-Buster Parfait might.

In one of those Swedish catalog stores where kids' pajamas cost what my wedding dress did, I picked up a little knit cap, tried it on my fist, and smiled. It was mostly green, a cheery Granny Smith with a few stripes, pink, yellow, blue. It was even on sale. But the last thing I needed was more baby clothes. By this point I knew I was having another girl, twenty-two months after my last one. Same age, same season, same clothes. Everything else about the pregnancy felt so overwhelming that it had been a great relief to know that I didn't have to buy a single thing. So I tossed the cap back in the pile, thinking of the Rubbermaid bins filled with little caps and other perfectly good girl stuff at home.

But as I left the store, I couldn't walk away. I told my friends I'd catch up, and I stood there, trying to figure out what I was feeling. There was no voice, but I knew God wanted me to buy that green hat. Yes, the Lord speaks to people in the language and means they best understand. So what does this say about me that God talks to me through shopping? Ignoring the slight, I obeyed the prompting, feeling a little foolish and superficial but glad to have any kind of divine communication in the midst of the depression that, more than anything else, left me feeling spiritually abandoned.

That night as I took the knit cap out of the bag, I imagined the tiny, warm head that it would adorn. I could imagine the soft cheeks against my breast. And, perhaps for the first time, I didn't think about the morning sickness or sciatica, the lack of space, my limited resources. I only thought about this baby as an individual. In that moment, I felt peace. There would be room enough in our house, in my heart, for this child. Motherhood is, after all, the story of the fishes and the loaves. I held the cap and cried.

The cap sat on my dresser for the next three months as a reminder of the comfort and knowledge I had received. After Camille's birth, which fortunately signaled the departure of my depression, she wore the cap many times. I joked to my husband that it was the "cap of many colors," representing my love for her. And now it is hard to imagine not having her in my life, hard to imagine that carrying her was such a burden on my body and spirit. I have given away many of her things, but I keep the hat. For me, it is holy, a talisman, a symbol that my baby and I had not been forgotten.

### In the Shadow of His Wings
Deborah Farmer Kris (as "Deborah")
2009 (vol. 29, no. 1)

She came in late. School started at 8:35 but it was nearly 9:30 when she shuffled into the classroom. She ignored the teacher's welcome, hung up her grease-stained backpack, walked to her desk, and put her head in her hands. Within ten minutes, her body slumped in slumber.

At lunch my cooperating teacher, Sandy, filled in the details. This was her 37th year teaching in the district—the poorest and poorest-performing district in the state. I was a 21-year-old student teacher, and we had 32 fourth graders between us. Tina, she said, had an older brother whose dark defiance had earned him a place in a special school after his fifth grade year. It was an open secret that her father was a major player in the local drug trade, she said. No one doubts he beats the wife; probably the kids. Yes, the social worker has filed with the state. If this kid were in Lexington she would have been removed years ago, but here... well, welcome to the neighborhood.

That afternoon, I followed the students to music. "I'm the old vet in this school," Sandy said, "so I get the tough ones in my class. These specialist teachers can't handle them on their own, yet. Go help them out." We hadn't finished the welcome song before Tina walked to the upright piano and curled herself beneath it, wrapping her arms around the leg. When I went to retrieve her, tears were streaming down her face, but I couldn't hear a sound—even her breathing was silent.

The silence lasted two days. "Don't you f**** touch my stuff!" I spun around to see Tina—a full head smaller than the smallest student—digging her nails into Jeffrey's arm. Her eyes were wild. Silence, fists, and an occasional simple addition problem. That was the best we could do for a few weeks.

One October day, Sandy pulled me aside. "Expect Tina to be a little off her game today. It's her birthday. Her brother was always a terror on his birthday—not much for a celebration at home." I rifled through my bag in search of something, some little present. I found two Halloween pencils and a sheet of pumpkin stickers. I made a card and placed them in her desk. She didn't acknowledge the gesture, didn't even look at me as she left that day.

When I arrived the next morning, a package was sitting in the center of my desk. Someone had ripped the book cover off a math book and used it for wrapping paper. A Dole banana sticker ripped in two served as tape.

And scrawled in black marker:

To Miss F. From your firend Tina

I unwrapped the package to find a rag doll—her face was smudged, her dress stained. When Tina walked in, she simply stared at me. I nodded and smiled. She practiced her spelling without complaint.

I am fairly certain I have never prayed more fervently than I did during those six months for those 32 students. My other teaching practicums had been almost effortless. But here I was, running a reading group with nine students who didn't have basic decoding skills, checking homework that was completed in homeless shelters, and feeling more than I had thought possible. And then there was Tina. She was beginning to trust me, and she was beginning to read; she even learned her times tables. But I knew the statistics were stacked against her. Her smudged face and fits of tears made me question all I knew about justice and mercy.

On my last day of student teaching, I once again followed the students to music. The students were well trained by now, and I could sit on the back bench and watch. After a few minutes, Tina came to sit next to me. She curled up on the bench and laid her head in my lap. I stroked her hair and listened to her breathing. I'm not sure how to explain what happened next. On a single inhale—for just a fraction of a second—I thought I saw her far from here, standing someplace warm and someplace gentle. Her face was clean. On her exhale, I felt a force from Elsewhere, felt more love than my body could hold, as if God wanted to touch her for a just moment in this lonely world and my lap was the nearest conduit. Tina fell fast asleep.

I don't know the ending to her story. I lost track of her after a year or two. Every fall, I pull out the doll and tell my students about Tina. They pass it around gingerly; they look at her picture peering from the old class photo, frozen in time.

I know I learned something of mercy that semester, something of God's love. But justice?

It still doesn't seem fair...

**Dress**
Brooke Jones (as "Brooke")
2009 (vol. 29, no. 1)

It had been wrinkled and awkward
for more than eight years
in the bottom of a chest.

Once in a while she would peek
down underneath the others just to
see if she remembered the
exact shade of blue.

Last week she pulled it out
to see if it would fit,
tried ironing out its shape,
but clumsily put fresh creases
here and there and then used
too much water.

She kept looking
for the round French collar,
dainty buttons,
and gorgeous pin tucks.
Thinking things, like
the waist didn't used to look like this.
Then she saw the whole cloth—
that it had never been sewn together,
never even been cut out
in the first place.

### Staking My Claim, Claiming My Stake: Mid-Singles
Sandra Lee (as "Dora")
2009 (vol. 29, no. 1)

A few months ago, I was reading an essay by Mary Lythgoe Bradford and was struck by her comments on being single again. As I read further and further, I found myself thinking, "Right on sister!" more times than I'd care to recount. One point that particularly spoke to me is that singlehood is not a punishment, a condemnation or a cruel joke. It's just a fact of some lives, and mine in particular at this point in time. And when I review my life, I can honestly say that I've chosen it over the marriage opportunities I've been presented with. I don't view this as being selfish, or too career-minded, or noncommittal, just realistic about my capacity to love and be loved by and to be happy with and foster happiness in certain people.

So, I'm single. And invested in living the best life I can. And I like to think that I've been doing a pretty good job of it so far. But there is always room for improvement, and the area that seems to have the most potential so far is my church experience. Not that I hate church. Far from it. But I have noticed that there are certain organizational quirks that could stand to be looked at again.

In my stake, the records of all singles over 31 years of age are moved out of the YSA ward into their geographic family ward. Frankly, I agree that YSA wards are no place for mid-singles. I think that being in multigenerational wards is a good thing for people who have attended their fair share of

Linger-longers and Flick 'n' Floats. However, reactions to the transition seem to be one of three varieties. Some people transition easily enough, faithfully attending the new wards that they're planted in, even though they may feel lonely as one of only a few mid-singles in their ward. Others seem to retreat into denial and continue going to the YSA ward despite time's relentless forward march. I can understand the rationales; that's where most of their friends are, who wants to be stuck in a family ward to molder away your thirties, and the fact that sometimes mid-singles can be a scary bunch. Still others just seem to "slip through the cracks," giving new incentive to overeager visiting teachers, home teachers and ward clerks.

A couple of months ago, the second counselor in my bishopric (who happens to be single and in his mid-forties) took a few of us mid-singles out to dinner to discuss how the ward/stake could better serve our needs. There was a lot said about having more activities, especially of the non-dance type, or segregating activities by age decades (ie: 30s, 40s, 50s), but I think my idea was the best. However, before I can amaze you with my brilliance, let me provide a little background info.

My stake is very diverse. It encapsulates two very affluent wards, three rather impoverished (both financially and leadership-wise) wards, two university wards, a YSA ward, and one non-English-speaking ward. The stake leaders have had to farm out YSA's and older couples to help with leadership and missionary work in the smaller wards that have many non-English speaking members or a lack of active adult members of both genders. As a stake missionary, I was assigned to one of these "growing" wards, and attended Sunday services there for six months to help out.

So, back to my brilliant idea. I told the counselor that I would love for the stake to designate one of the growing wards as the place where the mid-singles should attend, which would fulfill the two major needs of members of the Church: fellowship and service.

Fellowshipping is such a huge part of the gospel. What is visiting teaching and home teaching if not a formal take on fellowshipping? I believe that, important as VT/HT can be, the best type of fellowshipping is the informal and spontaneous kind, especially when entering a new ward. After having attended a vibrant YSA ward, sometimes it's just depressing to go to a family ward and be one of only a few mid-singles. We all have a need to be with our peers. Young mothers commiserate with each other about babies, and older ladies share menopause stories. Not that I won't benefit from their experience, but I do feel a need to share my own stories with those who will understand me best. On the other side of the gender divide, one of my guy buddies said that attending high priest group meeting in the family ward the first week was like feeling the prison bars slam shut on his dating years. Not that he didn't like the other HPs, but he suddenly felt as if he had aged thirty years, since the next oldest HP was in his 60s.

Members need callings to help feel invested in the ward, and to reap the blessings of service. Without a calling, it's just too easy to slip into inactivity. When my bishop asked me what calling I would like, I asked to be the RS pianist—not only because I wanted more incentive to practice piano, and because the old pianist was moving away, but because it would give me a reason to go to Relief Society that I couldn't shrug away because I didn't feel benefited by it. I admit that my current bishop does a better job than most, but it is bothersome that most of us mid-singles have been conveniently called to the activities committee, which also seems to be the catch-all place for in/less-actives. This one-size-fits-all calling can be particularly frustrating since the families in the ward are so busy with FHE, youth activities, Boy Scouts, sports and enrichment that they don't support other ward activities.

My last request of the stake leaders, assuming that they recognize the genius of my idea, would be to call as bishop someone who has some experience with mid-singles—either as having been one, having children or friends who have been in the situation, or just someone who is very empathetic. Sometimes, bishops just don't know what to do with mid-singles. When my roommate (who transitioned into the family ward a year ahead of me) had an interview with the bishop, he asked her what her plan was.

P: *Plan?*
B: *Yes, what is your plan?*
P: *For my career?*
B: *Hmmm, no. What is your plan for getting married?*
P: (Thinks to herself: Well yes, I *planned* on it about six years ago, thank you very much! Says:) *I'm not sure what you mean.*
B: *I think you need a plan. How are you going to get married without a plan? Maybe you should go online. It worked wonderfully for Jane. I think it would work for you.*

And really, the bishop was very well-meaning and earnest, but blanket solutions don't work for everyone. BTW, P was subsequently wooed by a prior home teacher, and they've been happily married for almost two years, sans internet hook-up.

## UNIT 4: 2010–2015

## Introduction by Aimee Evans Hickman

Thirty-five years after *Exponent II* printed its first paper, its relevance in a digital age was in question. A thriving blogosphere hosting a myriad of forums devoted to Mormon thought and experience had given longtime readers, as well as potential readers of *Exponent II*, a new place to exchange ideas in real time. These digital spaces were also introducing rising generations to discussions that had been ongoing for decades. This tension between those who'd been writing and reading about Mormon feminist issues in print since at least 1974 and those coming to these ideas for the first time in virtual spaces was amplified by the way thirty-five years of newsprint hid the sometimes unwieldy discussions that had taken place behind the scenes but were on full display in blogs and comment threads in the early 2000s. To some, blogs rendered print publications like *Exponent II* obsolete. In 2009, Emily Clyde Curtis and I trusted that *Exponent II* could have the best of both worlds as we committed our editorial tenure to a quarterly full-color magazine-style publication that would continue to hold a sampling of the historical moment in the archives of its pages while embracing the vibrancy and immediacy of the digital bloggernacle.[1]

Look no further than the first guest-edited issue of this era from the fall of 2011, our collaboration with the Mofem juggernaut *Feminist Mormon Housewives* (fMh), helmed by fMh founder Lisa Butterworth. In her Letter from the Editor, Butterworth shares the way doubt changed her faith even though she had "arrived at my destination of perfect Mormon womanhood." For those old or lucky enough to have been reading the pages of *Exponent II* for decades, the disillusionment Butterworth shares may have felt like revisiting well-worn roads. But as the success and vibrancy of the fMh blog demonstrated, the fact that these narratives are familiar makes them no less personal or urgent. This is poignantly felt in Lisa Van Orman Hadley's essay, "Waiting," which appeared in the Spring 2011 issue focused on the often fraught relationship many have with Mother's Day. Hadley struggles with the single Sunday a year that "all the women" of the Church are ostensibly celebrated entirely through the prism of motherhood as she experiences a prolonged period of infertility. Hadley achingly captures how unique and personal even these seemingly universal themes of Mormon womanhood are in a form that is true to *Exponent II*'s long publishing history and the urgent discussions taking place in comment threads throughout the bloggernacle.

During these years (2011–2012), "the Mormon Moment" was taking a new shape in American consciousness. The US Presidential campaign of Mitt

---

1. More on Aimee Evans Hickman and Emily Clyde Curtis's tenure in Chapter Nine.

Romney, the wild success of *The Book of Mormon Musical*, and the "I'm a Mormon" proselytizing ads, among other popular media, brought unprecedented public exposure to the Church and Mormon culture. Under this glaring spotlight, feminist grassroots organizations calling for structural change within Mormonism began to crop up online and in person as groups banded together to support women wearing pants to church, praying in general conference, and ultimately being ordained to the priesthood. As in the past, Exponent as an organization did not officially sign on to any of these efforts but instead made space for writers to share their experiences and ideas. Emily Clyde Curtis's Winter 2011 essay "Mourn With Those That Mourn: Being a Hospital Chaplain" explores her efforts to provide solace to patients and families using her faith and chaplaincy training without overstepping her beliefs or her authority as an unordained Mormon woman. In the Summer 2013 issue dedicated to women's experience with the temple, Amy Allebest's essay, "A Letter to the Brethren," gives voice to the heartache she experienced during temple rituals that she felt placed her husband as a wedge between her and God. Her letter, written as a direct appeal to Church leadership, implores them to consider the unfairness of temple rituals that could leave one feeling that man is "being punished for his own sins and not for Adam's transgression" while women are punished for Eve's in perpetuity. Many of Allbest's observations anticipate changes in temple language that would come to pass in endowment and sealing ceremonies in 2019.

But nowhere were the Exponent's efforts to remain a voice for all Mormon women more apparent than during the rise of Ordain Women and its moment in the national spotlight. *Exponent II* devoted a themed issue to the question of women and the priesthood in the spring of 2014, and in addition to including essays from Ordain Women founder Kate Kelly and other supporters, we included essays sharing a spectrum of viewpoints on women's ordination. In her essay "So Many Words," Diane Pritchett expresses exhaustion that the familiar Mormon feminist debates about female authority have followed her into middle age as she laments that "it is easy to get lost in words like authority, ordinances, keys, offices, administration, and power," when it is actually "God's presence [that] ordains the action." Where Pritchett expresses feeling inherently empowered by her faith regardless of her ordination status, in the same issue Abby Maxwell Hansen's essay, "Deployed Without the Priesthood," expresses a yearning for the ecclesiastical authority to minister to others that she feels excluded from as much when her priesthood-holding military husband is overseas as when he is home.

Sharing a plurality of voices has always been at the heart of Exponent's feminism. Whether that's been through scholarship invested in complicating simplified narratives about historical figures, like in Jana Riess and Linda

King Newell's Fall 2013 essay on "Reinventing Emma Smith," or reflecting on the ways that sharing perspectives unlikely to be found in official Church publications could reach those still finding their voice, as Maxine Hanks remembers in her Winter 2014 essay, "Remembering Exponent II: A Beacon in the East." In my own remarks at the 40th anniversary of the Exponent's founding in 2014, it felt important to me also to laud "the quiet voices that are often lost to history" as those contributions "may be where the biggest cultural shifts are manifested in the end."

Those cultural shifts included Church membership outside of the United States surpassing U.S. members at the end of the twentieth century and more conversations about how race and nationality impact individual experiences with Mormonism. Recognizing problems inherent to a global Church run by predominantly white, straight leaders required the Exponent to examine its own history and commitment to intersectional priorities going forward. Kailani Tonga's Spring 2015 essay, "The Color-blind Conundrum," explores how, as a biracial woman of Tongan/Swedish ancestry, she is often frustrated by attitudes that suggest "when it comes to race, it is easier to say, 'I don't see color' than to say, 'I see value in your color.'" She craves "a God that sees me for me and loves me because of who I am, not a God who erases the parts of me that make others uncomfortable." In that same issue, Averyl Dietering's essay, "As I Am," builds on how glossing over differences in the name of inclusion further fractures our community from a queer perspective. "When friends, family members, or Church leaders feel the need to tell me that I'm more than my sexuality, it's typically in situations when my sexuality is inconvenient or uncomfortable for them. They don't want to deal with all the complications that my queer sexuality causes, so they downplay it in order to emphasize other aspects of my identity." Dietering laments the empathy and compassion that is forfeited when we "fragment others in order to preserve our privileged perspectives," and the lost "opportunities to expand our horizons."

The determination to include a greater variety of voices in the pages of *Exponent II* during this era can also be seen as the work of visual artists slowly became a more integral part of the publication. A two-page spread dedicated to the art installation of multimedia artist Ginny Huo in Summer 2011 ushered in this new publishing priority. Under the direction of my dear friend, Margaret Olsen Hemming, named as art editor in 2012, works by painters, sculptors, textile artists, photographers, and others added density that, while aesthetically different, hearkened back to the early days of *Exponent II*'s hand-drawn illustrations from Carolyn Person (née Peters), when no inch of space went to waste. The Winter 2014 issue features the work of multimedia artist Page Turner. "The Sacred History of Remnants" is an exploration of the way found-objects pieced together from scraps that Turner's matriarchs had left behind could be transformed "back into sacred objects" via her sewing box "full of treasures from women long forgotten." Turner's process makes an apt metaphor, if ever there was one, for the entire *Exponent II* project of which I have been so very lucky to be a part.

## Waiting
Lisa Van Orman Hadley
Somerville, Massachusetts
Spring 2011 (vol. 30, no. 4)

At the end of sacrament meeting, an awkward new dad comes to the pulpit and says he needs to make a quick announcement. He clears his throat and says, "Um, the Elder's Quorum has a little something for all of the women in the ward. I'm going to pass this basket of treats around and all the women should take one." He is trying so hard and I appreciate the gesture, but there is no way around it: today is Mother's Day. This day was not created for women, it was created for mothers. And sitting here with my little bag of Hershey's Hugs and Kisses is not comforting. It is just another reminder of what I am not.

I remember Mother's Day when I was a kid. My mother had to conduct her cacophonous orchestra of children alone while my father sat up on the stand. They asked all of the mothers to please stand up, and the deacons brought around a carnation and baby's breath corsage for each woman standing. When my mother stood up, I felt proud. I looked forward to the day when I, too, would stand up and receive my corsage.

I'm thirty-two years old and still waiting for my carnation and baby's breath.

If there is one constant about infertility, it is waiting. Every month you wait to see whether your period will come. Every month the timer resets, every month another failure. You wait for appointments with your doctor—weeks, sometimes months. You wait two excruciating weeks after an in vitro cycle to take a blood test and then wait for the nurse to call and tell you whether you're pregnant. And then you wait for your period to come, that big red checkmark confirming what you already know. You wait for paperwork to be processed. You wait for the insurance company to approve another treatment. You wait for a birth mother to choose you, for a child to be matched to you. Sometimes it feels like putting coins into a slot machine and waiting for a payout. You worry about time running out. You wait and wait and wait and wonder if you will ever stop waiting.

I have been in this holding pattern for four years.

I remember when I went off birth control. My husband and I wondered if the timing was right, wondered if we should wait a little longer. But I was 28 and tired of waiting. We were sure that we wanted to be parents and certain that things would happen when they were supposed to. I figured it might take a few months. If worse came to worse, I would have to take Clomid for a month or two like my older sister.

But nothing happened. Clomid, surgery, in vitro cycles, adoption sessions, periods, periods, periods. Still waiting.

I've been in a lot of waiting rooms. At the doctor's office where I did my first two in vitro cycles, the waiting room for Infertility was shared with the waiting room for Obstetrics and Gynecology. It always seemed like a cruel punishment to have to wait with all of those pregnant women, all of those mother geese with their gaggles of cooing babies. The flyers pinned to the wall bore conflicting messages: a flyer for an infertility support group was pasted alongside a poster of a mother holding a newborn.

No one talks to each other in the waiting room. All the people on the Infertility side are there for the same reason, but they don't say anything to each other. You flip through magazines, make judgments about each other. Most of the women look to me like they're in their forties. They wear high heels and pearl necklaces and come in with briefcases. I, on the other hand, am usually wearing jeans and a t-shirt from the grocery store where I work. They probably think I'm just a kid. I'm 32, but it's not uncommon for people to think I'm in high school. A few years ago I was denied a sample at Costco because my mother wasn't with me. I see the way these women look at me, like, "What's she doing here?"

Sometimes I wonder that, too. Sometimes, actually pretty much all the time, I get sick of waiting and wonder how long I'll continue to do it.

A few months ago I decided I was going to try to talk to someone every time I'm waiting. I tried it out as I was waiting for an ultrasound during my last in vitro cycle. I started talking to the woman sitting next to me. She seemed nervous.

She told me it was her first in vitro cycle, and I told her how things worked. She told me how much she hated the nurse downstairs who drew her blood, and I told her about the time that nurse put the needle in my arm and forgot to attach anything to the other end. We talked until my name was called and I found myself wishing we could talk longer. For a minute, I forgot about waiting.

The thing about waiting is that you have to keep living life while you're doing it. You can travel the world, live at an artist colony, do all the other things you've always wanted to do. You can find other people who are waiting and wait it out together. I've found that it's almost always better to wait with someone than to wait alone.

## Letter from the Guest Editor
Lisa Butterworth
Salt Lake City, UT
Fall 2011 (vol. 31, no. 2)

As a little Mormon girl, I looked forward to many distinctly Mormon transitions and I knew that each transition had one ultimate goal: to ready me for transcendent Mormon motherhood. After which, hum, well nothing ... surely no further goals were necessary? I certainly could never have foreseen a transition that would lead to one day guest editing a Mormon feminist magazine like the *Exponent II*. No indeed, such an edgy eventuality did not figure into the picture.

At eight years old I took baptism seriously, relishing my new status as an official member of the Church of Jesus Christ of Latter-day Saints (and cherishing my shiny new CTR ring). After that, I couldn't wait to become a Beehive and join the ranks of the big girls who went to fun weekly activities with all the hip young leaders. I remember the first time I walked into the room of Young Women feeling like I didn't really belong, surprised that they didn't turn around and tell me to go back to Primary. By fourteen I had owned my identity as a Young Woman, and becoming a Mia Maid meant going to dances! The biggie though, was that as a Laurel I'd finally be able to date boys!

Joining Relief Society didn't really sink in, even after I was called to be in the RS presidency in a singles' ward. It felt like we were just playing at being grown-ups, because every good Mormon girl knows that the singles' ward is just a little layover. I'd be a real grown-up when I got married in the temple and went forth to multiply and replenish. And then I would live happily ever after, nurturing my 4.5 children and my protector/provider/presider/husband. Families are Forever.

Right on schedule, the returned missionary of my dreams showed up, but so did something that had not been on the docket—doubt. I had entered adulthood, married in the temple, and arrived at my destination of perfect Mormon womanhood, but ... here was doubt.

All my years of faithful Young Women attendance had not prepared me for doubt. Except perhaps to instill the fear that doubt meant I was a bad person. But ... I had read my scriptures every night. I had magnified my callings. I had prayed desperately and with all the hope of my heart. Okay, I admit I had looked upon my husband with lust, but we got married, so it was all supposed to be okay now. I'd been a good Mormon girl; what more could I do?

Losing certainty and rebuilding a new kind of faith was a lonely process. A process that led me to start a blog called *FeministMormonhousewives.org*.

Blogging introduced me to the long and noble history of Mormon feminists, a ground-breaking historical magazine called the *Woman's Exponent*, and to the impressive women who resurrected that project in the *Exponent II*. These feminists have made my transition from "perfect Mormon woman" to real Mormon woman a journey of love, support, friendship and hope. Their history changed the trajectory of my own.

The stories we tell each other, the lived experiences we share, this is the true history of Mormon womanhood. We are not a static ideal; through these stories we have the power to help each other heal and grow and transform. Reaching out to women online and in our own lives, we have collected some of these tales—stories of the myriad transitions we experience as real Mormon women. A series of women take us on a search for the feminine divine. We hear the voices of those who describe their transitions of citizenship, adoption, conversion, and loss. The writers help us awaken to our privilege, to the complexities of our faith lives, and the healing process for abuse survivors. And we threw in a few things for the laughs, because we're silly like that.

I never did arrive at my goal of transcendent Mormon motherhood—I never will. Truly, there is no one destination, no ideal Mormon woman. Rather, our lives are composed of thousands of journeys, millions of transitions, and countless unpredictable twists and turns along the way. This is Mormon women striving for eternal progression. These are our lives—varied, ever-changing, and unforgettably real.

## Mourn with those that Mourn: Being a Hospital Chaplain
Emily Clyde Curtis
Phoenix, Arizona
Winter 2011 (vol. 31, no. 3)

*This essay is based on an excerpt from the keynote address given in February 2011 for the Claremont College conference, "Women's Lives, Women's Voices."*[2]

My dad always said, "If you're the best at what you do, you can always find a job." So, as a Mormon woman who belonged to a church that didn't ordain women and belonged to a church that relied on a lay clergy, I think I put his words to the test when I told him I wanted to get a master's degree in divinity.

Although I didn't know what I was going to do in terms of a profession, I was confident that I could be true to the Church by going to Divinity School. While I was there, I had the option to participate in the Field Education program, which places students preparing for ordination in churches, hospitals,

---

2. This editorial note is part of the original publication.

prisons, group homes, and other places. After a lengthy chronic illness as a teenager, I knew I wanted to work in a hospital, and I was thrilled to get a placement as a chaplain at Brigham and Women's Hospital in Boston, Massachusetts.

At my job, I had the privilege of being with people in both the darkest moments of their lives and during moments of intense joy. I have held the hands of people as they died, and I have cradled dying newborns. I have sat with people waiting to hear about the severity of their loved ones' injuries, and I have rejoiced with people who had miraculous healings, even as I have also learned to redefine what miraculous healings are.

I remember walking into the hospital on my first day being thrilled that I would be embodying the scripture in the Book of Mormon, Mosiah 18:8–9.

> *Now, as ye are desirous to come into the fold of God, and to be called his people, and are willing to bear one another's burdens, that they may be light; Yea, and are willing to mourn with those that mourn; yea and comfort those that stand in need of comfort.*

I feel indebted to the chaplaincy staff there. I could say that going to my office each day sounded like the beginning of a joke ... "So, an imam, a rabbi, and a priest are sitting together ..." but these staff members taught me universal themes of spirituality, and they showed me through their examples how to let my differences be an asset in my church service and how to deal with my spiritual struggles while staying in my church community.

I watched my Muslim friends struggle to connect with patients after 9/11 when people judged them by the color of their skin and the way they dressed. I watched my Catholic friends deal with the issues of women in the priesthood that so mirrored my own experiences, and I saw them struggle with the sex abuse scandals in their church. I also learned different and beneficial ways of thinking about spirituality from my Buddhist friends and Christians from denominations different from my own. Still, in some areas, I was on my own. I didn't know any Mormon chaplains, much less ones who were women, and there were times when I had to grapple with theological issues, never being sure if I was doing the right thing. One of these situations arose when I was asked to perform Catholic infant baptisms as part of my job description.

Because BWH has one of the largest Neonatal Intensive Care Units in New England, the chaplaincy department deals with a lot of stillborns and babies that die soon after birth. Living in a predominantly Catholic city like Boston, this meant that we were often called on to baptize these babies.

While Vatican II has refuted the belief that babies who die before being baptized go to purgatory, many Catholics still believe this. And I met with a few parents who were desperate for the ritual. As a Mormon woman, I was reticent to perform this ritual because my church taught me that these babies would go straight to God and there was no need for baptism. I also was uncomfortable because even though the Roman Catholic Church does not require a person to be ordained to perform the rite of baptism, in my Church, baptism is a ritual done by people who hold the priesthood. I knew that by performing baptisms for another church, I would be questioned by other Mormons who would feel that I was leading people astray by sanctioning this form of baptism.

Still, as a chaplain trying to support grieving families, I wanted to do whatever I could to ease their pain. And I knew the power religious rituals can have to comfort and bring the presence of God into a room full of sorrow. I also was terrified of being in a tragic situation and having to explain my very minor issue when time was of the essence.

One of the most painful conversations I have had about my career choice was when a male Mormon friend of mine enthusiastically tried to convince me that I should not baptize these babies because by doing so I was participating in "priestcrafts." He left his living room to grab his Book of Mormon and proceeded to read me scriptures defining priestcrafts and what happened to those individuals who participated in them (Alma 1:16). I don't think he realized how hard it was for me, someone who is not permitted to have the priesthood, to be told that this other way I had found to express my pastoral authority was wrong and sinful.

My husband was concerned, too, and we argued for months about whether or not I would baptize babies. My husband, Nate, you must understand, loves nothing more than a good argument. He will often argue an opinion he doesn't agree with, or even believes is defensible, just to see if he can change your mind. It was incredibly frustrating to hear him say, "Yes, you should be allowed to baptize, but no, you shouldn't baptize in this way." Fortunately, my colleagues were patient and understanding while I tried to figure out what to do.

Chaplains are only permitted to baptize babies that will not live very long. If there's a chance that the child's parish priest can make it in time, we wait. Better yet, if there's a chance that the child can be baptized in her church with her community, we do not do this ritual because as in the LDS church, Catholics believe that baptism is a chance to not only wash away sins, but also a ritual that welcomes the child into the church community and begins her religious life.

After much prayer, thought, and discussion with my supervisor and good friend, a Catholic nun who could identify with the issue of priesthood authority that I was facing, I decided what I would do to bring comfort to these families and to assuage the concerns of Mormons who felt like I should not perform this ritual.

I realized that as a Catholic priest had taught me the way to perform a baptism, I could teach a baby's parents how to perform this ritual. What better gift could I give a mother or father than to give them a memory of sharing what would most likely be the only life ritual they would have with their child?

The first time I did this I remember a young father looking at me dumbfounded when I asked him if he wanted to baptize his 28-week-old son who had not been responding to medical treatments and had only hours to live. After explaining the ritual and putting the water in his hands, I asked him again if he wanted to do this or if I should find someone else. He said he did, and as tears streamed down all of our faces, this baby's mother cradled her dying son while his father softly said, "I baptize you in the name of the Father and of the Son and of the Holy Ghost."

Though I long to perform the baptism ritual, I saw in that moment that this was the right thing for me to do.

As I deliberated over whether or not to perform baptisms, I found a way to serve in a ministerial capacity while staying true to the current stance of my religious tradition, even as I struggle with that stance. By finding another way, I was blessed with a sacred moment with this young family as we worked to find peace amidst the tragedy of losing a child.

## A Letter to the Brethren
Amy McPhie Allebest
San Clemente, California
Summer 2013 (vol. 33, no. 1)

I have been mentally composing an essay about my experience with the temple since I was first endowed 15 years ago, and just this past spring I finally decided to write my thoughts in letter form to a member of the Quorum of the Twelve. It (not surprisingly) never reached him; instead, I received a well-intentioned but quite dismissive response from the secretary to the First Presidency. While exploring possible venues to make my voice heard I happened upon *Exponent II* and literally gasped when I saw the title of the call for submissions—this is exactly what I have been seeking all these years.

April 2, 2013

Dear Elder _____,

To introduce myself briefly, my name is Amy. I am a 36-year-old woman, a BYU graduate, a returned missionary (Chile Santiago West Mission), a teacher, the wife of the man of my dreams, and the mother of four beautiful children. I am coming to you now with a concern that is affecting many women of my generation, and I humbly ask if you would be willing to consider it.

Last year (yes, all in the same year), two family members and three of my dearest friends—each completely independently of each other—all left the Church. They each cited gender issues as among their primary reasons. With each dear sister, I talked, prayed, reasoned, shared testimonies, and wept. But with each one I found myself confronting issues that have their roots in our doctrine, and specifically in phrases found in the temple that have caused me anguish as well, and for which I have not found any answers.

At the time of my endowment I had read stacks of books, scriptures, and Hugh Nibley articles. I had my mission call and was eager and open-minded and full of excitement for what I had been taught would be the pinnacle of my spiritual experience on earth. Much of the ceremony was beautiful, but there were two issues that I found jarring from my very first time through, and with which I have continued to struggle. Both were mentioned by each of my sisters: the pattern of who hearkens to whom (and how that plays out in a real marriage) and the description of eternal destiny.

The first issue is the pattern of "hearkening" when seeking counsel. In my marriage, when my husband and I are seeking guidance, my husband counsels with his Heavenly Father, with whom he has always had his own personal relationship. I, next to him, counsel with my Heavenly Father, with whom I have always had my own personal relationship. We then talk with each other and compare notes. There have been times when I don't know what to do and I gratefully hearken to his counsel. There have been times when he doesn't know what to do and he gratefully hearkens to mine. If we're seeking an answer that affects both of us we nearly always get the same answer; if not, we counsel together until we reach a consensus. If no consensus is reached, we table the matter until later, and in the meantime the "no" trumps the "yes." This is a pattern that felt intuitively right to us, as well as being confirmed by teachings of general authorities such as Elder Perry, who said, "there is not a president and vice president in a family. We have co-presidents working together eternally for the good of their family.... They are on equal footing. They plan and organize the affairs of the family jointly and unanimously as they move forward." This is the pattern we model and explicitly teach our children.

This decision-making process has its foundation in our understanding that we stand before God as spiritual siblings—different of course in gender, spiritual gifts, and personality traits—but equally loved, equally worthy, equally powerful children of God. Some religions teach that a human being needs a priest to step in between him and the Divine; but we cherish our religion's teachings that no human being—be it a priest or any other person—has the right to step into the relationship between an individual and his or her maker. We are grateful for the knowledge that ours is a living God, who directs his children actively and directly through personal revelation. In many religions and cultures women are regarded as inferior because of Eve's original sin; we are proud to belong to the religion in the Judeo-Christian world that defends Mother Eve's choice as necessary and positive. Modern LDS revelation has done much to correct harmful interpretations of the Genesis story of Eve, a story which the *Washington Post* has described as having "a more profoundly negative impact on women throughout history than any other."

And so I was shocked when in the temple I watched as Eve made her courageous choice, but then was treated as if she had lost God's trust, going from active participant to silent observer as Adam was placed as an intermediary between her and the Lord. I remember how my chest and throat tightened and tears came to my eyes as I was told that I, by virtue of my being a daughter of Eve, would no longer hearken directly to my Father in Heaven, as I had always been taught to do, but to hearken to my husband as he hearkened to God. I have returned to the temple over and over and over hoping to understand it differently than it feels, because the way it feels creates a visual image of God telling me that I am no longer worthy or trusted to approach him directly. This was and still is confusing and devastating to me. If "man will be punished for his own sins, and not for Adam's transgression," why is woman forever punished for Eve's?

The second issue is the temple's description of eternal destiny. I was taught my whole life that if we live righteously and accept Christ as our Savior, we will inherit all that the Father has and will live eternally in Heaven with him and with our families. As I grew older I learned more of the details and as I studied coronation ceremonies during my semester in Jerusalem I became more excited for the additional truths the temple ceremony would provide about my divine nature and eternal destiny as a child of the Most High. I clearly remember when I first heard the blessing for the brothers in the room—it was as I expected and hoped, that they would be Kings and Priests to God the Father for eternity. I was thrilled as an identical, parallel phrase began, promising me that I would be crowned a queen and anointed as a priestess, until I heard the end of this parallel phrase—that my future husband would be a king and a priest to God, and I would be a queen and a priestess, not to God, but to a mortal man. This thought fills me not with peace and joy, but with panic. Does not a priest or priestess officiate in ordinances of worship? So as a man is to God the Father, so a woman is to a man. This is my eternal destiny? This is Heaven? I love and respect my husband, but that dear boy I met at BYU is not my god.

Throughout the past 15 years I have prayed, fasted, and reached out for help to a bishop, a stake president, a temple president, a trusted and insightful BYU professor, and a close circle of sisters and a few friends. None of these has brought me any answers. Usually the conversations with the women include tears and "I just tune out during that part," "I just have faith that that's not what it really means," or "I have faith that it will change someday." I spent some time last year on several LDS feminist websites and learned quickly that I have no desire to be an angry activist, and my spirit does not feel close to the Lord there. This is why I am turning to you. I am deeply troubled by the exodus of so many women, and I want to help them stay. I don't know how this will unfold, but I feel the Spirit strongly urging me to start with this letter.

Here are some of my questions. I do not expect you to answer them—it would just mean a lot to me to know that you are aware of them.

- Why does the temple's presentation of the Fall reflect the traditional interpretation (condemning and punishing Eve and her daughters), rather than the words of modern prophets?
- What does the hearkening covenant really mean? How is that supposed to play out in decision-making in a modern marriage? How can the partnership be equal if only one spouse is required to hearken to the other's counsel?
- What does the parallel phrase of king : priest to God :: queen : priestess to husband actually mean?
- What do I teach my children about the temple? It seems that the temple is telling me to teach my daughters that in their youth they will seek guidance directly from the Lord, but once they are married, they will receive their guidance from their husbands, who will be seeking guidance from the Lord. Remove Lord's face, insert husband's. I cannot do this. I have seen countless cases of deplorable abuse which would be termed "unrighteous dominion," but to think of my daughters even marrying good men who will nevertheless feel justified controlling their lives, disregarding their ideas and opinions, or telling them that if it comes down to it, their male 51% power allotment will trump their female 49%—as I have heard many male friends explain—feels absolutely wrong to me. So for now, I focus on teaching my children Christlike living and doctrines that I do know to be true. But in saying nothing about the temple (my current strategy, since I don't want to introduce these issues to them), I worry that I am not preparing them to make sense of the ordinances that once held so much promise of joy for me and are now a symbol of pain and fear.
- I have a testimony of Jesus Christ and of the Restoration, but whenever I go to the temple I feel alienated and hurt. What should I do? For years I have continued to go, trying to open my heart and puzzle through alternate meanings to those words, but I continue to feel like the Lord is telling me

that I, as a daughter of Eve, am not as worthy as his sons. This has become too painful for me now, so presently I just participate in baptisms. (The initiatory ceremony is beautiful and powerful, but still contains variations of those troubling words.)

I love the Lord. I love the Bible and the Book of Mormon. I feel Jesus there. I love the safety of the standards of the Church. I love watching my husband bless and baptize our children—I personally feel the Spirit and a great cosmic balance in men officiating in the ordinances of the priesthood. (I was filled with hope when I read V. H. Cassler's article "The Two Trees.") I love serving in my ward. I love the Church of Jesus Christ of Latter-day Saints, and am committed to my covenants and enduring to the end. My patriarchal blessing states that it is my destiny to testify of "the beauty and promise of womanhood." My hope is that one day, I will be able to feel that beauty and promise from the words chosen to convey God's message to his daughters in the temple, not in spite of them.

My request in writing this letter is not that you answer these questions or even give me advice. I don't even need a letter in the mail. What I feel prompted to ask is this: Would you, as an apostle of the Lord, be willing to take this matter to the Lord for us, the women of the Church? I believe that the Lord reveals his secrets unto his servants, the prophets, and these revelations are often precipitated by their asking questions. From Joseph Smith asking about baptism to President Kimball asking about priesthood, for example, the prophets are in a position to ask questions of the Lord that prompt new revelation. We women can speak to the Lord for our own lives and our own families, but in matters of doctrine and policy that affect the whole Church (and affect us and our daughters in fundamental ways), we rely on you to ask the questions. I am tired of people I love leaving the Church, and I am tired of hearing the women who stay tell me, "I have faith that it will change," but then they don't think about how it will change. I am also not interested in asking for change through angry blog posts or news articles. In my understanding, changes to Church policies and even the temple ceremonies have happened in the past because prophets have asked the Lord questions, and he has answered. Please ask him for us.

Very Sincerely,
Amy Allebest

## Reinventing Emma Smith
Jana Riess
Cincinnati, Ohio
with Linda King Newell
Salt Lake City, Utah
Fall 2013 (vol. 33, no. 2)

*This article is adapted from a blog post that Jana wrote April 23, 2013. Our version includes additional information and clarifications from Linda. Original post copyright 2013 Religion News Service. Used by permission.*[3]

At the recent Midwest Pilgrims retreat in Nauvoo, Illinois, I had the opportunity to listen to a fascinating talk by Linda King Newell, co-biographer of Emma Smith, first wife of LDS founding prophet Joseph Smith, Jr.

In 1984, Linda wrote, with Valeen Tippetts Avery, *Mormon Enigma: Emma Hale Smith*, which has stood for nearly three decades as the definitive biography of Emma. Until that time, Emma had been largely written out of official LDS history. In the early 1970s, when the two authors began piecing together Emma's life, there was only one small manila folder about her in the entire LDS Archives.

One item in that folder was a photograph of Emma's adopted daughter Julia, mislabeled as Emma herself. Other than a few other references to her being Joseph's wife and first president of the Relief Society, that was it.

One book about Emma was in print, a biographical novel by RLDS writer Margaret Gibson, *Emma Smith, the Elect Lady* (1954)—truly a work of fiction, according to Linda. In 1978 another publication appeared, a pamphlet by Erwin E. Wirkus, *Judge Me Dear Reader*. This sympathetic view of Emma excused her actions by suggesting that she had lost her mind and should be forgiven.

So, before Linda and Valeen published their book, existing materials about Mormonism's First Lady were unfair or inaccurate. The real Emma had disappeared. Why?

We all use history to suit our purposes, and Emma simply did not suit the purposes of the LDS Church in the years following her husband's death.

It wasn't just that she was the mother of a boy whom many Saints felt to be Smith's rightful prophetic heir, rather than Brigham Young.

It wasn't just that she clashed with Young so severely that he once claimed that "more hell was never wrapped up in any human being than there is in her."

And it wasn't just that her son became the leader of a rival church, coalescing the support of many former Mormons who had stayed behind in the Midwest.

---

3. This editorial note is part of the original publication.

It was that she hated polygamy and flatly refused to countenance its presence among the Mormon people.

Emma's disappearance from LDS history was so total that Linda says when she and Val co-authored an article about her for the *Ensign* in 1979, it was the first writing about her to appear in any official church publication in 113 years.

It's a beautiful article, but it's not a complete one; polygamy is not mentioned once anywhere—but Linda and Val were told in advance that Church policy did not permit that no-no subject on the pages of its official publications. That, nearly a century after the Church began distancing itself from polygamy.

The biography Linda and Valeen published with Doubleday several years later detailed Joseph's many polygamous alliances, his repeated lies to Emma about those marriages, and her conflicts with his plural wives—including a much-debated stair-pushing catfight with Eliza R. Snow. It's an outstanding and award-winning biography that was the product of countless hours of primary research.

The biography was an instant commercial success, selling out its first two printings. At the time of the third printing, however, Linda received word that the bishop of a friend's ward had received a call from a higher-up in Salt Lake who said that "two girls" had written a book about Emma Smith, and they were not to encourage the sale of the book by inviting the authors to speak in their ward. When pressed, Linda's bishop admitted that he, too, had received a similar call. The authors were alarmed, though Linda was comforted by her stake president, who told her, "You are my parishioner, and I will see you through this no matter how long it takes."

It turned out that such calls had gone out to bishops and stake presidents in Utah, Idaho, and Arizona, where Val lived. Within three weeks, the press got wind of the authors' ecclesiastical silencing and began to report about it—thereby tripling sales of the book.

Linda requested and was granted a meeting with some general authorities, including Dallin Oaks, to discuss the ban and discover what aspects of the book had been found objectionable. According to Linda, when they asked Elder Oaks if he had read the biography, he said that he had read the chapters containing paragraphs that others had complained about, and had read some other chapters in the middle. He found that the authors' views of Joseph Smith were "nontraditional."

Nontraditional. Which is another way of saying that a particular view of history does not suit institutional needs in the moment.

In the past three decades, more has been published about Emma Smith in official Church channels, including *Daughters in My Kingdom* (2011), which mentions her very positively as the founder of the Relief Society, and the Gospel Doctrine manual for Church history, which holds her up as an example—somewhat reproachfully—of how to support one's spouse.

It's an improvement that she's discussed at all. But the way Emma's story is carefully sculpted reveals as much about gender expectations and religious norms in our own era as it did when Brigham Young declared her *mormona non grata*. For example, in the support materials for the Joseph Smith manual, polygamy is once again nowhere mentioned. If that were the only document people used to learn about Joseph Smith and his life, they would naturally assume that he was married once, to Emma, and not to approximately three dozen other women.

The way that current Church materials deal with Emma's conflict with Brigham Young is ... to ignore it entirely. According to the official narrative, Emma stayed behind in Nauvoo rather than joining the majority of the Saints in Utah because she was a widow caring for five young children and Joseph's aging mother, not because she believed that, as she expressed it at the time, "the Twelve have made bogus of it."

Although she never lost her faith in the Mormon religion and in the sacred nature of the Book of Mormon, she had no testimony of Brigham Young and other polygamous LDS leaders.

What's especially interesting to me about the unfolding historiography of Emma Smith is that she herself would have been happy with the disappearance of polygamy and Joseph's other wives from Mormonism's official party line. This is exactly what she had tried to institute herself as a theological agent in her own right, so much so that when the Reorganization was founded in the 1860s she declared that Joseph had never been married to anyone but herself. Emma knew better, but she also knew that a polygamous history would not serve the needs of her son, Joseph III, in his role as president and prophet of the Reorganization.

In a remarkable twist of irony, her version of history is increasingly the LDS Church's as well.

## Artist Spotlight: The Sacred History of Remnants
Page Turner
Winter 2014 (vol. 33, no. 3)

As a child I was steeped in Mormon culture, which defines and enforces gender roles and responsibilities. Elder generations heavily emphasize domestic skills, which they bestow upon the younger women. The traditions of women were a major focus of my early development—learning how to mend and alter clothing, sew on buttons, the proper way to iron, food preparation and preservation, all taught to women by women. While under the tutelage of these church sisters, I discovered the sacredness of personal objects: sewing tins filled with specific tools, someone's favorite old spoon, drawers of handmade aprons.

After my lessons and chores were completed, I was free. There was an abandoned house deep in the forest that was my sanctuary. This was my secret home. The windows were boarded up but the interior was intact and its contents all in their place. The bedroom had a vanity where the former inhabitant's makeup and hair pieces were still in the drawers. The rooms had trunks filled with old family tintypes, linens and other family heirlooms. I made mud pies in her kitchen and played dress-up in her clothes while wearing her hair pieces and jewelry. Her home was a sacred place where I walked in her shoes and practiced being the kind of woman my elders were grooming me to become.

I blame these early adventures because I have always been bewitched by what is kept and saved, and by objects that are perceived to have little or no value. I am especially tuned into objects and tools owned by women. These remnants, the everyday mementos that someone saves—sentimental objects, trifles, trinkets and sundries—find me and resonate with the history of our lost sisters. In the way that hair, bone and teeth remain, so do many of these trinkets and tools.

While attending Brigham Young University in Idaho, I found myself lost in a world created by Mormon culture. I was confronted by the expectations of my gender and the role that I was intended to play. Social pressures to marry and start a family forced me to evaluate the faith and the responsibilities of my gender. I responded by going to the university's library where I sought to find my place within the faith. It was not long until I found myself alone in the dark back rooms of the library, like I had as a child, where the old books were stored. One book called out to me, a worn leather-bound journal written by an unknown woman. She endured the Mormon exodus from Nauvoo, Illinois, to Salt Lake City, Utah, during the 1840s as a result of the Mormon Extermination Order. This journal was the honest account of truly hard times; entire families perished on the trek. The journal told of her wavering faith and questions about Joseph Smith being a prophet of God. The margins were filled with tatting patterns and sketches of the landscape. I pored over and over the journal. There was something about her that was like me. I saw how she focused on her creativity during the most tragic times on her journey. The last pages were marked by pattern pieces of a dress she intended to make when she reached the "promised land," Zion. I sketched her pattern into my own journal. Many things have changed in the subsequent years, but the dress pattern has always stayed with me.

UNIT 4: 2010-2015

Page Turner's piece "The Sacred History of Remnants" is an artist spotlight with six accompanying pictures.

265

Some time ago a pile of sugar sacks found its way to me. The old adage "Use it up, wear it out, make it do, or do without" rang in my mind. And I never stopped thinking about the dress pattern. I returned to the traditions and skills taught to me in my youth. I hand-stitched the gown and dress form out of one of these sugar sacks, saved by a woman who kept it as a valuable resource (Photo #3: Sugar Sack Gown). After the emotional connection I experienced by making her dress, I felt obligated to go further. I gave shape to the unknown woman in whose home I used to hone my domestic skills as a child (Photo #5: Sugar Sack Crinoline).

During a visit to South Carolina to spend time with my 96-year-old grandmother, I realized just how much of my self-reliance and independence comes from her. I went back to my journal to sketch out the women in my life and the influence they have had on me, the gifts that each has given me. I made 20 more dress forms and gowns as effigies of these women. I hand-stitch each dress form and create my own patterns for each garment, in honor of the tradition of domestic high art, the skills developed by my ancestors out of necessity and honed out of passion into a consummate art form. My sewing tools are all vintage and antique; there is a connection I make by using the same tools that these sisters used. My thimbles have wear and scratches from years of use. My sewing box is full of treasures from women long forgotten. Paying respect to these sisters, I turn their scraps back into sacred objects.

## So Many Words
Diane Pritchett
Cambridge, Massachusetts
Spring 2014 (vol. 33, no. 4)

*Equality, Inequity, Superiority, Authority*
*Preside, Ordain, Manage, Administer*
*Offices, Appendages, Ordinances, Keys*
*Exclude, Include*
*Definitude, Disquietude*

God wants us to all equally share the burdens and blessings of the priesthood.[4]

We can have equality while having different roles.[5]

This is not the first time these words have roiled my religious life. When

---

4. The following note was published in the original essay: Kate Kelly, "LDS Church Responds to Priesthood Meeting Requests by Activists," *Deseret News*, September 24, 2013.

5. The following note was published in the original essay: Linda K. Burton, "LDS Church Responds to Priesthood Meeting Requests by Activists," *Deseret News*, September 24, 2013.

I was a Mia Maid, my Young Women's teacher told us our role as women was to get up early on Sunday to iron our brothers' shirts as a way of sustaining the priesthood. I found a way to stay.

I was in college when Sonia Johnson and the ERA came along. A stake president dedicated an entire talk at stake conference to the evils of feminism. The feminism class and the Women's Studies department at BYU were abolished. I found a way to stay.

Around the time the September Six were excommunicated, a bishop withheld my temple recommend when I gave him some of the writings of Maxine Hanks and the *Exponent II* women as part of a difficult discussion we were having about the early practice of women giving blessings of health. I found a way to stay.

And now. Here is the younger generation bringing up the same words, the same arguments, the same responses. On all sides of the discussion, opinions are strong. Voices are certain.

We thought that by staying, living our marriages differently, raising our sons and daughters thoughtfully, waiting hopefully and prayerfully, we could avoid these heavy words again. I am tired. I am confused. I am too middle-aged for certainty. Must we do this again?

People we love leave because of these words. Their absence hurts.

I turn to words that have comforted me in the past:

> *The rights of the priesthood are inseparably connected with the powers of heaven.... No power or influence can or ought to be maintained by virtue of the priesthood, only by persuasion, by long-suffering, by gentleness and meekness, and by love unfeigned. By kindness and pure knowledge which shall greatly enlarge the soul without hypocrisy and without guile.... Let thy bowels also be full of charity towards all men and to the household of faith ... then shall thy confidence wax strong in the presence of God; and the doctrine of the priesthood shall distill upon thy souls as the dews from heaven.*[6]

My father was the bishop in our ward in Manila, Philippines. A baby with a critical illness had been born to a recently converted family. At the baby's blessing, the mother asked if she could hold the baby during the blessing. My father, a lifetime member of the Church who had always held positions of traditional authority and leadership, welcomed the mother in the blessing circle. The baby died the week after the blessing. *Charity.*

When my mother had six children under the age of ten, she was assigned to visit teach Millie, a large amputee with equally large needs. She called her visiting teacher for every need, including, on one memorable occasion, Rice

---

6. The following note was published in the original essay: D&C 121: 36–45

Krispies for her dog. My mother was so involved with her that when we were in the midst of moving away from the area, and my sister found my mother weeping as she packed, she asked, "Are you crying because you are going to miss Millie?" *Love unfeigned*.

In church one Sunday a sister who was a recent convert from Catholicism, on stepping up to the stand to bear her testimony, knelt down to touch my father's feet, much like one would a cardinal or pope. As we watched in awkward horror, wondering what would happen next, my father gently took her hand and walked her to the podium, where he stood quietly by her side while she spoke. *Without guile*.

I was in a grocery store one day with my mother. Behind us in line was a young toddler who was screaming at the top of her lungs. The mother of the toddler was at her wit's end. She began to yell horrible things to her baby. Just as she was about to strike the child, my mother gently, with great sympathy, put her arm around the angry mother and pointed out the sun that was in the toddler's eyes. Together they calmed the crying toddler. *Persuasion*.

My father gave all his children annual blessings before the start of school. The memory of his hands on my head still comforts me when I feel scared. *Confidence wax strong*.

My mother stayed awake an entire night on her knees praying for my sick baby because I was afraid if I left him he would die, but I desperately needed sleep. Even though she was on the other side of the country, I knew I could call her and that she would stay awake watching over him. She prayed. I slept. He lived. *Presence of God*.

My mother-in-law went daily to a ward member's house for several years at bedtime to help a sister put on pressure stockings for bedtime because the sister was unable to do it herself. *Long-suffering*.

A bishop showed up at the hospital when my husband needed a blessing. No one called him. No one asked him to come. He just knew. *Pure knowledge*.

A home teacher showed up with a chainsaw and several other members of the ward to remove a large tree that had fallen on our car after a storm. *Kindness*.

A visiting teacher who had spent months helping me care for my sick baby gave him a blessing as she walked him around my living room helping him breathe. He had already received blessings by men, but she knew I needed him to have this female blessing. She didn't ask. She just did it. *Powers of Heaven*.

A bishop showed up early in the morning at the hospital the day our baby had his first heart surgery just to sit with us for a bit while we waited. *Patience*.

Actions of love conveying the connection to heaven. *Priesthood*.

It is easy to get lost in words like authority, ordinances, keys, offices, administration, and power. It is easy to forget that priesthood is "to wax strong in the presence of God." When God is not present, there is no priesthood. The words alone mean nothing. God's presence in the action means everything. God's presence ordains the action.

A woman in our ward was struggling with postpartum depression. The Relief Society had been arranging meals, caring for her children, and monitoring the family round the clock, but it became clear that we were working beyond our level of expertise. Hospitalization was essential. We knew that this was not news she would want to hear. Her husband, her visiting teachers, a member of the bishopric, and I gathered to discuss our options. As we prayed, it became clear to everyone in the room that before taking her to the hospital she needed a blessing and that this blessing must come from women.

This answer to our prayers distilled gently and clearly throughout the room. It was not a revolutionary or radical statement. We did not ask permission. We did not consult the handbook. Apart from deciding how we would proceed and that I would speak the words, we didn't even discuss it much. We took action. We gathered in her living room. Her husband and the member of the bishopric sat quietly in the background while the women embraced her in a circle.[7]

I do not remember the words I said that day. They were not from me.

I do not have words for *why* women should or should not be ordained to the priesthood, or for what God thinks about male and female roles. When I search for words, there is nothing but disquietude. And yet, again, I stay. Here, in this circle of my people—female and male—there are acts of kindness, charity and love unfeigned, infused with the power of heaven and the presence of God. Let others use words of *power, authority, ordinances, offices, keys and rights*. For me there is only the action of love.

Priesthood is there when love is there.

*gentleness, meekness, love unfeigned*
*kindness, pure knowledge, without hypocrisy,*
*without guile*
*inseparably connected to Heaven*
*charity, virtue, presence of God distill upon my soul*
*dew from Heaven*

---

7. For more on women's blessings, see pages 49–50, 87–89, and 347–49.

## Deployed Without the Priesthood
Abby Maxwell Hansen
Lehi, Utah
Spring 2014 (vol. 33, no. 4)

I have been married to a wonderful, active LDS man who honors his priesthood for over eleven years. He has treated me wonderfully in every aspect of our lives together. He is also a member of the Army Reserves and has spent significant time away from me and our children as the result of trainings and deployments. I've adjusted to this routine of married life, and accept it as part of the sacrifice I make to be married to such a great man and live in freedom.

A deployment caused my husband to miss the birth and most of the first year of our first son's life. He deployed a second time when that son had just turned four, we had a one-year-old daughter, and I was fifteen weeks pregnant with our third baby. Two days after he left, I had a miscarriage and lost the pregnancy. I came home from the hospital alone and grieved. Part of my healing process was when two friends came over and visited me one evening shortly after. I don't remember much about the conversation, other than feeling so safe and loved with these two women, both mothers and both women who had suffered miscarriages. I remember laughing and crying with them. They are still some of my closest friends.

As the visit neared its end, one of these women asked me, "Would you like a blessing? We could have our husbands come over and give you one." I remember hesitating for a moment. I was still bleeding and cramping. I was in my pajamas and had been crying, and I wasn't sure if I felt up to having two men who were not my husband come over to see me right then. On the other hand, I was really interested in hearing what God might have to say to me at that moment, and so I said yes, I would like a blessing.

My friends left to take over at home with their kids, and shortly after their husbands returned without them. While it felt a little awkward being alone with two men in that state, they gave me a sweet blessing that I am grateful for. I imagine my discomfort was probably surpassed by theirs, being asked on short notice to come alone and bless a married woman during such an intensely female time in her life.

I didn't consider at that time there could ever be another way of doing things. I now have a different point of view. From this new perspective I think, "How beautiful would it have been for my two friends, rather than their husbands, to have given me that blessing of healing and comfort?" There would have been no awkwardness, no discomfort, and certainly no less ability to speak the words that my Heavenly Parents wanted me to hear right then.

In my ward I have found myself on the other end of this spectrum as well, wanting to serve and yet being limited by my position as a woman in our Church. My husband went to the hospital instead of me when my neighbor's infant daughter lay within hours of her death to help administer a blessing. Only one of us could go to be with her, and it had to be him because he held the priesthood. How I wish I could have seen my friend and been there for her at that critical moment in her life. My other friend's husband left her and their three children after a decade of marriage. I can offer her my unfailing friendship, love, and help in many ways, but I can't help her bless her children in the middle of the night when one of them is sick. Another friend had her first baby but decided to forgo blessing her because her husband was no longer a member and they preferred not to have someone outside of their family perform the blessing.

My young neighbor who had been a child in my Nursery and Primary classes for several years was diagnosed with leukemia and went through years of chemotherapy. I was able to visit her at home with a Primary lesson when she couldn't attend church, but I was never able to help bless her or bring her the sacrament.

I watched my wonderful fourteen-year-old nephew be ordained a teacher by his dad just a couple of months ago. The ordination was at his aunt and uncle's house, and the family gathered together to participate and celebrate. It was even postponed a half hour while he waited for another uncle, a truck driver who had been driving all day, to arrive and join the circle of men. During the blessing, I noticed his mom, aunts, and grandmothers all sitting to the side, trying to keep children quiet. I also noticed his equally wonderful older sister, my niece, standing off to the side. Where was the ritual ordinance, increased responsibility, and celebration for her when she'd turned fourteen? It felt so lopsided and unequal. Another friend attended her all-male disciplinary council years ago and was asked very inappropriate and intrusive questions, leading to a long period of inactivity afterward. I want to ensure that any future girl or woman who confesses a sexual sin can meet with a female priesthood leader and be judged by a disciplinary council that includes women.

Two months ago my husband blessed our newest daughter in Sacrament Meeting. I wanted to be up there with him, even if it was just to hold her in my arms while he gave the blessing, as I would at home when he blesses a sick child. But it wasn't allowed. I didn't feel that longing with my first two babies, but something inside of me has changed. I still want to be a part of this Church, but I don't want to do it as a woman who is expected to sit and wait to receive blessings, depending on men for approval and availability in everything I do. I want to serve and give those blessings. I want women to be among my leaders and to make decisions. I want my daughters to look up on the stand and see women next to men, leading and teaching our congregations. I want to mean it when I say to them, "You can be ANYTHING when you grow up," and not have to add, "except in the Church," when she says, "I want to be the prophet!"

I want the Relief Society to be a true women's organization, not an auxiliary group under the leadership of male priesthood holders with veto power over any of their decisions. I want women to preside and conduct our meetings. I love hearing from our male leaders at these meetings, but in exchange I want women to attend the priesthood meetings and be speakers there as well.

In short, I want a church like the one Elder Uchtdorf described in the October 2013 General Conference. He said, "Regardless of your circumstances, your personal history, or the strength of your testimony, there is room for you in this Church." I want to belong to a church that has room enough, and a need for, women like me.

## Remembering *Exponent II*: A Beacon in the East
Maxine Hanks
Salt Lake City, Utah
Fall 2014/Winter 2015 (vol. 34, no. 2 & 3)

I was studying alone on the second floor of the Ricks College library, watching the snow cover icy sidewalks as students inched up the incline. Needing a break from biology, I roamed the shelves, inexplicably pulled toward an aisle where an apparently misplaced magazine attracted me. Its pages were covered in semi-psychedelic drawings and funky handmade typefaces. Surely this was a mistake that the librarians would soon remove. I took the paper in my hands and touched pages that seemed taboo. Glancing around, I sneaked it back to my carrel, where my eyes consumed each page, wondering who these Mormon women were, and how they found the courage to produce this paper.

Encountering *Exponent II* was an epiphany: I knew I wasn't alone. There were other women like me in the Church, feminists—in the 1970s. It was an unimagined validation to a stressed teen struggling for Self. I'd stumbled into a secret club, a hive of free-thinking feminists, ensconced in Boston, across the continent. Their voices streamed like a beacon light piercing the night in Idaho. These women were brave enough to put their inner selves onto paper, into print and send it across the country to my school. In 1976, I'd never seen anything like it. Yet it felt like home.

*Exponent II*'s artsy pages embraced headlines that blew my mind—visible assertions of inner truths and invisible struggles that were so controversial then: "*Woman's Exponent* Revisited," "What the ERA Will Mean to You," "Sisters and Suffragists," "women: education," "Notes on the Self Concept," "To Have A Career or Be a Homemaker?," "Me, A Sister Missionary?," "Women and the Priesthood," "The Mormon Female Experience," and "Closet Feminists." These women were not only thinking what I was thinking, they were speaking it, out loud. The headlines really said—"It's OK to Be Me"—after all. I wasn't the only alien in Mormondom. I was a feminist, "women's libber," avowed single, mission-hungry, honors student, and writer, co-chairing "Women's Week" with themes like "Woman Clothed with the Sun." I was a misfit: a liberal intellectual, nonconformist loner in a conservative workingclass family culture. God had dropped me in Idaho, but there were people like me in the East.

Boston seemed a world away, like a dream of Harvard or MIT. *Exponent II* bridged that distance with a glimpse of the Ivy League. Feminist writings from Claudia Bushman, Laurel T. Ulrich, Judy Dushku, Nancy Dredge, Carrel Sheldon, Lorie Winder, and Sue Paxman floated across pages illustrated by Carolyn Durham's feministic artistic flair. These were Eastern women; I never dreamed I would know them.

I missed *Exponent II* when I left school to work, then serve an LDS mission. However, its pages stayed with me, confirming my inner life. It had introduced me to Mormon women's studies, adding LDS history to my interests. When a mission quiz asked, "What magazine takes its name from an LDS women's publication of the 1880s?" I quipped, "*Exponent II*, named for the *Woman's Exponent*." "How did you know that?" the Elders asked. "I read *Exponent II*," I said. In 1979, I was privy to hidden discourse found only in liberal Mormon publications. *Exponent II* validated my Mormonism and my feminism, as a devoted LDS sister who entered men's work, and wouldn't oppose the ERA (Equal Rights Amendment) or the IWY (International Women's Year).

At BYU, I found *Exponent II* in the library and resumed my relationship. I worked for the College of Humanities in the 1980s editing manuscripts. Yet I envied my friends who went East to Boston for internships at *Exponent II*, as each returned a new person. I believed Boston could transform me too, but I couldn't fathom how to get there. *Exponent II* was East, and I was West, so I wrote for the Seventh East Press and *Sunstone*. Yet *Exponent II*'s deeply personal voices mentored me, helping me find my own. Mormon women's prose and poetry emerging in the '80s inspired me to write innumerable poems, texts, essays, manuscripts, and pieces of personal narrative, in private files and computers. It was enough just to get them out of me.

*Exponent II* stood nearly alone on the Mormon landscape in the 1980s; we had *Dialogue* and *Sunstone*, but the only feminist publications were

*Exponent II* and the Mormons for ERA newsletter. Mormon feminist writings in the '80s were flickering lights in the dark night between Sonia Johnson's excommunication in 1979 and the Mormon Women's Forum in 1988. Few remember how feared feminism was then—simply using the word was taboo. Women treaded water in a deluge of men's views. We could barely speak, much less find our own language. We had no voice nor vocabulary for our own voicelessness. We tried to write female texts in male words. We had no feminist context, no community, no internet, no blogs. We huddled in isolated groups at *Exponent II*, Mormons for ERA, the Algie Ballif Forum, BYU, U of U, and the Mormon Women's Forum. We didn't know we were a discourse, half a religion. We swam in a sea of malespeak, our voices like buoys, too far apart.

*Exponent II* kept Mormon feminism afloat in the 1980s by rafting women's voices together and reviving the memory of our feminist foremothers via "the spiritual descendent of the *Woman's Exponent*." *Exponent II* was our historical bridge between past and present. It was also a beacon in the East, guiding Mormon feminism safely into the 1990s, where we could finally know a discourse of our own.

The solution was simply more of the same—collect feminist texts from the beginning to the present, as evidence of another discourse amid the dominant one. Partly inspired by *Exponent II*, I compiled *Women and Authority: Re-emerging Mormon Feminism* in 1987–92, to bridge the gaps between Mormon feminists and their texts. It united feminists scattered across time and space, together in one place, one discourse. I excerpted feminist writings from the *Woman's Exponent, Exponent II, Dialogue, Sunstone*, the Algie Ballif Forum, MERA, BYU, MWE and personal interviews.

I chose thirty of my favorite pieces from *Exponent II*, Vols. 1–16, with phrases like, "I voted 'no' in sacrament meeting" ... "Understanding our Heavenly Mother by praying" ... "Girls get to pass the sacrament, too, right?" ... "Mother-in-heaven [sic] could be recognized as the head of the Relief Society" ... "Why not have a general conference when we hear only from the wives?" My selection ended with brave words about abortion.

Amazingly, *Exponent II* always told the truth while maintaining a middling image. When the Mormon Women's Forum emerged in 1988 (started by Karen Case), it was seen as more confrontational, political while *Exponent II* was viewed as more conciliatory, personal. Yet in 1990–92 when Utah and the nation opposed abortion rights, we protested at the Capitol, and *Exponent II* gave us wrenchingly real stories.

I'll never forget *Exponent II*, Vol. 15 no. 4, "Abortion: Learning to Speak from Experience," along with Vol.16 no. 1 "Adoption vs. Abortion." Mormon women asserted that "abortion does not kill the spirit; what it does mean is that spirit is forced to go elsewhere" and "adoption is not a solution to abortion.... I was not supposed to go through this tragedy so that some family could have my baby." At the Mormon Women's Forum we were so affected by *Exponent II*, we devoted an issue of the MWF Quarterly to abortion in 1992.

We were not more brave than *Exponent II*, but MWF countered the Church in Salt Lake City. Church discipline of feminists was rare before the 1990s. The one thing we "90s Five" had in common (Lynne Kanavel Whitesides, Lavina Fielding Anderson, Janice Allred, Margaret Toscano, and me—women disciplined in 1993–2000), was that we all worked on the Mormon Women's Forum. (I was on the Board 1989–99 and co-edited the *Quarterly*.)

In the aftermath of the "purge of 1993," Judy Dushku closed the distance between *Exponent II* and MWF by keynoting at Counterpoint in Salt Lake. She embraced us Forum heretics with *Exponent II* motherly love. She also symbolized an invisible link between East and West—Mormon feminists from Idaho who moved beyond their roots (like Sonia, Laurel, Judy, Lavina, me, and others).

A decade later, I went east. I was studying theology at Harvard, sitting with grad students in the basement of the HDS library, warming my soul in the fire of our ideas. It was 2006, the "50th Anniversary of Women at HDS," and I was on fellowship that semester, finally arriving in Boston. Judy took me to my first Exponent meeting—exactly thirty years after I first found *Exponent II* at Ricks.

The evening was surreal. We gathered in Nancy Dredge's living room with Laurel, Judy, Carrel, and Barbara Taylor, and younger women like Kate Holbrook and Aimee Evans Hickman. They wanted to hear about my fellowship, my work, and my story.

Yet they had been with me all along, from the beginning, in the mid-'70s. Their stories had always inhabited my heart, helping me write my own.

## The Radical Mission of Exponent II
Aimee Evans Hickman
Fall 2014/Winter 2015 (vol. 34, no. 2 & 3)

In response to a recent fundraiser, we received a generous $100 donation from one of our readers along with the following note: "Hoping you'll get a bit more radical." As *Exponent II* commences (what I hope will be at least) another 40 years of sharing women's experiences, this comment hints at how the question of *Exponent II*'s role in the larger discussion of Mormon women's issues is still as open to debate as it might have been 40 years ago.

When *Exponent II* was first conceived, its focus was not just in preserving women's voices but also in a radical project to engage them in difficult discussions while freeing them from the kinds of faith-promoting narratives that too often turn dynamic, personal experiences into static devotional objects all their own. The concept to "publish this paper as a living history in celebration of the strength and diversity of women," was in part a radical act to counter cultural platitudes and pieties about Mormon femininity that dominate so many of our correlated materials. Throughout its history, *Exponent II* has sought to expand the definition of a faithful Mormon woman, not by challenging people's faith, but by validating women's lives which both adhere to and diverge from idealized cultural narratives of Mormon womanhood. By exploring the way Mormon women grapple with their faith when life doesn't fit prescribed expectations or when the Church fails to live up to its own standards, *Exponent II* writers have been able to shift from viewing alternative life paths or Church failings as merely liabilities in their spiritual journey, to embracing those experiences in order to better understand the full picture of Mormon womanhood. Rather than seeing these detours and disappointments as events that women must simply use their faith to overcome, *Exponent II* has always endeavored to be a forum where diverse life-experiences and perspectives could be honestly shared, mourned, and celebrated.

The valorization of differing perspectives and life choices available to Mormon women anchors *Exponent II* in a feminist tradition which prioritizes the moral agency of women while giving full expression to women's voices. This broad scope offers some measure of validation to both those who are comforted by and struggle with being women in a patriarchal world and institution. Such free expression has also given *Exponent II* writers license to examine topics often considered too radical or taboo for most official Church publications, including subjects like abortion, LGBTQ issues, the Equal Rights Amendment, Church discipline, Heavenly Mother and many more. Rather than seeing such topics as subjects which must be skirted around to produce faithful, uplifting writing, many Mormon women have shown how grappling with these issues through honest spiritual inquiry and literary forms can become critical components in constructing an honest spiritual life.

So what does our loyal reader mean when she says that she "hopes [we'll] get more radical?" In the last two years alone, *Exponent II* has devoted entire issues to women's relationship to the priesthood and reflected honestly and critically on women's experience with temple worship. In 2014 we published an article praising the beauty of attending a gay wedding in Utah, and an article criticizing the Church for not putting as much political weight behind immigration reform as it did behind Prop 8. The truth is that for most modern LDS readers, the topics we explore radically exceed correlated boundaries.

So if the boldness of our subject matter isn't really in question, it seems that what our good reader is really asking is whether or not the act of validating a variety of lived experiences as authentically Mormon qualifies as "radical" in and of itself. In recent years as we've seen the formation of many activist Mormon feminist groups including WAVE (Women Advocating for Voice and Equality), Let Women Pray, Pants, and Ordain Women, whose explicit activist agendas are intent on changing minds, policies, and perhaps even doctrine, is *Exponent II*'s mission to share a variety of Mormon women's voices still seen as radical? This question was driven home to me a few months ago when a friend of mine who's heavily involved in one of these activist organizations commented that we Exponent women "just don't seem to have an activist bone in our bodies." I was taken aback. Every time we pay to put these words in print, a glorious hope rises up in me that feels simultaneously brave, holy, and defiant. But as our reader has proven, my friend doesn't seem to be alone in this assessment of what constitutes radicalism in this current moment. And it causes me to wonder, as a feminist organization, is *Exponent II* obligated to do more than share and support the variety of women's choices seen in the pages of our magazine? Or do we need to explicitly define and model a fully conceived Mormon feminist rhetoric and agenda of our own?

As Ordain Women was gaining steam and national media attention in 2014, *Exponent II* was contacted by media outlets who were interested in how our organization positioned itself in the conversation about women and the priesthood. I think that on all sides, many were disappointed in the stock response I offered, which was that *Exponent II* is not an "activist" organization lobbying for specific institutional changes. As we have since the ERA debates of the 1970s and 80s, *Exponent II* shares the thoughts and experiences of Mormon women considering their role within a patriarchal structure, without advocating a position of our own. *Exponent II*'s objective to provide a forum where Mormon women across the spectrum feel safe to explore these ideas, is in itself a feminist statement, I argued.

What I fear this argument inadvertently conveys to some is a wishy-washy feminism loosely defined as simply supporting all women's choices. And yet I believe that the work of *Exponent II* is so much more than that. If part of the work of feminism is to reveal a world which is fundamentally more limited for women than for men, *Exponent II* has done that both implicitly and explicitly throughout its history. But in the current Mormon feminist activist climate which aims not just to reveal but also to actively upend patriarchal structures, *should Exponent II* do more than validate the diverse experiences of Mormon women and instead insist that the experiences from which they choose be more expansive to begin with? In *Exponent II*'s mission statement the word "feminist" isn't even used, for example. Should it be? Laurel's remarks from earlier tonight are the first time I've ever heard that *Exponent II* was originally "poised on the dual platforms of Mormonism and Feminism," whose two aims, Claudia Bushman declared, were "to strengthen the Church of Jesus Christ of Latter-day Saints and to encourage and develop the talents of Mormon women." I'm not sure why this was removed from our mission statement, but I for one would like to see it brought back.

The implicit feminist project of *Exponent II*'s uncorrelated publication of living history was more than enough for many to consider us too radical or subversive throughout the first three decades of our existence. But then Feminist Mormon Housewives came on the scene in 2004, putting the "F" word at the center of the conversation. fMh and the Bloggernacle at large spawned even more online Mormon feminist forums and no doubt even influenced the formation and early content of *The Exponent* blog. I believe the authoritative and ubiquitous use of the "F" word has galvanized many of the activist-oriented organizations and rhetoric we have seen crop up in the last few years. It has in some ways also opened a chasm between women who feel a need for changes they themselves have not yet named, and those who know exactly what they want and are making efforts to effect those changes themselves.

There's no question in my mind that these activist groups have made an impact on the institution and culture of the Church in the last few years that many of us would applaud. Indeed, much of what has been percolating in the Mormon feminist echo chamber seems finally to have found its way into more mainstream or self-described "moderate Mormon" circles. While there's a healthy debate to be had about whether or not groups like "let women pray" or Ordain Women actually jeopardize the institutional changes they seek by putting the Church in a position where making any changes might appear as though the institution was succumbing to outside pressure, there's no question that these conversations are reaching lay members as well as those at the top of Church leadership.

So where does *Exponent II* fit into this landscape going forward? What do we need to do as an organization to stay relevant in broad Mormon feminist conversations while also staying true to our original mission? Does a project like our upcoming coloring book which will depict a diverse group of women from Mormon history have the capacity to grab the attention of both those in and outside mainstream Mormonism? Or are these subtler forms of feminist education seen as too dangerous by those already afraid of the "F" word, while being dismissed as merely paying tribute to a radical past without challenging the future by members of more activist feminist groups?

In my bones I believe in *Exponent II*'s mission to act as a living history of the current moment. In a world inundated with individual perspectives cropping up in dozens of public online forums daily, I believe more than ever in the importance of rigorously curating and publishing as broad a spectrum of Mormon women's voices as possible to represent our historical moment. Such even-handedness may not appear radical, but as our resident historians here will likely affirm, the quiet voices that are often lost to history may be where the biggest cultural shifts are manifested in the end.

And so this work requires that we capture not just the finely honed Mormon women's voices (whether they be radically feminist or radically anti-feminist), but the voice of the woman who is still seeking, still listening, and just beginning to wonder for the first time why she can't help bless and name the infant she brought into the world; why she can't hear a voice like hers trip-up the words to the sacrament prayer; why the grand promises of eternity given in the temple are not so much hers as they are unto her husband; why she feels uneasy everytime the word "feminist" is used; and how she, like all of us, begins to make sense of the internal dissonance these thoughts often produce.

In our church we are taught to stand as living witnesses to God's work. I believe that as *Exponent II* continues to procure and publish this living history that more fully reveals modern Mormon womanhood, we not only honor the emboldening legacy we've inherited, but that as we move forward collectively, creatively and wisely, 40 years from now our literal and figurative daughters, granddaughters, and great-granddaughters might be able to sing "Woman Rise" in the past tense. For myself, I cannot imagine a more radical change I'd like to see.

## As I Am
Averyl Dietering
Davis, California
Spring 2015 (vol. 34, no. 4)

"But you're so much more than your sexual orientation."

I hear those words a lot. I hear them from my mom when I try to explain to her how I can't hide my queer identity, even though I feel alienated and rejected because of it. I hear them from my well-meaning friends who don't understand why I "have to make *everything* about being queer." I hear them from Church leaders as they assure LGBTQIA+ members that it's possible to remain in the Church as long as you are celibate or married to an opposite-sex partner.

Most of the time I don't know how to respond when people remind me that I'm more than my sexual orientation. I am sure that they are well-meaning, that they are telling me this because they want me to know that they see me as a complex individual and not just another stereotype. But at the same time, there's also a subtext lying just under the surface of this sentiment. When friends, family members, or Church leaders feel the need to tell me that I'm more than my sexuality, it's typically in situations when my sexuality is inconvenient or uncomfortable for them. They don't want to deal with all the complications that my queer sexuality causes, so they downplay it in order to emphasize other aspects of my identity. I can sense their uneasiness as they scramble to affirm parts of my identity they can accept, while rejecting the others that they can't handle. What they mean to say is:

"I don't know how to respond to your needs as a queer person, and that frightens me. Maybe if I can convince you that the queer part of you is not as important as the other parts of you, then I can respond to the parts of you that I like, and pretend the others don't exist?"

And I am left fractured.

\*\*\*

I use the term "queer" to describe my sexual identity because it's the closest word I can find to describe how I feel. Some people are afraid to use "queer" because of its history as derogatory slang, but for many years the LGBTQIA+ community has been working to reclaim "queer" from its hurtful origins. I like identifying as queer because it allows for my sexual identity to be fluid and unrestrained by a prescriptive label. Some of my friends have found my identity as queer to be unsettling because they're not sure what it means. But that's the point. Queer is an unsettling identity that forces people to see me on my own terms. When I identify as queer, I retain the power to define myself. I refuse to fit your definition.

\*\*\*

What part of me is queer? Is it possible for me to isolate all of my non-heterosexuality into one fragment of myself and then close the door on it, as seems to be required of me? As a Mormon, it would be convenient if I could push every queer thought or feeling I've ever had into my right hand and then cut it off, a la Matthew 5:30. But it doesn't work that way. My sexuality isn't something I can pick out and isolate, like separating towels from sheets in the laundry. It's more like the ingredients in a cake: a portion of the cake is sugar, but it would be impossible to try to separate the sugar from the rest of the cake once it's baked. Not to mention that without any sugar, it wouldn't be much of a cake.

I am not always actively engaged in thinking about my sexual orientation, but it colors my life in more ways than I can expect or comprehend. My perspective as a queer person has varying, unpredictable effects on the way I see family, clothing, politics, movies, sports, religion, the economy ... the list goes on and on. Sometimes being queer is the last thing on my mind, like when I'm walking through a busy grocery store and trying not to bump into anyone. But then I hear someone jokingly call their friend a homoantagonistic slur, and suddenly I feel very queer.

***

"But you're so much more than your _____."

These words aren't only said to LGBTQIA+ Mormons. We could fill in the blank: you're so much more than your mental illness, than your ethnicity, your physical disabilities, your weight, age, gender, religion, race, sins, nationality. We all know what it's like to be on the receiving end of these words, to feel disappointed and even angry as a friend refuses to acknowledge part of our identity or experience because they're afraid to talk about it. On the other hand, we also probably know what it's like to speak these words to someone, in hopes that we can just move on from the part of them that makes us uncomfortable.

What happens to relationships when we fragment each other in this way? I think of times that I shied away from much-needed conversations with my Latina and Asian friends in high school about their experiences with racism and faulty immigration policies. Because I am white, their experiences were different from mine—but I didn't want to think about those differences because they exposed the cracks in what I thought was a flawless situation. What was lost in our relationship because I failed to talk about topics that made me feel uneasy, troubled, and even guilty? What was lost because I would rather fragment their identities rather than acknowledge the flaws in my own world view? When we fragment others in order to preserve our privileged perspectives, we fail to be empathetic and compassionate, and we lose opportunities to expand our horizons.

This does not mean that we must always see every aspect of everyone's personality from the beginning. That's simply not possible. And it's likely that our friends and family members will not share their entire identities with us from the beginning. What we can do, however, is acknowledge the complexity of their lives as they share it with us. We can affirm their identities, letting them know that we want to be better at seeing them in their wholeness, even if that means complicating our views or acknowledging problems that frighten us.

***

I have not often been with a friend who can appreciate fully both my queer and my Mormon identities. My Mormon friends tend to ignore my sexuality, while my non-Mormon friends often downplay my religious heritage. As a result, it is a rare and holy experience to be with someone who can understand how deeply interconnected my queerness and Mormon-ness are. At times like these, when I am in the company of someone who appreciates the complexities of my narrative, the claim that "you are so much more than your sexuality" rings true, for it means that I am whole as a queer Mormon woman, and that this wholeness is greater than the sum of its parts.

In the New Testament, Jesus often healed people by commanding them to be whole:

> And he said unto her, Daughter, thy faith hath made thee whole; go in peace.
> When Jesus saw him … he saith unto him, Wilt thou be made whole?
> Afterward Jesus findeth him in the temple, and said unto him, Behold, thou art made whole.
> When Jesus heard it, he answered him, saying, Fear not: believe only, and she shall be made whole.

Perhaps we can likewise heal each other by seeing one another as whole.

## The Color-Blind Conundrum
Kalani Tonga
Spring 2015 (vol. 34, no. 4)

A few years ago when I was employed as a paralegal, I worked for an attorney who taught me an important lesson about embracing differences and about our perceptions of group membership. When I first started working for him, he took me to lunch so that we could get to know each other. He told me he was Korean and told me a bit about his family. I revealed that I was biracial—half Tongan and half Swedish. We bonded over my ethnicity, as he had grown up in one of the few cities in Texas with a fairly large Tongan population. We chatted for a moment about the Tongan culture, and then he told me:

> I was in elementary school when the Tongans first started moving in. I remember talking to my classmates about a new Tongan kid in my class, and saying, "Yeah, who is this guy? He's not like us!" And, much to my surprise, my friends turned to me and said, "What do you mean 'US'? YOU'RE not like US either! You're Korean!" And that was the first time I realized that the group I thought I was a part of saw me as an outsider.

We went on to have a great conversation about being inclusive and finding commonalities. We also discussed the importance of seeing the value in difference. There is great value in variety, but I think it is often easier to focus on commonalities at the expense of appreciating the beauty of our differences. So often, especially when it comes to race, it is easier to say, "I don't see color" than to say, "I see value in your color."

I recently watched a video that a young Black man named Will Stack made after he was stopped in traffic and was not harassed, abused, shot, or killed by a policeman. Mr. Stack created the video to make the point that, as law abiding citizens, we have nothing to fear from officers of the law, and his video was in direct response to the current racial tensions between People of Color and law enforcement officers.

As I watched the video, something felt deeply uncomfortable to me, but I couldn't quite put my finger on it. When I engaged in conversation about both the video and the circumstances that led to the video going viral, my discomfort only deepened. There are several things about the video I find troubling, but I want to address just one. In his closing remarks, Mr. Stack states, "God doesn't see color. Why should we?" Here's the thing: I don't want a color-blind God. I don't want a God that doesn't see me for who I am. My friend, Kawehi Au, said it perfectly:

> I wouldn't say God doesn't see in color, but I would instead say God loves different colors. He doesn't look at us as all the same because in order to understand us all and have the Atonement really make sense, He needs to understand every part of us and that includes our color.

Amen, my friend. We are not the same. And that's ok. We don't need to all be the same to have equal value. I don't want to be colorless, and I don't want to live in a world where in order to be treated as equals we need to make the assertion that we don't see color. I want a God that delights in all colors, not one that removes color from the equation. I want a God that sees me for me and loves me *because* of who I am, not a God who erases the parts of me that make others uncomfortable. When you say, "Why should we see color?," you are asking me why an unchangeable and irrevocable piece of me is important. It is important because it is a part of me, a part of my earthly existence, and a part of the way I experience and interact with the world and its inhabitants.

The God I know is not color-blind. The God I know created beautiful variety and subtle variations and did so with intention and with love. We need a color-embracing gospel, not a color-blind one. Start seeing whole people. Start acknowledging the beauty and strength that come with diversity and difference. And for goodness sake, stop saying, "I don't see color," because when you say that, you erase an important part of a Person of Color's existence.

My God is not color-blind, and we shouldn't be either. When we choose to "not see color," the unintended result is to alienate and exclude the very people we claim to embrace. From the perspective of a Woman of Color, hearing that you don't see color is the equivalent of hearing that you are deliberately choosing not to see the parts of me that you find uncomfortable, and that suddenly puts me on the outside looking in on the group to which I once thought I belonged.

I think this phenomenon—feeling like you are part of an inner circle, and then abruptly realizing that you aren't—occurs fairly often when you are a Person of Color. Frequently, I find myself in conversations where I am nodding my head in agreement, engaged and feeling a sense of membership and belonging, and then suddenly I realize that the conversation I thought we were having is not at all what I thought it was. I am, in essence, my friend the Korean attorney, and I realize that the "we" being talked about somehow doesn't actually include me. The exclusion is almost always unintentional, but it's there. I am different. That often puts me on the outside looking in, or, at the very least, it puts me in a position where I am straddling the fence, often with my Tongan foot on one side and my Swedish foot on the other. Have you ever tried straddling a fence? Suffice it to say, it's an uncomfortable place to spend your time.

Last October, several of us "fence-straddlers" came together to talk because within our larger community, we saw several examples of Women of Color being silenced, discouraged, and, ultimately choosing to walk away from the conversation. We were losing our Sisters of Color to fatigue and frustration and wanted to figure out a way to better support each other. Through these discussions, the FEMWOC group was born.

FEMWOC initially was formed to fill a specific need for a small group of women, but it quickly became something much more than a little support group for Women of Color. I think we all realized that we had stumbled upon something really special when the conversations started flowing. We have stories. We have strength. We have powerful energy and fire and excitement. And because we have ideas and opinions that have often been silenced or overlooked, we started the FEMWOC blog, a blog for Women of Color, about Women of Color, written by Women of Color. So, we invite you to come and sit with us. Hear our stories. Share your own. Join us as we celebrate beautiful variety and seek to spread the good word of a color-embracing gospel. Our stories can be found at https://femwoc.wordpress.com

## UNIT 5: 2015-2024

## Introduction by Pandora Brewer

In the second to last chapter of *Charlotte's Web,* Wilbur the pig asks Charlotte the spider, "Why did you do all this for me?" Charlotte first assures Wilbur that he has been her friend and that she likes him. That would have been reason enough. But then, she characteristically shares deeper wisdom: "A spider's life can't help being something of a mess, with all this trapping and eating flies. By helping you, perhaps I was trying to lift up my life a trifle. Heaven knows anyone's life can stand a little of that." In this simple statement, she captures the ephemeral nature of life and, specifically, the representation of women's work. Often underappreciated, always busy taking care of what needs to be done only to see it consumed, unraveled, and scattered day after day. Charlotte knew that amid this "mess," her unique ability to create order and influence would have a lasting impact beyond the strands of her web. Her efforts would save Wilbur's life and, in doing so, create a permanent space for her legacy to grow and flourish.

Any work as difficult and time-consuming as publishing a quarterly magazine raises the question of why people would do it. With demands from work, family, and other commitments, volunteer (or practically volunteer) work on this level can feel overwhelming and discouraging. In my conversations at the time with Margaret Olsen Hemming—and our continued conversations with Rachel Rueckert and Carol Ann Litster Young[1]—we wondered aloud why we did this work and how we would find the time to do it. Eventually, we always found our way to Charlotte's empathy, pragmatism, and gratitude, opening our folders and tabs and spreadsheets and drafts and spinning words in our web. We actively chose this work in spite of, or perhaps because of, our own "messes." Choosing for ourselves, and for all the people who contribute to and appreciate the magazine, to lift up our lives "a trifle."

This act of finding our way from obligation to anticipation, reminding each other of why the work is meaningful was, for us, a centering and ultimately sustaining exercise. How Margaret and I, and now Rachel and Carol Ann, ask and answer these questions brings us back each week to why we originally accepted the responsibility of shepherding the magazine for a time.

For Margaret, the "why" began with her love for the Exponent II community. She worked with Aimee Evans Hickman and Emily Clyde Curtis as the art editor and then brought a knowledge of the publication process to the editor in chief role. She had a clear vision for how to honor the vibrant history of the organization, continue what Aimee and Emily had revived in the magazine, and shore up the structural gaps to build a succession plan

---

1. Sam Layco was also an associate editor in the first year of Rueckert's tenure. See page 105.

for the future. I said "yes" to the role of managing editor because I believed in Margaret and her vision. I have an operational and project management background and a passion for editing narrative essays, two very defined skill sets that complemented Margaret's broad experience.

Rachel came to the editorship viewing the process of reading, polishing, and publishing as sacred work. She believed it was a deep form of seeing and validating people whose voices have often gone unrecognized. Across our tenures, our shared "why" was and remains the desire to help people tell their stories.

The writing selected to represent the magazine during this time presents a map of what we carried forward, what we introduced, and what we grappled with as our writers and readers shared what conversations they were having and wanted to have within the pages. Sometimes we guided or sought out stories, but most often we were attentive to what was being submitted and what was on the collective mind of our community. Editing begins with curiosity, curiosity leads to a belief in the story, and this belief collaborates to amplify a voice that otherwise might stay quiet or even be lost. Curation became a journey to explore fresh points of view and discover writing that pushed us to think about the seemingly familiar in ways we had not considered.

Beginning with what we carried forward, the initial pieces selected in this unit reflect a menu of features that have provided consistency for readers over time. Emily Parker Updegraff's essay, "Arithmetic Rhetoric," was featured in Women's Theology. She delves deep into a series of often misinterpreted scriptures, leading us to mistake our relationship with God as transactional, a form of arithmetic rhetoric in which we "expect blessings in exchange for obedience and faith." Melody Newey, a contributor and poetry feature editor, asks us to remember when faith and love were not so complicated in her poem "Unfinished Business." Melody's verse is evocative of the best poetry features, a distilled visual and emotional oasis tucked amid the art and prose.

Features have also connected us to other parts of the organization, highlighting blog posts in Sisters Speak and publishing presentations from the annual retreat. The retreat talent show was the original stage for songs written by Heather Sundahl. Performed by The Red Hot Mamas, "Persisters in Zion/ Daughter of Exponent: a Medley" served as an antidote to divisive and toxic politics, empowering women to "stand up boldly for what we believe." Margaret Olsen Hemming's Spiritual Autobiography, "Claiming Space," was also given to a live audience before publication. Hemming shares her experiences growing up in her "liberal" family while finding comfort in community and faith in the scriptures. Refusing the societal pull to stand as either a feminist or a "true-blue Mormon," Margaret claims a space of her own choosing, a definition of devotion, love, and self-value more true than the one assigned by others.

Another *Exponent II* continuation from the tenures before us was themed issues: collecting or calling for a group of essays around a single topic, which gave potential contributors inspiration and a deadline. Themed issues, occurring two to three times per year between contest or open-themed issues, have included garden theology, loss, gifts of the spirit, food, arts and crafts, and many others. The issue on poverty was one of the most personally meaningful themes Margaret and I initiated. The power of the contributions was staggering, heartbreaking, and paradigm shifting. Tracy McKay Lamb's opening essay, "The Folly of Hedges," leads the collection. Tracy begins with the image of standing up in Relief Society and speaking against the "othering language" and marginalization of the Gospel of Prosperity. She shares the personal experience of losing everything and relying on public assistance to rebuild her life—a process painfully detailed and made almost unbearable by shame and stigma. She testifies that following Christ is more than saying the words; it requires real action tempered by humility, knowing that "nothing is earned ... anything we retain is solely through grace."

*Exponent II* has always been a forum for stories that reveal internal responses to external limitations as women explore friction and evolution within or movement away from roles they did not expect or design. In "During the Sacrament," a poem by beloved writer and activist Carol Lynn Pearson, we are inside a child's mind as she begins to reconcile the dawning awareness of her place in the church hierarchy. Her whispered longing is rooted in Christ's love, waiting, year by year, for an age where she can fully and equally participate. The title of Alixa Brobbey's poem, "After Dobbs," provides a frame to the searing portrait of a woman whose only choice is marriage, "her corset cinched so tight." The poem combines elemental and ancient imagery with a modern headline, connecting this one bride, in this one moment, to a universal loss of self for so many in her position. In "Gingerbread Girl," Falencia Jean-Francois describes a mother-daughter relationship where the mother is both victim and abuser. The vivid and painful imagery illustrates the layers from which the speaker must emerge, wondering if she will "recognize the body I find underneath." Allison Pingree's essay, "The Place that Does Not Exist," expresses the desire for her marriage and her life to be as it once was, sharing those seemingly insignificant moments between a couple that we may not notice until they are gone. The pain of her partner's cognitive decline ends with the joy of hearing him play music, "exquisite sounds that tether his soul to his body," knowing this "will be the last thing to go."

Contest issues inspired and attracted more contributors with provocative themes and a trip to a week-long writing retreat in Ireland (courtesy of former editor Sue Booth-Forbes) for the winner.[2] We could generate and publish more fiction, a rarely submitted genre. Carol Ann Litster Young's

---

2. Sue Booth-Forbes edited *Exponent II* from 1984–1997. She opened the Anam Cara Writer's and Artist Retreat in County Cork, Ireland, in 1998.

Letter from the Editor, "Holy in All its Forms," shows how the contests were presented and celebrated within the issues that featured them. In this editorial, Carol Ann explores what holy places have meant to her, growing up and then changing over time. She shares what it means to her today, finding holy places in the more "mundane ... less obvious places ... replenishing what was missing." She then weaves together the insights shared in the issue, ending by asking the reader to reflect on what holy means to each of us.

Several contest winners are featured in this unit's selections. In the Jewish tradition of filling in gaps or showing alternate points of view through fictional accounts, the Midrash contest was a call to create personal narratives for women in the scriptures, many of whom are mentioned only in passing. "Jael," a retelling of a few verses from Judges, is a stunning representative of what is possible in this genre. The author, Ellen McCammon, reveals two subtle love stories, one rooted in trust and responsibility, the other in loyalty and passion. "Wendell," by Susan Christiansen, responds to the prompt, "What do you believe and why?" Although she was never a pet person, Susan believes God led her to find her dog, Wendell. She writes that "his puppy energy" kept her tethered to the small joys in life when the questions of past and future were haunting and uncertain, realizing "that Wendell wasn't meant to rescue me from my problems so much as help me cope through them." The contest Spiritual Foremothers brought together stories of influential women with both honesty and reverence. Rachel Rueckert's winning essay, "Wonder Women," illustrates the complexity of mothering on multiple levels. She begins with purchasing a Wonder Woman crown and explores more history and context about her comic book idol. Underlying her search is the grief and loss of her own mother's capacity as the narrator reaches inward to find new sources of power. She discovers, "There is strength inside of me, and I don't even need a costume."

For all our planning and anticipation, there were critical conversations that required pushing against unconscious bias and assumed boundaries. Including marginalized voices continues to be an opportunity for the organization and magazine. We worked with many writers and artists who represent different and often intersecting identities, bringing perspectives outside the historical focus on a white, heteronormative LDS landscape. We agonized over how to respond to the exclusion policy of November 2015, waiting months to publish our LGBTQIA issue to ensure time for those impacted to process their experiences. Hannah MacDonald's essay "On Saying Yes to Boys" explores the expectations and assumptions that come with being a young woman in the church. She dutifully accepts all invitations from boys, increasingly resentful, her mind and complicated heart moving in sync with a propulsive, inherited *yes* despite feeling attraction for a female friend. In "Family History: Made for you but not for me," Ramona Morris feels "shut out of a narrative that wasn't created for people who looked like me." Feeling the pressure of completing her family history, specifically about her grandfather, she struggles with details she cannot find, feeling like she is failing, only to realize the act of searching is a gift to her and her mother, so much more than obedience to a commandment or discovering the perfect family. Allison Hong Merrill's essay "The Trench Coat of Multiple Colors" explores her decades-long love affair with a coat taken from her mother—"A lovechild of runway fashion and a rain poncho. It was, it was, it was my undoing"—that parallels her search for belonging. Andee Bowden's contest-winning essay "Shifting Sands" is a story about finding a true name to fit a true sense of self. As a nonbinary person, Andee wanted a name of their own choosing and found it on the shore of Lake Michigan, shaping letters in the sand, spelling a name that is "a gift that I carry with me from the most sacred land I have ever crossed."

With Ramona and Andee's reference to gifts, we arrive at Rosie Gochnour Serago, coming full circle to the question of why we do all we do for the magazine. In "Exponent Wrapped," Rosie's Letter from the Editor for the themed issue on creativity, she compares her role as the layout editor to wrapping presents for loved ones. In layout, she details the copy and pasting, laboring over font size, column gaps, orphan lines, and careful artwork sizing. She plays a "game of quarter inches," allocating as much space as possible to each contributor. All this work, why? "My layout and design work is my way of saying to all the women reading and contributing to *Exponent II*; your sentiments, whether written or illustrated, deserve to be wrapped." Rosie sums up beautifully the desire to share, amplify, and celebrate the voices in our community. She speaks for each volunteer as she articulates the joy in her reason: as we lift each other up a "trifle," we create together a permanent record of comfort and wisdom, connecting our busy and authentic lives to those busy and authentic lives of those who come next.

**Unfinished Business**
Melody Newey
Summer 2015 (vol. 35, no. 1)

Maybe when you see the bedroom door ajar,
you will think you hear a small voice behind it
inviting you to pray like you did when
you were a child—to a God both real and magic.

Remember how you knelt on knees
bruised from child's play that didn't hurt;
how primary songs were prayers
you didn't know you were singing?

Remember how you knew (without knowing):
love is neither cliché nor glorious illusion.
It is simply a reason to wake up and go outside.
Maybe you should play today. And maybe you should pray.

## Arithmetic Rhetoric
Emily Parker Updegraff
Summer 2015 (vol. 35, no. 1)

In "The Pacific," a short story by Mark Helprin, a newlywed young woman works feverishly at her job as a welder in hopes that her devoted, precise work will keep her husband safe in the Pacific theater of World War II. She "built the instruments with the disciplined ferocity that comes only from love." She felt that "somehow her devotion and her sharp attention would have repercussions, that, just as in a concert hall, where music could only truly rise within the hearts of its listeners, she could forge a connection over thin air." Feeling that her work had more significance than its immediate results, she bargained with the universe to buy a miracle with her labor, "though that miracle was not to be hers."[3]

We humans try to make bargains with God, with nature, and with other people. I remember thinking to my baby that if he'd just sleep through a task I needed to accomplish, he could stay up all night. While working in the lab on my graduate research I hoped to exchange prayers, fasting, and sleep for publishable results that would let me finish my degree. I think the inclination to make one-sided bargains is a widespread human tendency, but this can be amplified in a Mormon context, making us quite prone to viewing our relationship with God as transactional.

Latter-day Saint scripture describes God's response to human action this way:

> There is a law, irrevocably decreed in heaven before the foundations of this world, upon which all blessings are predicated—and when we obtain any blessing from God, it is by obedience to that law upon which it is predicated. (Doctrine & Covenants 130:20–21)

I, the Lord, am bound when ye do what I say; but when ye do not what I say, ye have no promise. (Doctrine & Covenants 82:10)

These scriptures are well-known to Church members, if only because they are Scripture Mastery verses that seminary students memorize. With words like *irrevocable, law, bound, promise,* and *obtain,* is it any wonder if our imaginations mingle these verses with a subconscious belief in bargain-making

---

3. Mark Helprin, *The Pacific and Other Stories* (New York: Penguin Books, 2005), 365–66.

and turn them around to create false meaning? A meaning that says we can promise ourselves blessings through obedience, allowing us to set the terms of a transaction with God?

These verses require careful reading to avoid being appropriated into wrong thinking. First, what is meant by law? A law that pre-dates the foundation of the world sounds like what we know of "intelligence," that is, something not created but co-existent with God.[4] From our mortal viewpoint the laws of physics appear to predate the foundation of the world as well. The most recognizable of these is the law of gravity, first mathematically described by Isaac Newton in the late 17th century. The word "law" in Renaissance and Enlightenment usage was a term for systematic and predictive descriptions of natural phenomena. Today scientists would use the word "theory" rather than "law" for such descriptions, and "law" in modern vernacular has a quite different meaning from how Isaac Newton would have understood the term.

To us, a law is a code established by an authoritative entity, enforced by monitors who punish infractions to that code. A law requires enforcement, a theory does not. I believe God's commandments are more like theories than laws because the consequences of following them follow naturally; they don't require a monitor to notice infractions and mete out consequences. Consider this restatement of the above verses:

> There is a theory, in place from before the foundations of this world, which describes and predicts all blessings—any blessing from God is obtained as a natural consequence of obedience to godly principles.

I am not suggesting rewriting the scriptures, but I find reframing these verses clarifying.

In graduate school, when I was working, fasting, and praying for results that my life in a very real sense depended on, I found the heavens closed to me. It was devastating at the time, and it's had far-reaching impact in my life. It was more disappointing than it needed to be, however, because if I hadn't heard so many times in church that God was in control (with no discussion of what that might mean), and that obedience would bring the blessings I prayed for, my expectations would have been different and I would have been less likely to have ended up on the brink of a loss of faith.

I suffered from naiveté and entitlement, but I'm not entirely at fault on those counts because this was my religious education, to expect blessings in exchange for obedience and faith. When people speak of obedience summing up to blessings or of equations for happiness I call it arithmetic rhetoric. This rhetoric is damaging because it sets people up for disappointment and

---

4. "Intelligence, or the light of truth, was not created or made, nor indeed can be," Doctrine & Covenants 93:30

conveys a falsehood. God is not a shopkeeper and blessings aren't commodities. As Dieter F. Uchtdorf said in the April 2015 General Conference, "Salvation cannot be bought with the currency of obedience." Neither can blessings. I think most people understand that ultimately, so where does arithmetic rhetoric come from?

In addition to a careless reading of D&C 82 and 130, I think arithmetic rhetoric could come from a misreading of King Benjamin.

> And now, in the first place, he hath created you, and granted unto you your lives, for which ye are indebted unto him. And secondly, he doth require that ye should do as he hath commanded you; for which if ye do, he doth immediately bless you; and therefore he hath paid you. And ye are still indebted unto him, and are, and will be, forever and ever; therefore, of what have ye to boast? (Mosiah 2:23–24)

The words "paid" and "indebted" certainly sound transactional. But looking at those verses in the context of the whole address, it's clear King Benjamin intends to instill humility, not encourage a sense of entitlement. We are forever in God's debt, and obedience does nothing to even the scales. King Benjamin is warning against the "pride cycle" that takes place throughout the Book of Mormon, where a state of blessedness leads people to forget God and oppress their neighbors. He is not putting forward an equation for extracting blessings from God.

Perhaps another reason people use arithmetic rhetoric is because they find it comforting. Believing that obedience brings payment of desired blessings is appealing because it gives a sense of control. But control is an illusion.

> I returned, and saw under the sun, that the race is not to the swift, nor the battle to the strong, neither yet bread to the wise, nor yet riches to men of understanding, nor yet favour to men of skill; but time and chance happeneth to them all. For man also knoweth not his time: as the fishes that are taken in an evil net, and as the birds that are caught in the snare; so are the sons of men snared in an evil time, when it falleth suddenly upon them. (Ecclesiastes 9:11–12)

As lived experience has taught you and me, bad things happen to the obedient and the good and to the innocent. How then to make sense of King Benjamin's talk of being "paid" with blessings? It helps to consider that Mormon aphorism from Alma 41:10: "wickedness never was happiness." I think this is true, not because of punishments applied by a divine monitor, but because the things God commands us to avoid are corrosive to relationships and as human, social beings, our relationships are a primary source of joy. Obedience to commandments at the very least saves us from torpedoing our relationships with others and with God and at best rewards us with joyful and lasting relationships. By not stealing or bearing false witness we gain the trust of our peers, by not committing adultery we create a safe space for relationships to flourish and by worshiping God we avoid wasting our time adoring entities that won't love us back. And thus we are "paid." The blessing is inherent to the act of obedience.

A final way people may use arithmetic rhetoric is its employment as a carrot. Not trusting that the blessings inherent to right conduct are sufficient, our leaders sometimes promise shinier ones. They promise happiness. While there absolutely are blessings from obedience, promising "happiness" seems a childlike approach, as if there's a sparkling reward for complying with the rules. In reality the blessings I enjoy really don't vary much day by day, nor does my obedience. I don't feel happy every day, but I'm no less blessed, and usually no less obedient, from one day to another. In fact God has not made promises about happiness, at least not in the short term. The scriptures do mention joy, as an underlying and ultimate satisfaction in a life lived in harmony with God. But "happiness" seems to me a transitory and vacuous substitute for joy, and a modern substitution too, that has little support in the scriptures.[5]

Thinking of obedience as a currency for acquiring blessings is wrongheaded, and in my opinion can even become a form of idolatry, of wrong worship. Ironically, focusing too much on God's commandments can take the focus away from God, away from a relationship with God that is personal and meaningful. This was the Pharisees' pitfall. Too much focus on obedience stunts our spiritual growth because it takes our attention away from the personal revelation and guidance by the Spirit that is so important to spiritual maturity. Perhaps as a child or teenager I would have responded to a promise of obedience summing up to happiness, but as an adult with more lived experience that rhetoric rings false. As a people we must speak truth about obedience and blessings. Blessings are real and God does ask obedience of us, but it serves no one to reduce them to integers to be plugged into a non-existent equation.

## Claiming Space: A Spiritual Autobiography
Margaret Olsen Hemming
Fall 2015 (vol. 35, no. 2)

If you spend much time around Mormon feminists, particularly those on blogs and Facebook, you might start to recognize a familiar story: a young woman is raised in a traditional Mormon family, discovers feminism in early adulthood, starts reading troubling church history online, and goes

---

5. The word "happiness" appears twenty-six times in the LDS scriptures, all in the Book of Mormon. "Joy" appears over 300 times, about half in the Book of Mormon, half in the Bible.

through a faith crisis of doubting what she was taught in childhood. This is my story, except the exact opposite. I was raised in a politically liberal, Mormon feminist family, and it wasn't until I was a teenager that I realized that the majority of the American church membership did not look like that. I was raised to be a Mormon feminist and discovered the conservatism of the church in early adulthood.

Let me back up a little. My great-great-great grandmother was Ane Andersen, born in 1823 in Flensted, Denmark. She married Peter Olsen in 1847 and they joined the LDS church, left Denmark, and crossed the plains to Utah in the early 1860s. They settled in Sanpete County, where there was a large Danish immigrant population, and so on my father's side, I'm almost entirely descended from Danish Mormon converts. My grandma took great pride in Peter and Ane's story and I heard it many times growing up. Even more than the pioneer history, however, my family emphasized its Danish roots. My father and grandmother often explained family habits and behaviors as Danish or Scandinavian. They see themselves as inheritors of the Danish culture.

My parents are devout Mormons—Mormonism was the center of our home and I knew, growing up, that they were dedicated to the church. This is an important point, because it framed how I saw committed Mormonism. They were steadfast as anyone I knew as a child. They are also pretty liberal. I always knew they were Democrats and feminists. My father is an anthropologist who studies traditional medicine in West Africa. During my childhood he regularly traveled there for research and brought home stories of healings from witchcraft and interactions with magical non-humans. Cultural relativism was part of how I was taught to understand the world, even though it wasn't until graduate school that I had the language to identify what that was.

My mother is a convert who was raised by civil rights and environmental activists. She ran an in-home daycare so that she could afford to be at home with us until my youngest sister went to kindergarten. Then she returned to school to get a master's degree in social work. The timing of her return to school was critical for me—I was twelve, and her increasing outspokenness about social justice and marginalized populations had a big effect.

What a child experiences is what they think is normal and universally experienced. I did not know that my parents were unusual. I knew that we were in the political minority at church, but I assumed it wasn't by much. I thought pretty much everyone I knew was a feminist, because the movement seemed so obvious to me. I was raised by people who never acted like being feminist was a caveat to their Mormonism. They are Mormons. They are feminists. That was my normal.

And then, when I was fourteen, we moved to Lehi, Utah. My high school was roughly 90 percent Mormon. It dawned on me pretty quickly that I did not fit in. People there talked about politics at church far more than we ever did in Michigan. It was the first time I had ever heard such viciousness in conversation at church. I had vaguely known in Michigan that my family was unusual, but in Utah it felt like a constant message, that people had to remind us with every interaction that we were different.

Rather than go silent, I started forming stronger opinions and speaking up about them. I protested against the racism I witnessed in school assemblies and the homophobia I heard in debate class. I also caused my church teachers headaches with my feminist questions. I unintentionally derailed Young Womens lessons with my questions. I grilled my bishop during a temple recommend interview about why we don't talk about Heavenly Mother. In BYC meetings I repeatedly argued against the budget gap between the Young Men's and Young Women's programs.

While my inclinations and identity solidified as a liberal, pro-LGBT rights feminist through high school, I also became increasingly devout. I read the entire Book of Mormon, getting up early on the morning of my sixteenth birthday to read the last chapter and pray about its truth as the sun rose. I went very willingly to church and activities every week, eagerly went to Girls Camp and EFY, wrote in my journal about my testimony, and planned to be a missionary.

Since I was too young to serve a mission, I had to spend all my do-gooder energy on something else. I had this sense of wanting to serve and also wanted to get out of Utah for a while. I applied and was accepted to AmeriCorps. During that year I worked in an elementary school in Charleston, built houses for Habitat for Humanity in rural Alabama, built trails at a youth camp in Georgia, lived in a tent and worked at a national park in Arkansas, and helped with children's art classes at a community college in Mississippi. My fellow teammates were the opposite of my Utah classmates: mostly liberal atheists. We talked about religion and politics frequently. I've dealt with lots of headaches since I was a child, and one time my team leader said to me, "I know why you get lots of headaches. It's because deep down you know you can't reconcile being Mormon with the rest of what you believe. Your body shows the stress from that through headaches."

It was the same message, but from the other side: you can't belong to both. Be a person who goes to church and follows the prophet, or be a person who advocates for feminism and LGBT rights. Choose one, because neither side wants you as you are.

But I was a believer. I got special permission from the AmeriCorps bureaucracy to use the government van to drive by myself to church every week, even when it was two hours away from our camp in Arkansas. That year I listened to Ani DiFranco, put dreadlocks in my hair, became a vegetarian, and protested against WalMart's labor practices, but I also read the entire Bible and went on missionary splits. I was filled with energy for both: I wanted to proclaim the gospel and stop human rights abuses. I felt the fire of righteousness.

I started at BYU the next fall still burning. That first semester was so hard. AmeriCorps had made my theoretical social beliefs into strong convictions. I no longer just believed in the need for social programs, I had worked side-by-side with a single mother in poverty-stricken Anniston, Alabama, for two months, and I had no patience with someone telling me that the poor just needed to work harder. My AmeriCorps teammates, women who had become my closest friends, sprang to my mind when my roommates said homophobic things. I had wielded a chainsaw, shingled a roof, held my own in heated religious conversations, and traveled by bus to Washington, DC, for a political protest. While I eventually found my people at BYU, there were lingering scars, particularly from the times that male classmates, coworkers, and administrators had made it clear that my opinions and willingness to verbalize them were not attractive in a woman.

Years later, I attended my first *Exponent II* retreat. One of the sessions was with a woman who had done graduate research in interviewing Mormon feminists about their dual identities. Women in the room talked about feeling pulled in two directions and the rejection from both communities for not fully conforming. For the first time in my adult life, I felt like I had found my people. These women understood me, all the parts of me, and accepted me completely. I called my husband and cried to him with happiness.

Soon after the retreat the following year, Aimee Hickman called me and asked if I wanted to be involved in reviving the magazine. "Yes," I responded. "Anything you want me to do, I'll do it." She took me at my word. In the last six years I have been the layout editor, the art editor, written fundraising letters and organized mailers, written articles, worked on our fundraising database, recruited articles for Sabbath Pastorals, been on the Readers Committee, started the silent auction at the retreat, and joined the board. I give you this list to emphasize that every single item here has *fed my soul*. I have come to love *Exponent II* and the women I have found here with a fierceness that matches my gratitude for them. It has become one of the pieces of my life that I could not do without.

So here I am, still a liberal feminist, still a Mormon. I go to church every week. I'm in my ward's Primary presidency. And I'm the editor of *Exponent II*. And I'm more at peace with all of that than I have been in a long time.

I've come to hate the phrase "true-blue-Mormon" that some people use to describe what I call McConkey-ite Mormons. I am a true blue Mormon. There is no one that gets to assert to being more Mormon than me. And

I'm a feminist, and no one gets to tell me that I'm not a real feminist. And if I'm living both identities, then no one gets to tell me that it's not possible to be both.

I was at the pool with my kids a few weeks ago, chatting with some other parents I had recently met. One of them asked me what I do, and I hesitated for only a moment. "Mostly I'm raising my kids," I said, "But I work part-time as the editor for a Mormon feminist magazine." In the ensuing conversation, one father said, "You're claiming both spaces for yourself. I think that's great." I hope that the work I'm doing personally and through the magazine will help more people acknowledge what he got so quickly: we get to claim the spaces where we are.

My thoughts keep returning to Peter and Ane. As I said at the beginning, I heard their story of leaving Denmark and traveling across the Atlantic and over the country to settle in Sanpete County, Utah, many times as a child. But I heard an extended version of that story just a few months ago. When Ane Andersen and Peter Olsen arrived in Utah, Brigham Young directed them to settle in Brigham City. But Ane spoke almost no English and she had heard that there was a large Danish immigrant population in Sanpete County. So she told Brigham Young that she wouldn't go to Brigham City, that she was going to where the other Danes were. She was willing to cross an ocean and a continent, but going to Brigham City was just too much to ask. I've been wondering since hearing that story what my family would have lost if she'd done as she was told, followed the prophet, and settled in an area that had few Danish immigrants. I probably would not have that sense of a strong Danish identity I spoke of earlier. So the effects of Ane's decisions have been passed down the generations. And maybe there's something genetic about my own insistence of living a devout Mormon life in a way that works for me. I think I come by it rightly.

## Jael
Ellen McCammon
Winter 2016 (vol. 35, no. 3)

> *Midrash Contest Winner. Judge's Response: This story holds a darkness that mirrors the horrific book of Judges. Judges is not a sweet scripture that ties up loose ends. The author here speaks to the undercurrent of violence and exploitation that runs through the Old Testament. The writing employs the power of suggestion as well as precision, while the relationships are complex and unexpected. This is a strong story for strong women.*[6]

---

6. This editorial note appeared in the original publication.

When you see me standing at the door of the tent I know what you think: here is sanctuary at last. I am your prize for fighting and living. The wife of your ally, alone and dressed in white in a quiet camp.

"Come inside," I say.

When I was a girl my mother told me: the women in our family have dark hearts, and they drink the cup of pain. I didn't understand what she meant. How could I? I knew little enough of pain, then.

She would brush out my shadow-black hair and tell me stories. About Isaac's wife Rebecca, the favored one, the first wife of his heart. About Lilith and Eve, Adam's two wives, one newer and better than the other.

"You're beautiful," she would say. "Use it."

There was little else we had, the two of us. She sent me outside to play in the shade of the neighbor's orchard while she entertained guests. They were always men and they always left with their jackets crooked and their pockets empty. After, we dined well, on fresh bread and olives and fish.

She would braid my hair up into a crown on my head, the gold bracelets on her arm winking. They jangled and clanged: both delicate and harsh. My mother's music. There came a time when my mother's guests started to linger at the back door before they left, watching me climb the orchard trees with my long legs swinging. Soon my blood came in. I was not afraid—my mother had told me of such things—but when I showed her the ruined shift she turned to stone. Cold and quiet.

I don't know how my mother made arrangements to sell me, but the temple cart came just days after my first blood, to give my mother the money and deliver me to the city. The man driving the cart counted out the coins into my mother's hands—a high price for a young virgin initiate. Soft new wood to be carved by the priestesses into one of their own.

The metal falling into her palms clink-clink-clinked like the links of chains moving together.

She clasped me to her. "They will give you what you want if only they think it was their idea," she whispered in my ear. "Never let them know you have a thought in your head, but command them all the same."

I wanted to hold her hand forever, but she turned away. She had nothing left to give me.

You look around the tent, at the embroidered hangings on the wall, the fine-woven bed roll over carpet. My husband is a merchant and a rich man.

"Please, drink." I pour wine into the finest bowl we have: shimmering, heavy stone. "You must be thirsty."

"I am." Your voice is a rasp. You look me up and down then take the bowl from me. Your hands are hot on my hands.

There is a dark spot on your leathers and I cannot tell if it is grime or blood.

They punished me in the temple. I was too loud and my steps too hard. I did not lower my gaze when the priestesses passed. Temple whores, they called them on the streets. But the whores of kings and lords, if so.

I broke a precious jar of kohl with my clumsy hands and laughed when I was scolded. I laughed again when the mistress of the initiates cracked me hard across the face. They put me in the laundry with the lowest of the slaves: not sold into the service of the goddess like I, but war-spoils handed to the temple in tribute. "A few days down there and you'll beg to come back up," the high priestess said. "Even to scrub the temple stones."

The laundry was all steam and smoke and burning skin. They fed us the scraps and leavings of the temple meals, less even than they gave the poor who came begging at the steps.

It was scalding and hunger and hands cracking like dry earth.

"Here," one of the slaves said. My age. "For your hands." A salve to tend the angry red welts splitting open my skin.

Her name was Deborah. We shared a pallet in the cramped slave's quarters. She was a restless sleeper, tossing and turning and crying out in the night.

Deborah was not a very good slave. At times, she would let the water in the laundry vat go still and stare into the flat milky surface. Her pale eyes went dark and her hands slack for minutes at a time. After these episodes the other women would gather around her. "What did you see?" Their soft whispers like the cries of gentle birds. "What is it?"

They did extra work so her trances went unnoticed. They loved her.

Her smiles were the full moon coming up over the water. She laid her hands on the tired slaves, the sick ones, and they were renewed.

A woman died one night. Deborah gently closed the staring eyes and keened over the body with great shaking sobs. They had to hold her back to let the guards take the corpse away to be burned. That day she stared into the water for hours and when the women asked her what she'd seen she just shook her head.

She was a peculiar woman. You finish the bowl of wine. It stains your mouth purple-red, dripping at the corners. I take the vessel from your hands and refill it.

"Enough," you say.

I stroke your shoulder and hold out the bowl. "Have more. Please. It's no trouble."

You look into my eyes and I look down, the shy blushing bride. You take the bowl from my hands again. I start to hum while you drink. My hand makes ever-widening circles on your shoulder.

You drift forward toward me. The bowl falls soundlessly against the carpets on the ground. "I must run," you mumble. "They will look for me. They will kill me if they find me."

"Rest." I run my hands up and down your arms. Pulling you down. "I will wake you before they come."

Your head falls into my lap, heavy arms around my waist. I keep humming the lullaby, one I learned in the temple. They left me in the laundry two weeks but it felt much longer than that.

"Are you ready to be an initiate now?" the mistress asked when she came down to fetch me. Her yellow dress shone bright against the drabness of the slaves in their frayed dun tunics. I looked at Deborah, where she stood slowly stirring the laundry drum. She did not look back. I nodded.

"Your hands aren't as bad as I thought they'd be," the high priestess said when I met her upstairs. They were pink and chapped, but no blood.

After that I submitted to their teaching. I learned to walk in a gentle glide, my long hems whispering against the stone. I learned to speak in different voices: soft and throaty and low, commanding and clear, dark and deep, high and sweet. I could sing their prayers and dance their dances. I made obeisance at their shrines. I knelt at the statue of the goddess in the center of the temple.

It was easy when I made up my mind. I hid myself inside layers of carmine lips and silk and perfume and became dormant in my own body—the body of a priestess, now.

After all, the temple was not so different from my mother's house. The men who came to the temple to worship sheltered themselves within us and sated themselves upon us.

The laundry was not so far away either, and nights in the temple were long and quiet. No one heard my silent steps as I descended to that warm gray space to utter different prayers.

I keep humming. I smooth your hair. Your breath is hot on my lap and your hair is coming loose from its queue. Gently, as though you were a child, I slide you off my lap and onto a pillow. I wait a moment but you do not wake. The spare tent stake is heavy and awkward in my hands. The mallet feels rough against my palm like the long wooden staves they used in the temple laundry. I expect to feel afraid but fear does not come.

There was a man who came to the temple who was not like the others. He bought our time but did not worship with our bodies. Heber, he was called, and richer than a king.

The other women said he only paid the temple for our company to keep up appearances. "He prefers to pray with the priests," an older priestess said with a laugh. "Courting his favor is a waste of time."

But I liked him. He told me of his affairs and asked for my advice. He listened to my answers with his live eyes flashing and needled me with questions. I almost felt my sleeping self wake beneath my incensed robes.

One day I was called to an audience with the high priestess. "Heber wishes to marry you," she said bluntly. "I told him such a thing is not done but he won't be put off. He's offered me a kingdom's worth to carry you away, more than you could ever bring in on your own, even such as you are." Beautiful, she meant, I suppose.

A strange fairy tale. Plucked like a rare trained bird from my jeweled cage to adorn another household. I was the enchanted artifact passed from hand to hand.

He came to speak with me later that day. "I wanted to ask you first, but I didn't know if it was possible."

"Anything is possible if you can pay enough."

He laughed. "See, that's why I asked for you. I'm not home often. I need someone clever to manage my household and my affairs in my absence. I don't need or expect … children. You'll be free. But only if this is what you want. I won't be angry if you'd rather stay in the temple."

His words came fast as falling water and I realized he cared enough to be discomposed.

"The slaves," I blurted out. "The laundry slaves."

"What about them?"

"Please buy them and set them free. I'll marry you then."

He blinked. "You know they'll just get fresh blood in tribute. There are always more slaves."

I shrugged. "They are my friends." His eyes on me were arrow-sharp.

I don't know how much he offered the high priestess but within a week it was done. The slaves of the laundry were free and I was wed. I cast off the flame colors of the temple and wore blues and greens. I stopped saying the temple prayers. I wore only silver jewelry. I brought nothing of the life of the priestess with me.

My husband, friend, and purchaser. My liberator. He taught me to tally his accounts and manage his servants, to meet with his tenants and scribes and husband his land. And then he left, for months at a time.

I cultivated allies for him and nursed his business agreements. "I trust you," he told me. "In everything." He smoothed my hair and went to his own bed.

When I hold the stake above your temple you groan for a moment and I wonder if you will open your eyes and kill me with your huge hands. I will not hesitate any more. I press the stake down against your skin and let the mallet fly with all my meager strength.

It makes a sound like an eggshell cracking, then a wet and sucking thud. The blood is a fountain and your eye bursts like a rancid olive.

I'm almost sick but my heart sings black-ripe in my chest and my own blood runs hot with power. You are nothing. You are nothing. I know I am damned now but I do not care; I cannot care.

I have conquered you when no one else could and I know that this is what it means to be a god. This dark pleasure.

My husband left several turns of the moon ago, after we entertained a new ally I had secured. General Sisera: a powerful man.

"What you are planning is risky," Heber said finally, late in the quiet hours when we two sat alone. "If you are found out I will have to disavow you. But I do not think you will be found out."

"Thank you."

He tipped his cup to me. "Thank me when you have what you desire." He tugs on my falling braids. "Clever scheming woman. You're almost more than I paid for."

There is love there, in its way.

I sit there soaked in your quiet blood and wait for the armies of Israel to ride into camp.

Hoofbeats, shouting. The rail and cacophony of martial men. "Where is Sisera?" A man's voice pierces like thunder. Barak.

I step from the tent. My dress is painted brown-red with gore. I stand tall and let my voice ring clear.

"The man you seek is inside." I point into the tent. "He is dead."

Another horse rides up besides Barak. A slight woman slides down from the saddle with a cry half-pained, half joyful. Her pale eyes find me like a touch.

"Deborah!" I call her name.

So long; it has been so long. She could not remain in Heber's household while I courted your favor, for you might recognize her. It was you who gave the laundry slaves to the temple. She showed me the scars you gave her.

And now she runs to the door of the tent and throws her arms around me, though I am stained all over with your blood. I kiss her and her mouth is sweet and fierce as it always is.

Her hands baptize me. She tastes like a flower. Her hands pull my hair almost to pain. My dark heart is in her hands and she drinks the pain from my lips.

# Wendell
Susan Christiansen
Winter 2017 (vol. 36, no. 3)

*Winning Essay:* Exponent II *Essay Contest*[7]

One Saturday in February 2015, my husband and I were driving to a funeral for the four-year-old daughter of two close friends. She had been born with serious medical difficulties, and although it was miraculous that she had lived as long as she had, we were all devastated by her sudden death. As we drove to the cemetery through brown farm fields in rural Maryland, I said to myself, "everything in my life is dead." It wasn't literally true, but it felt that way.

Migraines that I had lived with since I was a teenager had flared, incapacitating me five to seven days per week. This meant taking a leave from my PhD program—I couldn't stand to waste another semester of funding while lying in a dark room praying for sleep. I was living apart from my husband, partially because of the nature of our training programs, but also because our marriage hadn't been working.

I defined myself by my abilities to plan, work hard, and fix problems. But my plans had all failed. I physically could not work, and even when I could my efforts yielded little visible progress. I could find no answers for the cause of my migraines, no way to make headway on my dissertation, and no healing in my eroding marriage to my best friend.

No wonder I declared that everything was dead. But almost immediately, I had a clear, unbidden thought: *get a dog*.

I am emphatically *not* a dog person. I didn't grow up with dogs and never saw their value. A dog seemed to be just another hassle, but with shedding fur, sticky drool, and bad smells. I'm allergic to animals. I even have a very real fear of dogs.

But when I heard God telling me to get a dog, I also heard hope. So the following Monday morning I found myself in the living room of a quiet Mennonite family in Pennsylvania who had four puppies remaining from their dog's most recent litter. I thought I'd just take a look and test my feelings. I was biased toward a female dog, but a male puppy trotted over and wouldn't leave me. He curled up in my lap. He kept reaching for me with his paw. Less than an hour later I had handed over $500 and was on my way back to Baltimore with a nine-week-old puppy on my lap. I had not a clue how to care for him.

I named him Wendell, after the author Wendell Berry, who wrote of "the peace of wild things."

Learning to care for Wendell gave me something manageable that I could

---

7. This note appeared in the original publication.

do, and a source of joy in my life's otherwise bleak landscape. I took him to a puppy class. I rubbed his belly each morning when he lumbered over and flopped on me. I felt exhilarated when he learned to give me a double high five.

His puppy-sized bladder forced me out of my bed and out of my house sometimes ten times a day. He got me out of doors even more often once he learned to ring a bell whenever he "needed" to go outside. He helped me become more present in my community. My fluffy, happy dog made me appear more approachable. The introvert in me felt more comfortable greeting others because of Wendell. As we walked, we encountered people who lit up at his objective adorableness. I could sense that some needed a kind, brief hello and others needed someone to listen. I was able to connect with others in ways I would have missed by staying in my house. One day I sat with a thirteen-year-old girl who had been thrown out of a car by her abusive father. As I sat next to her on the curb, she held Wendell and cried as we waited together for the police and a social worker to arrive.

It's not an exaggeration to say that Wendell changed my life.

It was my dog and not my increasingly distant husband who curled up next to me on the couch on June 8, 2015, when I came home after learning that the cause of my recent migraines was a rapidly growing tumor in my head. My husband didn't offer, but I also didn't ask, and we were both at the point where we needed the other person to make the first move.

I realized then that Wendell wasn't meant to rescue me from my problems so much as help me cope through them. Wendell gave me hope when I arrived home exhausted after hours of medical tests, but still without answers or good odds of survival. He'd dance, want to be chased, and overwhelm me with love. I received miraculous and generous support from my community of friends and family that lifted and sustained me in unprecedented ways, but when they all left, it was Wendell and me alone in the house.

I was worried his puppy energy would be too much for me after the surgery that replaced one-third of my tumor-ridden skull with a polymer implant, but his happy dances gave my wrapped head a wide berth. He gently climbed onto the couch by my feet and slept with his head on my ankles.

I cried quiet, grateful tears when I went on the first walk with him after my surgery. It was a very short loop but it had been a rough recovery and that ritual of a morning walk—which he had made possible—helped me feel normal. I had felt so irredeemably broken, and I needed to see that I would heal.

Wendell's favorite room was supposed to be the bedroom for the baby I was carrying when we had bought the house eight years ago. That pregnancy turned out to be the first of innumerable miscarriages. As each successive pregnancy failed, I began keeping the door to that room closed. At times I wouldn't even enter it to sweep the oak floors. Once I stored a friend's items there for six months—I wanted it to be so full that I just might forget how empty it was.

Although I will praise my incredibly smart dog to anyone who will listen, I don't believe he sensed that this bedroom needed his presence. No, he chose it because the bed is next to a window positioned perfectly for people watching. Even so, seeing a creature I adore loving this space heals my heart and fills this sunny, quiet room perfectly.

Three weeks ago, my husband traveled to Baltimore to tell me he thought it was time to divorce. We had likely both come to that conclusion independently months ago. I even felt grateful we were finally talking about it. Even so, I was floored by the endless waves of loss and pain I also felt. When I dropped him off at the train station with few moments to spare, my husband of over ten years jumped out of the car, grabbed his bags, mumbled a "see ya," and hurried away to catch his bus. I have never seen as much pain and sadness in his eyes as I did in that moment.

Anticipating that this parting would be difficult, I brought Wendell along. As I sat stunned and crying in the car, my peaceful, wild thing nuzzled my arm and crawled onto my lap. We drove to the lake and ran loops around it until we were both exhausted.

I'm adjusting to the idea of my new reality: life in a house with just my dog and me. For the first time in my life, I have no plan, no idea what my life or my career will look like. I don't know how much longer I'll be living in this city or when I'll complete my PhD. But we—Wendell and I—will be just fine.

I know so little right now, but I do believe this: if God tells you to get a dog, go find your Wendell.

## Persisters in Zion/Daughters of Exponent: a Medley
Heather Sundahl
September 13, 2017 (exponentii.org)

Every year at the Exponent retreat I find myself belting it out at the talent show. Which is hilarious because I am no singer. But I have a strange gift that I trot out annually: I'm sort of a Mormon housewife version of Weird Al. Taking hymns and substituting wacky lyrics for reverent ones gives me deep, deep joy. Past songs have included "Come ye Husbands of the Ward" and "The Modesty Song." This year Liz Johnson inspired me to take the oft-sung YW/YM medley, "Sisters in Zion" and "Army of Helaman," and give it a political twist. For dramatic effect, the Red Hot Mamas sang it through all the way, then divided and blended verses 3 and 4, singing the final chorus together. Of course there were props. There are always props. Be inspired to come up with your own.

*As Persisters in Zion we'll stand up to douchebags,*
*We'll try to build bridges instead of huge walls.*
*And those who insist upon grabbing our kitties*
*Will find out that bravery does not come from balls.*

*Persisters in Zion are women of action—*
*Calling out haters and shouting the truth.*
*Let's not hang with Nazis; let's fight for the Dreamers*
*And show off our power in the voting booth!*

*We have been shown, like our mother Eve*
*To stand up boldly for what we believe.*
*We have been taught by first lady Michelle*
*That we should go high while they go to hell!*

*Oh we are here as daughters of Exponent.*
*Enlarging the circle of love.*
*And we will try to make this a safe place*
*To honor our Mother above.*

## Wonder Women
Rachel Rueckert
Winter 2018 (vol. 37, no. 3)

*Winning Essay:* Exponent II *Essay Contest.*[8]

> *"If men do not comprehend the character of God, they do not comprehend themselves."* —Joseph Smith

I paused to admire a Wonder Woman tiara for sale during the silent auction at the last Exponent II retreat. The wooden crown seemed well made, perhaps even hand carved. I wrote my name down on the bidding sheet.

"Ten dollars."

I checked back again later. My signature was buried behind several others.

"Twenty-five dollars," I wrote. I could justify the cost. This was for a good cause, right?

I was outbid again. "Thirty-two," I added with more hesitation.

I'm not one for spontaneous spending, but I surprised myself and kept bidding.

"Forty five," I scribbled.

Despite my detestation for princess culture, my heart raced as I competed

---

8. This note was in the original publication.

to take the crown home. I knew I could get the same thing online for a fraction of the price, but something about purchasing the object from the sacred space I'd inhabited for two days propelled me to keep bidding.

The total kept going up. But I was relieved and giddy when, after negotiating with my fierce competition, I won. I immediately demanded all of my friends try it on. They relented, put the crown on, and grinned. The joy over the crown was contagious.

I thought my shopping spree and moment of fun was the end of the whole affair. I was wrong. In the following days, I caught myself putting the crown on before starting a difficult writing project. Then after a long day at work. Then I put it on again before eating my breakfast one Saturday morning. My husband walked into the kitchen and found me in a robe, wearing the crown, eating yogurt. He smiled, then laughed. "What are you doing?"

I wasn't sure.

At therapy a few weeks later, I decided to take a break from talking about my mother's debilitating psychosis and the legal steps I was taking towards guardianship to process what was happening with the Wonder Woman crown.

"Can you say more about why you admire Wonder Woman?" my therapist said.

The list was easy to generate. "She is kind, strong, compassionate, fierce, confident, capable of learning, beautiful, an advocate ..."

Then there was a pause, a burning in my throat.

"She is a goddess," I said, mildly horrified when my eyes sprung tears. I thought of Heavenly Mother, whose vague presence I have felt at various points in my life, especially during times when I felt an absence of female role models and mentors. The parallel finally hit me.

\*\*\*

You, I, and the box office all agreed that the 2017 Wonder Woman movie featuring Gal Gadot spoke to us. Part of the film's resonating success can be attributed to depicting a powerful woman in cinema; the world needs more female representation. But there was another layer, a deeper draw within me. After my therapy session, I decided to learn more. What was it about Wonder Woman I found so meaningful?

I read a book called *The Secret History of Wonder Woman* by Jill Lepore; I was certain some of my admiration would be challenged. Wonder Woman was created by Dr. William Moulton Marston, the inventor of the lie detector test.

Marston, a staunch feminist, became a failed academic before turning to comic book writing. Wonder Woman was influenced by the early suffragist ideals and political cartoons featuring women escaping bonds symbolizing the patriarchy.

Marston also secretly practiced polygamy. He married two brilliant, consenting women who had a tremendous influence on Wonder Woman: Sadie Holloway and Olive Bryne. Bryne's mother, Ethel, gained national recognition in a hunger strike to bring awareness to birth control access. Bryne's aunt was Margaret Sanger, founder of the early version of Planned Parenthood. These strong women inspired and, at times, even wrote the character of Wonder Woman.

Lepore's book paints a messy history. Wonder Woman has been through a lot since her creation in 1941. People critiqued the length of her skirt, criticized her reluctance to marry, objectified her body, sexualized her bondage and struggle against evil men. But people also praised her hatred of guns, valued her commitment to truth, applauded her enthusiasm for women's education, praised her moral courage, and celebrated her promotion to the Justice League of superheroes during WWII (though, much to Marston's dismay, the editor only allowed her to serve in the war effort as a secretary).

Obsession with modesty? Occasional aspirational shame? Polygamy? Built on the backs of strong, forgotten women? This all hit home. Wonder Woman, in all her complex history, only became more real to me. Much like people's nervousness about discussing or defining Heavenly Mother today, people fretted over whether Wonder Woman's influence was for the collective good.

But one thing is certain; Wonder Woman to date has been one of the most popular comic book superheroes of all time, despite the relentless debates about who she is and what she stands for. Our craving for the Feminine Divine is here to stay.

***

My mother continued to spiral, and if I had to admit it, I felt I was spiraling too. I had spent hours salvaging her mortgage, gathering evidence, and calling different lawyers to take on our contested guardianship case. I needed something else to look forward to in October. So for Halloween, I hunted down a convincing Wonder Woman costume to go with the crown. I got a velvet cape, gladiator sandals, and epic body armor. Then my spontaneous spending resurfaced. At a costume shop, I caught sight of a plastic sword from the 2017 movie adaptation. This time my husband, sensing my excitement, insisted I go for it.

As I walked home from the costume shop, I kept swinging the sword around, a bit thrilled by a sense of power. For the first time in my life, I felt like I understood the scriptural messages about the "armor of god." I now had a visual for an ideal female warrior. The physical sword of truth in my hand somehow made me feel as if my figurative truth had more weight and meaning, even if the sword was only plastic. I could see it! I could swing it! I could point the way! I could hold onto it for dear life. I could feel less afraid. I could fight for what was right.

But as I brandished the sword on Cambridge Street, not caring what the passing cars were thinking, I remembered a key moment in the film. After spending a lifetime relying on her sword for strength, Wonder Woman reaches a crisis point. She learns it isn't the object that possesses power, but herself.

She realizes she is a goddess, stronger than she ever believed.

\*\*\*

Maybe Wonder Woman is no more than a sexy comic book figure, a money-maker for the capitalists in Hollywood. Maybe my pull towards a mysterious Heavenly Mother is nothing more than an earthly pining for the motherly void in my current life. But I don't think so. Like everyone, I have crises to face. I want an inspiring woman to channel on the days when I don't want to get out of bed, call another lawyer, or continue on the harrowing path of rescuing my suffering mother without her consent. And if there is a goddess looking out for us, a goddess we are all supposed to emulate, I think she'd act like Wonder Woman.

Lepore insists that Wonder Woman "wasn't meant to be a superwoman; she was meant to be an everywoman" (220). I see that kind of divinity as I watch the women in my life—I want them all to try on the crown. I see glimpses of the divine in their lessons at church, in their bravery in standing up for what is right despite opposition, in their courageous careers and parenting. I see the divine in their art, in their unspoken care, in their academic achievements, and in their written words. I see the divine in their broken hearts, their best efforts, and their unique intuition. Collectively, they are wonder women. And they remind me that I too have divinity within myself. There is strength inside of me, and I don't even need a costume.

But after the cape, armor, and sword go into storage, I'll keep the crown on my desk, ready at a moment's notice when I need the reminder.

## Letter from the Editor: Exponent Wrapped
Rosie Gochnour Serago
Fall 2018 (vol. 38, no. 2)

We've all had times in life when we've given someone a gift that wasn't wrapped. I don't mean a gift that couldn't be wrapped; I mean a gift that, with a little more planning and effort, with just a smidgen more time in your day, could have been wrapped.

An unwrapped gift is still meaningful. The wrapping is superfluous in many ways. But after gifting many an unwrapped gift, I've learned again and again that wrapped gifts are better.

When I feel best about a gift I've wrapped, the process usually goes something like this. I search through my miscellaneous drawers for a simple, natural fiber paper. The wrapping paper is a reflection of me. It's not Hallmark and it's not glittery. It's likely tan butcher's paper. I dig through more miscellaneous drawers for something that would make a nice tie. I like string or twine, not ribbon. Maybe the earthy cord that bound my farmer's market carrots. My bows are floppy, not crisp. To top it off, I find a thick marker and I write a note, directly on the paper. I choose my words with care.

When I'm done, the result is not gorgeous. It's not award winning. Sometimes the paper is newspaper. (But if it is, I probably picked from a good section, carefully avoiding the stock report.) If it's the semi-annual gift for my domestic goddess, lime green-loving mother-in-law, she's not going to give the wrapping job any awards.

But to me, it signals that I finished the job. It says I care about this gift—paired with the powerful act of giving—enough to see it through to the end. To tie it up with a simple bow.

This is the philosophy that I carry with me as I digitally pull together the pieces that make up every issue of *Exponent II*.

I'm the layout editor. What does that mean?

Women send *Exponent II* their words. Their stories. Their pain. Their joy. Their questions. And I lay out their paragraphs. Column by column, spread by spread. I type the titles and author names, letter by letter.

For the bulk of the body text, I copy and paste, but I carefully look for orphan lines and consider the nuances of breathing room and white space.

Did you know the font size of the body text of every *Exponent II* article is 9.75? Not 9 or 10. 9.75. A terribly odd font size. But it's the font size I've found gives just enough readability to still be economical with space.

And between each column is a .25" gap. Someone makes that decision, and it's me. It could be bigger, it could be smaller.

If these decisions sound fussy and somewhat frivolous, that's fair. They mostly are. But added up, they weave intention through the magazine. All the small details are intentional. That's what makes a good wrapping job.

And the art. Oh, the art! I am constantly fighting, re-thinking that 9.75 font size. Could we make the words fit a little bit tighter so this beautiful painting could be just a touch larger? When laying out 25,000 words, a handful of poems and 15 pieces of art in 40 pages, it's a game of quarter inches. And I fight for every quarter inch to give each component—and by extension each artist, author and poet—as much space as they deserve.

Because that is my gift to this community.

These women write their words. The artists share their beauty. The proofreaders, copy editors and editors strive for thoroughness and accuracy. And when it comes time to hand it off to our eager readers, I have a chance to wrap the gift.

It would be a lovely gift without any wrapping.

But my layout and design work is my way of saying to all the women reading and contributing to *Exponent II*: your sentiments, whether written or illustrated, deserve to be wrapped.

## The Folly of Hedges
Tracy McKay Lamb
Summer 2019 (vol. 39, no. 1)

> "'*look to the poor and needy and administer to their relief, that they shall not suffer.*' Now note the imperative verb in that passage: 'They shall not suffer.' That is language God uses when he means business." —Jeffrey R. Holland, October 2013

Last year, I stood up in Relief Society and I made the teacher cry. The woman at the front of the class was teaching a lesson on self-reliance. It doesn't always happen, but it's a frequent enough occurrence that I usually steel myself and sure enough, she veered into the Gospel of Prosperity. I sat on my hands, then shifted and dug my nails into my palms. I didn't know this woman and wanted to give her the benefit of the doubt. I hoped someone else would speak up, stand up, say something, say anything…

And then suddenly there was me, standing. Shaking. Struggling for words. My body trembled with indignation and anger as I struggled to make my voice clear and calm. You do not use the words "welfare mothers" and the othering language of "they/them" around me—a fact I am certain my entire Relief Society now knows.

Mormon theology is very clear about our obligation to one another—not only in our scriptures, but in the promises we make in our highest places. We are a communitarian people, covenanted to "succor the weak [and] lift up the hands which hang down" (D&C 81:5). The very promise of Zion is that we shall have no poor among us (Moses 7:18). Being a follower of the Savior means acknowledging very real commandments, not mere suggestions, on what it means to dedicate our lives to following the Son of Man. I will never sit quietly while anyone tramples this fundamental cornerstone of my faith.

There was a time where I was able to spin fairy tales and build hedges around the world to give myself a false sense of security. That's all the prosperity gospel is—whistling past the graveyard, pretending if we do everything correctly that we will be immune from the realities of a fallen world. And maybe for some people it works. At least for a while. But it behooves us as we grow, as we more fully mature and come unto Christ, that we understand the folly of our hedges and walls.

I did everything right. I got married, I had a baby, I joined the church. I made my life fit the ideal, in a desire to fully integrate.

I attended church faithfully, cultivated family life, and added two more babies in quick succession. And then it didn't work. My husband started doing opiates. I went to the temple. My husband lost his job. I wore out my knees praying. My husband overdosed. I did my visiting teaching, counseled with my bishop, volunteered at the storehouse. My husband ordered drugs online and the house went into foreclosure. I honored his priesthood as I was counseled, and tried harder to be perfect. My husband overdosed again.

When you get knocked down that hard, when your entire life and identity is coming undone around you, you have to face some hard truths. At that point, my faith was transactional. I thought if I followed the rules and did what I was supposed to do, that I would be rewarded. I was confusing living an embodied, rich life for a child's game. We don't do good things because we expect a tidy reward from a benevolent Father. There are cautions against this very notion everywhere in the scriptures. I had received my just reward—in pride.

My hedges and rows came tumbling down along with the rest of my life and I was standing in the rubble of not only my suburban dream and marriage, but of my adopted faith too. If none of this was reliable, then what was? It was time for me to sort what mattered, to figure out what in the rubble was worth salvaging and nurturing, and what was destined for the ash heap.

I had been praying for the wrong things. I had been childishly expecting the Lord to reward my actions with the manipulation of the world and other humans. There is no gospel of prosperity. We don't get earthly blessings for being good, not ever. God is pretty clear that that's not in the cards. But we miss it. So often, we miss it. When I let go of what I thought I was supposed to be doing, and actually asked God with a humbled and crushed heart what I needed to do, the answers came pouring in.

One of the answers that surprised me was counsel from my bishop to apply for state welfare assistance. The day I walked into the county welfare office was a Rubicon. I was suddenly everything I thought my faith had promised to protect me from: I was poor. I was divorced. I was a single mother. I was facing homelessness. Everything I had feared, every stigma I had hoped to avoid, had become a part of my life. In the prevailing narrative distilled down, my ex-husband was a drug addict and I was an uneducated single mother on welfare.

I felt so much shame when I walked through the nondescript sliding doors of the county welfare office. I had done as much paperwork ahead of time as possible, and all three of my young children were with me, as required. The county would need to see the children and verify they were taken care of and there were no signs of abuse.

Let's dispel a common myth immediately: applying for and receiving welfare isn't easy. There are a million unanticipated but unsurprising indignities in the application process. Along with all the basic information about yourself and your children, you must show detailed financial and court documents regarding legal separation, divorce, child support, and your housing arrangement. You must show documentation on bank accounts, retirement, titles on cars, or any other asset you might have access to. Any vehicle you have must be under a certain value or you are required to sell it. It's a detailed assessment, and it's a high bar. It's also one that you are required to return to examine every six months for the entire time you receive welfare. But the people working in the welfare office were kind and professional. They had dedicated their professional lives to helping people like me get help.

As I left the welfare office, trailing behind my children and clutching a printout telling me I would hear our results in about a week, I was conflicted and confused. I didn't want to be a welfare mother. I didn't want to lay bare my dire straits to strangers and I didn't want to need help. But I also couldn't pretend I didn't need it.

I hadn't necessarily subscribed to the derision around welfare, but I had absolutely internalized the stigma, and my stupid pride had made me resist help much longer than I should have. My impressions of what welfare meant that morning shifted and changed in real time as I helped my children buckle into our (older, paid for) car.

The enormity of what it meant to think of an entire class of sisters and brothers as a monolith hit me. Comfortably labeling people who qualified for public assistance as "them" allowed me and allowed society to distance ourselves—to build those hedges of the prosperity gospel—believing they could never be us. I suddenly felt deep shame. But it was a shame changed. It wasn't about my personal pride in my lack of means. It was a shame for failing to understand what it meant to love and serve my brothers and sisters, to be a true follower of Christ as I wished to be.

Despite the sometimes catastrophic consequences of agency, there were mechanisms and safety nets and hands outstretched waiting to help. I lost my home, but because of the hard work by women's-rights advocates, I was able to get a divorce and protect myself and my kids. My ex-husband was swallowed by addiction but there were laws, judges, and courts who ensured that my children were protected, and that their father was protected too—from himself and from doing further damage. Addiction was a nasty, slouching beast, but there were programs and help for that, too. I may have been without home or child support, but there were programs in place for people just like me. I didn't have an education, but there were low-interest student loans so I could find a way out of my situation. It was all imperfect, and sometimes difficult to navigate, and required work. It was work I could not have done had the help not been available.

Any lingering notion that life's blessings were somehow earned was obliterated in me that day, along with my pride.

I ended up spending a total of six years on some form of public assistance. My children received Medicaid, though I did not qualify—I spent a lot of time hoping I didn't get sick. We received SNAP food benefits, and my children qualified for free school lunches. These benefits kept my little family afloat while I went to school full time and graduated with a college degree at the age of 40, after which I was able to find good employment that helped support us. My kids still received school lunches and Medicaid, since my work didn't offer medical benefits. We did not need SNAP any longer, and were able to transition off of that assistance. We were right on the edge of security, able to stretch and make it work, and deeply thankful for the resources that helped us get there.

Through all of this, the church was there to help me and my children with the gaps and limits of the government systems. The official church counsel for bishops is to advise the ward members in need to seek whatever governmental assistance is available, and then to help from that point. It's a wise plan. The church can do a lot, but a strong social safety net that is available to all is a moral imperative that we should strive to support as a people.

From the rubble that I was forced to sort through, I learned that nothing we have is earned. Not a single thing. We can work, we can try, we can build ourselves and our families and communities up. Not only can we, but we have a covenant obligation to do so. But the truth is, everything we are and have already belongs to the Lord and we are only the stewards. Anything we retain is solely through grace.

So when someone in church stands up and begins a lesson starting with the premise of "us" and "them" I will shove my hands down and try to wait and see where it goes. I owe everyone the same grace I hope to receive. If they veer into talking about welfare, my heart might race. If they start defending the building of hedges or give a little whistle, the chances are good that my racing heart is going to lead me to stand gingerly on legs that, I assure you, are shaking, but I have conquered greater fears and I will open my mouth and testify:

Being a follower of the Savior means acknowledging very real commandments, not mere suggestions, on what it means to dedicate our lives to following the Son of Man.

And I will go from there.

## Gingerbread Girl
Falencia Jean-Francois
Spring 2020 (vol. 39, no. 4)

My mother was a gingerbread woman pulled from the oven too soon.
Her gingerbread man already on the run
she stood alone, under-cooked, and ill-equipped to care
for the cold little lump of gingerbread dough they had made together, but
    that somehow fell to her
to keep alive.
This new, strange kitchen she found herself in was empty,
but no matter. She set to work.
Lacking the calm, even pressure of a rolling pin, she made do with what she
    had—
her belt, her shoe, her brush, her open hand, her closed fist, her fingernails,
    her foot, shod and unshod—
to beat me
into a shape resembling her idea of a person. (I never could quite measure up.)
When the instructions for carving out my femininity, written in the language of kindness,
eluded her,
she substituted cruelty and criticism.
When the controls for the oven from which she came
proved too complicated to operate,
she toughened my dough with impossible expectations.
BUT! What she lacked in baking skill she more than made up for
with a steady piping hand.
Barrettes, bows, and ribbons; braids, weaves, and ponytails; gold necklaces
    and gold bracelets;
diamond and emerald earrings; silk, satin, and lace; designer, designer,
    designer!
She coated us both in thick layers of the most royal of icing,
lest anyone see her scars or my still bleeding wounds;
lest anyone notice my burnt edges;
lest anyone judge our misshapen parts;
lest anyone feel the need to offer us help.

Seventeen years later, my mother is gone,
consumed from the inside by an insatiable disease that gave no thought
to her appearance,
and I have begun the work of unlearning everything she taught me.

As I chip away at the layers of hardened icing,
I wonder if I'll recognize
the body I find
underneath.

## Family History: Made for You But Not For Me
Ramona Morris
Spring 2021 (vol. 40, no. 4)

It was in Sacrament Meeting that I first saw myself, and my family, as "other."

I was visiting friends in Idaho and Utah following my grandmother's death, and in the middle of the meeting, members were asked to pull up a family history application to locate "Family Members Near Me." This was uncomfortable for two reasons.
1. I'm Black and probably was the only person of color in the room.
2. The act felt like a slap in the face for those who simply didn't have the typical LDS family or couldn't trace their genealogy.

As an Afro-Caribbean Latter-day Saint, I was already managing identity issues relating to being the "token" Black person in an extremely white space. I really struggled when it came to the less-than-subtle pressure for perfection. (Someone actually thought I was a refugee and assumed I came to Utah by boat. I told them sassily there are planes flying to and from my country.) While sitting in that service, I immediately felt shut out of a narrative that wasn't created for people who looked like me. Chances are that I would never find my family by simply clicking a link on a phone app.

Compared to most of my LDS friends, I cannot boast of having generations of ancestors who were members of the church. I cannot brag about family members who have served missions or feel delight that members of my family were sealed in the temple for time and all eternity. I have found myself time after time struggling to find my place as a member of the church when my family tree looks vastly different than most members'.

My family's history has always been complicated. While growing up, I heard tales of my great-grandfather, that he was possibly about to be sent to the army or to do some job which he didn't want to do (in Ireland? Scotland?) and that he left by stowing away on a boat to Barbados.

I learned the story of my grandmother who became a nurse in the 1940s. At that time, there was a massive stigma around the nursing profession, and my grandmother's desire to study went against the expectations of her family and the community. She ended up being highly trained in the nursing field and left Barbados during the Windrush era where skilled workers were able to work and live in England. England was where she met my grandfather and where my mother was born. They stayed in England until my mother was three years old.

Even as a young girl, I was always proud of my grandmother and her accomplishments. I grew used to the stories about her qualifications and how she had defied her town and her parents who believed that she should've gotten married instead of studying to become a nurse.

It was only when I entered my teenage years that I learned about my grandfather. I only have a name. *Ernest Taylor.* I know that he was an engineer. Apart from this, the only other valuable information my grandmother would share was that he was African, and his family had undermined the relationship which had led to their breakup. After this, my grandmother moved my mom back to Barbados and stopped talking about my granddad; she preferred to speak only about my mother who was born as a result of her failed love story.

I relished any snippets of information that my grandmother would provide about my grandfather. I never asked why it was painful for her, but I knew she wasn't fond of the topic. What I did learn was that she loved my grandfather, but knew that she could support my mom with her salary as a nurse and didn't need to settle for his family and the drama that would come with it.

Why would I share this bit of my family's telenovela although it has caused such pain for my grandmother and mother? In many ways, speaking so openly about my family explains why I believe that the pressure for members of the Church of Jesus Christ of Latter-day Saints to successfully find distant family members doesn't always come with puffs of magical smoke and fanfare. In the years since my grandmother's death and in my attempt to be a good daughter, I have struggled with anxiety, tears, and confusion when it relates to completing family history work.

But the uncomfortable pressure remains and I have found myself over the years trying to complete the missing branches on my family's history. I sat in on a class at Utah State University that offered a few hints. However, once I returned home, continuing to focus on family history work has led to even more tears and setback after setback in hopes of learning anything more, especially about my grandfather. Although I know more about my grandmother's journey, the information related to my grandfather is practically invisible. And each time I fail, I feel immense Mormon guilt.

I tell myself that this is all due to toxic positivity. Even if I say that it doesn't matter, I want others to see that I too have a history I can be proud of. I want others to see that I'm doing well. In my heart, I want others, instead of looking down at me for my less-than-ideal family, to see that I, that we, have accomplished something that goes beyond the stereotype of the dysfunctional or absent Black family.

I know that I need to silence this voice. Family history isn't about the church. It's for my mom who has no memory of her father. It's for the little girl who only got to spend less than four years knowing the man who is responsible for her proud African spirit.

And although he never knew me, I really want to feel as though I have made my grandfather proud in some way.

This is the hardest part about not knowing who he was.

## On Saying Yes to Boys
Hannah MacDonald (pseudonym)
Fall 2021 (vol. 41, no. 2)

I don't remember who told me first—my mom? My dad? My Young Women's president, the one with the indestructible, gravity-defying, blonde hair? Whoever it was, here is what they told me: *say yes to boys*. If a boy asks you to slow dance, you say yes. It doesn't matter if his list of hobbies begins and ends with Rubik's Cube or if he's wearing a Star Wars tie or if the DJ is playing "Say Something" by A Great Big World featuring Christina Aguilera or if you're feeling like your glitter cat eyeliner is a little too cool for this Stake Dance. It was very courageous of him to ask. You say yes. You put your hands on his shoulders, and when the only conversational opening he can come up with is, "What color is your toothbrush?" you smile as if that's a normal thing to say and you answer honestly, "It's pink with a little blue stripe down the middle. How about yours?" The yes rule also applies to dates, homecomings and proms, church callings (obviously), light hand holding, the question "Did you have a nice time tonight?" and eventually, to marriage proposals (or, more accurately, marriage propo*sal*, singular, because you should really only be saying that particular "yes" one time).

Neither I nor my two sisters were natural daters in high school, which might explain why the yes rule was so big in our family. Even getting the chance to say yes in the first place was a rare blessing. All three of us were (and are) "too intimidating" for most boys, whatever that means. We were about average height, and none of us could bench more than 50 lbs, so the source of our menacing power remained a mystery.

I said my first major yes when I was sixteen years old. According to the intricacies of the almost-but-not-quite-canonized Mormon dating timeline, I was too young to be in an exclusive relationship, but my parents were surprisingly supportive. After all, I was setting a good example for my non-dating sisters. In this household, We! Date! Boys! The boy in question was a grade above me, tall-ish, skinny-ish, a wearer of nice shoes and soft, vintage T-shirts with photographs of dead jazz musicians on them. It was late spring and we sat side-by-side in the itchy yellow grass of the foothills, sneezing. He said we needed a song, an anthem for our relationship, and asked if I had any suggestions. I didn't. He pulled up "La Vie En Rose" on his iPhone and we listened to it as the sun set. I was half certain that he was joking. *Obviously not this one*, I thought. *It's just so ... romantic.*

"It's perfect," he said.

It might be wrong for me to criticize the yes rule too harshly, considering the fact that I am a product of it. My dad returned from his mission sure that my mom was the one. My mom did not share this certainty, but Dad was unfazed. He waited patiently, asked for her hand, asked again. Eventually, she said yes. The day of the wedding, when she was crying in her temple clothes, he had to convince her yet again to marry him. They're together to this day, and one of the most loyal couples I know of. Just say yes, I guess.

During my senior year of high school, New Year's Eve was on a Sunday. I was at home watching the BBC's *Pride and Prejudice* miniseries with my family, feeling put-upon, texting my friend, Sarah, and hoping against hope that I would be allowed to go out once the clock struck midnight and Monday arrived.

> omg mr Collins is proposing
> so is there even anything going on still?

HAPPY NEW YEAR
yeah we're all in campbells backyard

> any dodge-sam action?

a smooch. but many smooches were past around
cOME OVER

Midnight came and went, and my parents concluded that it was too late to go out. My mom and I lay next to each other on the living room floor with the lights off. The rest of our family had already gone to bed. I stared at the ceiling, almost sure that I could see patterns swirling in the darkness. Oil slick shadows. I thought about Sarah. She had beautiful, full lips, thick hair, nearly invisible eyebrows. By second period, her drugstore mascara would disintegrate into tiny black flecks that collected under her eyes. Her fingernails were rounder than mine and her skin was pinker and I liked it when we danced together. I wondered about the smooches that were being passed around without me.

"Mom?" I asked.

"Hmm?"

"I think I'm attracted to women."

Two sets of eyes bored into the ceiling, looking at nothing.

"No, honey," she said. "You're not. You have a lot of gay friends, so you think you're gay too. You're a follower."

Even after three years at an East-Coast-hotbed-of-liberalism university, countless rewatches of Beyoncé's "Partition" video, and a single secret kiss, I've never stopped saying yes to boys.

Ben and I became friends in high school and spent years in a you-like-me-but-I-don't-like-you standstill. When I came home for the summer, we biked around Salt Lake together, laughing, gossiping about our classmates, discussing semiotics (him) and wait-just-a-minute-how-do-the-gears-on-this-thing-work-anyway (me). After dark, he offered to escort me to my doorstep. As we drew close to my house, the conversation became sparser and sparser until eventually, about a block away, it petered out altogether. I could feel the question coming and I pedaled faster. Maybe I could escape. Maybe, if I played my cards right, he wouldn't ask me at all; *she's too far away*, he'd think to himself, *she looks tired, I bet she really wants to get inside, better luck next time*. I put a bike length and a half between us when he called out to me: "Hey! Hannah! Wait up."

I waited up.

"I have something I want to ask you."

"Yeah?"

"Will you go out with me? On a date?"

I had never hated Ben before that moment, but there's a first time for everything. My summer flashed before my eyes: all the expired eyeshadow I'd apply, all the sit-down dinners I'd eat and the bad movies I'd watch, all the times I'd say "haha please don't touch me there," or worse, all the times I *wouldn't* say "haha please don't touch me there." I'd break things off in August, tell him I couldn't handle the distance.

"Yes," I said.

We kissed goodnight.

## During the Sacrament
Carol Lynn Pearson
Fall 2021 (vol. 41, no. 2)

The eight-year-old, newly baptized
  takes the blessed bit of bread
    from the silver tray in her brother's hand
      glances at her father
        who is always on the stand

And whispers to her mother
  "When I'm twelve I'll get to
  pass the sacrament, won't I?"

"Shhhhh!"

The voice of her ten-year-old brother
  in a loud whisper across their mother's folded arms:

"No!"
"Why?"
"Shhhhh!"
"'Cuse you're a gurrl!"

The eight-year-old's mind
  full of every Harry Potter book
  half of Louisa May Alcott
   and many other worthy friends
    speaks silently:

"Maybe when I'm thirteen."

The voice of her sixteen-year-old brother
  who kneels at the white table on the stand
  to bless the tiny cups of water:

"... that they do always remember him ..."

"I love Jesus ... maybe when I'm fourteen ...
... absolutely when I'm fifteen ...
he will remember me ...."

Silence.

Then the voice of her Other Brother
  sweeter than Goodnight Moon:

"... I ... do always ... remember you."

## Letter from the Editor: Holy in All its Forms
Carol Ann Litster Young
Winter 2023 (vol. 42, no. 3)

    We get to decide what, or where, is a holy place for ourselves. When we were younger, perhaps we were told which places were holy. For me, that was the temple. Maybe nature, slightly. My church experience made connections with nature through ward campouts, Girls Camp, and Scout Camp. There seemed to be a set criteria for what made a place holy—quiet, clearly feeling God, being in a specific, separated area. However, I don't think it was explicitly explained to me growing up that I could decide what makes a place holy.

No one else could decide this for me—or for anyone else. Others might say somewhere is holy, and perhaps you might feel it too. But only individuals can answer that question for themselves.

My holy places have changed over time. Perhaps when I was a youth I needed the pattern and example of temple trips and ward and family campouts to explore what was holy. Now, I find that my holy places include a mix of wonderment—like when you can see the night sky clearly, how small you feel looking at the great expanse of the stars and realizing how very old they are—and connection. One way I know a place is holy is feeling that mix of connecting with our inner knowing and an outside presence that both connects and distances ourselves with its grandeur.

I also find holy places in the mundane parts of my life. That life includes real constraints such as the threat of sickness, lack of paid time off, being a parent, and money concerns. As a result, I have shifted away from searching for the grand and epic and I now seek holy places in less obvious spaces—like taking a minute when I'm losing my patience to take deep breaths outside while my toddler's screams of "I don't want you to have alone time" are barely muffled on the other side of the sliding glass door. Or walking slowly through the snow, hearing the crunch of my feet and the muting effect of the snowfall. Finding ways to be present and accepting it's winter instead of wishing I was somewhere else. The cheesy but profound Peloton yoga instructor reminding us at the end of each class that everything we need is already within us. Connecting with our holy places can be recharging, recommitting to ourselves and our lives to try again, respecting ourselves, replenishing what was missing.

A brief summary of holy places from all of the writing in this contest issue might be: "it's complicated." Many of the writers explore places that used to be holy or find holy in unexpected places or times. Several others reimagine a holy place....

We invite you to reflect: What are your holy places, and what makes them holy to you?

## Shifting Sands
Andee Bowden
Winter 2023 (vol. 42, no. 3)

*Winning Essay:* Exponent II *Essay Contest.*[9]

My life began in Michigan. Two peninsulas surrounded by lakes that are so much more than lakes. The Great Lakes are aptly named. Lake Michigan is massive, stretching across hundreds of miles and a wide variety of landscapes. Some Lake Michigan beaches have sand that squeaks when it gets hot. Some are perfect for hunting Petoskey stones, Leland Blues, and Charlevoix Stones. Some have dunes that reach to the clouds and carry history and myth in their sands. Lighthouses, in a variety of colors and styles, each with their own rich stories, dot the vast shoreline. Looking into a Great Lake is like looking across an ocean—there is the shore you are standing on, and then endless, stretching, careening water, hiding life and death beneath its ebbs and flows.

For all of these reasons and more, Lake Michigan is a sacred space to me. But what makes Lake Michigan sacred isn't just the water or the lighthouses or the memories. I found my name, myself, on its shores.

While my life began in Michigan, it didn't stay there long. I have lived across the wide world, seen oceans and seas and straits, mountains and valleys and plains. But Lake Michigan will always be my home, and I will always return, whisper "hello," and dip my toes in her icy ruffles.

I call the lake my home not because great things happened to me there, or happened in Michigan generally. Quite the opposite. Michigan is where my family was homeless, living in a campground as the soil froze and the winds turned icy, our camper trailer heated by a single gas burner flickering in the night, while my sister and I curled our bodies to fit on narrow dining benches as we tried to sleep. Michigan is where my family moved from house to house to house, and school to school to school (six elementary schools in four years), as my parents sought cheaper rents and new jobs that would pay enough to feed and clothe their four young children.

When we could afford the gas to drive to the shore, we would pack up our car and drive to the lake, scant camping gear in tow. It got cold at night, and often rained, but the roar of the waves crashing into the sand easily made up for the damp chill and soggy campfires.

When I was growing up, one special part of beach days was a visit to a grocery store deli. Each time we were headed to the lake, we would make a quick stop to purchase a few items to pack into a picnic. I remember the excitement of visiting the deli—all of us decked out in our hand-me-down swimwear and

---

[9]. This note is part of the original publication.

sandals—as we lined up at the counter to let our mouths water at the sight of the variety of salads and meats. Chicken salad was always a staple of our summer beach days.

But as much as I loved going to the beach, I hated that swimwear. It always felt wrong to me, for my body. I wanted to wear board shorts and feel the cool, refreshing water unencumbered against my skin. My tight-fitting, stretchy leotard felt wrong, holding scratchy sand against my tender flesh. And then, as the years went by, my body also grew to feel wrong. With time, I learned the words that describe this experience.

I am a nonbinary person. I have a female-presenting body and androgynous hormones. I don't feel strongly female-ish, and I also don't feel male-ish. I'm just a person, in a body. And that body isn't who or even what I am—it's just what I'm walking around in.

When I was born, I received a name. But that name given to me by my parents was chosen before they knew who I was or what I would be like or would want to become. In the United States, my birth name is commonly given to female-bodied infants. In other countries the name is more common for male-bodied infants. This is because the name means "masculine," but it's an adjective that modifies nouns that have a feminine grammatical gender. But in the United States, and with English not having grammatical gender as a feature, the name became associated with feminine. If you look up this name in baby naming books, they will tell you that it means "womanly" or "lovely." This is not the case; in Ancient Greek it means "masculine."

It's actually fitting to me, as a nonbinary person in a body with androgynous hormones and female-ish features that my very name would be yet another gendered piece that doesn't fit me well. My birth name didn't fit my sense of myself. It itched like an allergic reaction, or like rough sand scratching me from the inside out, flaring up each time it was uttered.

I needed to find a name that gave me peace, rather than pain. I needed to find myself in a name, and I went to my sacred place to seek it. And so, on the shores of my lake, at the age of fifteen, I sought MY name.

While on a family camping trip, I took myself on a walk, hiking through the woods and down a dune to get close to the shore. With wind furiously whipping my hair, fresh water and pine filling my nostrils, and silky sand beneath my body, I sat with her, my lake, and asked her to help me find my name.

I took my fingers and slid them through the satin sands, looping curls and dots and stark lines until I found it: ANDEE. There I was, all at once. It was me. It was neither feminine nor masculine. It was unique, but not bizarre. It was playful and memorable and not like anyone else's. I loved it immediately. I loved the me I could be as Andee.

When I first started using my chosen name, there was a lot of resistance. My mother seemed to take the change quite personally, waxing poetic about how beautiful she finds my legal name, and describing how hurt she is that I don't care for it. But liking or not liking the name is not the point. The name assigned to me at birth is not who I am, and I cannot live with being called a name that feels like someone else. The name I chose on Lake Michigan's shores is so much more meaningful and beautiful and holy to me than the one given to me at birth.

It has been 25 years since my lake graciously gave me my name. I use it exclusively, and resent when people ask me what Andee is short for. It's not short for anything—it is ME. All of me, not a piece of something else. Quite the opposite—when I used my birth name, I didn't feel like I could be completely, authentically me. I felt pigeonholed into being and acting like a specific kind of person—a person that I am not. So no, Andee is not short for anything at all—they are completely me, and I am them.

I often return to my favorite beach. There is a broad swath of soft sand and a pier that stretches out to a square, red lighthouse. The first half of the pier has railings—the final half does not. Some days the waves break violently over the top of the walkway; it's not always safe to walk the full length of the pier. While breakwater stones line both sides, they are not always enough to keep the crashing waves at bay. Knowing this, I always try to walk out to the lighthouse. Some days the water is too high and, with regret, I have to turn back. But when I can, when it's safe, I walk along the pier through the waves, and make my way to the end.

My name, myself, began in Michigan. A chosen name, or a found name, is holy, is sacred to the bearer. For me, it is a gift that I carry with me from the most sacred land I have ever crossed. I will bear it, with honor and pride, always remembering how the gentle crush of the waves on the satin sands whispered to me my own song, helping me find my way to myself.

## The Place that Doesn't Exist
Allison Pingree
Spring 2023 (vol. 42, no. 4)

In the place that doesn't exist, my husband and I lace our fingers and stroll the streets on a summer Saturday evening. We catch the sunset, laugh at a joke he tells, brush up against each other and melt into passionate kissing … and he remembers it all the next morning.

There's an outdoor cafe where we meet up with friends and pass the hours telling stories over crusty bread, wedges of cheese, bittersweet chocolate, and strawberries bursting with juice. He remembers our friends' names, the stories they tell, and what we ate.

In this place, we gather with my mom, my daughter, and my five brothers and their families for a reunion. As we make meals, spend afternoons building sandcastles at the beach, and watch slides from my dad's old projector, some childhood pathologies play out again while others are healed. My husband catches my eye at the right time, recalling what I told him years ago about those patterns, and understanding what these changes mean to me now.

On the drive home, we stop for fuel, and he knows how to insert his credit card, choose the type of gas to pump, and hold the nozzle in place, rather than throwing it to the ground in frustration—gas spilling over my legs and shoes.

Our home in this place that doesn't exist has a kitchen with cupboards—cupboards where he remembers to put the measuring cups, and the cans of diced tomatoes, and the glass bowls with lids. In this kitchen he knows to turn the stove off, and to heat his flannel bean bag neck warmer in the microwave, not the toaster oven. On Valentine's Day, the card that he leaves me on the kitchen counter tells me what he loves about me and why I'm his Valentine, instead of wishing me both "Happy Birthday" and "Happy Mother's Day."

In this place that doesn't exist, there's one that *does*: my husband's music. In the living room, here and now, he lifts his 1732 Sanctus Seraphin violin and plays Bach's *Chaconne*, his fingers quivering in yearning vibratos and his bow flying in lightning-speed arpeggios. This music—exquisite sounds that tether his soul to his body and alchemize my despair into amazement—will be the last thing to go.

## After Dobbs
Alixa Brobbey
Spring 2023 (vol. 42, no. 4)

My friend stares directly at
the sun, cups his cheeks
with her palm—risking blister
and burn.    She is the picture

of bliss. Rosy cheeks stark
against white lace. They sway
as one, slice through the cake
with giddy imprecision. Her corset

cinched so tight, she kneels
by the bleach bowl in prayer.

She folds over, like a hanger's hook. Bile stains the air.

## The Trench Coat of Multiple Colors
Allison Hong Merrill
Fall 2023 (vol. 43, no. 2)

### 1. 眉飛色舞 Brows Fly and Countenance Dances in Rapture
Taipei, Taiwan, July 1995

She looked into her pocket mirror, lipstick in her trembling hand. Furrowed brows. Labored breaths. Rose pink slipped out of the upper lip line. She finger-wiped it and reapplied. I watched from the backseat. The tag sticking out of her dress read *size petite*. I traced the contours of her face in my mind: a mouth that hardly smiled, deep-carved forehead creases, high cheekbones that pushed up her glasses, a tiny mole on her tiny nose. *Remember Mama. Remember her. Remember the past we had together, even though much was unshared.* I inhaled and filled my lungs with her scent. Essential oils. Cough drops. Baby lotion. *Remember Mama. Remember her. Remember the hours we hold in our hands, unspent.*

Forty-eight years old, Mama lived with diabetes and Alzheimer's. Discharged from the hospital only two months earlier. Weak and weary. Weepy and dreary. It was agreed, my sisters traveled with me. Mama insisted on tagging along. Repeatedly promised to stay strong. Fear of missing out, no doubt. Four-hour ride from our hometown to Chiang Kai-Shek International Airport in Taipei. Mamma Mia! She vomited the entire way. Disgorged and discharged. Moaned and groaned. Sour air. Silent tears. Head against window. Mother of sorrow.

Twenty-two years old, I lived with youthful arrogance and egocentricity. Engaged to an American young man only two months earlier. Elated and enthusiastic. Overwhelmed and rhapsodic. Flying to the US, my future felt exotic. Finally able to talk about my childhood as if telling someone else's story. Family drama, I would live without. Excuse me while I embraced the joy of missing out. The ride to the airport, daydreamed the entire way. Clapped and giggled. Hummed and whistled.

Time for farewell photos outside airport security. Sheepishly put on the trench coat I'd taken from Mama's closet. Stole sideways glances at her reaction to my thievery. Relieved she didn't chastise me. Mama's final gift, allowing me to bask in the bride-to-be euphoria, to fantasize about a new destiny in America.

2. 攘人之美 Rob Others of Their Beautiful Possessions
Hualien, Taiwan, October 1987

Mama only shopped at indent houses on Import Street. Brought home Japanese designer clothes on layaway. Tossed them onto her unmade bed. On the sticky floor. On the back of a chair. Price tags dangled. New items added to the pile: a red belted dress. A flowery-patterned blouse with puffy sleeves. A wide-lapel trench coat with pink lining, metallic silver trim, and a turquoise shell.

Oh my gosh, that trench coat! A lovechild of runway fashion and a rain poncho. It was, it was, it was my undoing. Even though I was only fourteen years old—a child, really, with friends who wore Hello Kitty overalls—I was obsessed with a mom coat. I wanted, I wanted, I wanted it. And I wanted nobody to tell me it was wrong to covet.

A few days after my parents' divorce, Mama was kicked out of our house, in the dark of the night. Single, alone, had zero visitation rights. Baba had sole custody. Remarried soon after. Forbade us to see our mother. Threatened to break our legs if we dared. *Pfft!* I thought. *You've broken bones, hearts, and other body parts. Don't you think that's quite enough?*

I snuck over to Mama's house anyway, after school every Saturday. Sat on Mama's bedroom floor. Stared at the trench coat of multiple colors. Imagined myself in it someday. Oooh, would you look at me! A sophisticated, striking socialite.

3. 兩全其美 One Thing that Beautifully Serves Two Purposes
Utah, USA, October 2000

In my American neighborhood, I was the only immigrant, the only person of color. The local ward of the church contacted me. Introduce your culture to the youth, they asked. Bring Chinese stuff for a display, they said.

*Hmmm—my entire being is Chinese stuff,* I thought. *How about I clothe my Chinese body in a thieving trench coat?*

A Caucasian teenage girl eyed my coat. Asked to borrow it. Wanted to dress up as Tanake Trang. "Y'know, that Asian-looking Jedi?"

I shook my head. I didn't know. "Does Ta-Ta-Ta—that Jedi—does she wear a trench coat?"

She shook her head. "Well, no, but your coat looks like a cloak. It's perfect for Halloween."

My beloved coat. A cloak. And a Halloween costume, no joke. Like a photography prop. Like toy blocks. Like an apple box. Like the stuff people sometimes chuck into a garbage can and turn their backs on.

4. 棄如弁髦 Disposing of a Black Headpiece after a Rite of Passage Ceremony
Utah, USA, November 2005

A familiar sound. Dump truck brakes. I stiffened. Straightened my back. Outside the window, the truck picked up the trash next door.

*Oh no.*

From the back of a chair, I grabbed the trench coat. Slipped it on. Braced against the cold. Ran out into the snow. Pushed down the garbage can lid. Rushed it out to the street. Watched the dump truck round the corner, I could almost weep.

I missed it again, again, and again. Like all those times my husband missed the chance to chuck out the trench coat. "You haven't worn it for years, it's taking up closet space," he would complain. I always stopped him from touching that thieving thing, even though it now seemed lifeless, purposeless, and meaningless. It had become something I wore once in a while, and then tossed in the closet, at the top of a clothes pile.

But how could I dispose of my teenage desire, yearning, and obsession? How could I get rid of a part of Mama that I wore on my body, besides my body? How could I treat the coat like the three layers of a black headpiece worn in an ancient Chinese Rite of Passage ceremony? Worn one layer at a time. Worn three times. Served the purpose, then deemed useless. Worse than a prop. Thrown out post hoc.

5. 後悔莫及 Belated Penance
Utah, USA

My birthday. Forty-eight years old. The same age as Mama was when I left Taiwan. I remembered her face. Not her voice. Thought of the coat. Where did it go? Upstairs. Bathroom. Basement. Storage room. Garage. Laundry room. Closet. Guest bedroom. Nowhere. Nowhere. Nowhere in sight. Possibly, my husband had thrown it out. Secretly. Quietly. Quickly.

No. Maybe not. Maybe he donated it to a local thrift store. Maybe a teenage girl bought it for $1, maybe more. Paid more for it than I did. Maybe she loved it more than I did. Maybe she wore it better than I did.

How did she feel when she wore it, a child born in 2007 wearing a trench coat made in 1987? Did she wear it to not look like herself? Did she also wear it for Halloween? Or for a school play? For a photoshoot? For a dress-up party? Where could I find her? How could I tell her about the world tour of the coat, journeying from Japan to Taiwan to America? How could I tell her it was the only physical possession I had of my mother, who passed away in an ambulance, wearing only a thin cotton slip when she closed her eyes for the last time? How could I tell anyone that I wished I had apologized to her for coveting and thieving? How I wished I could've draped the trench coat of multiple colors over her frail, shivering body when she silently left this world. Left her tearful life. On that cold winter night. On her fiftieth birthday.

# UNIT 6: REFLECTIONS ON NEARLY TWO DECADES OF THE EXPONENT II BLOG

PREVIOUS PAGE

1. A circle of women join Caroline Kline in blessing her son, Anthony, at the 2012 Sofia Gathering in Southern California.

2. Bloggers at the Exponent II fortieth anniversary gala, 2014. Back row: Aimee Evans Hickman, Libby Potter Boss, Emily Clyde Curtis, Chelsea Shields, Suzette Smith, Sandra Lee, Heather Sundahl, Caroline Kline. Front row: Sherrie Gavin, Emily Parker Updegraff, Rachel Hunt Steenblik (holding Cora), Brooke Jones, April Carlson.

3. Ramona Morris on a visit to Utah from Barbados with Jody England Hansen, 2022.

4. Katie Ludlow Rich, Natasha Rogers, Lindsay Denton, and Amy Freeman at Walden Pond on their way to the 2023 Exponent II retreat.

5. Bloggers and MoFem friends at the River Rock Roasting Company in La Verkin, Utah, 2019.

6. Nancy Ross, April Young-Bennett, and Rosie Gochnour Serago at the Sunstone Symposium, 2019.

7. Abby Maxwell Hansen reads from one of her blog posts at an Exponent II Women's History Month event at Writ and Vision in Provo, Utah, 2024.

## Introduction by Caroline Kline

Juanita Brooks's father once told her that it is the cowboy who rides on the edge of the herd, "who sings and calls and makes himself heard, who helps direct the course." A brilliant historian, Brooks had things to say about Mormon history, the scriptures, and more. As she contemplated her own relationship to the LDS Church, her father said to her, "Ride the edge of the herd and be alert, but know your directions, and call out loud and clear. Chances are, you won't make any difference, but on the other hand, you just might."[1]

Brooks's clear voice did make a difference. And so, I believe, has the Exponent II blog, which has been riding the edges of the herd and calling out loud and clear for nearly two decades. In its almost 6,000 posts, the blog has covered an astonishing amount of territory, including critiques of LDS gender roles, expressions of solidarity with LGBTQ members, diverse intersectional voices, and much more. Ultimately, this online forum, unbounded by geography and available to anyone with an internet connection, has created a sisterhood that so many of us would not have known otherwise.

### The Genesis of the Blog[2]

The Exponent II blog was born in 2006 as a new generation of Mormon feminists were yearning for online forums for conversation and solidarity. I was in my mid-twenties at the time, and I had recently discovered *Exponent II* through the woman I visit taught, Jana Remy, who let me borrow her stack of issues.

Reading those issues was life-changing for me. Here I found a community of women who for decades had been asking the kinds of questions that preoccupied me. Exponent II was the organization I had been looking for, and I was determined to contribute to it. A blog sprang to mind. Mormon-themed blogs in the mid-2000s were becoming hives for energetic conversation, idea sharing, and solidarity. Jana and I thought that an Exponent II blog could help connect younger feminists to this organization that had been the bedrock of the Mormon feminist movement for decades.

We, along with other founding members Emily Clyde Curtis, Brooke Jones, Deborah Farmer Kris, and Amelia Parkin, launched the blog in January 2006. Since then, it has featured a new post nearly every day, serving as both a bridge to more orthodox Mormons (mainly through its wildly popular, feminist-friendly Relief Society lesson plans) and as a haven for feminists

---

1. Davis Bitton and Maureen Ursenbach, "Riding Herd: A Conversation with Juanita Brooks," *Dialogue: A Journal of Mormon Thought* 9, no. 1 (Spring 1974): 12.

2. For more on the blog's founding, see pages 75–78.

yearning to share their questions, pain, and hopes for the tradition. Unlike the magazine's lengthier and beautifully edited pieces, blog posts often feature a degree of rawness, immediacy, informality, and frankness. This is not a liability; rather, it's the unique power of the blog.

## The Selections

This unit features a selection of Exponent II blog posts, highlighting a variety of Mormon feminist thought and experience. As these posts show, the blog has been at the forefront of both calling out the limitations and harms of LDS discourse and policy and of envisioning new inclusive paths forward for the tradition.

Jana Remy's "Radical Mormon Feminist Manifesto" (2007) was ahead of its time, taking the stance of radical inclusion toward LGBTQIA members among other visions of a future of equal opportunity for men and women in the church. This post garnered significant outrage at the time, but now it stands as prophetic, laying out the path so many Mormon feminists would tread over the next two decades.

The subject of LDS modesty discourse and objectification of women has been fertile ground for bloggers throughout the years. Amelia Parkin's "The Modesty Myth" (2011) shines in its clear, systematic unveiling of the damage of so much LDS modesty rhetoric, arguing that this discourse reduces girls to bodies and ultimately sexualizes them. She proposes a different path forward for the tradition: teaching girls that their value as human beings is unconnected to their sex organs. In her post "The Harms of Projecting the Mormon Male Gaze Onto Young Women" (2018), Caroline Salisbury (as "Violadiva") likewise points to the damage of objectifying rhetoric and practices within Mormonism, which so often—and at great expense to women—center the male gaze. April Carlson (as "Cruelest Month") tackles the same topic of modesty and objectification, but humor is the weapon of choice in her "Neckties: Priesthood Attire or Lucifer's Lust Pointer?" (2014). Her satirical (and hilarious) takedown of men's neckties as "phallic phallus pointers" turns LDS modesty rhetoric on its head, treating men's clothing and bodies as temptations that must be contained.

Meghan Raynes's "Now I Have the Power" (2011) arose in a moment when many young Mormon feminists were starting to explore their own spiritual power apart from that which the LDS Church authorizes. The post stands as a moving vision of what often came to be known as "priestesshood," as the author recounts the power of her experience with female blessings. April Young-Bennett's "Rejected Offerings" (2014) highlights a different Mormon feminist vision: full inclusion of women into the LDS priesthood. Her post arose in a seminal moment for Mormon feminists, as the Ordain

Women organization broke onto the scene and inspired thousands of Mormon feminists with the hope that structural change within the institutional church was possible. April's experience with rejection and dashed hopes is one that so many would also later experience when Kate Kelly, one of the founders of Ordain Women, was excommunicated.

Rachel Hunt Steenblik's "What I First Learned About Heavenly Mother" (2013) showcases another strategy Mormon feminists have long used to elevate women's status in Mormonism: emphasizing Heavenly Mother's existence and exploring her character and identity. Steenblik's post challenges the taboo against speaking about Heavenly Mother and brings to light little-known discourses about her.

Throughout the years, blog posts have often touched on hot-button topics in society. Heather Sundahl's moving "Baby Killer" (2008) sheds far more light than heat on the topic of abortion as she processes her grief at her lost pregnancy and her gratitude for safe and competent clinics able to help women of varying circumstances. As "Em," Emily Gilkey Palmer's "Freedom of Religion Under Attack Again" (2020) takes on the religious freedom rhetoric that arose among some church leaders during the COVID-19 pandemic. As a historian, Em was well positioned to correct misleading statements about government overreach.

Intersectional feminism began to play a significant role in Mormon feminist blog discourse in the 2010s. Greater understanding and increasing articulation that women's experiences with Mormonism were highly dependent on the intersection of gender, race, sexuality, gender identity, class and more began to permeate many posts. Blogging as "Spunky," Sherrie Gavin's poem "After" (2014) gives voice to the unique experiences, exclusions, and journeys of LGBTQIA Mormon women, as it features her own story and quest to become a mother. Melissa-Malcolm King's "Come Come Ye Queer Saints" (2020), a poignant discussion of her own experience with exclusion within Mormonism due to race and sexuality, came in the wake of BYU Honor Code changes prohibiting same-sex romantic behavior.

Queer voices and experiences were central topics of Mormon feminist interest and concern in recent years. In "Gender Affirming Care: Simple Words, Complex Emotions" (2023), Valerie Green shares her experience as a transgender woman and the pain she has felt upon being misgendered. Nancy Ross and Emily Holsinger Butler's "Poems of Exclusion" (2016) points to the devastation so many Mormon feminists felt in the wake of the 2015 policy excluding children of gay members from baptism and mandating church discipline for lesbian or gay couples who marry. Yet, hope and love were also central themes for LGBTQIA allies, as Mormon feminists proactively stood beside their LGBTQIA brothers and sisters. This is evidenced by Jody England Hansen's

"The Unconditional Act of Hugging" (2023), which recounts the soul-feeding joy the author has given, shared, and received hugging folks at Pride parades.

And finally, the #hearLDSwomen project (2018–19), born in the Exponent II Facebook group and then amplified and extended on the blog, became the blog's longest-running series. Spearheaded by Lindsay Denton, this series ran for a year and documented the various ways, large and small, women felt dismissed, unheard, or belittled within the church.

### The Difference We Made

For nearly two decades, Exponent II bloggers have bravely and courageously ridden the edges of the tradition and even of the Exponent II organization itself, calling out Mormonism's problems and excavating its most liberating possibilities. I believe the blog has made a difference, as it familiarized a generation of younger Mormon feminists around the world with critical language and empowering insights that might be brought back to their own immediate communities.

Bloggers have also made a difference throughout the years by articulating radical positions of inclusion and equality. As Margaret Toscano once told me, the outer edges of movements for change are important. Those at the edges create room for people who want moderate change to look reasonable. By staking out the revolutionary position, those at the edges shift the needle, moving the outer boundaries farther so that things between the outer boundaries and the status quo now seem more possible.

I believe our 6,000 blog posts have been a significant part of the swell of voices articulating new visions and shifting that needle over the last two decades. I think there's a good chance various posts have helped some in powerful positions within the institution imagine new possibilities. But more important than any impact we might have had on the institutional church, I believe, is the impact our blogging has had on our own lives. We have imagined and worked for a better world for our daughters and nieces. We have forged friendships that will stand the test of time and distance. I may never see the church become what I would like it to become. But how I treasure my Mormon feminist blogging community, those women who share similar hopes and dreams, who understand the struggle as no one else ever could. That has been life-changing and life-enlivening and will always remain, no matter what the institution does.

## Radical Mormon Feminist Manifesto
Jana Remy (as "Jana")
February 16, 2007

I really like the ideas that Caroline and others have recently proposed. Such feminist assertions are heartening, and are evidence of a growing activist consciousness that's quite encouraging.

I'd like to take this one step further by posting this **Radical Mormon Feminist Manifesto** that I've been drafting with some fellow feminists. For now, I see this document as a work-in-progress. I hope that you will comment on whether or not you agree with its assertions or you will suggest edits. It is my hope that this document can become a "proclamation" that will speak for many Mormon women who are invested in social change.

We are Radical Mormon Feminists. We are men and women, gay and straight, white and of color, of varying ages and abilities, from many nationalities and economic backgrounds. As such, we write this proclamation to assert our needs and our agenda for those oppressed by the church's stand on issues of gender and sexuality.

We affirm that as the LDS Church moves into the 21st century, it can no longer ignore and reproduce the multiple oppressions of sexism, racism, and ableism that are endemic in its patriarchal hierarchy.

As such, we assert that we will no longer passively submit to secondary status within the church for ourselves or our friends and family who are members. We subscribe to the tenet that our "God is no respecter of persons," and that God looks upon and understands the motives of our hearts as no leader—priesthood or otherwise—can. We embrace a Savior who reached out to all people regardless of their sexuality, gender, national origin, or ability; and commit to striving to reach out to all in the same way.

Additionally, we reject church teachings about the eternal nature of traditional gender roles and will not sustain official proclamations from the church leaders that reify such notions of women and men conforming to specific narrow roles such as submissive wives, full-time mothers, bread-winning fathers, traditional family members, head-of-household males, and priesthood-leading husbands. Instead, we sustain expansive acceptance of equal partnership between two adults in marriage; co-parenting by natural and adoptive parents; community support for single parents whether natural or adoptive; equal career encouragement and opportunities for both genders; and family teams that head households together in love and togetherness.

We believe that God ordains both men and women to have spiritual power for blessing, healing, and leading and desire women to be recognized in such roles. As radical Mormon feminists, we call for women and people of color to be included in all levels of leadership and where homosexual, intersexual, and transgendered people participate in full fellowship and temple ordinances.

While we affirm the free agency of each individual to make their own choices about Mormon belief and practice, as radical Mormon feminists we take a stand and assert our unwillingness to support patriarchy and the gendered hierarchy and oppression that results from it. We recognize the many righteous, well-meaning men who preside as faithful and loving leaders. We do not wish to remove them from their leadership roles. We only wish for the opportunity to join them as we work as one people to build the peaceful Zion community imagined and sought after by our ancestors. We do so with millennial fervor, calling for the day that all children of God are welcomed equally into the Mormon fold.

We acknowledge that large changes seldom happen overnight. We suggest the following as beginning steps to achieving the goals discussed above:

1) Call couples to serve in bishoprics together. Allow women to interview and hear the confessions of other women.
2) Jettison Boy Scouts and create the same youth programs for girls and boys.
3) Drop the "preside" language about marriage. Focus on co-equal partnerships.
4) Make priesthood ordinations optional and/or given as a young person desires it—sort of like a patriarchal blessing. Allow both girls and boys the same opportunities for ordination.
5) Let women learn their husbands' new names at the temple veil.
6) Allow same-sex couples to be sealed in the temple, even when local laws don't allow legal marriage.
7) Let women plan and speak at their own RS Conferences w/o men involved.
8) Allow women to preside over official meetings, such as sacrament meeting.
9) Turn the focus from bishops making the callings to self-callings—let both men and women volunteer and seek out roles they are interested in (even if men want to be in primary or women want to be in leadership).

## Baby Killer
Heather Sundahl (as "Heather")
November 11, 2008

When I dialed the number for the Newton Women's Health Clinic, I had no idea what I was going to say. I started with, "Hi, I'm about 17 weeks pregnant and …" I paused. "Miscarriage" felt so inadequate and I was struggling to remember the term my doctor had used. The phrase "fetal demise" came to me too late. Apparently, many of the women who call that office are tongue-tied because the receptionist jumped in for me "—and you need an abortion." "No. Yes. Sort of. I'm in my second trimester and the baby died. I need to schedule a D&E."

I didn't want to call or go there. How could I go to a place where women went to get rid of their thriving feti when I was so desperate to hang on to mine? "Baby killers," one friend called them. "You are going to be surrounded by Baby Killers." She clearly thought I was crazy to go to the clinic for a D&E instead of having it at the Brigham, the preeminent women's hospital here in Boston. But at the appointment when my eight-months pregnant OB couldn't find a heartbeat, she'd held my hands and shared with me that the year prior when she'd lost a baby at 20 weeks, this doctor at this clinic was the place to go. "For later term dilation and evacuations, the clinic knows their stuff better than any hospital."

I drove home sobbing, saying over and over, "I lost the baby. I lost the baby." My poor 2½-year-old in the backseat offered her help, saying, "Me help you find baby?" I cried harder as I imagined Millie thinking I was a mom who'd set a child down someplace and then "lose" it.

I was 36, had 3 kids, taught Primary, and was going to an abortion clinic. I'm not sure I've ever felt so low. This was my third miscarriage in less than a year and I swear the young mommies at church were afraid to use the drinking fountain after me, lest their fecundity swirl down the drain as well. The phrase "Baby Killer" haunted me because I felt like it fit. We'd bought and moved into our first house just days prior and my mother's warning rang in my head: "Don't you lift any heavy boxes or you could lose that baby." Of course I'd lifted boxes and though my OB assured me there was no connection, I still wondered if I had killed my baby. I was desperate for *any* explanation.

Spiritually I felt so adrift. Six months prior, I'd been 9 weeks along when I started spotting. I was reading the Book of Mormon, in Second Nephi when Isaiah takes over, so I wasn't expecting much when I opened the scriptures that night. Just a little comfort would be nice. Instead, I got Revelation as I read, "For unto us a child is born, unto us a son is given ... " A calm warm feeling came over me and I *knew* it would be okay and I *knew* I was carrying a boy. The blessing my husband gave me the next day talked about a normal pregnancy and a healthy child. Ah. Peace. But the ultrasound told another story: the fetus had expired at 7 weeks. An autopsy after the D&E showed the baby suffered chromosomal problems. But I was half right. It was a boy.

I got that D&E at the Brigham. The whole thing was ironic. You go to the maternity wing and have the procedure in a labor and delivery room. Mine had a shared bathroom. As I peed I could hear a baby crying. I flushed to drown out the sound. When I woke up, I had my husband, Dave, holding one hand, and my dear friend EmilyCC, a chaplain at the Brigham, holding the other. I was surrounded by love. But the newborn's cries echoed off my hollow insides. I could feel my emptiness.

I had a hell of a time trying to make sense of that whole experience. I wanted to be mad at God. I felt like he'd pulled a joke on me: "It's all fine—just kidding! Gotcha!" But I also felt the Spirit working overtime to comfort me, giving me a sense of peace and calm that pushed all anger aside. So I did the old, "Well maybe that feeling and that blessing are about the kid I'm GO-ING to have in the future." God's time and all that. Ha ha.

Driving to the clinic for part one of a two-part Field Trip of Horrors, I had no idea what to expect. I think I imagined a rundown shack in a back alley. Instead, it was an inconspicuous building in a nice part of town. That afternoon the clinic was only seeing the hospital-referred patients and I was the only one there. The staff was nice and the doctor competent as she prepped my cervix for the next day's procedure, but I could not get out of there fast enough. (Let me just add that while "laminaria" may sound like those pretty paper bags people use to illuminate their walkways for parties, there is nothing festive about those sticks of torture.)

Friday, July 16, 2004, Dave drove me back to the clinic. We parked our car and made our way through the crowded lot. I saw him before Dave did. I froze, and Dave turned to see why I'd stopped. An older man, perhaps in his sixties, stood in front of me with a sign. He looked like a temple worker on his day off. On the poster was a picture of a dead fetus and the words "Baby Killer" in red. "Baby Killers," he said to us. Or maybe he didn't and I just imagined it. Whatever the case, the words were like a slap. Part of me longed to explain to this man that I wasn't a baby killer like the other women in there. I was a Mormon, a baby maker. Though I'd shifted from a Pro-Life to a Pro-Choice stance in college, I felt like most abortions were a result of irresponsibility. Demographically I'm sure I shared a lot with the protestor in front of me, probably more than with the women inside. Who knows? But this man had drawn a line, and I was clearly on the other side.

Every muscle in Dave's body was taut and he started to say something to the man but I shook my head. Years of visiting teaching has taught me that you can't reason with crazy people. I started to laugh. When faced with the surreal, I giggle. I held my head up and we walked into the clinic. I felt relief to see an armed guard inside.

As I waited in chairs to be called, I couldn't help but sneak glances at the other women. White. Asian. An African American. I wondered at their stories and wanted to cry for the ones who were clearly there alone. One thing for sure, none of us *wanted* to be there. The woman who was in recovery with me was 10 years my senior and just stared out the window the whole time.

On the drive home I made Dave take me to McDonald's for fries and a Diet Coke to wash down my antibiotics and painkillers. I needed whatever comfort I could find.

I healed quickly and felt blessed to have had such excellent medical care. That fall I was asked to speak the Sunday prior to Thanksgiving and as I wrote my talk, I imagined sharing from the pulpit, "I am thankful for the gospel, for my family, and for safe and competent abortion clinics...." Writing that talk made me realize the contradictory nature of my loss. How could my heart, so aching for my lost children, still overflow with love for the three I had? And how could I feel such faith and hope in the Lord even though I could not quite kick the feeling that I'd been jerked around? Emptiness and love; faith and doubt. I don't know how it's possible to feel such things simultaneously, but I know that I did.

I didn't mention the clinic in my talk. I'm not that brave. I've realized that for many Mormons, where one stands on the abortion issue is the ultimate litmus test. The elections, of course, bring the "choice" debate to the forefront. Just today a friend told me about her nephew in Logan. Apparently, his school had held a mock election and only one kid was voting for Obama. That lone kid was ostracized and threatened. His peers' objection? "How can you vote for a man who wants to murder babies?!"

About a month ago a woman in another ward lost her baby at 21 weeks. A mutual friend called me and asked if I recommended the clinic or the hospital for the D&E. Hmmm. Listening to cries of newborn babies, or being called "Baby Killer." It's a terrible choice to have to make, but in my opinion, it's a blessing that she has one.

## The Modesty Myth: Why Covering Up Just Won't Do (excerpts)
Amelia Parkin (as "Amelia")
April 21, 2011

The Mormon emphasis on external, clothing-oriented modesty is just another form of sexualization. We attempt to negate the sexualization of young girls' and women's bodies by covering them up and locking them behind the door called Chastity. But when the female body is taboo because of its inherent sexuality (a sexuality so powerful that a woman literally turns herself into pornography for some men by dressing immodestly, according to that canard advanced by Dallin Oaks), and when women are celebrated almost exclusively because of their potential as breeders and nurturers of children, then we successfully sexualize the female body every bit as much as pushing heels, padded bras, plunging necklines, and miniskirts for pre-teens does. The invisibility of the female body, or of the attributes of the female body that stand for Sex, does not mean we have refused to grant the female body a sexualized status.

> According to the APA, "sexualization" occurs when:
> - a person's value comes only from his or her sexual appeal or behavior, to the exclusion of other characteristics;
> - a person is held to a standard that equates physical attractiveness (narrowly defined) with being sexy;
> - a person is sexually objectified—that is, made into a thing for others' sexual use, rather than seen as a person with the capacity for independent action and decision-making;
> - and/or sexuality is inappropriately imposed upon a person.[3]

As a culture in which we begin telling our girls as toddlers that their value comes from their ability to attract and retain a mate in the interest of fulfilling their divine role "Mother" and in which we far too often pay too little attention to other characteristics of our girls; in which there are externally imposed standards of what it means to be physically attractive, which standards often conflict with the message to physically attract men; in which girls' capacity for independent action and decision making outside the realm of their role as mother-in-training is downplayed; in such a culture I can only conclude that girls' sexuality is inappropriately imposed upon them as a class.

I have a radical proposal: the church and Mormon parents should teach girls that they have value without connecting that value to the sexiness of their bodies, their attractiveness to men, their capacity to make babies. Rather than lessons in which girls make lists of characteristics they should look for in a worthy, Priesthood-holding husband, have them make lists of the characteristics they should foster in themselves to be loving human beings in relationship with others, successful employees, and contributing members of their larger society. Rather than teaching them how to iron their future husbands' dress shirts, teach them appropriate grooming and behavior for success in the workplace, as civic volunteers, as adult women. In addition to YW activities during which they learn new recipes or make crafts, offer activities during which they learn less stereotypically female skills. I guarantee that if we prepare our daughters to be successful, well-rounded **individuals** rather than spending so much effort to prepare them to fill a preconceived concept of "wife and mother," then we'll have a sure way to get away from both ends—extreme cover up and extreme exposure—of the sexualization spectrum.

When we do so, we will see women and girls as **human** beings with

---

3. "Report of the APA Task Force on the Sexualizaiton of Girls," American Psychological Association, 2008, APA.org.

enormous worth and potential, with wonderful things to offer the world rather than as **sexual** beings who offer primarily their ovaries, vaginas, mammary glands, and uteri. And then, when we see a girl's bare shoulders because she's wearing a perfectly decent tank top or an expanse of skin on her thigh because it's hot and she's wearing shorts, when her neckline makes it recognizable that she does indeed have breasts, we'll be a hell of a lot less likely to see her as salacious and hypersexualized and instead register little beyond the lived reality of the female body.

**Now I Have the Power**
Meghan Raynes (as "MRaynes")
November 6, 2011

Several days ago I was at a park with my children. There was nothing particularly interesting about this park except for two older boys at one corner play-fighting. I don't like my children to watch or engage in violent behavior so I tried to keep their attention on the other side of the park. But we kept hearing snippets from their dialogue: "I have the power." "Ha ha, I just took your power." "You can't take it because I'm invincible." "I have your power, I have your power." "No. I have THE POWER."

My daughter, Sylvia, became more and more distracted by their exchange and before I could stop her, marched over to the two boys. Sylvia stared at them intently and then proclaimed, "Now I have the Power." She snatched at the air in front of their faces as if, in this one single gesture, all of their power and the power of the universe would be instantly transferred to her. The look on their faces was priceless because, at least momentarily, my three-year-old daughter *had* taken the power.

I was stunned but also delighted and so proud that this spirited little girl is my daughter. Sylvia is in that beautiful time before the forces of the world try to convince her she is smaller than she actually is. But along with my pride there was also a twinge of sadness and a jaded feeling of "if only it was that easy."

But what if it is?

As I've reflected on this experience over the past couple of days I've come to think that maybe Sylvia is on to something. In her little brain Sylvia knew that these boys would never just come over and bestow power upon her. No, she had to take what she felt was rightfully hers to have.

I wonder if this isn't analogous to the situation that we Mormon women find ourselves in? The issue of women and the priesthood has been talked to death but one thing is for sure, the male leaders of our church aren't going to walk over any time soon and bestow the priesthood upon us just because we ask nicely.

But the Power of God is available to us all. We as women have every right to declare, "I have the Power." To be clear, I am not talking about the institutional power that comes in the form of priesthood. I don't believe it would do women any good to all of a sudden start to perform living ordinances just because we declare we have the power to do so. But I believe the scriptures are very clear that we are all—man, woman, child—endowed with the ability to access God's power and utilize it for the good of our sisters and brothers. So many of us sit on the sidelines blaming our inaction on powerlessness and a lack of authority. This is a great lie that has been perpetrated and the fact that so many sisters feel as if they have no right or ability to be a conduit of God's love and power is to the detriment of us all.

Two years ago I received a blessing. I have been the fortunate recipient of many blessings in my life, and while they have all been meaningful, this one was special. I had been suffering for some months from a major depressive episode and was in a very dark place. While I was never in immediate danger, I longed for and sometimes considered a permanent end to my suffering. It was during that time that I left my home to meet with some old friends. I had become adept at hiding just how serious my situation was; nobody in my family or ward knew and even mr. mraynes was unaware of the extent of my depression. Though I had my brave face on these women knew intuitively that I was in trouble.

Towards the end of our time together my dear friend asked if she and the other women could give me a blessing. I stalled at first, not wanting to admit that I needed help and also a little afraid of going down that path, but I was so tired and so desperate that in the end I agreed.

It was like so many of the priesthood blessings I have received from my husband and father; a kitchen chair was pulled into the middle of the room and the women gathered around me except that they placed their hands all over my body. A pair on my head, another on my shoulders, some on my arms and my hands, thighs and feet. The feeling was amazing, warmth and connection emanating from those hands and coursing through my body. And then she spoke. She did not use priesthood parlance but the more informal rhetoric of love, friendship and intimacy. My friend spoke of the things that she loved about me, how she knew I was in pain and blessed me that I would be able to escape it. Then another woman spoke, sharing her thoughts and hopes for me. And another, telling me that God knew me and had a special work for me to do. Each woman in that circle spoke, some blessing me, some just expressing love. And I wept, tears of sadness and gratitude. When they were done my body felt alive again. After months of feeling only numb, the energy in my body was overwhelming but also exquisite.

This blessing was my life raft. I was drowning and these women used the power of God in every sense of what that means to save me. Within two weeks my depression had lifted and has yet to return. I made it through an unexpected pregnancy and the start of my graduate program without any relapse at all. I was healed. This is nothing short of a miracle and it was all because these wonderful women stood up against everything they were ever taught about authority and power and rejected it. Instead, they saw a sister in need of comfort and said, "I have the power to help her." My gratitude to these women knows no bounds.

Utilizing the power of God requires faith, confidence and a willingness to serve the children of God. There is no regulating this and exclusively assigning it to one sex. I am reminded of those two little boys in the park, bickering about who has the power and how they can use it. This is a ridiculous exercise that has no meaning unless we give it meaning. How sad that we as a church have done exactly this. What a tragedy that we are losing out on the unique blessings women can provide if only they were encouraged to fully access the power of God. It's time to stop waiting for that encouragement, it's not coming. Now is the time to reach out and grab the power that God has for us. I have a feeling They have just been waiting for us to say, "Now I have the Power."

## What I First Learned About Heavenly Mother (excerpts)
Rachel Hunt Steenblik (as "Rachel")
September 25, 2013

Once upon a time, I had the rich opportunity to research Heavenly Mother full-time. For BYU. I had just finished my BA in philosophy, when one of my professors invited me to work for him that spring and summer before I headed East for grad school. He had received a grant from the Women's Research Institute. My answer was a resounding, "Yes." I remain sincerely glad that it was, despite the fact that the thing that I remember most from that period was that I was exhausted—spiritually, mentally, and emotionally. This may be because the thing that I remember second most, is that I was also full—spiritually, mentally, and emotionally. It was beautiful to read and read about our Eternal Mother, as it was beautiful to learn that there were things to read and read. Much of my research contributed to the 2011 *BYU Studies* article, "'A Mother There': A Survey of Historical Teachings about Mother in Heaven."

Just the other day, I was given another rich opportunity: to talk about the things I learned during that time with my Relief Society sisters. It felt sacred (as did the conversation that followed). The first things I shared were the things I remember feeling very new to me then. The second things I shared were a few of my very favorite themes, threading throughout many of the writings and discourses. I share both with you now.

**New to me in 2008:**

- The hymn, "O My Father," was initially titled, "Invocation, or the Eternal Father and Mother," suggesting that Eliza herself viewed her words as a prayer to both Heavenly Parents. (Jill Mulvay Derr, "The Significance of 'O My Father' in the Personal Journey of Eliza R. Snow," *BYU Studies,* vol. 36, 1996–97.)
- Eliza's poem was not the first recorded expression of LDS belief in an Eternal Mother. W.W. Phelps published a hymn ten months before that he had written for the dedication of a Seventies Hall. It was titled, "A Voice From the Prophet: Come to Me." The relevant lyric says, "Come to me; here's the myst'ry that man hath not seen; Here's our Father in heaven, and Mother; the Queen, Here are worlds that have been, and the worlds yet to be, Here's eternity,—endless; amen; Come to me." (*The History of the Church,* vol. 7, Chapter XXVI; *Times and Seasons,* February 4, 1845.)
- This suggests that the doctrine did not stem with Eliza, but was common knowledge at that time. Eliza explained, "I got my inspiration from the Prophet's teaching. All that I was required to do was use my Poetical gift and give that Eternal principal in Poetry." (Maureen Ursenbach Beecher, Janath Russell Cannon, Jill Mulvay Derr's *Women of Covenant: The Story of Relief Society*.) There is additional evidence that Joseph Smith taught it. When Zina D. Huntington Young's mother passed away, she asked Joseph, "Will I know my mother as my mother when I get over on the Other Side?" He responded, "Certainly you will. More than that, you will meet and become acquainted with your eternal Mother, the wife of your Father in Heaven." (Suza Young Gates, *History of the Young Ladies MIA,* 16.) Abraham H. Cannon recorded in his journal that Joseph Smith invited Sidney Rigdon and Zebedee Coltrin to "accompany him into the woods to pray," where they experienced a succession of four visions—two of which included Heavenly Mother. (Abraham H. Cannon Journal, Aug. 25, 1880, LDS Archives, cited in Linda Wilcox's *The Mormon Concept of a Mother in Heaven,* 10.)
- The earliest recorded expression intimating that Heavenly Mother is too sacred to talk about was written by a 20th century seminary teacher, named Melvin R. Brooks: "Considering the way man has profaned the name of God, the Father, and His Son, Jesus Christ, is it any wonder that the name of our Mother in Heaven has been withheld, not to mention the fact that the mention of Her is practically nil in scripture?" (Melvin R. Brooks, *LDS Reference Encyclopedia,* Salt Lake City: Bookcraft, 1960, 309–310.) It has not been repeated by any church president, apostle, or other general authority. (Before sharing this truth, I first asked the sisters to raise their hands if they had ever been taught this well-meaning, but incorrect conjecture. Every single woman had.)
- President Joseph Fielding Smith said, "How uplifting, comforting, is this thought, that the Father of Jesus Christ is in very deed our Father—that we

are in very deed his offspring, and this is the doctrine of the Bible.... And A Mother in Heaven! Latter-day Saints believe that not only have we a Father in heaven, but a mother there. Why not have a mother as well as a Father? Is there any blasphemy in this teaching?" ("The Eternity of the Family," Ch. 26, Address delivered Sunday, December 3, 1944.)

- It was extremely common for early leaders to testify of Heavenly Mother. In fact, they would do so as simply and easily as we might stand on Fast Sunday and say, "I know that Heavenly Father and Jesus Christ love me." Whatever they were talking about, they included Her. Talking about the pre-mortal existence? Include Her! Talking about adversity? Include Her! For instance, on one occasion, Apostle Orson F. Whitney said, "We are taught that men and women, the sons and daughters of God, who were spirits in his presence, were sent here to take mortal tabernacles and undergo experiences that would in due time exalt them to the plane occupied by their Father and Mother in heaven." ("The Apocalypse." In *Collected Discourses 1886–1898*, vol. 5, edited by Brian H. Stuy. Woodland Hills, Utah: B.H.S. Publishing.)
- Almost every Church President has spoken specifically of Heavenly Mother, but none did so more often than Spencer W. Kimball.
- Apostle Neal A. Maxwell referred to truths concerning our Heavenly Mother as one of the "truths that [is] most relevant and most needed in the times in which [we] live." ("Things as They Really Are," Chapter 4, *Living Prophets*.)
- Most General Authorities today verbally pair Heavenly Father and Mother together with the phrase, "Heavenly Parents." This may be because it mirrors the well-known language of the Family Proclamation, but it also might be to emphasize the closeness and unity of the Father and Mother. An earlier Apostle, Erastus Snow, said, "If I believe anything that God has ever said about himself, and anything pertaining to the creation and organization of man upon the earth, I must believe that deity consists of man and woman.... There can be no God except he is composed of the man and woman united, and there is not in all the eternities that exist, or ever will be a God in any other way." (*Journal of Discourses* 19:269–270, March 3, 1878, cited in Linda Wilcox's *The Mormon Concept of a Mother in Heaven*, 11.)

**A few of my favorite themes:**

Women are created in the image of Heavenly Mother.
- President Spencer W. Kimball instructed a group of women, "You are daughters of God.... You are made in the image of our heavenly mother." (Conference Report, Mexico City and Central America Area Conference 1973, 108.) At another time he said, "God made man in his own image and certainly he made woman in the image of his wife-partner.... You [women] are daughters of God. You are precious. You are made in the image of our heavenly Mother." (*The Teachings of Spencer W. Kimball*, ed. Edward L. Kimball, Salt Lake City: Bookcraft, 1982, 24–25.)

Heavenly Mother is like the Father in perfection, glory, and attributes.
- Elder Melvin J. Ballard taught, "No matter to what heights God has attained or may attain, he does not stand alone; for side by side with him, in all her glory, a glory like unto his, stands a companion, the Mother of his children. For as we have a Father in heaven, so also we have a Mother there, a glorified, exalted, ennobled Mother." (Bryant S. Hinckley, *Sermons and Mission Services of Melvin Joseph Ballard,* Salt Lake City: Deseret Book, 1949, 205.)

Heavenly Mother's influence on us here.
- President Harold B. Lee once said, "There are forces that work beyond our sight. Sometimes we think the whole job is up to us, forgetful that there are loved ones beyond our sight who are thinking about us and our children. We forget that we have a Heavenly Father and a Heavenly Mother who are even more concerned, probably, than our earthly father and mother, and that influences from beyond are constantly working to try to help us when we do all we can." ("A Sure Trumpet Sound: Quotations from President Lee," *Ensign,* Feb 1974, 77.)

(The third thing I shared was the sadness I felt for a long time afterward, because I knew that we *could* talk about our Heavenly Mother, but did not hear that speech when I went to church on Sunday. After one particular Relief Society lesson, I understood 1) how desperately I needed to hear someone talk about Heavenly Mother, and 2) that *I* was someone, and that *I* could talk about Her. I did, out loud, in front of my entire ward during the very next Fast and Testimony meeting. It took all of the courage I could muster, and even when I walked away from the podium and found my seat, my body shook. Thankfully, when the meeting ended an individual I hadn't met yet gave me a tight hug and thanked me for my "non-traditional testimony." I didn't know it then, but he would soon become one of my truest friends. Something else I didn't know then, is that reclaiming my voice and reclaiming my Mother would change everything for me. Above all, it would make me feel calmer in the Church that I (still) love, and would make it easier for me to continue claiming my voice years into the future.)

## After
Sherrie Gavin (as "Spunky")
January 8, 2014

After becoming impatient at the GYN, so I went out and listened at her door
After I overheard her speak of a diagnosis, and thinking, "Wow. Glad that isn't me!"
After finding out that it *was* me

After being told words like hermaphrodite, intersex, transsexual
After being told I might be male; and wondering if I was male. And gay.
After being told my chromosomes were female, but I could choose
After being told I needed to be a lesbian, because I wanted to be a mother
After deciding I wanted to marry a man
After hearing that God's plan for women was only to be mothers
After knowing that was a lie.
After I decided I wanted to be a mother
After a friend offered to be a surrogate
After being dumped by an RM because I could not give him natural children
After dumping a boyfriend who was not open to adopting outside of his ethnicity
After another friend offered to be a surrogate
After a gay man proposed, because he wanted to be a parent.
After I decided that I wanted sex with marriage, so said no.
After marrying someone else. And divorcing.
After again questioning my womanhood because of the desire to have children.
After accepting that I am enough
After a boyfriend said we should adopt from China.
After he became a fiancé and said this was our problem together.
After marrying him.
After yet another friend offered to be a surrogate.
After going to India for IVF and surrogacy.
After coming home childless.
After two women seeking huge financial retribution offered to be surrogates.
After we said "no, thank you" to them.
After a fourth friend offered to be a surrogate for us.
After going through IVF three more times.
After feeling the warmth of Exponent prayers—more powerful than I have ever felt before. Or since.
After going through two more surrogacy transfers.
And still being childless.
After my beloved giraffe blanket arrived, and brought me back to life.
After being told a family wanted to give away some kids, and thinking the situation too volatile.
After deciding to call the police and leave the situation to them.
After hearing a voice tell me that those children were mine. So I didn't call the police.
After I took these beaten girls home with me.
After a thousand angry, belittling, menacing text messages from the monsters.

After fearing daily the girls would be lost to us.
After contacting the birth mother, and finding her to be an angel.
After we found the attorney.
After two more giraffe blankets came to heal the girls from the monsters. And it worked.
After the birth mother signed over her rights.
After menacing monsters and apathetic courts with flexible, disinterested schedules.
After finally legally excluding the monsters from our lives.
After a very long four more weeks.

After the birth mother arrived at court to plea for the girls to stay with us.
After the birth father failed to show up to contest our application.

I became a mother.

**Rejected Offerings**
April Young-Bennett
April 6, 2014

    I didn't ask the woman at the door of the tabernacle if I could come to the priesthood session. Elder Oaks had already answered my question, although he had not directed his answer to me. I strained to hear him talking to the men about me, a female member of Christ's church who wanted to serve God as a priesthood holder. I listened through a cell phone as I waited outside in the rain, where I had been waiting in a line labeled "Standby" for nearly two hours.
    It wasn't a real standby line, even though it was labeled as such. Where I stood, behind hundreds of women hoping against hope to be admitted to the priesthood session, I saw men who entered the line behind me redirected to the real, unlabeled standby line. A man with a Temple Square name badge was saying, "This is not the priesthood standby line, I'll tell you that."
    There wasn't much point to asking the woman at the end of the fake standby line if she would let me into the priesthood session after she had already refused hundreds of other women. Instead, I asked her about church PR. I wanted to know why the church PR department had ignored our many written requests for meetings with general authorities but responded to our request for tickets to the priesthood session with an open letter, addressed to me and three other women, with our names across the top, that was published in the *Deseret News* before I even received it. I wanted to know why that open letter made false claims that Ordain Women had said things that none of us had ever said.
    I guess what I really wanted to know was why the church had rejected

my offering. I asked to speak with my church leaders. I asked that my questions be taken to God by His prophets. I asked for the opportunity to serve my God and my church in expanded ways. With the exception of this one woman, who had patiently received us at the end of that line, most of what I received was cutthroat PR tactics that treated me as an enemy.

I suppose that Elder Oaks answered my questions, explaining that a woman is just an "appendage" to the priesthood. But he wasn't speaking to me. He was speaking to other men at a session I wasn't allowed to attend.

It wasn't the first time the leaders of our church had talked about me and my female peers at the priesthood session. When I was 21 years-old, I was two months into my mission when President Hinckley, the very person who had signed my mission call and sent me to the far-away land where I was serving, gave a talk about sister missionaries during the priesthood session of General Conference.[4] The first thing one of the male missionaries said to me after returning from the priesthood session was, "Boy, President Hinckley sure doesn't like sister missionaries!" When I read it, I learned that the offering that I was making right then, serving my God and my church as a missionary, had been rejected by the prophet, who would have preferred that women like me stay home. Acknowledging that an all-male session was an odd place to talk about sister missionaries, Hinckley added, "Now, that may appear to be something of a strange thing to say in priesthood meeting. I say it here because I do not know where else to say it. The bishops and stake presidents of the Church have now heard it. And they must be the ones who make the judgment in this matter."

And so, that idealistic, excited 21-year-old missionary version of myself died a little that day. It was one of the first times I realized that men, attending male-only sessions and serving in male-only callings, would make judgments in matters of how I should serve my God in my church without my input.

Yet, I served with all my heart, might, mind and strength. I led people to God. I tolerated leadership from teenage boys who were younger, less mature and often less knowledgeable than I was, but eligible for leadership positions that I was excluded from. I worried about mission goals to seek out male converts instead of female. My mission president explained that the church needed priesthood holders—men—to administer the church. Women weren't needed.

Today, I mourn for the idealistic young missionary I used to be. I miss her. I remember her desire to serve. I remember her faith and love for the gospel.

I also mourn for the 12-year-old girl I used to be. I endured a Sunday School

---

4. The following note was included as a link to the talk in the original post: Gordon B. Hinckley, "Some Thoughts on Temples, Retention of Converts, and Missionary Service," October 1997, churchofjesuschrist.org.

class that went through eight different Sunday School teachers in one year because none of them could tolerate the gang of young, male, priesthood-bearing bullies who spent each Sunday School hour shooting spit wads, knocking over chairs, and tormenting the girls and the teachers in the class. Unlike my teachers, it never occurred to me to quit that class. I came every week, bracing myself for the boys' torture but still eager to hear God's words at my church. My 12-year-old self loved the church too much to let bullies keep me away.

And I mourn for the 8-year-old girl I used to be. I set a goal to read a dozen volumes of Bible stories in preparation for my baptism and memorized tales of my scripture heroes. I remember my joy as I stepped into the baptismal font, my resolve to keep my covenants. I remember my father smiling and waiting in the water to baptize me. I don't remember what my mother was doing at that moment.

What is left of these younger versions of myself has been tainted, if not lost. I feel like these qualities in me were intentionally quenched by my faith community. My church has rejected my offerings again and again, refusing my service because I am a woman.

I wonder how I will continue to protect my faith while I endure yet another rejection. Today, I read new falsehoods written by the Church PR Department about our efforts at Temple Square yesterday and news stories from church-owned media outlets that underestimate our numbers by less than half. I struggle to reconcile the fact that the church that taught me honesty and kindness does not employ these virtues toward me and other women like me.

I worry about younger girls who remind me of myself. What if they, like me, can never honestly say, "I don't want the responsibility of the priesthood"? How will they avoid the censure of their Mormon peers, their church leaders and the PR professionals the church hires? Will they grow up like me, never able to understand how a desire to avoid responsibility in God's work is a virtue? Will they be satisfied as "appendages to the priesthood"? Will their offerings be rejected? Will their faith and idealism and excitement for the gospel dwindle?

I hope not, but sometimes it is so hard to hope.

**Neckties: Priesthood Attire or Lucifer's Lust Pointer? (excerpts)**
April Carlson (as "Cruelest Month")
August 19, 2014

Neckties are arrows that point to the male genitalia. Why are they considered "priesthood attire" in the LDS community? In some congregations otherwise worthy men are not allowed to participate in priesthood ordinances unless wearing a white shirt and necktie. The male missionary uniform is a white shirt and conservative necktie, symbols of orthodoxy in the LDS Church. *Salt Lake Tribune* columnist Robert Kirby recently noted, "Neckties are so important to Mormons that it's only a matter of time before we start seeing them airbrushed onto young men in church publications."

Oh, the horror! Before such a perilous day dawns, I must sound a warning. Neckties are leading women far from the iron rod of righteousness into the shadowy mists of lust. The influence of the necktie is subtle and pernicious and has infiltrated every level of Church leadership. The white shirt and necktie are ubiquitous symbols for male professional conformity and power, but some Christians contend that a man in a suit is too much temptation for the modern Christian sister.

Justin Timberlake and Jay-Z acknowledge the power of the well-dressed man in the song "Suit and Tie." Brother Timberlake croons in the chorus, "And as long as I got my suit and tie, Ima leave it all on the floor tonight." You are mistaken in hoping Brother Timberlake took off his suit and tie to put on his pajamas. In the accompanying video Brother Timberlake sings these seductive lyrics without wearing a necktie. But there must be neckties in the video of the man that brought sexy back. The video cuts to men in neckties dancing provocatively and women in bikinis getting wet. The equivalency is obvious: suit and necktie is to man as bikini is to woman.

Yes, suits are very sexy. But, let us focus on harm reduction. Small measured steps we can take to increase the pure thoughts of our congregation. For now, let us imagine the buttoned suit jacket as a protective shield. I have rarely witnessed a general authority or other prominent church leader with a necktie nakedly exposed by an open jacket. (It does happen. Google at your own risk.) Instead, a neatly buttoned armor covers the pointy end of the necktie, diminishing the downward gaze towards the Telestial Kingdom. Modesty restored and lustful gaze averted.

The general male membership of the church is not so noble. They blatantly display their phallic pointers with seductively unbuttoned jackets or no jacket at all. Few are the modest Mormon men who wear a bow tie, vest, or thick sweater to cover the pointy end of the necktie. I say a little prayer of gratitude for each of them when they pass me the sacrament in a modest bow tie. In these latter days of rampant wickedness upon the earth, can we afford to ignore these frivolous fabric phallic pointers and their devastating impact on women and homosexual men?

Images of early Church leaders depict virile bearded men who had many wives and much progeny. Although they followed the fashion of their day, the cravat or bow tie maintains the viewer's gaze upward towards celestial glory and the face (where one can observe the light of Christ). Early church leaders didn't wear a fabric phallic phallus pointer. A cravat or bow tie was good enough.

In contrast, modern leaders walk a fine line: following the winds of fashion by donning the necktie, but diminishing the lust-inducing power of Lucifer's Lust Pointer by keeping their suit jackets closed....

Perhaps some of you are thinking that the necktie as phallic phallus pointer is a limited problem. Maybe Cruelest Month is the only woman in the world having lustful thoughts? Sociology professor Lisa Wade, Ph.D., has written about how the purchasing power of lusty women is driving the rise in "hunkvertising." She warns that female desire should not be underestimated, stating, "It's funny to us to think of women being lustful because we don't really take women's sexuality very seriously ... we don't *really* believe that women are the way we imagine men to be." In the age of battery-operated boyfriends and "mommy porn," can we continue to promote the phallic necktie as modest "priesthood attire"? We are putting the rising generation at risk with our reckless participation in dangerous haberdashery....

Neckties as tools of lust are not a new problem, but they are getting harder to ignore. We must take seriously the spiritual gauntlet women face as they attend church in a sea of phallic pointers. The time has come to speak of the modesty of men and stop promoting neckties as a symbol of orthodoxy.

What does it mean to be a modest man? The convicted sodomite Oscar Wilde stated in the play *A Woman of No Importance*, "A well-tied tie is the first serious step in life."

Truly. The first step in leading women (and gay men) astray and the first tender step in a path that does not take female sexuality seriously. A mindset that values a necktie above the pure thoughts of others is selfish and prideful. Modesty conveys simplicity, decency, humility, and propriety. A modest man cares enough about daughters of God to not come to church wearing a giant arrow that points to his member....

Engage in a brief exercise of empathy and imagine something more radical than women wearing pants to church. What if women started wearing bikinis to church? How about giant arrows that point to their breasts and vagina? What if we only let sisters teach and pray in church if they were wearing a bikini or accessorized in a breast/vagina pointer? Well, church attendance would probably increase, but not for the right reasons! Pure thoughts would wither and fail. Yet this is what the women and gay men of our community must endure each day of worship....

Finally, ponder on a portion of the Word of Wisdom, "A principle with promise, adapted to the capacity of the weak and the weakest of all saints, who are or can be called saints." As you dress for church on Sunday, think of the weakest of all saints. Those who struggle to meet your gaze and look into your eyes instead of at that place in your pants. Those who try to think on a hymn but only recall the primary song, "I have Two Little Hands." Think of the weak among us. Just as you abstain from tea, coffee, tobacco, alcohol, and drugs to make life easier for the addicts, set aside your neckties. Adapt to the capacity of the weakest saints suffering from necktie-induced lust addiction. Choose modesty and leave the necktie in the bedroom.

**Poems of Exclusion**
Nancy Ross and Emily Holsinger Butler (as "EmilyHB")
November 5, 2016

The new Exclusion Policy was leaked to social media on November 5, 2015, which labels same-sex married couples as apostates and prohibits baptism and other ordinances for their children. EmilyHB and I wrote poems soon after the event that discuss the impact of the policy on our personal lives. Today we are sharing them with our readers to commemorate the anniversary of this terrible day.

\*\*\*

my Mormon dream, and getting over it.

by EmilyHB (written 13 Nov 2015)

my dream is gone and with it went my plan
to stay the course and be there for the dawn
of some great thing. but I don't think I can,
and this because my lovely dream is gone.

a lifeboat made of little more than hope
(not watertight and also slightly frayed),
it carried me through storms and helped me cope,
and stay! of such was my good lifeboat made.

I didn't need the ocean to be true.
the faith (and miracles it would precede)
were not my gift; the hope would have to do.
my dream is gone, and *that* I didn't need.

whether it is true or whether counterfeit,
still the work to do is getting over it.

\*\*\*

Dear God, I'm a zombie

by Nancy Ross (written November 11, 2015)

Dear God,
I'm a zombie.

I have wandered through my week
With a slowness I don't fully comprehend
Distracted by the pain in my mind
Not picking up on the details of life
And dragging my feet at home and at work.
Please bring me back to life.

Please help me to love my neighbor.
I'm worried that when she finds out who I am
And that I will leave our beloved church
That will be the end of friendship
And children playing together.

Please be with me when I leave.
Please continue to watch over my children,
And my husband and myself.
Please don't abandon us
Wherever we go.
Amen.

## The Harms of Projecting the Mormon Male Gaze Onto Young Women (excerpts)
Caroline Salisbury (as "Violadiva")
November 20, 2018

Last Sunday a male speaker visiting my ward repeated a variation of a joke that always makes me cringe: "The more doors that get slammed in your face as a missionary, the prettier your wife will be."

All the versions I've heard of this joke have something to do with the hardships or accolades a young man experiences as a missionary (knocking doors, saying prayers, being an AP, changing flat tires, days spent fasting, etc) and their inevitable reward of a "pretty" wife for doing so.

My heart rate rushed and my face burned as I heard the congregation titter in response. I looked around to see if I could find any other horrified or embarrassed faces. The young women near the back deadpanned the joke.

I approached the man afterward, thanked him for visiting our ward and for the other nice remarks he made in his talk, then asked, "When you made the joke about slamming doors and pretty wives, what did you mean by that?"

He smiled and told me it was something that he and the other missionaries would say to each other during tough times as a way to keep their spirits up. I was really glad to hear him explain the context and it gave me an appreciation for how difficult it can be for missionaries to stay positive about their work when everything feels like a failure.

I said, "I've heard this joke a lot, and I've also heard how it affects the young women and girls, including me. It can make us feel like a young man expects to be rewarded with a pretty wife after serving a mission, or that we're a trophy he earns for enduring hardship. It's also hurtful because it makes us feel like we're only valued for our looks, not for our kindness, or our personality, or our spirituality. And for the women who consider their looks to be a little plain, it can make us feel like we're not deserving of a man who worked hard on his mission."

The man's face was instantly compassionate and he said, "Oh, I'm so sorry! I never even thought of it that way, but what you're saying makes sense. Thank you so much for telling me."

I continued, "Thank you for hearing what I had to say, it means a lot to me that you'll consider my experience. From the perspective of the person who is made the butt of the joke, it can really sting. If you're going to speak to audiences that include women and girls in the future, I'd recommend not using that joke again."

He said, "Oh, absolutely. You're totally right. Thank you so much for telling me. I'll be sure to do that."

We shook hands, wished each other well, and I breathed a sigh of relief, thankful that he was so receptive to the effects of perpetuating the joke. I have full faith in his integrity that he will think differently about addressing audiences with girls and women present, and I hope he'll also think of what the young men internalize about women from jokes like that.

\*\*\*

The joke described above is one of the ways the Mormon Male Gaze is projected onto the young women of our church.

The Mormon Male Gaze (from "male gaze"[5]) is rooted in the flawed idea that a young woman's body is automatically, inherently sexually alluring to the priesthood holding men all around her. She is alternately seen as a temptation to be eschewed or a reward to be given. Both interpretations objectify the young woman for her body. When the Mormon Male Gaze befalls a girl, the young woman herself bears the burden of being appropriately alluring, so as to be a reward to "worthy" young men, while not being overly alluring to "tempt" other men. According to the many accounts I gathered, the projection of this Mormon Male Gaze is usually done by adult women to younger

---

5. The following note was included as a link in the original post: tekanji, "FAQ: What is the 'Male Gaze'?". *Finally, A Feminism 101 Blog*, August 26, 2007, finallyfeminism101.wordpress.com.

girls, or by women to each other. The projection of the gaze exists even when the threat of actual gaze does not.

From a young girl's first lessons on modesty, she is educated in the inevitability of the Mormon Male Gaze being upon her at all times. Girls are informed of this gaze by their parents, church leaders, seminary teachers, and sometimes even by the men or boys themselves. She is told that men and boys will be looking at her, noticing her clothing, appearance and exposed body parts, and likely having sexually arousing thoughts about her if they find her "too" attractive. The effects of this projection are deeply harmful to a young woman's developing self-esteem, body image and internal sense of worth and beauty. It breeds tremendous amounts of sexual shame, which may follow her throughout her life. It flies in the face of other teachings our young women receive about their individual worth, and emphasizes that man truly does look on the outward appearance, despite assurances that the Lord looketh on the heart.

Projecting the Mormon Male Gaze onto girls is horribly insulting to men and young men as well, as it ungenerously presupposes that all men and young men default to seeing young women primarily as sexual objects. It unfairly characterizes young men as walking erections, waiting to go off at any time, in no control of their own thoughts, and without ability to process their attraction or arousal in appropriate ways. It is debasing to men and young men to speak of them having so little control over their minds and actions....

As leaders, parents, teachers and friends, we must stop ourselves and others from perpetuating these harmful ways of speaking to young women and young men. We should encourage our youth toward autonomy of mind and body, of dressing appropriately for their own comfort according to the activity they're attending. We should build the confidence of our young women by emphasizing their positive attributes and character as the most valuable contributions to their relationships. We must stop projecting our own irrational fears and insecurities onto them.

## Come Come Ye Queer Saints: Pride, Prejudice, Persecution
Melissa-Malcolm King
March 7, 2020

As a Queer, Disabled, Person of Color, I have suffered much in this life at the hands of those claiming to act in God's name. The message is loud and clear: You are not worthy and you are not wanted here. I am mentally exhausted by the narrative given and the harshness of its supporters. In other words, get straight, get white, don't fight and then you'll be alright. With recent events surrounding BYU and the CES system, I stand in solidarity with my rainbow family.

Don't get me wrong this message is not new. The issue of Pride, Prejudice and Persecution is an ongoing, never-ending battle for freedom in a land where pain, suicide and broken families reside. My rainbow family is being slaughtered emotionally and physically each and every day. We are tired of begging to cut the shackles that the church continues to demand we carry to demonstrate worthiness. We are disgusted by the fact that so many just stand idly by and silently help the platform be pulled from under us. We are sick and tired of watching others bask in the privilege of a cisgender, heteronormative, white male-centric land with blinders on.

This is not an issue of policy or procedure, guideline or honor code, this is an issue of humanity. It doesn't matter how many changes occur or how the manuals are edited unless church leadership begins to change perspective. Church leadership needs to claim responsibility for the blood on their hands and the hate in their heart towards the LGBTQ+ community. Until then no amount of changes that come from church headquarters will provoke any difference in attitude. It will simply be lip service from people who are cowering down to societal pressures rather than following the Savior's command to love one another unconditionally.

My rainbow family and I are not trying to flaunt our homosexuality, gender identity and expressions that come with it. We are simply showing pride in who we are and who God made us to be. We want to give hope to those who are silently suffering so that they will have the strength to live another day. We are trying to save lives, and for some of us, we are looking to have a spiritual life. We fight to be visible in this community while most world religions have deemed the LGBTQ+ community to be unworthy, satanic, and with having little chance at eternity.

We will not be erased. We will not be cast aside. We are not your measure of humanity. We are human beings just like you who believe in family, community service and kindness to all. It is the callous thinking of society and church leaders that leads many to believe that somehow our lives are devoid of this and that is not of merit for our rainbow community. In actuality, we want it more because we have to work harder to achieve it.

We are grateful for allies who do not stand idly by. We are grateful for allies who not only protest with us in public media forums, but speak out in Sunday School and other spaces where our voices are not heard. We are grateful for allies who provide safe spaces and resources that not only keep us alive but give us hope. We need allies who not only will stand with us but will carry us when we are too tired to walk any longer. We need allies who will not speak for us but use their privilege to allow our voices to be heard louder.

Yesterday, I was stuck on a train as I watched my rainbow family march. As I tried to exit the train, a person called me the "N" word several times and

I watched as people stood by and said nothing. It was not the words I was called but the echo of silence that pierced my soul.

It is this silence that allows hatred to grow and become acceptable in society. In contrast, many are being silent about the very issues that are tearing down humanity and building walls instead of more seats at the table. I am imploring church leadership, its members and the world at large to stand up and recognize the suffering they have caused and work actively to do something about it.

We are tired of being second-class citizens. We are tired of being cast out of our families. We are tired of laws that allow for housing and employment discrimination. We are tired of not being able to even use the restroom without fear of retaliation. We are tired of policies and procedures that spread hate in the name of serving a just and loving God. We are tired of burying our friends who have died by suicide. We are tired of wiping aside our tears where joy should abound. We are tired, but we will continue our fight so long as injustice and persecution exist. Will you take a step out of your privilege and into the shadow of the suffering? Let us all press on ... until victory is won.

## Freedom of Religion Under Attack ... Again
Emily Gilkey Palmer (as "Em")
June 25, 2020

I recently read the transcript of Elder Bednar's address on religious freedom.[6] Several of the things he said were troubling and problematic in my view. He said:

> "I believe it is vital for us to recognize that the sweeping governmental restrictions that were placed on religious gatherings at the outset of the COVID-19 crisis truly were extraordinary," Elder Bednar explained. "No other event in our lifetime—and perhaps no other event since the founding of this nation—has caused quite this kind of widespread disruption of religious gatherings and worship."

As a historian I feel bound to note that this is untrue, the Spanish Flu being an obvious example of a previous disruption of religious gatherings. It is also an America-centric view, as Latter-Day Saints have had their religious services disrupted for far longer periods of time due to authoritarian anti-religious regimes like the Nazis or the Soviets. It is also incorrect to

---

6. The following note was included as a link to the talk in the original post: David A. Bednar, "And When He Came to Himself (Luke 15:17)," Newsroom, June 17, 2020, newsroom.churchofjesuschrist.org.

suggest that the shuttering of our church meetings came from "sweeping governmental restrictions" at the outset. The Church issued its order to suspend church meetings on March 11th, which was within days of several states (including Oregon, my state) making the same ruling. Many other states did so much later. And as we all know, there was no "sweeping governmental" (if by that we mean federal guidelines or assistance) anything. You can easily look at the state-by-state executive orders to see that there was a great deal of variation. Some states included banning church gatherings in stay-at-home restrictions (Maine, California, Oregon many others). Some allowed only gatherings that could maintain social distance and limited the numbers of participants, usually to ten or fewer (Connecticut, North Carolina, Oklahoma, many others). Still others deemed religious services to be essential and placed no significant restrictions (Florida, North Dakota, others). The Church's own guidelines for re-opening regionally involve local and regional authorization first, so there isn't any direct confrontation that I can see. The Church is not trying to do something that States are preventing them from doing. So from a purely factual standpoint, Elder Bednar's point was misleading at best.

> "Americans and many others throughout the free world learned firsthand what it means for government to directly prohibit the free exercise of religion."

Freedom of religion, as put forth in the Establishment Clause of the First Amendment, prohibits the government from encouraging or promoting religion in any way. The government cannot declare an official religion or give financial support to religion. The government cannot penalize you for your religious beliefs. No one has stopped members from reading scriptures, praying, sharing their beliefs online, having Zoom meetings, sharing the Gospel, having the Sacrament at home or any other religious expression. You can't do it in a large group. But that is freedom of assembly, not freedom of religion.

I'm not denying the importance of gathering to religious expression. But my own experience has been that it is the Church, and not my State, that is denying me that. Oregon prohibits gatherings, including religious gatherings. But it is my Area Authority who decided we aren't allowed to have Sunday devotionals on Zoom anymore. We did for about a month, and then he decided they were wrong, and now I've had no spiritual contact with my ward in about two months. But that isn't Oregon. That's the Area Presidency, for no discernible reason and with no coherency of policy. Other areas are having meetings. The Oregon Eugene missionaries have an hour-long virtual Sacrament Meeting every Sunday. So if gathering is so essential to our religion, perhaps we can look within before we start pointing fingers at the deficiencies of our government.

"As we have just experienced, religious freedom can quickly be swept aside in the name of protecting other societal interests. Despite COVID-19 risks, North American jurisdictions declared as essential numerous services related to alcohol, animals, marijuana, and other concerns. But often religious organizations and their services were simply deemed nonessential, even when their activities could be conducted safely. In the name of protecting physical health and security or advancing other social values, government often acted without regard to the importance of protecting spiritual health and security. It often seemed to forget that securing religious freedom is as vital as physical health."

The fundamental difficulty here lies in the question of whose freedom. Is it right for me to decide that my religious freedom is more important than your physical health? The well-known adage goes "my right to swing my fist ends where the other fellow's nose begins." The government's obligation is to protect everyone's safety. If your religion endangers someone else's life, then your religion is going to get some restrictions slapped on it. Civil liberties do not give anyone an absolute right to do what they want regardless of endangering other people. I go to church with my ward, then three days later sneeze when bringing groceries to my non-member father. Suddenly my freedom of religion has become an infringement on his freedom not to die.

I'm not going to argue about whether pets or marijuana are essential. I will say, however, that it is much easier to carry forward these services with minimal exposure risk than it would be to have a large in-person church service. Like any other retail or medical field, there are adaptations that allow these businesses to continue in modified conditions. Just like, I might add, the Church has continued in modified conditions. The states weren't authorizing big ol' pet *or* pot parties....

I have a lot to object to, clearly. But I have two much larger concerns. First, this is a dangerous pronouncement to make in a national environment where disdain for safety is high while the cases continue to skyrocket. When you start to paint government restrictions as attacks on freedom of religion, it gives a powerful justifier to people who didn't want to wear a mask anyway to go out and endanger other people. In addition to the many nebulous claims of "freedom" that we hear about why individuals shouldn't have to keep six feet away or avoid having parties or wear uncomfortable masks or constantly wash themselves you now get to add the very powerful and very persuasive "an Apostle said the government is putting forward restrictions that are an attack on freedom of religion." Did Elder Bednar say masks were an attack on freedom of religion? No. But it provides a very easy justification for rejection of government authority as inherently malevolent and intrusive, an attack on God and God's people.

Second, the timing of this public complaint of attack is bad. Right now there are millions of Americans who are calling out very real governmental oppression—oppression that results in death, maiming, wrongful imprisonment, poverty, hunger. Not the "oppression" of having small gatherings or meeting virtually instead of in person. Real oppression. Right now members of the Church *should* be addressing racism. Since Church membership is majority white, that means that Church members should be doing the hard work of thinking about the ways that we are complicit in oppression. It is time to wrestle with the reality that in some important ways, I am the bad guy and I need to try to fix it. It is not comfortable, or pleasant, or easy. But it is what God is calling white people to do.

However, Elder Bednar's narrative is one of victimhood and oppression. The ones who are suffering at the hands of the government and who deserve relief are us! Well that was a relief! For about two weeks there I was really feeling upset and rotten because of my white privilege. It sure is nice to go back to believing that *I* am the real victim here! I am not only a good guy but am in fact a righteous warrior for freedom! My freedom, not someone else's freedom that might involve me doing some hard thinking and changing.

I agree with Elder Bednar that our government has some serious problems and we need to be awake and alive to them. I do not agree that temporary restrictions to protect the most vulnerable in a time of pandemic are a form of persecution. If we could be trusted to put the safety and freedom of other people first with our every thought and deed, governing ourselves with those principles ever in mind then yes, these restrictions would be inappropriate and unnecessary. That is not who we are as a people right now.

## Acknowledging Institutional Mistakes is a Strength Not a Weakness: Wisdom from Oral Histories with Mormon Women of Color
Caroline Kline (as "Caroline")
September 4, 2022

I was elated to interview Nadine in 2015 for my dissertation on Mormon women of color navigating issues of race and gender (now a book[7]). As an older professional Southern Black woman and somewhat recent convert, Nadine gave me a window into what attracted her to the church—clarity on religious questions, community, and opportunities for involvement. She also showed me a powerful strategy for dealing with some of Mormonism's

---

[7]. The following note was included as a link to the book in the original post: Caroline Kline, *Mormon Women at the Crossroads: Global Narratives and the Power of Connectedness* (Urbana: University of Illinois Press, 2022).

thorniest problems like polygamy and the priesthood-temple ban: prayerfully reject them.

*What I eventually used was the principle of personal revelation, which I had believed as a Baptist and which was key to me in looking at the LDS faith. I prayed and the answer I received was that neither the priesthood ban and the temple ban nor polygamy had been of God.... [Joseph Smith] said that the key part of our religion is the atoning sacrifice of Jesus Christ. And that everything else—everything else—was all just appendages to that key tenet. And I was like, I can go for that. And you know, all these other things, they are appendages, so I don't really have to worry my head about that. I had already received clear revelation that the priesthood ban and the temple ban and polygamy were not of God—so I could join the church.*

Interesting, right? By rejecting these practices and teachings that were confirmed to her through personal revelation as not being authored by God, she was able to embrace the church. She was able to choose baptism. She was able to participate and love all the good things the church did offer.

Nadine didn't need the historical church to be perfect. She was a child of the South, raised in a context of overt racism. Historical racism from white-led institutions did not surprise her. She could accept that reality. What she couldn't accept was the idea that racist practices—and practices which she found harmful to women and families—were authored by God.

Nadine's experience of finding space to choose the church—through rejecting church practices she knew in her bones to be harmful and ungodly—has made me consider a) why more Mormons don't do this and b) how the church might create space for members to do this and thus retain and gain more members.

Why don't more Mormons who see troubling and hurtful teachings feel free to reject them and embrace the good in the church, like Nadine did? I think this is due to both Mormon culture and institutional church emphases. Mormon culture too often advocates a black or white, all or nothing, it's all true or it's all false mindset when it comes to church truth claims. It's a very rare Sunday at church when I hear someone acknowledge something they find problematic or don't accept regarding church teachings or practices. Rather, there are strong cultural norms to not dissent or challenge basically any teaching. Faith in Mormonland is generally characterized by agreement with institutional discourse—not by doing the hard work of sorting out what is godly and what isn't in our culture and institution.

Institutional church discourse has certainly helped contribute to the above cultural phenomenon. Repeated emphases on prophetic authority and God/Jesus directing the church imply that basically all church policies and teachings are authored by God. There is some lip service to the idea that church leaders are fallible, but as the old joke about Catholics and Mormons goes, Mormons don't tend to believe it.[8]

But what if church leaders could shift their discourse by offering more institutional humility? I for one would be a far more comfortable member if I saw church leaders acknowledging and yes, apologizing, for mistakes and harmful practices. I'd feel comforted if my leaders were people who were willing to admit to institutional shortcomings. That would build my confidence in my leaders and in this institution far more than repeated assertions of prophetic authority and God directing the church. The unwillingness to acknowledge shortcomings (so evident in the defensive tone of the church's PR response to the recent horrific AP story on sexual abuse) indicates a serious weakness to me. Robustness, strength, and maturity entail recognizing humanity, acknowledging missteps, and committing to do better.

One of the most impactful articles I read as a young Mormon feminist is "Lusterware" by Laurel Thatcher Ulrich. She makes the excellent point that too often we church members mistake things in the church that are earthly, weak, and fault-ridden for things that are godly, perfect, and just as they should be. This can lead to disillusionment and the questioning of one's membership when those things (or people) we held up as godly turn out to be fallible.

Like the essay indicates, members need to be more judicious about the things they pedestalize. But church leaders could certainly help members do this if they opened up more space for them to develop discernment in church contexts. Opening up space could entail introducing discourses that acknowledge institutional fallibility; that talk about how the institutional church is on a journey of progression; that its leadership is listening, learning, and making mistakes, but committed to doing better.

I've thought a lot about Nadine's oral history, and I think she was really onto something. The freedom she felt to privilege her personal revelation and reject unjust and hurtful church practices ultimately enabled her to embrace the church. I wish more people could self-authorize and find that freedom. I'd like more people to feel free to stay or join, if that's what they would like to do. I wish the institutional church would help create room for that through discourses of humility and progression.

---

8. The joke is that Catholic doctrine states that the pope is infallible, but Catholics don't believe it; Mormon doctrine states that the prophet is fallible, but Mormons don't believe it.

## The Unconditional Act of Hugging (excerpts)
Jody England Hansen
July 6, 2023

I marched in my first Pride Parade with Mormons Building Bridges nine years ago. At the time, I lived in Colorado, and had traveled to Salt Lake City in order to march with friends and family in the parade....

Back then, the number of people participating in the Mormons Building Bridges entry was in the hundreds, and the reception was loud and generous. A group of people dressed in Sunday best, many marching with spouses, and strollers, carrying rainbow signs declaring that God is Love, or covered in Primary song lyrics. We were greeted with cheers, and waves and people running out from the sides to hug someone. In my practice of presencing God by presencing love, this was one of the most spiritual experiences of my life. At least up to that point.

After returning to Colorado the next day, several of my Mormon feminist friends started talking about marching in the Denver Pride Parade (which was 2 weeks later), and wondering what it would take to have a Mormons Building Bridges entry. None of them (at that time) knew if any of their loved ones were gay, but they felt they needed to show up to give a message that God is Love. I shared my experience with them. Within a few days, they had arranged for the MBB banner, and funding for the entry, and spread the word about a meeting place for those who wanted to participate. I sent the information out to some Utah groups as well.

The Sunday morning of the parade, I met my friend near downtown Denver, and we unfurled the Mormons Building Bridges banner. We made our way to the parade staging area in a nearby park, looking for anyone who was joining us. We were excited to see a few dozen people there, and listened to different accounts of people finding subs for their primary or Sunday school teaching assignments, or council meetings. As we held the banner out and walked to our assigned position, several of the parade organizers came over to us with shocked expressions on their faces.

"Wait a minute ... You're Mormons?!?! Here? I thought you had to kick your kids out if they were gay! This is fabulous! I can't believe it! I have got to get a picture of this and send it to my mom. She won't believe it!"

They welcomed us warmly, even as they were amazed and incredulous that we were there. Soon, they were bringing others from the parade committee over to meet us and talk with us, saying, "Hey, you gotta come over here and see this. There are Mormons here!" They made sure we were going to walk behind one of the water trucks so that we would have plenty of water while marching. Costumed people from the entries around us came to talk with us, share their stories, and ask us about what brought us there. It was the best kind of missionary experience on all sides.

Finally, it was time to start marching. As we followed other entries through the park, making our way to the main parade route, several young men came running over to us. They were members of Affirmation, and they had traveled from Utah, driving all night so they could join us for the parade. As we marched with the banner, they would continually run along on either side while calling out, "Hi! Would you like to hug a gay Mormon?" I saw them throwing their arms around everyone who wanted a hug. Fabulous doesn't begin to describe them.

A young man at the edge of the park called out to me, asking for a hug from a Mormon. I ran over to him and gave my first MBB hug. As I held him close, he whispered in my ear, "I am a child of God. And He has sent me here." I whispered back, "Yes, They have. And They love you."

He looked at me and started crying. He said, "I really needed to know that my people still love me."

The rest of the parade, I was the one crying. People cheered us constantly. Only one time did I hear someone yell anything less than positive. "It's about time you showed up!" Several of us called out, "We are sorry we are late!" But I really thought there would be more hurt expressed. Because we are late. Regardless of what any official message is, individual members have not shown up in places like this to really speak up as people who try to follow Christ and the gospel of love.

Afterward, when we were walking back to our car, a woman called out to us, asking if we were really Mormons. She came over and told us how she had struggled as an adult, wondering if all the things she had loved about being a child raised in the Church were a lie. She had been so hurt by harmful rhetoric against LGBTQ people, and she had left the church. When she saw us, she had to know how we felt about God, and what brought us there. She asked for a hug, and as I held her, she said, "For the first time in a long time, I feel love and belonging from my tribe."

A few months later, I spoke on a panel for a Gender Inclusive Family conference at the University of Utah. During the Q and A at the end, a young man in the audience asked the question, "Have any of you learned anything new about gender in recent years?" I was the only panel member who had an answer. "Yes. I learned that there are as many ways to experience and express gender as there are people." As I said that, I could see him visibly change from seeming tense to seeming relaxed.

After the panel, he talked to me a bit about what I said. Then he told me that he was a 27-year-old transgender man. I immediately asked how he was doing. He said he was doing well, and he and his husband were happy together. Then, after he hesitated for a moment, he said, "My mom hasn't spoken to me in 8 years."

I paused, trying not to express shock or anger. I looked at this amazing young man who was clearly in pain at the loss of connection with his mother, and all I could say was, "I am so sorry." Then I said, "I can't change things with your mom. But I am really good at giving Mom Hugs." And I held out my arms. He hesitated again, said he was probably okay, but then he leaned into my arms and let me hold him as he laid his head on my shoulder. After a moment, he whispered, "I had forgotten how much I miss this." I whispered back, "I don't know how things will work out, or how long it takes, but I really believe love will always overcome."

And he held on to the hug for a while.

After that, I volunteered at the Mormons Building Bridges Free Hugs booth whenever I could. We would set up at Pride Festivals, but also at art fairs or town events. One of the first times I volunteered was with MBB founders Erika Munson and Kendall Wilcox at a concert festival in downtown Provo.

But my favorite hugging booths were the ones we set up at Pride Festivals....

Usually, if someone came by covered in glitter, they might hesitate as they looked at me in my church clothes with my arms held out ready to hug anyone who wanted. Some would say, "I don't know if you want to hug me. I might get glitter/paint/make-up on your clothes." I loved saying it would only make me feel pretty and loved. Then they would hurry over to get hugs. There was a woman who was only wearing a g-string and two pasties, covered in glitter, and she loved being hugged for a long time. I told her there was no limit on free hugs. She kept coming back for more hugs from me, and she wanted a "Hugged by a Mormon" sticker each time. Soon, the stickers covered more of her than the pasties did, and I had glitter and body paint all over me.

This was a visual image of how unconditional a welcomed hug can be. She was covered with a part of what I gave her. I was covered with a part of her that rubbed off on me.

When I have an opportunity to hug, I ask myself—"Is there a part of me that I can let go of, so I can have space to receive what someone else is offering?"

This act of offering an embrace, without conditions or agenda, often to strangers—people who might never know my name or that I likely will never see again—this is a small but also powerful practice of having room for people, right now. Of loving without condition....

Practicing the act of an unconditional hug is a practice of love.

## Gender Affirming Care: Simple Words, Complex Emotions (excerpts)
Valerie Nicole Green
July 19, 2023

I knew I was different for practically my entire life. I have memories of yearning for a life in the feminine world from my earliest memories, around four years old. I became aware that surgical reassignment was possible in my early teens (I remember it as 10 or 11, but facts prove me wrong) when I read about Dr. Renée Richards, the first and only (that we know of) transgender woman to play professional tennis.

What follows are more recent experiences. These are experiences that I found painful. They are experiences I may have avoided with early gender-affirming care that could have spared me the ravages of a puberty that I did not want to experience. I desperately hope that younger transgender people can be spared.

I attended a [Mormon feminist] retreat in 2022 as a first-year attendee. I attended again this year. But I can tell you that I had second thoughts about staying (or just continuing participation) for the remainder of the retreat that first year and questioned whether I'd ever be returning.

I was welcomed. I was included. I was loved.

I was also strongly triggered.

I walk into any female space with just a bit of trepidation and with my shields up because I know I have physical characteristics that belie my development before transition. Will those characteristics affect the way I am seen, included, treated, trusted? To some extent, yes.

On the first evening, we were all standing around in a common room and chatting. I'm an introvert, so this is already hard for me. I'm also aware of the timbre and resonance of my voice and that it can be a dead giveaway of the puberty I experienced, so I don't like talking in general in women's spaces. But I was slowly fitting in. Just as I was feeling comfortable, a woman joined our small group. She walked up to me and said (paraphrasing) "Oh, a tall person. I always like to be near people who are taller than me so I don't stand out so much." To be clear, this was a perfectly reasonable and friendly thing to say. It's a way to break an awkward silence. How could she have known how much I hate being taller than the other women around me? At 5'11" (apparently, I lost an inch somewhere in my middle age), I often tower above other women. I hate it.

It's not as though I don't know other women who are as tall or taller than me. A dear friend, a cisgender woman, is 6'3" and I know that no one would ever peg her as anything other than a cisgender woman. I also don't know whether she would be similarly bothered by comments about her height. Maybe. I've never asked her. If I'd been seen as a girl/woman my entire life, perhaps my height wouldn't bother me so much. As it is, it's a painful reminder. In my mind, my height is still a dead giveaway and is one of those physical characteristics that early care might have helped me avoid.

This 2022 retreat was attended solely by women. Everyone was asked to indicate their pronouns upon registration, and at the opening group session we confirmed that everyone in attendance was using she/her pronouns. That should make it simple to avoid misgendering someone. Nope. At lunch on the second day, I got misgendered. That is always painful. It's gut-wrenching. It instantly brings up an unpleasant past that I would rather just forget ever existed.

Everyone has been socially conditioned to recognize and react to physical characteristics in gendered ways. Clothing, hair, makeup (or lack thereof), size, and voice qualities are all things we are socially trained to interpret in gendered terms, and we are then socialized to respond in gendered language and actions. Sitting at lunch, the most likely thing to trigger a misgendering is my voice. Consequently, I hate my voice. I've made some attempts to change it. I may take further actions in the future to change it.

Most transgender people I know are very much aware of the difference between an accidental slip and a malicious use of gendered terms. We give a lot of grace to those who make the occasional mistake. I'm grateful when someone instantly realizes it, quickly and simply apologizes, and moves on. That's the right thing to do for such a mistake.

So, if I understand simple mistakes and offer grace to the other party, why is it still such a painful experience? Because it reinforces the idea that I'm not fully seen as a woman. It tells me that no matter what I've done to this point, no matter how many steps I've taken in my journey, no matter what has been done to make me feel included and that I belong, I'm still being seen as "a man in a dress." It tells me that the other person still sees me as, at worst, male, or, at best, a transgender woman—not simply a woman, but a transgender woman. It reinforces the idea of being different (in an unwelcome way) and being othered. It hurts. I'm proud to represent, in some small way, the transgender community. I don't shy away from it. But that distinction between being a transgender or a cisgender woman only belongs in discussions when the distinctions are important such as during discussions with my medical professionals or discussions about gender identity....

You might think that this pain goes away over time. It actually gets worse. I can go months without being misgendered and suddenly it occurs out of the blue. It is always a gut punch. I think it's worse when I've interacted with someone a lot and it suddenly pops out. The message I get is always the same. It tells me that I'm still seen as AMAB (Assigned Male At Birth). Something they perceive about me still tells them that I'm transgender rather than cisgender. It's something I wish would go away and never come back.

Being misgendered hurts. Quickly apologizing and moving on is the right thing to do. But consider that your one act of misgendering may be a transgender person's fifth time that day or the tenth time that week. If you love your transgender siblings, please make every effort to use appropriately gendered language. Being reminded of the physical characteristics that resulted from the wrong puberty also hurts. Please endeavor to use language that doesn't highlight their physical characteristics.

**#hearLDSwomen series**
edited by Lindsay Denton

In September of 2018, a post in the Exponent II Facebook group by Lisa Torcasso Downing asked women to share instances when they felt silenced, inferior or invisible at church because of their gender. Within two hours, there were over 200 comments. Within 24 hours, there were over 900.

I came back to the post again and again, reading each new comment and subthread. The stories ranged from one spare sentence to multiple paragraphs, from the tiniest slights to the deepest violations, but each of them was connected by the same pain, the same hopeless resignation that results from the complete lack of recourse for women in the Church. I wrote to the blogger backlist to express my overwhelming drive to DO SOMETHING. "If even one third of the people on that thread gave permission for their stories to be shared," I wrote, "we'd have enough to post every day for almost a year."

Over the next week, bloggers chimed in with suggestions for the name of the series and how to structure it. Two weeks after the Facebook thread, #hearLDSwomen was launched, and the stories came pouring in. The series was aimed at priesthood leadership, and each post contained a "pro tip" to encourage men to be better in their own spheres.

A year and 365 stories later, #hearLDSwomen was among the largest-scale series on the blog. From the introduction post:

> The Exponent is launching a series to document the small and large ways women in the Church are dismissed and unheard due to patriarchy. The series will show by sheer volume that the silencing, underutilizing and discrediting of women is a systemic problem in the Church of Jesus Christ of Latter-day Saints. By giving space to these stories on this platform, we are adding to the comprehensive record of the hurts endured by women in the Church so that these testimonies will stand as a witness before God and man that these occurrences are not a blip here or there; they are the all too common result of a deeply-rooted and endemic flaw in the structure of our church.

These experiences span decades with most of them having occurred in the past few years. This is not a problem that is getting better. This is not a problem that is going to fix itself. Women's experiences need to be heard before they can be believed, and they need to be believed before there can be meaningful change. The first step toward this goal is recording and sharing these stories. Only then can we achieve change going forward in policy and in practice.

"In the words of Jesus Christ, whose name our church bears, "if any man have ears to hear, let him hear" (Mark 4:23).

\*\*\*

I am great with symbolism. Going through the temple was PAINFUL, and confusing. I honestly assumed that SURELY I didn't understand it. Surely.

It took me over ten years to realize that I had understood and wasn't alone in my concerns.

—HHB

I was Primary president in a ward that wasn't huge, but we did definitely have plenty of adults who could've helped out in Primary. I suggested name after name and nothing. ever. happened. So one week, I dismissed all the classes that didn't have teachers. I said, "Tell your parents that you don't have class today because we don't have a teacher for you." Guess what? The next week, five new teachers were called.

—Amy Giauque Chamberlain

Some time ago my ward began to let women be the last speaker in Sacrament meeting. It happened about once a month, and I appreciated it so I mentioned it to one of the counselors and he responded that they had checked the handbook and saw no reason why a woman couldn't speak last. Fast forward to a new Bishopric that was put in about two years ago and since then that ward has not had a woman speak last. It showed me that it doesn't matter how forward-thinking local leadership may be, you're just one spin of leadership roulette away from where you started.

—JG

Our ward's Relief Society had a book club, and all book choices had to be approved by the bishop.

—Sherry Work

I was asked to be on a committee to plan our Stake Relief Society meeting. We met 4 times and had a great program planned—a lady was going to come talk about her art and what inspired her (she painted women from the scriptures). We really spent a lot of time planning this.

The 5th time we met, the group was informed that the Stake President had insisted that he was going to talk instead, and his topic was "honoring the priesthood."

I was so furious that I couldn't come to any more planning meetings. I've never felt so worthless and so blatantly disrespected!

—Nicole B.

About 6–7 years ago my bishop came into the Young Women room and quoted Spencer Kimball at the girls. He told them that if they survived a rape, it wasn't really rape because clearly, they hadn't fought hard enough to protect their virtue. None of the female leaders corrected him. He was the bishop and his word outranked ours.

—Amy H.

At one of my mutual activities, all the young women were required to wear a t-shirt over their suits–regardless if it was a one-piece–while all the boys were, of course, shirtless. Any push back and we were not allowed to attend.

—Sarah A.

A bishop (who is still currently serving) told me I needed to be a better Mormon wife so my husband wouldn't abuse me. Then he asked me sexually explicit questions about things I did as a teenager right after I disclosed that I was being abused in my home. I was 34.

—Lesley

It took me four years to get my sealing canceled from my abusive ex-husband. I knew it was possible because a friend had gotten it done. I also knew it was a recent change in the handbook. I went through four bishops and two stake presidents during that time who all drug the process out longer to keep me from going through with it. Despite me clearly having expressed that I had prayed about it and had peace in moving forward with the cancellation was right for me, they dug their heels in and refused to let me move forward. This happened in multiple wards.

—Anonymous

I felt invisible today when I was reminded that the ward boundaries are dependent on numbers of active tithe-paying priesthood-holders in the area, and my presence in our ward boundaries has no bearing.

—Anonymous

While preparing to bless our baby, I had wanted to participate by holding her since that would be the only church ordinance for our children that I would be able to be a (small) part of. But I was worried about making a fuss, I was worried that my Bishop would say no, and I was worried people would judge me. I also wanted to let my husband have this special moment with our child.

We chose only close family, one friend, and the Bishop to join in the blessing. I wanted it to be men who love my baby and who would be there for her through all of life's ups and downs. So imagine my surprise when everyone invited to participate joins in a circle around my baby, and a complete stranger from the Stake steps in beside my husband. Sitting in the pews, there was nothing I could do. So I watched as a stranger participated in this sacred moment with my child because he held the priesthood, while I sat beneath them, powerless because I am a woman.
—Anonymous

I had all my tithing put under my husband's name after marriage. I asked to have it moved back to under my own name and was told it didn't matter.
—Ashley Groesbeck

When I went in for my missionary interview with my stake president, the first thing he said to me was, "Sisters are 10% of the missionary force, but they cause 90% of the problems." Way to discourage me! I felt so humiliated. But I went anyway. End of story is that the sisters' district was the highest-baptizing district in the mission.
—Laurie Lisonbee

I'm not sure how best to put this, but one of the things I find most annoying is what I call the "Jedi hand wave" answers that we get as single sisters—"we don't know, but ... ah, it'll all work out."

We're told in the temple our salvation apparently requires not just Christ's intercession but the intercession of our spouse—with no information on who will fulfill that role for me. "It will all work out in the eternities."

We're called through the veil by a man—married sisters by their husbands, but who will call me? Best answer I got was "Someone who loves you."

Add to that the worship (to the point of fetishization) of The Family and being told weekly that the best and divine role of women is to have and raise children... where does that leave us? (Hand wave) "You still count. It'll all work out. These are not the droids you're looking for."

It's not good enough.
—Kristin

# An Afterword in the Form of a Personal Essay

Laurel Thatcher Ulrich

*Exponent II* helped me find my voice. I've long known that, but to understand how it happened, I needed to confront a sequence of my own diary entries that had always made me cringe. In my life, those thirty pages from the early 1960s are the prequel to the prequel of the history you have just read.

I met Gael Ulrich on a blind date in January 1958. We married the following September, just before I began my junior year at the University of Utah. I graduated in June 1960. In September we headed to Boston. He would begin graduate work at the Massachusetts Institute of Technology. I was about to become a mother. On October 18, 1960, at Boston's Lying-in Hospital I gave birth to our first-born child, a son we named Karl.

When Karl was three months old, I opened a newly purchased journal and entered a passionate but cringingly awkward essay about the joys of motherhood. I was confident that, unfettered by a profession, a mother had the opportunity "to become 'woman thinking.'" The key was to "strip her mind of nonessentials and think deeply on the great questions." (Without question, Thoreau's *Walden* hovered unacknowledged over this essay). "Cowardice," I concluded, "makes a woman jealous of a man's role. It is much easier to let a job—an important job—think for you and become you." Notice the pronouns in this essay. There was no "I" in my prose.

The same aversion to personal pronouns showed up on January 20, when I reported on JFK's inaugural address. "What is an individual, anonymous life in history?" I was thinking about Dr. Zhivago, the book as well as the movie, and about Auden's "Musée Des Beaux Arts" as well as Kennedy's "New Frontier." I asked, "In the great scheme of things—what do men care for? What does a sense of history do for man?" Without question I was thinking of *man* in its generic sense, although you can be sure I included myself in the next sentence: "The great majority of lives are lived out wrapped in domestic care."

On January 25, I tried composing a set of "Household Proverbs." But I soon gave up. "Books due at the library!" I wrote. "I suppose I don't 'hunger

& thirst after righteousness' as I should, but I hunger and thirst after books." On April 12, I apologized for a two-month gap in my diary: "Reason: another child to take care of—this for pay." I added, "My idealized thoughts about the role of homemaker are still o.k. I suppose—but the real problem is how to get through the next half hour."

After our second child, Melinda, was born in February 1963, I filled several pages with descriptions of her charms and those of her brother, but months went by before I picked up the diary again. Then on August 24, 1963, I had something to share: "Just finished Betty Freidan's book *The Feminine Mystique*. It was like a breath of air—suddenly all the cycle of depression-insight-energy of the last 3 years started to fit together."

I wasn't very specific about what it was about Frieden's book that had given me such a boost, but in imagination at least, I was no longer a frazzled young mother but a woman with a plan, a not very specific plan or even an immediately practical one, but a plan for sure.

I was now determined to embrace *both* motherhood and "a meaningful career outside the home (part-time or in 'soil-bank' now—full time later)." I insisted that such a decision did not indicate selfishness. It was simply acknowledging "the talents God gave me." Having made that decision, I abandoned the diary. I didn't pick it up again for thirteen years.

So what happened to my plan? What happened to me? The book you have just read contains part of the answer. I edited *A Beginner's Boston*. I invited women to my house to talk about emerging feminism. I co-edited a women's issue of *Dialogue*. I contributed to an Institute course and later an anthology on early Mormon women. I finished an M.A. in English at Simmons College, taking 5 years to complete a one-year program. I began an Ph.D. in history at the University of New Hampshire, where my husband was a professor of chemical engineering. I had three more children. I taught primary, Relief Society, and seminary, and as ward activity leader helped produce a three-act play and a Christmas pageant with a live donkey.

And I found my voice, allowing its passion, if not its pronouns, access to my academic writing. I was not superwoman. I was simply blessed with good health and a strong support system as I learned to do everything everywhere all at once.

A few months ago, while searching *Exponent II* papers, Katie Rich came across a letter I wrote to Claudia Bushman on March 14, 1975. I believe I was responding to a letter in which Claudia, who was working on a Ph.D. at Boston University, assured me it was possible to pursue a graduate degree part-time as long as you weren't too ambitious. In my reply I informed her that *American Quarterly* had provisionally accepted an article I had submitted but wanted revisions. I told her that "Instead of being elated I was depressed for two days.

I think it has something to do with being pregnant and realizing I *am* ambitious." I added a P.S. in blue ink, "Time is the only cure for morning sickness."

Despite the pregnancy, I completed the requested revisions. My article on Puritan funeral sermons was published in the spring 1976 issue of *American Quarterly*. The opening paragraph contained a sentence you all know well, although it took another twenty years for it to enter pop culture and give me my one true claim to internet fame.

In my 2007 book, *Well-Behaved Women Seldom Make History*, I acknowledged the importance of *Exponent II* in my own personal and professional journey. In my discussion of the importance of history in second-wave feminism, I told the story of Susan Kohler's discovery of bound volumes of the *Woman's Exponent* and the enormous impact that periodical had on our lives. Somehow, we found in the writings of long forgotten women "models for religious commitment, social activism, and personal achievement that seemed far more powerful than the complacent domesticity portrayed in popular magazines or in our own congregations."[1]

Some of the challenges women face today are unique. Others are grounded in enduring traditions. Serious engagement with the past can help us distinguish one from the other. This remarkable book is a starting place for anyone striving to understand the impact of so-called "Second Wave feminism" on the lives of Latter-day Saint women.

---

1. Laurel Thatcher Ulrich, *Well-behaved Women Seldom Make History* (New York: Alfred A. Knopf, 2007): xxix-xxx.

# Acknowledgments

Exponent II has always been about community, and the creation of this book is no exception. We appreciate everyone who shared their stories via interviews, filled out our Google Forms surveys, allowed us to anthologize their work, responded to our queries, and for the myriad other ways people have shown up for us.

We could not have done this without Caroline Kline, Aimee Evans Hickman, Emily Clyde Curtis, and Pandora Brewer. They have been our dream team and our informal history committee. They spent hours with us conducting interviews on Zoom, writing essays, answering questions, and saying "yes" to anything we asked and more. From start to finish, their contributions have been as integral to this project as these women have been to Exponent II.

Trying to tell the story of a community with so many writers, editors, and historians feels audacious. Luckily for us, they share their talents. Each person who read and gave feedback on earlier drafts or chapters has made this book better—Susan Rugh, Martha Bradley Evans, Margaret Olsen Hemming, and Nancy Ross. We are so grateful for the unique contributions of Laurel Thatcher Ulrich, who reviewed multiple drafts, sent us her diary entries, checked facts, and wrote the Afterword. Nancy Dredge's comments on our drafts and the timeline she compiled for Exponent II's fortieth anniversary were invaluable. And Rachel Rueckert, who captained the editing of this manuscript, is an absolute treasure.

Our work has been blessed by the collective efforts of Exponent II volunteers and friends who have documented events, preserved materials, added to the archive, cleaned up interview transcripts, scanned photos, granted us access to electronic documents, tracked down details, and more. Cheryl Howard DiVito's scrapbooks and binders of the organization's records are a gold mine. While it is impossible to name everyone, we want to acknowledge the contributions of Carol Ann Litster Young, Rosie Gochnour Serago, Lori LeVar Pierce, Jeanine Bean, Kirsten Campbell, Emily Fisher Gray, Emily Updegraff, Barbara Christiansen, Susan Christiansen, Diane McKinney Kellogg, Judy Dushku, Sue Booth-Forbes, Claudia Bushman, Grethe Peterson, Helen Claire Sievers, Jim and Mimmu Hartiala-Sloan, Marti Lythgoe, Jonah Sundahl, Allison

Pingree, April Young-Bennett, Abby Maxwell Hansen, Annie Dredge Kuntz, Margaret Dredge Moore, Fara Sneddon, Jackelyn Durfey, and Sarah Pierce.

As Claudia Bushman says, if you don't write it down, it never happened. We add that if it's not archived, it will be forgotten. Since 1977, Brigham Young University has been the repository of Exponent II's papers—minutes, correspondence, drafts, scrapbooks, etc. We are thankful to the librarians and digitization team at the Harold B. Lee Library who have scanned, uploaded, and improved the searchability of the entire run of *Exponent II*'s quarterly publication—Elizabeth Smart, Marissa Bischoff, Greg Seppi, and all those who worked alongside them. We consulted the digital collection daily. We also thank the L. Tom Perry Special Collections team—John Murphy, Karen Glenn, David Whittaker, and all who have curated and cared for Exponent II's materials over the decades and made them accessible to patrons. Their work matters.

We are forever grateful to the entire team at Signature Books. They take us seriously.

From Katie: Many thanks to my husband, Joey, and my children, Jackson, Daniel, Scarlett, and Hayden, for your unwavering support and sacrifices that made this work possible. Rachel Hunt Steenblik, your encouragement helped me believe I could do this. My "Write or Dies"—Lisa Van Orman Hadley, Kimberly Ence, Barbara Jones Brown, and Rachel Rueckert—both my writing and my life are enriched because of you. My "Lakeview Relief Society" sisters, Lindsay Denton, Natasha Rogers, and Amy Freeman, you make feminism fascinating. And to my co-writer and friend, Heather, I could not have done this without you, and I certainly would not have laughed so much in the process.

From Heather: I am grateful to my mother, Marilyn Bickmore, who raised me to value women's organizations, and my sister, Angela Whitman, for always showing up. My twenty-eight years of Exponent endeavors were facilitated by the love and sacrifices of my family: Dave and our kids, Jonah, Georgia, Millie, and Bea. I am indebted to Judy Dushku for bringing me into the Exponent fold, and Nancy Dredge for taking me under her editorial wing. Denise Kelly, Kirsten Campbell, and Pandora Brewer, being bunk mates at retreats fed my soul with wisdom and laughter. From Susan Christiansen I learned that Exponent could survive just about anything. Much love and gratitude go to my Marco Polo sisters, Emily Clyde Curtis, Aimee Hickman, Caroline Kline, and Brooke Jones who are everything good about Mormonism and feminism. To my dear besties who fix things they did not break and keep me afloat. And finally, to Katie, an extraordinary scholar and friend, now you too know where the bodies are buried.

# Cover Artist Acknowledgments

*Exponent II*'s cover art is a collaborative process with editors and contributing artists. Here we seek to acknowledge the work of contributing artists for the covers that appear in this volume. When no artist is identifiable, most often because the work came from pieces in the public domain, the art, design, or layout editor is acknowledged.

**Unit 1 Cover Montage (pg. 111)**
October 1974 (vol. 1, no. 2)—Carolyn Peters (Person)
March 1975 (vol. 1, no. 4)—Carolyn Peters (Person)
September 1975 (vol. 2, no. 1)—Carolyn Peters (Person)
June 1976 (vol. 2, no. 4)—George Anderson Collection, Brigham Young University
March 1977 (vol. 3, no. 3)—Kathleen Watt
Fall 1981 (vol. 8, no. 1)—Del Thornock
Fall 1982 (vol. 9, no. 1)—Renee Tietjen
Winter 1983 (vol. 9, no. 2)—Jan L. Braithwaite
Spring 1983 (vol. 9, no. 3)—Ondre Pettingill

**Unit 2 Cover Montage (pg. 157)**
Fall 1985 (vol. 12, no. 1)—Sallie Warton Latimer
Winter 1986 (vol. 12, no. 3)—Eileen Perry Lambert
1988 (vol. 14, no. 2)—Linda Hoffman Kimball
1988 (vol. 14, no. 3)— Eileen Perry Lambert
1990 (vol. 15, no. 4)— Eileen Perry Lambert
1992 (vol. 17, no. 1)—Dell J. Fox, "Paper Snowflake, 1966"
1993 (vol. 18, no. 1)—Linda Hoffman Kimball
1996 (vol. 19, no. 4)—Eileen Perry Lambert
1996 (vol. 20, no. 1)—Rick Rawlins

**Unit 3 Cover Montage (pg. 201)**
Fall 1997 (vol. 21, no. 1)—Sarah Bush
Fall 1998 (vol. 22, no. 1)—Fae Ellsworth, "Fire Woman"
Winter 1999 (vol. 22, no. 2)—Anneliese Warnick Shapiro

Spring 1999 (vol. 22, no. 3)—Kristen Ellsworth Applebee
Summer 2000 (vol. 23, no. 4)—Connie Chow
Summer 2001 (vol. 24, no. 4)—Eileen Lambert
Fall 2002 (vol. 26, no. 1)—Shraga Weil, "A Time to Seek"
2004 (vol. 27, no. 2)—Lena Dibble
2009 (vol. 29, no. 1)—Galen Bell Smith, "Wave [Womb]"

**Unit 4 Cover Montage (pg. 245)**
Summer 2010 (vol. 30, no. 1)—Tessa Lindsey
Fall 2011 (vol. 31, no. 2)—Lindsay Hansen Park
Spring 2012 (vol. 31, no. 4)—Rae Farmer (as Rachel), "Under Wyoming Skies"
Fall 2012 (vol. 32, no. 2)— Sculptor, Anne Gregerson, Photographer, David Hawkinson, "In the Room"
Winter 2012 (vol. 32, no. 3)—Valerie Atkisson, "Jungle Totem"
Winter 2014 (vol. 33, no. 3)—Page Turner
Summer 2013 (vol. 33, no. 1)—Amy Zeleski, "St. George Temple"
Spring 2014 (vol. 33, no. 4)—Caitlin Connolly, "They Listened at the Same Time"
Fall 2014 (vol. 34, no. 2)—Angela Ellsworth, "Seer Bonnets: A Continuing Offense"

**Unit 5 Cover Montage (pg. 285)**
Summer 2015 (vol. 35, no. 1)—Emily McPhie, "What Would You Do"
Spring 2016 (vol. 35, no. 4)—Katrina Whitney, "Blessing"
Spring 2018 (vol. 37, no. 4)—Beth Allen, "A Quiet Strength"
Spring 2019 (vol. 38, no. 4)—Kwani Povi Winder, "My Prayer"
Winter 2021 (vol. 40, no. 3)—Rosie Gochnour Serago, "Pandemic Postcards"
Spring 2021 (vol. 40, no. 4)—Herikita, "Mujeres"
Spring 2022 (vol. 41, no. 4)—Aïsha Lehmann, "Ashley"
Summer 2023 (vol. 43, no. 1)—Hayley Labrum Morrison, "Lot's Wife"
Winter 2024 (vol. 43, no. 3)—Heather Holm, "Trek"

# COVER ARTIST ACKNOWLEDGMENTS

### *Exponent II*'s logos over the years

1. 1974. "Tree of Knowledge," created by Carolyn Peters (Person) for the 1971 "Pink Issue" of *Dialogue: A Journal of Mormon Thought* and adopted as *Exponent II*'s first logo.

2. 1989. Created by April Perry, sister of art editor Eileen Perry Lambert, and first appearing in vol. 16, no. 4.

3. 2004. Updated tree logo, collaboratively designed by Aimee Evans Hickman, Nancy Dredge, and Evelyn Harvill based off a woodcut image made by Kim Kelly (Hickman's sister-in-law). It first appeared in vol. 27, no. 1, in celebration of *Exponent II*'s thirtieth anniversary.

4. 2014. *Exponent II*'s current logo as of this writing, created by layout designer/editor Stefanie Carson to celebrate the organization's fortieth anniversary. It first appeared in the special double issue vol. 34, no. 2 & 3.

# Index

## A

ableism, 341
abortion and reproductive rights, xiii, xix, 44–45, 159–61, 179–83, 192, 274–75, 276, 329–30, 339, 342–45; *see also* adoption; birth control; family planning
abuse, xiii, 41–44, 46, 94, 160–61, 172–74, 200, 259, 377; domestic violence, 41–44, 172–74, 189–91, 199–200, 307, 318–19, 331, 353; ecclesiastical/spiritual, 136, 179–80, 191–94, 376–78; emotional, 161, 172–74; sexual, 161, 172–74, 189–91, 377
activism (by Mormon women), 69, 78, 92, 94–96; *see also* LDS Wave; Let Women Pray campaign; Mormons for ERA; Mormon Women for Ethical Government; Ordain Women; Wear Pants to Church Day
Adam and Eve (Bible), 248, 258–60, 300; *see also* Eve (Biblical figure); temple (LDS): depictions of Eve in
Adams-Cooper, Jan, 46
Adams-Cooper, Scott, 25, 38, 46
adoption, xiii, 44, 160, 180–83, 213, 251, 274–75, 352–54
Affirmation/Gay & Lesbian Mormons (later LGBTQ Mormon Families and Friends), 34, 161, 197–98, 371; *see also* LGBTQ+ issues
African Americans. *See* Black identity; race
agency, xx, 110, 121, 135, 165, 188, 220–21, 276, 316, 342
aging, 141, 174–77, 215, 226–28
Alabama, 297–98
Algie Ballif Forum, 274
*All God's Critters Got a Place in the Choir* (book), xiii, 115
Allebest, Amy McPhie, 83, 248, 256–60

Allred, Janice, 74, 275
Alzheimer's, 107, 328–29, 330
*American Quarterly* (journal), 380
AmeriCorps, 297–98
Anam Cara Writer's and Artist's Retreat, 62, 289n2
Anthony, Susan B., 28, 124
Anti-war movement/sentiment, 3, 160, 184
Anderson, Lavina Fielding, xi–xiii, 24, 34–36, 54, 57–59, 115, 139–40, 275
Anderson, Lynn Matthews, 66, 70–71
Andrews, Linda, 40, 49, 66, 81, 86, 203
anger, 31, 35, 42, 118, 150, 156, 195, 210, 220, 235, 253, 259–60, 268, 281, 344, 372
Annan-Mensah, Gifty, xiv
Applebee, Kristen Ellsworth, 386
Arizona, 71, 76, 79, 129, 184, 253, 262
Arkansas, 297
Arrington, Chris Rigby, xii, 24–25, 113, 127–29
Arrington, Leonard J., 5, 11–13
Association for Mormon Letters, 76
Atkinson, Jenny, xiii, 62–68, 186–89, 203, 223
Atkisson, Valerie, 386
Atonement, 150, 168, 283; *see also* Jesus Christ
Attwood, Polly, 195–96
Austin, Michael, 100
Avery, Valeen Tippetts, 261–63

## B

baby blessings (ritual), 88–89, 267, 271, 336–37, 377
baptism, 5n15, 94, 129, 214, 216–17, 252, 253–56, 255–56, 260, 323, 339, 356, 359, 368
Baptist(s), 188
Bagley, Lacey, xvi

Baker, Katrina Vinck, 100, 107
Baker, Robin, 60–62, 70, 72, 100, 160, 180–83, 203
Ballard, Melvin J., 352
Ballard, M. Russell, 56
Bankhead, Lucille, 127
Barbados, 106, 319–21
Barlow, Cindy, 116, 150–51
Barney, Cassandra, 93
Barrett, Kristine, 114, 131–33
Bates, Irene, 59
BCC Press, 100
Bean, Jeanine, 103–4
Beattie, Melonie, 41
Bednar, David A., 364–67
Beecher, Maureen Ursenbach, xi–xii, 7–8, 12, 34–35
*Beginner's Boston, A* (book), xi, xx, 1–4, 15, 380
Bell, Elouise, xii, xv, 24
Bennion, Kate, 107
Benson, Ezra Taft, xiii, 28, 159, 177
Berry, Blanche, 5
Beutler, Elizabeth Dredge, 70
Bible (Old and New Testament), 136, 187, 258–60, 280, 282, 290, 298, 356, 376; women in, 126, 132–33, 290, 299–305; *see also* Adam and Eve; Eve (biblical figure)
Biden, Joe, 101
birth control, 3, 12, 28, 44, 123, 160–61, 164–65, 250, 311; *see also* abortion and reproductive rights; family planning
bishop or bishoprics (LDS), 1, 3, 10, 13, 23, 39, 43, 44n10, 46, 53–54, 57, 61, 85, 87–88, 129, 143, 155, 160, 161, 173, 179–80, 186, 193, 194, 197, 199–200, 220, 243–44, 259, 262, 267–69, 297, 315–17, 342, 355, 376–78
Bishop, Marion, xvi
Black identity, 25–26, 101, 127–29, 233–37, 319–21, 362–64; *see also* race: ban on Black priesthood ordination and temple participation
Black Lives Matter (BLM), 101
Black, Margaret M., 113, 129–31
blessings. *See* baby blessings; priesthood (LDS): blessings, male given; women's blessings

"bloggernacle," 69, 75–78, 96, 107, 247–48, 278
body image, 65, 362
Book of Mormon, 100, 154, 187–88, 254–55, 260, 263, 294–95, 297, 343
*Book of Mormon, The* (musical), 82, 248
*Book of Mormon for the Least of These* (book series), 100
Bookstaber, Pam, 29
Boss, Libby Potter, 94, 335–36
Boston/Boston area. *See* Massachusetts, Boston/Boston area
Boston Female Liberation, 6
*Boston Globe* (newspaper), 1–2, 13, 17, 25, 52, 56, 153, 189, 225
Boston University, xvii, 380
Boston Women's Health Book Collective, 6, 6n17, 44
Bowden, Andee, 103, 291, 326–28
Boy Scouts, 114, 141, 244, 325, 342
Bradford, Mary Lythgoe, xi, 5, 38, 65, 114, 141, 223, 242
Braithwaite, Jan, 68, 385
Brandeis University, 43, 161
Braude, Ann, 72
breastfeeding/nursing, 5, 113, 122, 203, 213
Bridgeforth, Ruffin, 25, 127
Brigham Young University, Idaho (formerly Ricks College), 264, 272–73
Brigham Young University, Provo (BYU), 18, 24, 27–29, 35, 40, 52–55, 60, 72, 127–28, 165, 187–88, 208–10, 216, 227, 256–59, 267, 273–74, 298, 349, 362–64; Board of Trustees, 52–55; *BYU Studies* (journal), 349; Harold B. Lee Library, xx; Honor Code, 339, 362–64; L. Tom Perry Special Collections, xii, xix, 40, 156; Women's Conference, xii, 52–55; Women's Research Institute, 43, 267, 349
Brobbey, Alixa, 107, 289, 329–30
Brodie, Fawn, 52
Booth-Forbes, Sue, xiii, xvi, 33, 35–40, 41–3, 46–50, 52, 58–60, 61–65, 86, 159–62, 186–89, 191–94, 223, 273, 289
Brewer, Pandora, xvi, 65, 90–95, 99, 104, 206–12, 223, 287–91
Brooks, Joanna, xvi, 87
Brooks, Juanita, xi, 5, 154, 337
Brooks, Melvin R., 350

Brown, Diane, 223
Buddhist/Buddhism, 72, 254
Bulger, Stephanie, 128
Burke, Tarana, 96
Burnett, Kimberly, 70, 78, 203
Busath, Anne Castleton, 39
Bush, George H. W., 184
Bush, Sarah, 64, 385
Bushman, Claudia, xi–xii, xv–xvii, 2–21, 25, 42, 52, 55, 63, 72, 86, 113, 116–17, 153–56, 192, 205, 223, 273, 380–81
Bushman, Richard, 9, 13–15, 22, 55, 72
Butler, Emily Holsinger, 359
Butler, Tricia (Trish) 11, 15n26, 23
Butterworth, Lisa, xiv, 82, 247, 252–53
Buys, Sandra, 15, 23
*By Common Consent* (blog), 75

## C

Cabus, Sylvia, 65, 205, 216–17
California, 37, 59, 165, 189, 194, 208–09, 226, 238, 256, 279; Bay Area, 56, 213; Irvine, 73–75; Pasadena, xii, 24–25, 198; Southern California, xiii, 69, 73–78, 204, 335–36
Cambridge Women's Center, xvii
*Camelot*, 209, 222
Camp Windigo (western Massachusetts), xi, 9
Campbell, Joyce, 10, 15–16, 22
Campbell, Kirsten, 80–81, 90, 95, 99, 107
cancer, 40, 68, 71, 175–77, 206, 218, 306–08
Candari, Esther Hi'ilani, xv
Canfield, Bonnie Brackett, 86
Cannon, Connie D., xii, 9–11, 15, 24, 116, 155
Cannon, George Q., 124
Cannon, Heather, 9–10, 15–16, 86, 116, 149–50
Cadge, Wendy, 72
caregiving: child care, xvii, xix, 12, 100, 296; elder care, 144, 226–28; illness, 144–45, 218, 328–29; *see also* motherhood
Carlson, April, 335–36, 338, 356–59
Carson, Stefanie, 90, 86, 387
Case, Karen, 274
Cassler, Valerie Hudson, 260
Catholic/Catholicism, 26, 234, 254–56, 268, 369n8
Celestial marriage. *See* plural marriage

"Cell 16," 6
Chamberlain, Amy Giauque, 376
Chandler, Bob, 43
Chandler, Rebecca, xii, 24
Charles, Melodie M., 35–36
*Charlotte's Web* (book), 287
chastity, 345
childbirth, 122, 181–82, 232–33, 235, 379; *see also* pregnancy, pregnancy loss, infertility
childless/childfree, 212–16
Choi, Hanna, xiv
Chow, Connie, 70, 386
Christiansen, Barbara, 99–100, 103–04
Christiansen, Susan, 78n21, 96–100, 103, 290, 306–08
Christmas, 39, 48, 121, 176, 183–84, 186, 206, 218, 223–25, 228, 380
Church of Jesus Christ of Latter-day Saints xvii, 252, 260, 278; All-Church Coordinating Council, 51; correlation, 4, 14, 115, 134–35, 162, 276–78; disciplinary councils, xiii, xviii, 30–32, 51, 56–59, 94, 159, 162, 271, 275, 276, 339; First Presidency, xii, 4, 18n31, 25, 53, 114, 135, 256; general authorities, xii, 13–34, 19, 21, 22, 59, 85n18, 257, 262, 351, 354; general conference, xiii, 30–31, 59, 84–85, 248, 272, 274, 294, 354–56; General Handbook of Instructions, 44, 87, 94, 269, 376–77; history department, 5, 8, 11–13; members leaving church, 61, 67, 110, 193, 259–60, 267, 359–60; Mormon Tabernacle Choir, 95, 127–129, 195; Office Building, 13, 59; prophet, 17, 109, 127, 134, 148, 178, 189, 214, 237, 259–60, 261–63, 264, 272, 297, 299, 350–51, 355, 368–69; Quorum of the Twelve Apostles, 4, 13, 16, 27, 53, 55, 129, 135, 256, 260, 263; retrenchment, xiii, xviii, 51–55, 57–60, 162; Strengthening Church Members Committee, 51; structural or systemic sexism in, 117–19, 133–37, 191–94, 270–72, 323–24, 341–42, 354–56, 375–78; Sunday School/Gospel Doctrine, 77, 109, 121, 155, 176, 194, 262, 355–6, 363, 370; Temple Square, 30, 75, 84, 354–56; testimony meeting, 36, 194, 268, 352; *see also*

Book of Mormon; disfellowshipment; Brigham Young University (BYU); Equal Rights Amendment; excommunication; institute of religion (LDS); International Women's Year; missions/missionary work (LDS); Ordain Women; patriarchal blessings; priesthood; Policy of Exclusion (POX); Primary (auxiliary for children); race: ban on Black priesthood ordination and temple participation; Relief Society (auxiliary for women); sacrament, administration of and gender; sacrament meeting (LDS worship service); scripture; temples (LDS); Young Women's (auxiliary for youth)
Civil Rights Movement, 3, 296
Clarke, Nancy Richards, 35
Clarke, Vicki Boyack, 11, 13, 15, 22
Claremont College or Graduate University, 253
class and social divisions, 3, 7, 101–02, 124–25, 165; *see also* intersectionality; poverty
Clay, Kaye, 11
Cluff, Sasha, 32
Clyde, Aileen, xv, 71, 187
Clyde Curtis, Emily, xiii–xiv, 70–73, 76–83, 91–92, 247–48, 253–56, 287, 335–36, 337, 343
*Codependent No More* (book), 41
Colorado, xii, 24, 40, 71, 168, 370
Columbia University, 105
community involvement/service, 5–6, 17, 116, 134–36, 148–49, 196, 200, 216, 243, 297–98, 363
complementarity. *See* gender roles
Connecticut, 72, 75
Connel, Cynthia W., 107
Connolly, Caitlin, 386
consciousness-raising groups, xi, xviii, 3–4, 24, 153, 380
Cook, Helen Mar, 159, 162–63
Coons, Lela B., xi
#CopingWithCOVID19, 100
Cornwall, Rebecca, 28, 114, 122–23
Counterpoint Conference, 54–55, 69, 275
COVID-19 pandemic, xv–xvi, 100–2, 364–67
Cowdery, Oliver, 140

Coyle, Abigail, 23
Crall, Shari Siebers, 160–61, 189–91
creativity, 38, 160, 168–71, 291
Crenshaw, Kimberlé Williams, 101
Curtis, Judith, 204, 232–33

## D

Dall, Rose Datac, 93
Dalton-Bradford, Melissa, 96
Darley, Lucille, 56
*Daughters in my Kingdom*, 262
*Daughters of Sarah* (feminist newspaper), 32
death, 45, 140, 141, 144, 146, 175–77, 206, 214, 226–28, 254–56, 267, 271, 302, 306, 319, 333, 364, 367; *see also* miscarriage/pregnancy loss; suicide
Decker, Jeanne, 23
Degn, Louise, 24
DeLong, Camille, xv
Democrats, 296
Denton, Lindsay, 335–36, 340, 375–78
depression, xii, 24, 87, 89, 113, 118, 145, 149–50, 179–80, 192, 204, 238–39, 269, 348–49, 380; *see also* mental health; postpartum depression
Derr, C. Brooklyn, xiii, 34
Derr, Jill Mulvay, xi–xii, 8, 34–36, 115, 133–37
Deseret Book, 43
*Deseret News* (Newspaper), 29, 354
*Dialogue: A Journal of Mormon Thought*, xi–xii, xv, xviii, 3–6, 12–14, 38, 57, 59, 85, 88, 100, 153, 273–74, 380
diaspora (Mormon), xviii, 1, 115
Dibble, Lena, 386
Dietering, Averyl, 249, 279–82
disability, 161, 198–99, 281, 362
disfellowship or disfellowshipment, 43, 57–59, 58n31, 187–88; *see also* Church of Jesus Christ of Latter-day Saints: disciplinary councils; excommunication
DiVito, Cheryl Howard, 40, 66, 68, 70, 86, 90, 159, 166–68, 222–23
divorce, 61–62, 194, 198, 213–14, 235, 308, 315–16, 316–17, 331
*Dobbs v. Jackson Women's Health Organization*, 289, 329–30
Doctrine and Covenants (D&C, LDS scripture), 109, 119, 140, 154, 188, 267, 292–94, 314; *see also* scripture

INDEX

domestic violence. *See* abuse
Downing, Lisa Torcasso, 375
Dredge, Nancy Tate, xii–xiii, 11, 15n26, 19–24, 30, 33–35, 42, 48, 67, 69–71, 74–75, 78, 86, 103, 113, 192, 203–4, 222–23, 273–75, 387
Dredge, Paul, 21, 33
Dudley, Karyn, xiv
Dunsson, Judy, 128
Durham, Christine, xi, 8
Dushku, Judith (Judy) Rasmussen, 3, 8, 9–12, 15–16, 23, 31–32, 35, 38–39, 42–47, 54–58, 62, 65, 70, 72, 79–80, 82, 86, 103, 115–16, 151–56, 161–62, 188, 194–97, 203, 273–75

# E

Eagle Forum, 28–29
Eastley, Mikelle Fisher, 203
eating disorders, 46, 65
education, 124, 164, 209, 234–36, 296–98, 315; and children, 100, 119–22, 131, 226, 240–41; women and higher education, xvii, xix, 3, 5, 10, 23, 33, 34, 40, 62, 73–74, 91, 143, 155, 216, 236, 253, 293, 296, 306–08, 317, 380
Eldridge, Allison, 72
ELWC (Electronic LDS Women's Caucus) (internet listserv), 71
Eliot, T.S., 171
Elizabeth II, 186
Ellerby, Linda, 183
Ellsworth, Angela, 386
Ellsworth, Fae, 385
Emmeline Press, xii, 8
Employment: discrimination, 364; Mormon mothers and, 12, 62, 69, 123, 177–79, 317, 380; women in the workforce, 12, 178, 204
England, Eugene, 4–5
*Ensign* (magazine), 4, 47, 144, 147, 262
Equal Rights Amendment, 113–15, 267, 273, 276–77; in *Exponent II*, 21, 28–31, 74, 122–25; history of, xi, 26–29; LDS Church opposition to, 17, 21, 26–30, 74, 114, 122–25; *see also* International Women's Year; Mormons for ERA; Sonia Johnson
Eve (biblical figure), 5, 133, 220, 229, 258–60, 300, 309; *see also* Adam and Eve; temple (LDS): representations of Eve in
Eves, Rosalyn Collings, 106
Exponent Day Dinner, xi, 8, 36, 114, 154
Exponent II: BIPOC Art and Writing Scholarship, xiv–xv, 105–06; art and design in, 6, 10, 14, 24, 46–47, 79–80, 91–94, 210, 249–50, 312–14; circulation/distribution, 12, 59–60, 63, 152; coming back into print, xiv, 79–82; covers, 111, 157, 201, 245, 285, 335; editorial operations move out of Boston, 79; embracing gender expansiveness and gender minorities, xix, 101; Facebook discussion group, 102, 340, 375–78; fortieth anniversary, xiv, 85–87, 249, 275–79, 335–36; founding/launching the paper, xvii, 9–12; finances, 11, 46, 60, 73, 96–100, 103–6; friendship and community, xvii, 39–40, 155, 203, 206–12, 353; meetings with general authorities, 14–19; mission/purpose, xvii, 101, 106, 113, 116–17, 275–79; modernizing production, 46–48; Mormon feminist identity and, xix, 19, 21, 26, 31, 52, 67, 78, 83, 109–10, 113–16, 162, 272–75, 276, 298–99; paste-up parties, xvii, 10, 33, 47, 59, 63; podcast, 106; temporarily moving online-only, xiv, 78; tenth anniversary, 36–39; website, xv, 66, 70, 107; Writer Workshop Series, 106–07
Exponent II Features/Columns: Artist Spotlight, 249–50, 263–66; East/West, xiii, 34, 55, 115, 142–45, 169–70; Frugal Housewife, 10, 113–14, 145–48; Goodness Gracious, 65, 223–25; Sisters Speak, 10–11, 24, 45–46, 65, 80, 84, 115–16, 148–51, 288; Women's Theology, 288, 292–95
Exponent II Retreats, 75–76, 79, 80, 86–89, 95, 97–101, 103–07, 151–56, 185, 207–12, 222–23, 224–25, 309–10; Barbara C. Harris Episcopal Camp and Conference Center, 72, 86–89, 103; Friday night welcome ceremony, 48–49; Hillsboro Camp, xiii, 36–39, 45, 48–50, 63, 71, 160, 223; Keynote speakers/speeches, xv–xvi, 38, 48, 71, 87, 103, 160, 168–72; staff retreats, xi, 9–11, 14, 65–66, 203; Quaker Meetings, 38, 49–50, 88, 103;

393

Spiritual Autobiography, 36, 115, 139–40, 288, 295–99; Talent/Variety show, 49, 308–09; Workshops, 116, 150–56, 205, 219–22

*The Exponent* (blog), 77, 79–80, 82–55, 94, 96, 98, 100, 102, 106n8, 107–08, 204–07, 247, 278, 288, 335–36; blog content in selected works, 240–44, 341–78; blog founding, xiii, 75–78, 337–38

excommunication, xii–xiv, xviii, 30–32, 43, 44, 51–52, 57–59, 74, 85, 160–61, 179–80, 187–88, 192, 267, 274, 339; *see also* Church of Jesus Christ of Latter-day Saints: disciplinary councils, retrenchment; disfellowshipment; September Six; Sonia Johnson

## F

faith, xvii, 14–15, 34, 50, 51–52, 87, 109, 115, 127–29, 136, 139–40, 159, 162–63, 185, 188, 193, 198, 204, 220, 248, 252–53, 256–60, 263, 264, 266–69, 275–79, 282, 292–95, 295–99, 314–17, 345, 347–49, 354–56, 359–60, 367–99

family, 3–4, 21–24, 119–22, 141, 142–43, 143–45, 145–48, 212–26, 226–28, 233–37, 314–17, 323–24, 326–28, 330–33; in LDS theology, xiii, 70, 161, 256–60, 341, 351; *see also* gender roles; LGBTQ+ issues, marriage; motherhood

"The Family: A Proclamation to the World," xiii, 70, 161, 341, 351

family history, 92, 120, 290–91, 319–21

family planning, 24, 44, 65, 160–61, 164–65; *see also* abortion and reproductive rights; birth control

Farmer, Gladys, 71

Farmer, Rae, 71, 386

Farmer, Sarah, 65, 68

Fascinating Womanhood, 122

fasting, 15, 39, 196, 293

FBI (Federal Bureau of Investigation), 97

*Feminine Mystique, The* (book), 3, 124, 380

feminine divine, 131–33, 253, 311; *see also* Heavenly Mother

Feminism: feminist advocacy, 41–46, 56–57, 77–78, 83–85, 94–96, 105–06, 161–62, 297; second-wave, xvii–xviii, 3–7, 381; women's march and, 84, 95–96; women's history and, 6–8, 51–55, 64–65, 154, 159, 381; *see also* Equal Rights Amendment; Exponent II; International Women's Year; Mormon feminist identity; Ordain Women; suffrage movement

*Feminist Mormon Housewives* (blog), 75, 78, 82, 247, 252–53, 278

*FEMWOC* (Feminist Women of Color, blog), 284

Finland, 154–55

Finnigan, Jessica, 83

Flake, Kathleen, xv, 113, 117–19

Fleishacher, Sharon, 43, 200

Floyd, George, 101

food storage, 121, 145–47

Fox, Dell J., 385

Fox, Laura, 45

freedom of religion, 364–67

Freeman, Amy Clark, 335–36

Friedan, Betty, 3, 124, 380

*Friend* (magazine), 4, 55

## G

garments (LDS), 205–06, 216–17

Gavin, Sherrie, 335–36, 339, 352–54

gay. *See* LGBTQ+ issues

gender identity. *See* LGBTQ+ issues

gender roles, 3, 17–18, 34, 56–57, 62, 74, 85, 109, 117–19, 210, 230–32, 256–60, 263–66; critique of, 141, 230–32, 337, 341–42, 375; partnership, 34, 341–42; *see also* consciousness-raising groups; LGBTQ+ issues; priesthood (LDS): women and

genealogy. *See* family history

Genesis Group, 25, 127–29

Georgia, 174, 297

Gileadi, Avraham, xiii, 58

Gillette, David, 56

Gilliland, Steve, 6

Givens, Fiona, xvi, 83

*Giving Tree, The* (book), 230–32

Glenn, Sharlee Mullins, 95

God, 139, 171, 220, 227, 235–37, 239, 241, 248, 255–56, 257–60, 265, 266–69, 270, 273, 283, 291, 292–95, 306, 308, 309, 341, 343, 348–49, 350–52, 354–56, 358, 362–64, 366–67, 370–72; *see also* Heavenly Father; Heavenly Mother; Jesus Christ

*Goodbye, I Love You* (book), 45
Goodfellow, Jennifer, 48
Goodfellow, Vanda, 59
Goodson, Stephanie, 9–10, 16, 155–56
Gordon, Suzanne, 52
Graves, Kristen, 64
Gray, Darius, 25
Gray, Emily Fisher, 81, 92, 95
Gray, Sharon, 90
Green, Valerie, 339, 373–75
Gregerson, Anne, 386
grief, 69, 85, 149–50, 175–77, 226–28, 253–56, 290, 328–29, 339, 342–45
Griffiths, Jeannie Decker, 86
Groesbeck, Ashley, 378
Groesbeck, Joan D., 161, 198–99
Grover, E. Victoria, 205, 219–22, 223
Gulf War, 160, 183–86

# H

*Habits of Being: Mormon Women's Material Culture* (book), xiv
Hadfield, Molly Cannon, xiv
Hadley, Lisa Van Orman, 105, 247, 250–51
Hafen, Bruce, 53–54
Haglund, Anna, 70
Haglund, Karen, 48, 62, 66, 68, 70, 85
Haglund, Kristine, 85
Haight, Dana, 223
Hales, Robert D., xii, 14–15
Halloween, 240, 311–12, 331–32
Hammond, Robin, 23
Hanisch, Carol, 32
Hanks, Maxine, xiii, 57–59, 249, 267, 272–75
Hansen, Abby Maxwell, 248, 270–72, 335–36
Hansen, Jody England, 335–36, 339–40, 370–72
happiness, 24, 140, 242, 293–95, 298; *see also* joy
Hardy, Diana Bate, 96
Harris, Claudia W., 159, 174–77
Hartiala-Sloan, Mimmu, 8, 11, 39, 43, 47, 86, 116, 151–56
Harvard Divinity School, 66, 71, 72, 253, 275
Harvard University, xi, 4, 7, 16, 22–23, 33, 53, 55, 63, 86, 106, 109, 153, 273
Harvill, Evelyn, 43, 49, 70, 387
Harward, Nancy, xiv, 82
Hatch, Orrin, 30

Hawaii, 138–39, 236
Hawkinson, David, 386
Haynie, Janna, 23
healing, by the laying on of hands. *See* priesthood (LDS): blessings (male given); women's blessings
health. *See* cancer; death; depression; infertility; mental health; miscarriage/pregnancy loss; childbirth; postpartum depression; pregnancy
#HearLDSWomen, 340, 375–78
Heavenly Father, 145, 151, 172, 188, 256, 257–58, 315, 350–52
Heavenly Mother, 145, 159, 164, 172, 188, 274, 276, 297, 310–12, 339, 349–52
Heavenly Parents, 160, 168, 270, 350–51
Hemming, Margaret Olsen, xiv–xv, 80–81, 91–95, 99–100, 104–05, 249, 287–91, 295–99
Herikita, 386
Hickman, Aimee Evans, xiv, 70–73, 75, 79–83, 91–92, 110, 275, 275–79, 287, 298, 335–36, 387
Hill, Anita, 41
Hill, Susan Arrington, 113, 119–22
Hillsboro Camp. *See* Exponent II retreat: Hillsboro Camp
Hinckley, Gordon B., xiii, 195, 199, 222, 355
Holbrook, Kate, xvi, 66, 69, 72, 86, 203, 206, 223, 226–28, 275
Holland, Jeffrey R., 18, 314
Holland, Patricia (Pat), 18
Holm, Heather, 386
Holy Ghost, 139, 170–71, 220, 238–39, 256, 259–60, 295
Homemaking, 119–22, 129–31, 142–43, 145–48, 177–79; *see also* gender roles; motherhood
Home teacher/teaching (LDS), 5n15, 120, 173, 186, 197, 243–44, 268
Homosexuality. *See* LGBTQ+ issues
Horne, Bonnie, 1, 8, 10–11, 15–16, 23, 35, 68, 151–56
Hornography (brass band), 86
"How Firm a Foundation," 87
Howe, Susan Elizabeth, xii, xv, 23, 33–34, 40, 42, 86, 113–14, 137, 160, 192
Hunter, Howard W., 12, 129, 189
Huo, Ginny, 249

## I

Idaho, 109, 184–86, 198, 236, 262, 264, 272, 275, 319
Illinois, Chicago, xii–xiii, 24–26, 32, 36, 65, 77, 233–37; Evanston, 224; Nauvoo, xii, 34–37, 261–63, 264
*Illuminating Ladies: A Coloring Book of Mormon Women*, xiv, 278
"I'm a Mormon" campaign, 82, 84, 248
immigration, 276, 281, 330–33
Indiana, 80, 178, 211
*Internet Archive* (website), xx
infertility, 125, 250–51, 352–54
International Women's Year (IWY) xii, 26–29, 114, 122–25, 273
Intersectionality or intersectional feminism, 92, 100–2, 105–06, 249, 339
intersex. *See* LGBTQ+ issues
institute of religion (LDS), xi, 6–8, 7n20, 11, 21, 72, 144, 380
Iowa, 209
Ireland, 62, 289
*Irreantum* (magazine), 76
IRS (Internal Revenue Service), 99
Islam, 72, 217, 254

## J

Jacobsen, Florence, 135
James, Jane Elizabeth Manning, 127
Japan, 211–12
Jean–Francois, Falencia, 289, 318–19
Jesus Christ, 15, 26, 47, 140, 150–51, 187–88, 193, 196, 219–22, 227–28, 236–37, 239, 256, 258–60, 282, 289, 314–17, 324, 341, 350–51, 354, 357, 371, 376–78
John Birch Society or Birchers, 124
Johnson, Jane Clayson, 72
Johnson, Sonia, xii, 29–32, 52, 85, 150–52, 267, 274
Johnston, Charlotte Cannon, 5
Johnston, Mary, 223
Jones, Brooke xiii, 76–77, 206, 241–42, 335–37
*Journal of Mormon History*, xviii; *see also* Mormon History Association
joy, 122, 140, 165, 178, 214, 295, 295n5; *see also* happiness
judgment (interpersonal), 164–65, 179–80, 187, 251, 254–55, 318, 377

## K

Kazmi, Salma, 72
Kelley, Clydia, M., 129
Kellogg, Diane McKinney, 23–24, 30–31, 35, 68, 86, 160, 164–65
Kelly, Denise, 81, 95
Kelly, Kate, xiv, 84–85, 248, 339
Kelly, Kim, 387
Kimball, Chris, 24
Kimball, Linda Hoffman, xiv, xvi, 23–24, 47, 62–63, 65, 77, 81–82, 90, 96, 203–07, 223–25, 233–37, 385
Kimball, Spencer W., 25, 136, 260, 351, 377
Kimball, Violet Tew, 159, 163–64
King Benjamin, 294
King, Melissa–Malcolm, 339, 362–64
Kline, Caroline, xiii, 73–78, 80–81, 84, 335–41, 367–69
Knight–Zimmer, Claudia, 160, 183–86
Kohler, Susan, xi, 6–7, 10, 15–16, 86, 109, 151–56, 381
Krakos, Kyra, 88
Kris, Deborah Farmer, xiii, 76–77, 80, 206, 240–41, 337
Ku Klux Klan (KKK) or Klansmen, 29, 124
Kuntz, Annie Dredge, 70, 88–89
Kuntz, Toby, 89

## L

Lamb, Tracy McKay, 289, 314–17
Lambert, Eileen Perry, 38, 45, 46, 49, 59, 64, 385–87
Latimer, Sallie Warton, 385
Lauritzen, Stephanie, 83
Layco, Sam, 105–06
Lazenby, Margaret, 64
LDS Church. *See* Church of Jesus Christ of Latter-day Saints
LDS Women Advocating Voice and Equality (WAVE), 78, 78n21, 277
Lee, Harold B., 352
Lee, Rex E., 55
Lee, Sandra "Dora," xiii, 76, 205, 242–44, 335–36
Lehmann, Aïsha, 386
Leify, DeTiare, xiv
Lepore, Jill, 310–12
lesbian/lesbianism. *See* LGBTQ+ issues

# INDEX

Let Women Pray campaign, 85n18, 248, 277–78
Levine, Stephanie Wellen, 72
LGBTQ+ issues, 27, 34, 45, 51, 83, 94–95, 161–62, 194–98, 214, 224, 249, 276, 279–82, 290, 297, 321–23, 326–28, 337–40, 341–42, 352–54, 358, 362–64, 370–72, 373–75; allyship, 94–95, 194–97, 337, 370–72; BYU Honor Code, 339, 362–64; homophobia, 51, 297–98, 323; intersex, 342, 352–54; lesbian/lesbianism, 51, 161–62, 194–98, 210, 339, 353; non-binary, 326–28; Pride Festivals, 370–72; queer identity in selected works, 197–98, 279–82, 321–24, 326–28, 352–54, 362–64, 373–75; same-sex marriage, 94–95, 276, 342, 359; special issues of *Exponent II,* xiii, 83, 95; transgender, 83, 339, 342, 371, 373–75; *see also* "Policy of Exclusion"
Lindsey, Tessa, 386
Lisonbee, Laurie, 378
Litster Young, Carol Ann, 104–06, 287–91, 324–25
Littke, Lael J., xii, 24, 37, 74
Little, Debbie, 72
Longfellow Park LDS Chapel, 2
Lord. *See* Jesus Christ
Lythgoe, Dennis, 38, 43, 161, 199–200
Lythgoe, Marti, 38, 63, 86

## M

Maas, Susan J., 18
MacArthur, Mary Ellen Romney, 25, 38
MacDonald, Hannah, 290, 321–23
MacMurray, Maryann, 10, 16
Madsen, Carol Cornwall, xii, 34
Madsen, Laurel, xv, 223
Maitland, Jo, 68
Manifesto (1890), 135
marriage, xix, 9, 12, 24, 45–46, 113, 119–22, 141, 144, 146–48, 172–74, 212–16, 217, 289, 306–08, 314–17, 328–29, 329–30; abuse in, 172–74, 199–200; childless, 212–16; gender roles and, 12, 61, 109, 129–31, 173, 230–32, 256–60, 270–72, 341–2; same-sex marriage, 94–95; sex and, 33–34, 141, 165; *see also* divorce; gender roles; LGBTQ+ issues; plural marriage; singlehood; temple (LDS): weddings/marriage/sealings; widowhood
Marston, William Moulton, 310–11
Martin, Michelle, 70
Maryland, Baltimore, 79–80, 306–8
Mary Magdalene, 227–28
Massachusetts, 28; Arlington, 33, 149; Belmont, 13, 15, 64; Boston/Boston–area, xvii–iii, 1–79, 91, 148, 180, 203, 254–56, 272–75; Brockton, 183; Cambridge, xvii, 1–3, 13, 20–22, 33, 37, 63, 91, 105–6, 109, 137, 154, 207–12, 266; Cape Cod, 72; Framingham, 43, 200; Hingham, 199; Newton, xi; Plymouth, 71; Sommerville, 250; Watertown, 70; Winchendon, 11, 14
Massachusetts Institute of Technology (MIT), 104, 152, 273, 379
Matisse, Henri, 170–71
Mauss, Ruth Hathaway, 74
Maxwell, Neal A., 351
McBaine, Neylan, xiv, 82
McCammon, Ellen, 290, 299–305
McConkie, Bruce R., 12
McDannell, Colleen, 83
McKinney, Diane. *See* Kellogg, Diane McKinney
McKinnon, Janice, 23
McPhie, Emily, 386
*Melrose Place*, 64
Memorial Day, 189–91
menopause, 188
menstruation, 206, 218–19, 250
mental health, xix, 24, 49, 281; *see also* depression; postpartum depression
Merrill, Allison Hong, xvi, 103, 291, 330–33
#MeToo, 96
Michigan, 297, 326–28
Middle East, 184, 225
Midrash, xiv, 92, 290, 299–305
Midwest Pilgrims, xiv, 36, 71, 82, 204–6, 261
*A Midwife's Tale: The Life of Martha Ballard, Based on Her Diary, 1789–1812* (book), 52–53
Midwifery, 88
Milano, Alyssa, 96
Miller, Sharon, 23
Minnesota, 106, 119
miscarriage/pregnancy loss, 204, 229, 270, 307, 339, 342–45

397

missions/missionary work (LDS), 56, 65, 113, 117–19, 131, 154–55, 185, 194–97, 216–17, 236–37, 256–57, 273, 298, 319, 322, 355, 356, 360–62, 365, 378
Mitchell, Joni, 209
modesty, 216–17, 338, 345–47, 356–59
Momma Dragons, 94; *see also* LGBTQ+ issues
Moore, Margaret Dredge, 70, 80–81
Mormon Battalion, 127
*Mormon Enigma: Emma Hale Smith* (book), 261–63
*Mormon Feminism: Essential Writings* (book), xvi, 87
Mormon feminist identity, xix, 19, 21, 26, 31, 52, 67, 78, 83, 109–10, 113–16, 162, 272–75, 276, 298–99
Mormon History Association, xviii
Mormon Land (*Salt Lake Tribune*), 96
"Mormon Male" xiii, 3
#MormonMeToo, 96
Mormon Moment, 82, 94, 247–48
Mormon Sisters, Inc., xvii, 14–15
*Mormon Sisters: Women in Early Utah* (book), xii, 8, 10, 19, 154
Mormon Studies, xviii, 7, 64
Mormon Women for Ethical Government, 95–96
Mormon Women Project, xiv, 82
Mormon Women's Forum, 54–55, 69, 274–75
Mormons Building Bridges, 370–72
Mormons for ERA, xii, 29–32, 274; *see also* Sonia Johnson
Moroni (angel), 224–25
Morris, Ramona, 106, 290–91, 319–21, 335–36
Morrison, Hayley Labrum, 386
motherhood, xix, 34, 69, 70, 119–22, 142–43, 143–45, 180–83, 183–86, 252–53, 325, 342–45, 347–49, 352–54, 379–81; childless, 212–16; daughter relationships, 70, 143–45, 177–79, 218–19, 226–28, 235, 238–39, 250, 266, 309–12, 318–19, 322–23, 330–33; debate about mothers working, 12, 62, 69, 123, 177–79, 380; depression and, 179–80, 204, 238–39; grandmothers/grandmotherhood, 71, 122, 131, 143–45, 162–63, 206, 226–28, 232–33, 236, 296, 299, 319–21; identity beyond motherhood, 63, 142–43, 159, 177–79; LDS Teachings on, xiii, 5, 17–18, 177–79; satire about, 129–31; self-sacrifice and, 145–48, 230–32; single mothers, 190, 233–37; *see also* abortion and reproductive rights; adoption; family; gender roles; marriage; miscarriage/pregnancy loss; pregnancy
Mother's Day, 125, 147, 178, 190, 231, 247
*Ms.* (magazine), 33, 187
Munk, Margaret Rampton, 114, 125–26
Munson, Erika, 372
Murri, Ina Mae, 161
music, 26, 35, 39, 49, 87, 117–18, 120, 130, 170–71, 224–25, 289, 300, 329, 350
Mutual Improvement Association, 133, 140, 143

# N

nature, 125, 131, 137–39, 292, 324–25, 326–28
Nelson, Russell M., 96, 101
Nephites, 100
Nevada, Las Vegas, 209
Newell, Linda King, xi–xii, 34, 248–49, 261–63
*New Era* (magazine), 4
New Hampshire, 34, 99; Durham, xi, 5, 10, 154; Greenfield, 72, 100–1, 103; Hillsboro, xiii, 36–39, 72; *see also* Exponent II Retreat: Hillsboro Camp
New Mormon History, 7
New Year (holiday), 224, 322
New York City, 105
New York (special issue), xii, 24
*New York Times* (news agency), 102
Newey, Melody, 288, 291–92
*Newsweek*, 82, 129
Nibley, Hugh, 257
Nielsen, Midge W., 113, 129–31
*Ninety-Nine Fire Hoops* (book), 103
Nissen, Harriet (Toxie), 37, 71
Nissen, Puffy (Patricia), 37, 71
nonbinary. *See* LGBTQ+ issues.

# O

"O My Father" (hymn), 350
Oaks, Dallin H., 262, 345, 354–55
*Obergefell v. Hodges*, 94

Obama, Michelle, 309
O'Connor, Flannery, 169–70
Official Declaration 2 (LDS Church), xii; *see also* race: ban on Black priesthood ordination and temple participation
Ohio issue, xii, 24
Ordain Women, xiv, 84–85, 248, 277–78, 338–39, 354–56
Oregon, 364–67
Orr, Eugene, 25
Othote, Linda Collins, 33, 39–40
*Our Bodies, Ourselves* (book), 6n17, 44

## P

Pace, Eunice, 38
Packer, Boyd K., xiii, 51
Palmer, Emily Gilkey, 339
Parcell, Abby, 106
Parenting/parenthood. *See* gender roles; marriage; motherhood
Park, Benjamin E., 6
Park, Lindsay Hansen, 386
Parkin, Amelia, xiii, 76–77, 337–38, 345–47
Partridge, Kody, 54
Pasifika identity, 114, 138, 249; *see also* FEMWOC, race
patriarchal blessings, 216, 260, 342
patriarchy, 117–19, 123, 177–79, 276–77, 309–12, 341–42, 375–78; *see also* LGBTQ+ issues; race; sexism
Patterson, Dayna, 88–89
Patterson, Sara M., 51
Patton, Ellen, 46
Paxman, Shirley B., 59
Paxman, Susan L. *See* Booth–Forbes, Sue
Pearl of Great Price (LDS scripture), 314; *see also* scriptures
Pearson, Carol Lynn, xvi, 45, 289, 323–24
Pellett, Alma Frances, 107
Pere, Vernice Wineera, 114, 138
perfectionism, 129–31, 145–48, 319
periods. *See* menstruation
Perry, April, 47, 387
Perry, L. Tom, xii., 13–19, 22, 25, 257
personal revelation, 36, 117, 137, 193, 205, 219–22, 238–39, 258–60, 295, 343, 368–69
Person, Carolyn Peters, xi, 1, 5–6, 10, 16, 20, 86, 249, 273, 385, 387

Peterson, Chase, 22–23
Peterson, Esther Eggertson, xv, 38
Peterson, Grethe Ballif, xv, 11, 14–15, 19, 22–24, 28
Pettingill, Ondre, 385
Phelps, W. W., 350
Pierce, Lori LeVar, 84, 103–04, 107, 108
Pierce, Sarah, 108
Pilgrimage (1982 retreat), xii, 34–37; *see also* Exponent II Retreat; Midwest Pilgrims; retreats, and Mormon feminism
Pinborough, Elizabeth, xiv
Pingree, Allison, 106–07, 289, 328–29
pioneers (LDS), 127–28, 162–63, 264, 296, 299
Plummer, Louise, xv
plural marriage, 5, 21, 123, 159, 163–64, 262–63, 311
poetry, 125–26, 131–33, 137–39, 141, 162–64, 218–19, 232–33, 241, 291, 329, 359–60
"Policy of Exclusion" (POX), xiv, 94–95, 290, 339, 359–60
politics, 24, 82–83, 147, 148–49, 212, 280, 295–99; *see also* abuse; anti-war movement/sentiment; *Dobbs v. Jackson*; Women's Health Organization; Equal Rights Amendment (ERA); International Women's Year (IWY); Mitt Romney; Mormon Moment; *Obergefell v. Hodges*; Policy of Exclusion (POX); women's march
polygamy. *See* plural marriage
pornography, 78, 204, 345
Porter, Susan H., 23, 27, 29
postpartum depression, 87, 269
poverty, xv, 92, 234, 240–41, 289, 314–17, 318–19, 326
"Power Hungry," 74
prayer, 15, 30, 39, 40, 55, 58, 85, 87, 127, 150–51, 184–86, 196, 226, 237, 238–39, 241, 252, 257, 266–69, 291–92, 292–93, 315, 350–53, 368
pregnancy, 41, 88, 91, 143, 144, 160, 164–65, 179–83, 190, 204, 235, 238–39, 250–51, 270, 349, 379, 381; *see also* miscarriage/ pregnancy loss; motherhood; postpartum depression
priestesshood, 338; *see also* women's blessings; Ordain Women

Priesthood Correlation Program. *See* Church of Jesus Christ of Latter-day Saints, correlation
priesthood (LDS), 5, 119, 250, 266–69, 270–72, 276, 342; blessings (male given), 239, 260, 267–68, 270–71, 348; Women and, 57, 69, 74, 84–85, 87, 100, 133–37, 248, 253–56, 266–69, 276–78, 338–39, 342, 347–49, 254–56; *see also* Church of Jesus Christ of Latter-day Saints; baby blessings; Ordain Women; race: ban on Black priesthood ordination and temple participation; women's blessings
Primary (LDS Church auxiliary for children), 18, 55, 80, 127, 133–35, 214, 252, 271, 291, 298, 342, 343, 358, 370, 376, 380
Pritchett, Diane, 87–88, 248, 266–69
Proposition 8 (California), 278
prosperity gospel, 289, 314–17
Provo Canyon Retreat, 71

## Q

Quaker meetings (Mormon feminist), 35–38, 49–50, 88, 103
Quakers, 185
quilts/quilting, 40, 95, 98, 131, 206, 214, 218–19
Quinn, D. Michael, xiii, 58

## R

Race: as a feminist issue, 87, 113, 284; ban on Black priesthood ordination and temple participation, xii, 13, 25, 113, 127–29, 168, 260, 368; and Exponent II, 24–26, 101–02, 105–06, 205; racial identity, 25–26, 138–39, 233–37, 249, 282–84, 319–21, 330–33, 362–64; racism, 13, 101, 127–29, 254, 281, 282–84, 297, 331, 341, 363–64, 367–68; *see also* Black Lives Matter (BLM); intersectionality; FEM-WOC; Pasifika identity; Women of Color
Radke-Moss, Andrea, xvi
rape, 44, 65 190, 377; *see also* sexual assault
Rawlins, Rick, 385
Raynes, Mary Beth, xv
Raynes, Meghan ("MRaynes") 338, 347–49
Red Hot Mamas, 288, 308–09
Rees, Robert A., 5–6, 12, 14
Relief Society, xi, xviii, 2, 8, 10, 12, 34–36, 43, 53, 56, 77, 87–88, 109, 128, 148–49, 160, 173, 175, 179–80, 193, 200, 213, 244, 252, 269, 272, 274, 289, 314–17, 337, 342, 349–52, 376–77, 380; Cambridge Ward(s), 1–3, 23–24, 153–56; General Presidency and Board, 18, 27, 50, 53, 55, 71, 148; loss of autonomy and financial independence, 4, 28, 64, 115, 123, 133–37, 272; Nauvoo Relief Society, 34–36, 261–63
*Relief Society Magazine*, 1, 4, 134
Remy, Jana, xiii, 73–77, 337–38, 341–42
Reorganized Church of Jesus Christ of Latter-day Saints, 261–63
reproductive rights. *See* abortion and reproductive rights; birth control; family planning
retreats, and Mormon feminism, xi–xiii, 34–37, 46–50, 71, 373; *see also* Exponent II Retreat; Midwest Pilgrims; Pilgrimage (1982 retreat)
Revelation on Priesthood. *See* race: ban on Black priesthood ordination and temple participation
Rhode Island, 38, 46, 203
Rhytting, Ann, 38
Rich, Katie Ludlow, 108, 335–36, 380
Richards, LeGrand, 14n20
Riess, Jana, xvi, 248–49, 261–63
Rigby, Hazel, xii, 29; *see also* Mormons for ERA
Rocky Mountain Retreat, 71
*Roe v. Wade*. *See* abortion
Rogers, Natasha, 335–36
Romish, John, 13
Romney, Mitt, 44, 56–57, 82, 195, 247–48
Rosenbaum, Karen, 65, 204–05, 212–15, 223
Ross, Nancy, 83, 335–36, 339, 359–60
Roto, Anna-Kaarina, xv
Roto, Anzu, 15
Rueckert, Rachel, xv, 104–09, 287–91, 309–12
Rugh, Susan Sessions, xii, 24
Rugh, Tom, 25–26
Russell, RevaBeth, 63, 114, 141
Russell, Sylvia, 66
Rutgers University, 29

## S

Sacrament, administration of, and gender, 49, 100, 271, 274, 279, 289, 323–24

# INDEX

Sacrament Meeting (LDS Worship service), 36, 38, 49, 185, 193, 227, 250, 271, 274, 319, 342, 357, 365, 376
Salisbury, Caroline, 102, 338, 360–62
Salleh, Fatimah, xvi, 100
*Salt Lake Tribune*, 54–55, 69, 95, 357
Same-sex marriage. *See* LGBTQ+ issues
Sanger, Margaret, 165, 311
Savage, Julie Hemming, 80, 205, 230–32
Schlafly, Phyllis, 26–29
Scriptures, 77, 121, 139, 252, 255, 257, 288, 290, 292–95, 314–15, 337, 343, 348, 365, 375; *see also* Bible; Book of Mormon; Doctrine and Covenants; Pearl of Great Price
Second-wave feminism. *See* feminism: second-wave
*Secret Life of Wonder Woman, The* (book), 310–12
*Segullah* (blog and magazine), 77–78
September 11, 2001, attacks, 206, 223–25, 254
September Six, xiii, 51, 57–59, 69, 162, 187, 267
Serago, Rosie Gochnour, 93–94, 108, 291, 312–14, 335–36, 386
sewing, 167, 206, 241, 249, 263–66
sex and sexuality, 33–34, 38, 45, 101, 113, 141, 164–65, 197–98, 205–06, 249, 279–82, 339, 341–42
sexism, xix, 35, 69, 83, 117–19, 122–23, 139, 141, 172–74, 189–91, 191–94, 197–98, 230–32, 256–60, 261–63, 308–9, 323–24, 341–42, 345–47, 356, 360–62, 375–78; *see also* priesthood (LDS): women
sexual assault, 65, 95–96, 173, 189–91, 192; *see also* abuse; rape
sexual harassment, 33, 41, 94, 96
sexual identity. *See* LGBTQ+ issues
sexualization of women and girls, 338, 345–47, 360–62
Shaffer, Anja, 80–81, 86
Shapiro, Anneliese Warnick, 385
Sheldon, Carrel Hilton, 9–10, 15–19, 23, 33, 35, 39–40, 47–49, 66, 86, 103, 151–56, 160, 179–80, 205, 273–75
Sheldon, Garret, 10, 40, 46, 152
Shields, Chelsea, 336
Shipps, Jan, xviii, 52, 64–65

Sievers, Helen Claire, 23, 29, 56–57, 84
Sillitoe, Linda, xv, 114
Silverstein, Shel, 230–32
singlehood, 23–24, 33, 65, 192, 204–05, 216–17, 237, 242–44
*60 Minutes* (news program), 195, 217
Smith, Barbara, 27
Smith, Bathsheba, 124
Smith, Emma Hale, 35–36, 249, 261–63
Smith, Galen Bell, 386
Smith, Joseph, III, 263
Smith, Joseph F., 140
Smith, Joseph Fielding, 50, 350–51
Smith, Joseph, Jr., 35–36, 127, 140, 148, 214, 221, 224, 260, 261–63, 264, 309, 350
Smith, Marilyn Y., 127–29
Smith, Suzette, 80–81, 96–98, 335–36
Sneddon, Fara, 88
Snow, Eliza R., 8, 12, 124, 133–37, 262, 350
Snow, Erastus, 351
social media, 83–85, 93, 96, 101–02, 107, 110, 359, 375–78
Sofia Gathering, 78, 335–36
Soper, Kathryn Lynn, 77
*Sophie's Choice* (film), 209
Sorensen, Virginia Eggerson, xv, 38
South Carolina, 266
South Korea, 21–22
Spafford, Belle, 135
spirit. *See* Holy Ghost
spiritual gifts, 119, 134, 139–40
Stack, Peggy Fletcher, xii, xv, 54, 69
stake president or stake presidency, 13–15, 21, 44, 56, 85, 180, 197, 259, 262, 267, 376–78
Stark, Helen Candland, 113–14, 145–48
Steed, Jessica Oberon, 78, 80
Steenblik, Rachel Hunt, 87–88, 335–36, 339
Steinem, Gloria, 33, 54, 187; *see also Ms.* (magazine)
Stokes, Cathy, 26, 35, 205, 233–37
Stone, Ann Gardner, xv, 206, 218–19
STOP ERA, 26–29
Stromberg, Lorie Winder, xiv, 29–31, 74, 84, 116, 148–49, 273
Suffolk University, 3
Suffrage movement, Mormon women and, 7–8, 28–29, 124
suicide, 189, 363–64

401

Sundahl, Dave, 344–45
Sundahl, Heather, xvi, 65, 69–71, 78, 81, 87, 96–99, 106–07, 203–07, 223, 238–39, 288, 308–09, 335–36, 339
Sunstone Education Foundation magazine and symposium, xi–xii, xviii, 43, 54, 59, 198, 273–74, 335–36
Swenson, Sharon, xvi
Swett, Katrina, 72

## T

Taiwan, 330–33
Taylor, Barbara, 44, 46, 48, 64, 66, 68, 70, 73, 82, 275
Taylor, Breonna, 101
Taylor, Elmina S., 140
Taylor, John, 135
temple (LDS), 83, 85, 100–1, 129, 131, 195, 205–6, 217, 236, 248, 256–60, 276, 315, 324–25, 342, 376; Biblical temple, 282, 299–305; covenants, 83, 173, 216–17; initiatory and endowment ceremony, 50, 85, 258–60, 342; recommend interviews and recommends, 85, 101, 267, 297; representations of Eve in, 248, 258–60; unequal or sexist covenants and language, 173, 248, 256–60, 279, 342, 376, 378; weddings/marriage/sealings, 46, 85, 129, 173, 198, 252, 256–60, 319, 322; *see also* Church of Jesus Christ of Latter-day Saints: Temple Square; garments; race: ban on Black priesthood ordination and temple participation
Tennessee, Nashville, 106, 195
Texas, 183, 282
Thanksgiving, 208, 345
Thayne, Emma Lou, xi, xiii, xv–xvi, 18, 34, 65, 115, 169–70, 223
Thornock, Del, 385
Tietjen, Renee, 23, 29, 33, 38, 46, 86, 385
*Times and Seasons* (blog), 75
Tobler-Preece, Lisa, 48
Toiaivao, Courtney, 105
Tonga, Kalani, 249, 282–84
Toscano, Margaret Merrill, 74, 83, 275, 340
Toscano, Paul J., xiii, 58
"To the Mothers in Zion," (Benson), xiii, 159, 177–79
transgender. *See* LGBTQ+ issues

tree of knowledge, 5–6, 78, 86
Trump, Donald, 95, 101; *see also* Women's March (2017)
Turley, Kylie Nielson, 204
Turner, Page, 89, 93–94, 249–50, 263–66, 386
Tyler, Jan, 27–28

## U

Uchtdorf, Dieter F., 272, 294
Udall, Roslyn (Roz), 33, 46, 86
Ulrich, Gael, 1, 5, 379
Ulrich, Laurel Thatcher, xi, xiii, xvi, 1–6, 10–11, 15n26, 18–19, 34–36, 52–55, 64, 72, 84, 109, 115–16, 142–43, 151–56, 195, 273–75, 277–78, 379–81
Ulrich, Mindy, 40, 380
Ulrich, Wendy, xv
*United States of America v. Suzette M. Smith*, 97–98
United States Postal Service (USPS), 10, 18, 60, 152
University of California, Berkeley, 216
University of California, Irvine, 73–75
University of New Hampshire, 5, 34, 380
University of Utah, 33, 54, 133, 143, 209–10, 274, 371, 379
Updegraff, Emily Parker, 288, 292–95, 335–36
US Capitol, 101
US Congress, 26, 28, 41, 101
US military, 160–61, 183–86, 248, 270
US Senate, 30
US Supreme Court, 41, 94
Utah, 63, 106, 133, 162, 195, 209–10, 226, 262, 270, 296–99, 319, 331–32, 371; Provo, xii, 24, 108, 123, 177, 335–36, 372; Salt Lake City, 12–14, 25, 30, 34, 54, 63, 84, 122–25, 139, 194, 215, 252, 264, 272, 275, 323

## V

van Uitert, Bert, 1
van Uitert, LuAnne, 1
van Uitert, Rebecca, xvi
Vietnam War, 3, 128, 160
violence against women, 189–91; *see also* abuse; rape; sexual assault
Violence Against Women Act (1994), 41–42

Virginia, 29, 41, 80, 141; *see also* Mormons for ERA
Visiting teaching/teacher, 1, 1n3, 14, 34, 87, 173, 197, 243, 267–69, 315, 344

## W

Washington, DC, 30, 38, 217, 298
*Washington Post*, 82, 258
Watt, Kathleen, 20, 23, 385
Wear Pants to Church Day, 83, 248, 277
Weil, Shraga, 386
*Well-Behaved Women Seldom Make History* (book), 381
Wellesley College, 62
Wells, Emmeline B., 29, 49–50, 124, 159, 163–64
Wheatley, Meg, 38
Wheelwright, Hannah, 87
"Where have all the Mormon feminists gone?," 69
White-Hammond, Gloria, 72
White Roses campaign, 58
Whitesides, Lynne Knavel, xiii, 54, 57–59, 275
Whitman, Wendy, 23
Whitney, Katrina, 386
Whitney, Orson F., 351
Widener Library (Harvard), xi, 7, 109, 116, 152
widowhood, 159, 175–77, 235, 263
Wilcox, Kendall, 372
Wilding, Marlena, xiv
Winder, Kwani Povi, xiv, 386
Withers, Maida Rust, xii, 29; *see also* Mormons for ERA
*Woman's Exponent* (newspaper), xi, 7–10, 29, 36, 64, 80, 109, 152, 154, 253, 273–74, 381
A Woman's Place Bookstore, 54
*Women and Authority: Re-Emerging Mormon Feminism* (book), 57, 274; *see also* Hanks, Maxine
Women of Color, xiv, 24, 87, 106, 284, 367; *see also* Black identity; intersectionality; Pasifika identity; race
women's blessings (ritual healings), 49–50, 55, 63, 87–89, 178–79, 266–69, 270–71, 338, 341, 347–49; *see also* priesthood (LDS): blessings (male given)
women's health. *See* cancer; death; depression; infertility; mental health; miscarriage/pregnancy loss; childbirth; postpartum depression; pregnancy
women's march (2017), 84, 95–96
women's movement. *See* consciousness-raising groups; Equal Rights Amendment; feminism: second-wave; International Women's Year
Wonder Woman, 290, 309–12
Wood, Bonnie, 38
Wood, Teddie, xii, 29; *see also* Mormons for ERA
Woodworth, M. and W., 28–29, 115, 123–25
Word of Wisdom, 358
Work, Sherry, 376
World War II, 183, 292, 311
Writ and Vision, 108, 335–36
Wunderli, Anne, 94
Wyoming, 132, 137

## Y

Young-Bennett, April, 85, 335–36, 338–39, 354–56
Young, Brigham, 127, 135, 261–63, 299
Young, Margaret Blair, xvi, 159, 177–79
Young Men's (LDS auxiliary), 297
Young Single Adult (YSA) wards/activities, 23–24, 242–44, 252
young women, modesty and, 260–62, 345–47, 377
Young Women's (LDS auxiliary), 18, 53, 77, 119, 143, 252, 267, 297, 377, 321, 377
Young, Zina D. Huntington, 350

## Z

Zeleski, Amy, 386
*Zelophehad's Daughters* (blog), 77
Zion, as Mormon ideal, 81, 164, 177–79, 220, 264, 288, 308–09, 314, 342, 308–09, 314, 342

# About the Authors

**Katie Ludlow Rich** is a writer and independent scholar of Mormon women's history. Her work focuses on centering women's voices and their agentive decisions even when functioning within a patriarchal tradition. She has a bachelor's in history and a master's in English, both from Brigham Young University. Her writing has appeared in *Exponent II*, *Dialogue: A Journal of Mormon Thought*, the *Journal of Mormon History*, and the *Salt Lake Tribune*. She lives in Saratoga Springs, Utah.

**Heather Sundahl** believes in the power of stories. In pursuit of this, she has volunteered with Exponent II for twenty-eight years. As a writer and editor, Heather works to amplify the voices of marginalized folks and has collected the oral histories of Batswana, South African, Native American, and queer Mormon women. She received an MA in English from BYU in 1994 and an MA in Marriage & Family Therapy from UVU in 2023. Heather currently works at a residential treatment center where she helps her teenage clients find narratives that promote growth and healing. She lives in Orem, Utah.

Made in United States
Orlando, FL
01 April 2025